The Aranda's Pepa

An Introduction to Carl Strehlow's Masterpiece
Die Aranda- und Loritja-Stämme in Zentral-Australien (1907-1920)

The Aranda's Pepa

An Introduction to Carl Strehlow's Masterpiece
Die Aranda- und Loritja-Stämme in Zentral-Australien (1907-1920)

Anna Kenny

Australian
National
University

PRESS

ANU PRESS

Published by ANU Press
The Australian National University
Acton ACT 2601, Australia
Email: anupress@anu.edu.au
This title is also available online at press.anu.edu.au

National Library of Australia Cataloguing-in-Publication entry

Author:	Kenny, Anna, author.
Title:	The Aranda's Pepa : an introduction to Carl Strehlow's masterpiece, Die Aranda-und Loritja-Stamme in Zentral-Australien (1907-1920) / Anna Kenny.
ISBN:	9781921536762 (paperback) 9781921536779 (ebook)
Subjects:	Aranda (Australian people)--Social life and customs. Kukatja (Australian people)--Social life and customs. Aranda (Australian people)--Kinship. Kukatja (Australian people)--Kinship. Aranda (Australian people)--Religion. Kukatja (Australian people)--Religion.
Other Authors/Contributors:	Strehlow, C. (Carl), 1871-1922. Aranda-und Loritja-Stamme in Zentral-Australien.
Dewey Number:	305.89915

Cover design and layout by ANU Press

Cover image: Carl Strehlow's map, 1910 and Carl Strehlow's 'Aussendungsphoto', 1892. Archiv/Mission Eine Welt, Neuendettelsau.

Contents

Sign 316. pepa (book, letter): With index finger one makes quick movements on the palm of the left hand, as if one were writing.[1]

Carl Strehlow, 1915

Plates, Diagrams and Maps

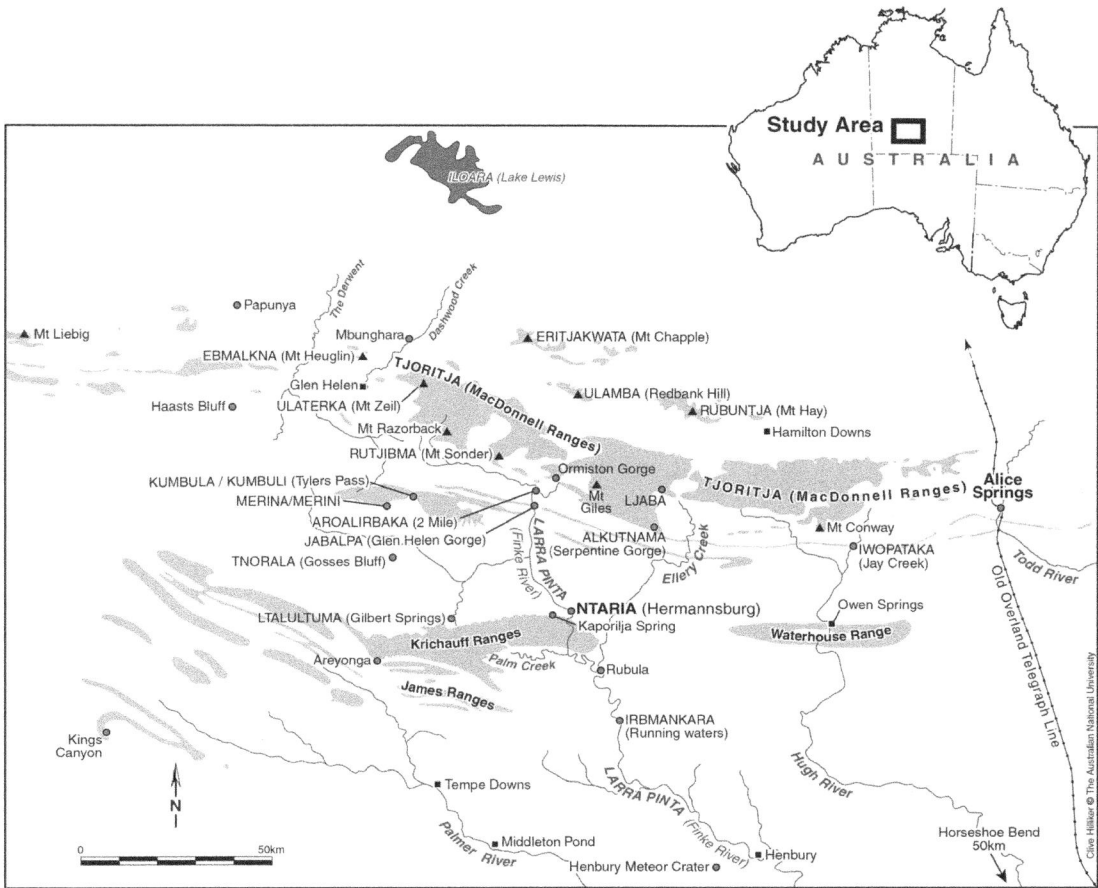

1. Map of central Australia.

Source: Clivie Hilliker, The Australian National University.

Acknowledgments

Work on this book, which has been developed from my thesis, was made possible by a postdoctoral fellowship funded by an ARC Linkage grant (LP110200803) between The Australian National University, the Central Land Council and the Strehlow Research Centre titled, 'Rescuing Carl Strehlow's indigenous cultural heritage legacy: the neglected German tradition of Arandic ethnography'. Foremost I am indebted to my Aranda friends in central Australia who have been generous, lenient and patient with me over the years we have known each other, while living in central Australia and working on many native title claims since early 1994. At ANU I am deeply indebted to Professor Nicolas Peterson who has been my teacher and mentor for nearly 20 years. I am also very thankful for the support given to this project by David Ross and Brian Connelly from the Central Land Council and Michael Cawthorn from the Strehlow Research Centre.

I wish to thank Professor Emeritus Diane Austin-Broos, my PhD supervisor, without whose guidance and critical comments some ideas would not have emerged. Under her supervision my understanding of intellectual histories that have impacted on anthropology's development greatly expanded and opened up various new ways to approach aspects of intellectual history in Australia. I am deeply indebted to her. I am also indebted to Dr Lee Sackett, Dr John Morton, Professor Fred Myers and Professor Andre Gingrich who have encouraged my work.

I am particularly thankful for the assistance given to me by the staff of the Strehlow Research Centre, Graeme Shaughnessy, Scott Mitchell, Penny Joy and Adam Macfie in Alice Springs, and by Lyall Kupke of the Lutheran Archives in Adelaide. Thanks are also due to the librarian at the Central Land Council, Amy O'Donoghue.

I would also like to thank Dr Miklos Szalay, Garry Stoll, Dr Maurice Schild, Dr Gavan Breen, Dr John Henderson, Dr Jenny Green, Dr Walter Veit, Craig Elliott, Helen Wilmot, Chris Nobbs, Geoff Hunt and my brother Urs Kenny who have provided comments and constructive criticism on various manuscripts. A special thanks to Peter Latz for pointing out some important details about the perception of Western Aranda people of Carl Strehlow's persona; to Professor Karl Heinz Kohl who welcomed me at the University of Frankfurt; to John Strehlow for our initial conversations about his grandfather; and to Peter von Leonhardi for inviting me to Gross Karben to see where his great-uncle Moritz von Leonhardi edited Carl Strehlow's masterpiece.

I am especially grateful to my very good friend Julia Munster who has always been supportive and provided helpful comments and advice. Lastly, and most of all, I thank my loving family, Shane and Roisin Mulcahy, for their constant support and critical comments.

Preface

I first encountered Carl Strehlow's work over 25 years ago whilst studying ethnology, Germanistic (German studies) and linguistics in Zürich. At the time *Die Aranda- und Loritja-Stämme in Zentral-Australien* did not strike a chord in me, although I was keenly interested in Aboriginal cultures and particularly interested in language *per se*. My interest in oral literatures was sparked by my father. In my childhood he had read to me every available collection of mythology ranging from Swiss legends, to Greek myths and Tibetan fairy-tales. Carl Strehlow's work did not seem unusual among other collections of *Mythen, Sagen und Märchen* (myths, legends and fairy-tales) found in a German context, although it seemed rather cryptic due to the lack of a glossary that explained Aranda and Loritja terms used in the translations of the indigenous texts. The collection presupposed an enormous amount of knowledge and language proficiency which I did not have at the time. It was soon returned to the library shelf.

Many years later, having worked with Aboriginal people on land and native title claims as well as on mining related issues in central Australia, I again encountered Carl Strehlow's ethnographic work during research into Western Aranda culture and country. The nature of my work provided me the opportunity to travel with Central Australian indigenous people over their traditional lands, and in time I became attuned to mythology associated with landscape and the mastery of Carl Strehlow's work, compiled in the first decade of the last century, revealed itself. *Die Aranda- und Loritja-Stämme in Zentral-Australien* and his unpublished materials described the sophistication of Aboriginal cultures that other Australian works of the time lacked.

Not only had he written the base for a successful 'claim book', which is a legal anthropological report, and compiled family trees of the people who own the country featured in these narratives, he had also compiled as Marcel Mauss expressed it 'un précieux recueil de 1500 vers aranda qui forme une sorte de Rig Veda australien' (Mauss 1913: 103).

Orthography

In this book I have used mainly the original orthography of Carl Strehlow which includes well known spellings of polysemic key terms such as 'altjira' and 'tjurunga' and the language labels 'Aranda' and 'Loritja'. I have only used contemporary spellings of Aranda and Loritja words in citations from contemporary publications and reports (including my own previous work) that use spelling systems developed by the Institute for Aboriginal Development ('IAD'). In the IAD system the language name 'Aranda' is spelled 'Arrernte', for example. Spellings from the published works of early writers such as Spencer and Gillen, Howitt, Roth, Róheim and Pink have been retained and their usage is referenced.

Generally, the spelling of Aboriginal words, including names of individuals, languages (Luritja, Pertame, Eastern Arrernte, Central Arrernte, etc.), groups of people, subsections, sites, countries (estates) and dreamings that are in use today follow the IAD spelling systems unless they are established place names, personal names of people who have long passed away or no longer in use. Currently a new system is developing for the Arandic language used at and around Ntaria (Hermannsburg) and may replace the current IAD system. The people belonging to these Western Arandic areas prefer to spell their language name 'Arrarnta' or 'Aranda'. Thus, I have included in Appendix A pronunciation guides for both systems and where available I have included recent spellings of words used at Ntaria in the glossary in Appendix B.

Primary Sources and Translations

The main body of my primary research material is held at the Strehlow Research Centre in Alice Springs, Central Australia. Other primary sources are held in capital cities of Australia, Germany and England.

English quotations from Carl Strehlow's magnum opus *Die Aranda- und Loritja-Stämme in Zentral-Australien* are extracted from the unpublished Oberscheidt translation (1991), all other quotations from Carl Strehlow's unpublished manuscripts and letters are based on my translations if not otherwise indicated.

Introduction

Around the turn of the twentieth century three outstanding researchers were investigating societies of central Australia. The writings of Baldwin Spencer, Professor of Biology at the University of Melbourne, Frank Gillen, Post and Telegraph Stationmaster in Alice Springs, and the Lutheran missionary Carl Strehlow at Hermannsburg contain unique documentation of Australian indigenous cultures as they may have been pre-contact. Yet, while Spencer's and Gillen's work and achievements are a celebrated part of Australian intellectual history, Carl Strehlow's contribution to our knowledge and understanding of Aranda and Loritja language, oral literature and culture remains almost unknown.

Spencer and Gillen became central figures in international anthropology. British, German, French and American social scientists, such as Frazer, Malinowski or Durkheim, used *The Native Tribes of Central Australia* (1899) and *The Northern Tribes of Central Australia* (1904) to illustrate their theories and acknowledged these works as major contributions to the discipline. In contrast, Carl Strehlow, although known in Germany and cited by N.W. Thomas, Durkheim and Lévi-Strauss, has been consigned to obscurity in Australia and elsewhere. His magnum opus *Die Aranda- und Loritja-Stämme in Zentral-Australien* (1907–1920), a masterpiece of classical Australian anthropology written at Hermannsburg in central Australia, is nearly unrecognised in English-speaking anthropological circles, although it always seems to have been a sort of omnipresent shadow that ghosted the better known Anglophone ethnography of central Australia.[1] Even though this work has been in the public domain for nearly 100 years, and two unpublished translations exist, one by Charles Chewings and the other by Hans Oberscheidt (1991), it has not been republished, which is astonishing, considering the ongoing general interest in Australian indigenous cultures in Australia and overseas.

Carl Strehlow's work is often inaccurately attributed to his youngest son, Theodor George Heinrich Strehlow, who also conducted extensive research in central Australia. The latter's research, however, received its initial impetus from his father's outstanding work. T.G.H. Strehlow was strongly influenced by his father and is unlikely to have been able to achieve what he did without his father's material.

---

1   John Morton, pers. comm., 13.11.2012.

The significance of Carl Strehlow's *Die Aranda- und Loritja-Stämme in Zentral-Australien* was recognised by some of his contemporaries. The reviews were favourable. By the time the second volume of the work was published in 1908, N.W. Thomas noted:

> Strehlow writes with full knowledge of the language, and we cannot but feel the enormous advantage which this knowledge gives him over all other enquirers. Further memoirs are to appear, and they will be eagerly awaited, for the two already published are masterly. (Thomas 1909: 127)

Andrew Lang wrote in *Man* that 'No one should henceforth write on Mr. Strehlow's tribes who has not mastered his valuable volumes' (Lang 1909a: 28). Lang suggested that the work should be translated into English, but World War I intervened and the leading figures of the British anthropological establishment had reservations about the German Lutheran who had spent over half his life in central Australia (Mulvaney and Calaby 1985: 124, 195, 379, 391; Veit 1991, 2004). Another attempt was made in the late 1930s by Charles Chewings, who had translated Carl Strehlow's monograph, and Adelaide Professor of Classics and English literature, J.A. FitzHerbert.[2] However, the publication of the translation was again eclipsed by war.

Other reasons for the 'disappearance' of *Die Aranda- und Loritja-Stämme in Zentral-Australien* in Australia and elsewhere are anti-mission sentiment past and present, the impact of Nazism on anthropology in Germany, Australian hostility towards the German Lutherans of central Australia in the first half of the twentieth century, and finally the antagonistic debate between T.G.H. Strehlow and the Australian anthropological establishment in the 1960s and 1970s. Strehlow junior's unique relations with Aranda people, his idiosyncratic interpretation of that relationship, and his intellectual style all made him marginal to academic anthropology. His peripheral status seemed to transfer back to his father's work.[3]

Carl Strehlow's ethnographic oeuvre as well as Spencer's and Gillen's were written at a time when the discipline of anthropology was still 'transitional'. They preceded the development of modern field anthropology as the empirical study of cultures and social systems that underpin particular peoples (Morphy 2001: 41–43). Carl Strehlow and Spencer and Gillen were turn of the century empiricists, who collected data out in the field and referred it to mentors in Europe. These were the 'armchair anthropologists' of the discipline's mythic history. Strehlow collaborated with Baron Moritz von Leonhardi, a German

---

2 FitzHerbert Papers (Barr Smith Special Collection) and Tindale Collection Acc. No. 1539 (South Australian Museum Archives).
3 Also T.G.H. Strehlow's tragic 'Stern Case' in 1978 contributed to the marginalisation of his and his father's work and gave the name Strehlow a negative tinge. See Kaiser (2004: 66–75).

intellectual with interests in philosophy and anthropology. In England, Spencer's interlocutor was James Frazer although Spencer's dominant influence came from the natural sciences.

Baldwin Spencer was a biology professor in the Darwinian mould (Mulvaney 2001: 20), a representative of the evolutionary thinking in the British Isles. He believed that the Arunta [Aranda] belonged to a lower form of human beings (Spencer and Gillen 1927: vii). Morphy writes that Spencer and Gillen were 'both strongly influenced by Darwinian evolutionary theory' (Morphy 2001: 30) and 'concerned to affirm the position of Aborigines at the lower end of the hierarchy of the evolution of society' (Morphy 2012: 551). Jones (2005: 17) remarks that 'Spencer was constrained by the natural historical framework and the evolutionist approach' in which 'rudimentary customs and beliefs' among the Aranda were identified 'just as he had located primitive forms in the Australian biota' during the Horn Expedition. He quotes Spencer and Gillen as follows:

> … it seems that in the evolution of the social organisation and customs of a savage tribe, such features as those which we are now discussing are clearly comparable to the well known rudimentary organs, which are often of great importance in understanding the phylogeny of the animal in which at some time of its development they are present … we may recognise in them an abbreviated record of a stage passed through in the development of the customs of the tribe amongst which they are found. (Spencer and Gillen 1899: 105)

Their views influenced attitudes and policies towards indigenous people in Australia and elsewhere during the twentieth century and even today are manifest in policy making. In the nineteenth century, evolutionism was a common presumption of anthropology in the British colonial world and influenced, in some degree, the foci in ethnography. Baldwin Spencer's particular interest in biology gave his work an added evolutionary emphasis. The ethnographic material collected by Gillen and published in *The Native Tribes of Central Australia* (1899), *The Northern Tribes of Central Australia* (1904) and *The Arunta* (1927) is still valuable as a reference for scholarly research. In this case, the broad ranging empirical work of the collaboration outlasted Spencer's Darwinian backdrop. If anything, the latter is regarded now as a period anachronism. Still, Spencer never abandoned his view that they were 'Stone Age' people. He maintained this position as late as 1927 in *The Arunta* (Spencer 1927: vii) as did Frazer until he died. The majority of the British establishment saw the original central Australians as representatives of an early and inferior stage of human development.

This view was embodied in museum collections. Terminology derived from the natural sciences was applied to Aboriginal artefacts as well as people. For example, in 1907 the South Australian Museum's director Edward Stirling called all the artefacts of Reuther's Diyari collection, 'specimens' (Jones 1996: 384). In his expedition diary of Wednesday, 11 February 1917, another director of the South Australian Museum Edward Waite described Nellie, an Aboriginal woman, as the finest specimen he had yet seen:

> Had a hurried breakfast and then walked to the Black's camp and took photos of 4 youngsters and some gins, the latter objecting to undress, or rather I had not time enough to humour them. I then went across to another camp and found 3 gins. They all soon posed for me in the altogether. Returned to our own camp and the manager of the station (Battams) introduced the belle of the tribe (Nellie) to give me a sitting, she is a finer specimen than I have yet seen.[4]

In contrast, on the same issue Carl Strehlow commented: 'And these people with such mental capacities should form the "missing link"? Never.'[5] Like his editor and mentor, von Leonhardi, Strehlow's views were shaped by German humanistic thinking. As a consequence, his monograph *Die Aranda- und Loritja-Stämme in Zentral-Australien* is significantly different from other Australian anthropological work of the period. Guided by von Leonhardi's interrogations and his own sense derived from empirical observation and a Lutheran training, Carl's work reflected the aims of this tradition, 'centred on efforts to document the plurality and historical specificity of cultures' (Penny and Bunzl 2003: 1). Its central concern was language and the mythic corpus that was seen to be culture's main manifestation. Unlike the British anthropological tradition, which dominated Australian discourse, German anthropology was largely based on a humanistic agenda, and as a result it was anti-evolutionist, anti-racist and anti-colonial. The permanent general secretary of the German Anthropological Society, for example, took advantage of his position between 1878 and 1908 'to drum into his colleagues, at the annual assemblies, the unity of mankind and the equality of feelings and mental life of all humanity' (Massin 1996: 87).

The two most influential figures in nineteenth century German anthropology, Adolf Bastian (1826–1905) and Rudolf Virchow (1821–1902), rejected socio-cultural evolutionism. Bastian was particularly opposed to social Darwinism (Petermann 2004: 535), warning explicitly against over simplification and generalisation, and did not believe in a straight line of stages of progression for one particular culture or for that matter for the whole of mankind. Bastian's

---

4 E.R. Waite Diary No. 63, 7.10.1916 to 30.6.1917. The Diaries of Edgar Ravenswood Waite are held at the South Australian Museum Archives.
5 Carl Strehlow, *The Register*, 7.12.1921.

anthropology was governed by methodological convictions rather than an overarching theory. He drew on induction and empirical observation to avoid the classification of data according to predetermined categories, regarding schemes of classification as work in progress rather than definite models (Penny 2003: 93). Also Rudolf Virchow, the leading physical anthropologist and pathologist at the time in Germany, maintained that no one race or people was superior to another (Evans 2003: 200). With most of his other colleagues he professed the unity of humankind.

One of the main reasons for this humanistic and pluralistic position was that Germany (like other politically less significant European countries) was not an imperial or colonial power until the last quarter of the nineteenth century.[6] It was therefore not committed to an ideology of racial superiority 'that is virtually a political necessity for colonial powers' (Adams 1998: 264; Gingrich 2005: 68). The intellectual roots of nineteenth century German anthropology reached back to philosophers who emphasised the ideas of particularism opposing progressivism and deduction. Johann Gottfried Herder (1744–1803), the founder of German historical particularism, exerted a major influence on the development of anthropological thinking, as he was interested in the differences of cultures from age to age, and from one people to another (Adams 1998: 271). He rejected the concept of race (Mühlmann 1968: 62) as well as the French dogma of the uniform development of civilisation. Instead Herder recognised unique sets of values transmitted through history and maintained that outlooks and civilisations had to be viewed from within; in terms of their own development and purpose (Berlin 1976: 174). Thus, humanity was made up of a great diversity, language being one of its main manifestations. Herder's concepts of *Volk*, a cultural group or entity, and *Volksgeist*,[7] the individual expression of the being of a group of people, which sets it apart from others, provided the basis for this particularism. They were to become central tenets of German nineteenth century anthropological thought. The *Volksgeist* of a people, he believed, was embodied in their language and their literature, which included the oral traditions of indigenous peoples. Therefore language became crucial in German anthropological research. It became the pre-condition of authoritative ethnography. It is this tradition that led to a concept of cultures in the plural.

To achieve their Herderian goal, (i.e. to cover the various manifestations of cultures as completely as possible), German anthropologists were committed to inductive science and an empirical methodology. They stressed the need to gather as much information as possible before attempting to generate theories

6   Before Germany's unification in 1871 under Bismarck, it was made up of a large number of autocratic principalities.

7   The German word *Geist* is very difficult to translate. Literally *Geist* means 'spirit' or 'ghost', however, in this context it means something like 'the essence of a people' or 'the mind/intellect/genius and spirit of a people'.

about human difference (Penny and Bunzl 2003: 15). These aims made German nineteenth century anthropology a bustling enterprise. German anthropologists had networks of collectors, officials, missionaries and scientists throughout the world gathering information and examples of material culture. They launched some of the largest anthropological expeditions, sent researchers all around the globe, and were an influential presence at international conferences engaging in debates about human history, culture, environment and race. They founded the best equipped anthropological museums (Berlin, Leipzig, Hamburg and Munich) and a number of internationally recognised periodicals devoted to the discipline. The humanism of German anthropology with its pluralistic outlook and its anti-evolutionist position lasted nearly to the eve of World War I. This German humanism generated a number of humanist traditions as well as diverging streams of thought. It was ultimately contested and so marginalised that Franz Boas decided to leave Germany in the late nineteenth century exporting the German anthropological tradition to the United States.[8] Its fate in a post-Imperial and Nazi Europe was replicated in Australia: to become a 'nontradition of good anthropology … forgotten, repressed, and noticed only after tremendous time lags' (Gingrich 2005: 103).

Two routes to Empiricism

Carl Strehlow's route to empirical anthropology was traced through German philology, the German Romantic Movement, Humboldtian cosmography, history and comparative geography. Baldwin Spencer's, on the other hand, came through Charles Darwin, Herbert Spencer and other evolutionists. This route was also shaped by the role of biology in the late nineteenth century. The excitement with which advances in biology were received meant that the discipline's procedures became a model for others, and a model for empirical science generally. Later, this method would be known as 'the organic' model for social sciences. The idea was that societies, like natural species, exhibit organic structure. Such a view influenced Radcliffe-Brown to term anthropology 'a natural science of society' (Barnard 2000: 62–63, 70–71).

The ethnographic classics of these very different field-researchers illustrate two distinctive pathways to empirical studies in social-cultural anthropology. One leads through natural science as method using the taxonomic process of collecting, describing and identifying specimens. The other uses mainly the study of language, its semantics, syntax and semiology to specify a social life and its oral traditions. I will trace the path to empiricism that Carl Strehlow

---

8   The antihumanism of anthropology of imperial Germany has been elsewhere well covered see for example Massin (1996), Zimmerman (2001), Gingrich (2005: 111–136) and Monteath (2013); its racism forshadowed the developments in Nazi Germany.

and his editor Baron Moritz von Leonhardi followed. On this pathway language featured prominently as methodology and ultimately as evidence that Aranda and Loritja people were not by virtue of their material culture inferior human beings.

Carl Strehlow's *Die Aranda- und Loritja-Stämme in Zentral-Australien* is the richest and densest ethnographic text written on Western Aranda and Loritja cultures of central Australia at the beginning of the twentieth century. It is the first Australian work that comprehensively records the oral literature of Australian Aboriginal people in their own languages. The German tradition that grew out of Herder's seminal thoughts on language, the particularity of the 'other' and his humanism, which profoundly influenced German and North American anthropology, is also present in Carl Strehlow's work. It is not that Strehlow cites the scholars of German historical and philosophical thought. He does not. Like Boas, however, his work follows a distinctive form that privileges language and particularism. Moreover, his interests and emphasis reflect a pattern typical of the German tradition. Beyond diffuse influences, his teachers of Lutheran hermeneutics and von Leonhardi's probing questions secured him on this course. Like Spencer, Strehlow reflects his society and time.

Because his monograph was written in the German nineteenth century humanistic style, which was strictly descriptive, ethnographic and resistant to grand theory, nearly 100 years after its publication, *Die Aranda- und Loritja-Stämme in Zentral-Australien* remains an invaluable resource for Aranda and Loritja people. In documenting the complexity and richness of central Australian cultures, this classic allows regional comparisons, and an opportunity to chart change and continuity across a century. These issues are particularly significant in the contemporary setting of state-sponsored recognition of land and native title rights for indigenous Australians. Strehlow's masterpiece, among other things, bolsters the evidence for the continuation of traditional laws and customs in relation to Aboriginal land ownership and has been used as evidence in land right claims, native title claims and the protection of large tracts of country from mineral exploration in central Australia.

Considering Carl Strehlow's opus from the vantage point of the twenty-first century tells us something about both Strehlow and his German tradition, and the nature of modern professional anthropology. Importantly, this latter development routinised fieldwork and with the beginnings of a global modernity also began to shrink its significance. Strehlow's lifetime 'in the field' provided a unique opportunity for his empirical work but also necessitated a mentor to guide him through the demands of scholarly production. Like Spencer's relationship with Frazer, and Gillen's with Spencer, the relation between von Leonhardi and Strehlow is a specific intellectual mode.

Central concern and overview of the book

The main aim of this book is to make a contribution to overcoming the longstanding omission of the role of the German humanistic tradition, represented by Carl Strehlow, in Australian anthropology and intellectual history. The German missionary Carl Strehlow had a deep ethnographic interest in Aboriginal Australian songs, cosmology and social life which he documented in his seven volume work, *Die Aranda- und Loritja-Stämme in Zentral-Australien* (1907–1920) at the beginning of the twentieth century. This immensely rich corpus, based on a lifetime on the central Australian frontier, is barely known in the English-speaking world and is the last major classic ethnographic corpus on central Australian cultures that is to be discovered and evaluated in the English speaking world. I address with this book a long neglected research problem of the histories of Australian anthropology and intellectual history that have been almost purely Anglophone in their orientation so that untranslated work has been ignored. It is the first step towards an account of how this other anthropological tradition informed Carl Strehlow's work and highlights the key elements of his ethnography and brilliant scholarship.

Part One of this book (Chapters I to IV) positions Carl Strehlow's anthropological opus in its intellectual milieux: the German anthropological tradition of the nineteenth century and the Lutheran missionary background. His work falls in a German tradition of anthropological specification pursued through language which bears a strong resemblance to Franz Boas' approach. In this style of work language is a recurring theme because early German anthropologists believed it was the key to both a people's thought and sentiment. This language-based form of anthropology took hold in North America through Boas and his students, such as Edward Sapir, a crucial representative of early twentieth century linguistic anthropology, and Ruth Benedict who wrote on patterns of culture.

Chapter I begins with a general outline of Carl Strehlow's life and work in central Australia, a brief contact history of the Aranda and Loritja and an overview of the contents of *Die Aranda- und Loritja-Stämme in Zentral-Australien*. Carl Strehlow was interested, as it seems, in all aspects of religious and secular life, with special attention to song and myth. In this chapter I introduce 'altjira', a key Aranda term. This concept and its polysemy will be gradually explained, as it appears throughout the book. My discussion demonstrates how the term's meaning has changed in the course of 100 years.

Chapter II introduces the German anthropological tradition of the nineteenth century which is based on late eighteenth century German philosophy and in turn shaped a style of ethnography. The roots of this tradition are mainly to be found in Johann Gottfried Herder's concepts of *Volksgeist*, *Humanität* and language that together provide the bases for a form of cultural particularism. The inherent cultural pluralism and particularism of German anthropology contrasts with biologically-based theories of human difference and evolutionary sequencing of nineteenth century Anglo-American and French schools. To position Carl Strehlow within a framework of late nineteenth century and early twentieth century anthropology, I discuss briefly Franz Boas and Fritz Graebner, two important representatives of German anthropology. Strehlow's masterpiece *Die Aranda- und Loritja-Stämme in Zentral-Australien* is a typical example of German particularism and can be called Boasian.

In Chapter III I discuss the major influences on Carl Strehlow as a frontier scholar other than the German anthropological tradition. To understand his scholarship it is necessary to look at his missionary background which reveals some characteristics shared with the German anthropological tradition. The Lutheran language tradition in conjunction with the theological work of Warneck, Löhe and Deinzer, had a significant bearing on the manner in which Strehlow approached both his missionary and ethnographic work. Finally, von Leonhardi was indisputably Strehlow's major influence, as their heady intellectual partnership opened the questioning world of science to the pastor in the Australian desert.

Chapter IV is devoted to the letter exchange and dialogue between Strehlow and von Leonhardi and how this intellectual friendship between two diametrically opposed people, the missionary and the armchair anthropologist, produced a complementary partnership and a major ethnographic work. It is doubtful that Strehlow's classic monograph *Die Aranda- und Loritja-Stämme in Zentral-Australien* would have been published without his mentor and editor who helped shape his ethnographic insights. It is noteworthy that this, like Spencer and Gillen's work, was collaboration. Where Spencer brought an evolutionary frame to Gillen's observation, von Leonhardi brought rigorous particularism to Carl Strehlow's Christian humanism. If Strehlow was in a sense 'pre-anthropological', then it was von Leonhardi's incessant questioning and probing, as he responded to a scholarly community that shaped Strehlow's work into an opus that would connect with other anthropology.

These three influences, the German philosophical-cum-anthropological tradition, missionary hermeneutics and cosmopolitan scholarship shaped Strehlow's major work. The meeting point for these three was an intense engagement with the particulars of human experience. Herder and his successors, such as the von Humboldts, the Neuendettelsau seminary and von Leonhardi, each required real engagements with the meaning that 'others' might give to their lives. Both through training and through personal propensity, Carl Strehlow responded to these demands. He wrote within a tradition that acknowledged that all cultures are equal, notwithstanding their different moral values, and have individual features that cannot be rendered in terms of generalised stages of development. This position, though, did not prevent him from making remarks about certain customs he perceived as barbaric – for example, institutionalised homosexuality.

Part Two of this book (Chapters V to VIII) discusses the content and limitations of his masterpiece and how to position him in a history of anthropology. It shows the way in which Carl Strehlow, like Spencer and Gillen, represents a transitional phase in modern anthropology. An effective fieldworker, a committed empiricist, he nonetheless brought with him implicit models from Europe that did not fit indigenous Australian cultures. Still, his European preconceptions and assumptions allowed him to begin systematic data collection in a way that was rare for the period and remains of immense value. This data exemplifies many 'take-off points' for central developments in the modern field of twentieth century anthropology. I have chosen three areas of his work that demonstrate this paradox: his studies of myths, social classification and territorial organisation. The treatment of myth and kin build towards the understanding of land tenure because the former constitute the nature of traditional ownership.

Chapter V examines Carl Strehlow's focal interests, mythology and cosmology, which he recorded for both Aranda and Loritja groups. His linear and free translations of myth are innovative and provide some of the earliest insight into the true sophistication of Aboriginal cultures. Strehlow's explicit framework of Grimmian *Mythen, Sagen und Märchen* (myths, legends and fairy-tales) reflects his transitional status as a modern ethnographer. There are no traces of the more conventional approaches to myth of twentieth century anthropology. Among these one might list metaphoric or symbolic accounts that treat myth as integral to a particular culture specified by its master symbols and genres of metaphor. One would also include the twentieth century's three major comparative approaches: functionalism, structuralism and psychoanalysis that in their different ways address particular aspects of cognition taken to underlie all myth.

In Chapter VI, I discuss Carl Strehlow's studies on social classification, which he examined through 'marriage', the subsection system, kinship terminology, and family trees. Carl Strehlow had only a limited sense of comparative social analysis: subsections were mainly identified with 'marriage rule', and kinship with family trees. His ethnographic groundwork provides a point of departure to pursue an analysis of kinship systems. It gives a comprehensive overview of the subsection system and kinship terms that are still used today by Aranda and Loritja. His lists of relatives by generation and their totems, for example, provided the basis for his son's extraordinary genealogical exercise in data collection.

I examine in Chapter VII issues of land tenure and traditional ownership. Carl Strehlow did not study territorial organisation, which would become important in Australia in the mid-twentieth century. Nonetheless he provides significant information on the system at a particular time, one which resonates with current trends in Aranda and Loritja land tenure. His material informs modern views on these subjects and has been used in land and native title claims.

In Chapter VIII I discuss how Carl Strehlow might be positioned in Australian anthropology, how this might bear on the work of his son, T.G.H. Strehlow, and on more general issues of intellectual history in Australian anthropology. I discuss how I suggest that this history may be approached. My brief account of contemporaneous literature makes a beginning for other scholars who might, for instance, wish to compare and contrast Strehlow's and Spencer and Gillen's work with the numerous travellers tales that began Australian ethnography. My short address to current work in the history of Australian anthropology and ideas that is not well explored locates an area of scholarship in which much more could be done.

Part I

I. Carl Strehlow and the Aranda and Loritja of Central Australia

On the 23 December 1871 in a little village called Fredersdorf in Northern Germany, Carl Friedrich Theodore Strehlow was born as the seventh child of the village school teacher (Liebermeister 1998: 16). Carl grew up in modest circumstances that offered few opportunities. In the Germany of the late nineteenth century, clerical institutions were the only source of education for the talented poor. The Lutheran Seminary at Neuendettelsau where Carl trained offered a rich and intense intellectual grounding for the bright and gifted student. As Carl Strehlow was finding a calling that would take him to the remotest place on earth – as Europeans imagined it – the world in which he would spend 30 years was being uprooted.

At the time, the Overland Telegraph Line was making its way north traversing traditional Aboriginal countries in central Australia. In just a very few years, this initiative was followed by the Lutheran missionaries, A.H. Kempe and W.F. Schwarz. In 1877, they built a small mission settlement at Ntaria, a sacred site associated with the ratapa dreaming.[1] The missionaries called this mission 'Hermannsburg' in recognition of the seminary that had trained them. Their journey from Bethany in South Australia to the centre of Australia had lasted nearly 18 months because they had been travelling with an entourage consisting of 37 horses, 20 cattle and nearly 2000 sheep (Leske 1977, 1996; Scherer 1963; Harms 2003). Not long after their arrival Kempe and Schwarz were joined by Louis and Charlotte Schulze (nee Gutmann), and their future wives Dorethea (nee Queckenstedt) and Dorethea (nee Schulz), who were the first European women to settle in central Australia.

One year after the missionaries' arrival in 1878 a group of Western Aranda men led by Nameia[2] returned from a long revenge expedition into the southern territories of the Matuntara and must have observed with great surprise and indignation 'the first structures erected at Hermannsburg' that 'greeted their eye' (Strehlow 1970: 125). These were not the only wary or hostile eyes trained on the missionaries. By 1879 the mission lease was surrounded by squatters who were backed by local police (Hartwig 1965; Donovan 1988: 60, 87). Both groups tended to disparage the missionaries.

---

1   See Carl Strehlow (1907: 80–81; 1908: 72 f.3; 1911: 122–124) and T.G.H. Strehlow (1971: 758).

2   Nameia was murdered in 1889 at constable William Willshire's police camp on the Finke River. It seems the murderers were never identified with certainty (Nettelbeck and Foster 2007: 71–73). See also T.G.H. Strehlow's *Journey to Horseshoe Bend* (1969).

2. Map of route of the Lutheran missionaries to Hermannsburg.

Source: Clivie Hilliker, The Australian National University. Adapted from Leske 1977.

At Ntaria, the newcomers immediately built pens for their livestock. They also began their crusade to evangelise the indigenous people who chose to stay temporarily at the new settlement. This proximity allowed the Lutherans to begin their study of language and culture. The missionaries called these people Aldolinga meaning 'from the west'. However, the progress in spreading the gospel among the 'Aldolinga' was slow and life on the frontier incredibly harsh due to droughts, isolation, disease and the aggression of other white settlers. By 1891 the little mission was abandoned, the missionaries had been defeated by the challenges and the loss of their families (Austin-Broos 1994: 132).

The Aranda and Kukatja-Loritja peoples

Carl Strehlow's ethnographic data relates mainly to two distinct groups whom he broadly labelled Aranda and Loritja in the title of his publication, although these names can also be used for other neighbouring groups. One was an Arandic group and the other was a Western Desert group that did not display all the typical features of a Western Desert culture due to social and environmental circumstances.

Carl Strehlow refers often to the Western, North-Western, Eastern and Southern Aranda in his writings, but he does not define exactly where their territories lie; and on his map (1910) he shows language and dialect distribution rather than territories belonging to particular groups. He placed the western Arandic language, Aranda Ulbma, on the upper Finke River, roughly between the MacDonnell and James Ranges (including Hermannsburg Mission), the Aranda Roara between the eastern part of the MacDonnell Ranges and James Ranges including Alice Springs, the Aranda Lada from approximately Henbury along the Finke River and the Aranda Tanka between Charlotte Waters and Oodnadatta along the lower Finke River. His son, T.G.H. Strehlow (1971: xx), wrote that Carl Strehlow's information came mainly from the north-western and Hermannsburg sectors of the Western Aranda area.

The Arandic group whose culture Carl Strehlow documented in great detail identify themselves today as Western Aranda or Arrarnta. They call themselves sometimes 'Tyurretyerenye', meaning 'belonging to Tyurretye', and refer to their Arandic dialect as Western or 'Tyurretye Arrernte' (Kenny 2010: 6). Their ancestors lived in an area bounded roughly in the north by the Western MacDonnell Ranges (Strehlow 1907: 32, 42; T.G.H. Strehlow 1971: 670, note 19)[3] that separates them from the Anmatyerr and Northern Aranda peoples. In the south, their country stretches along the Finke River past the James Range, to the countries of Southern Aranda and Matuntara peoples. To the west, it extends to the Derwent River and to the east it abuts the territory of today's Central Arrernte people (see also T.G.H. Strehlow 1947: 59).

---

3   Tjoritja (Tyurretye) was not only the name for the MacDonnell Ranges, but also for Alice Springs which lies in the MacDonnell Ranges. Carl Strehlow also wrote that 'Lately, Alice Springs has been called Kapmanta; kap is an abbreviation of kaputa = head, and manta = dense. Kapmanta literally means: dense head. What it refers to are the roofs close together (roof = head of the house) because here the natives had first seen roofs of corrugated iron' (Strehlow 1907: 42).

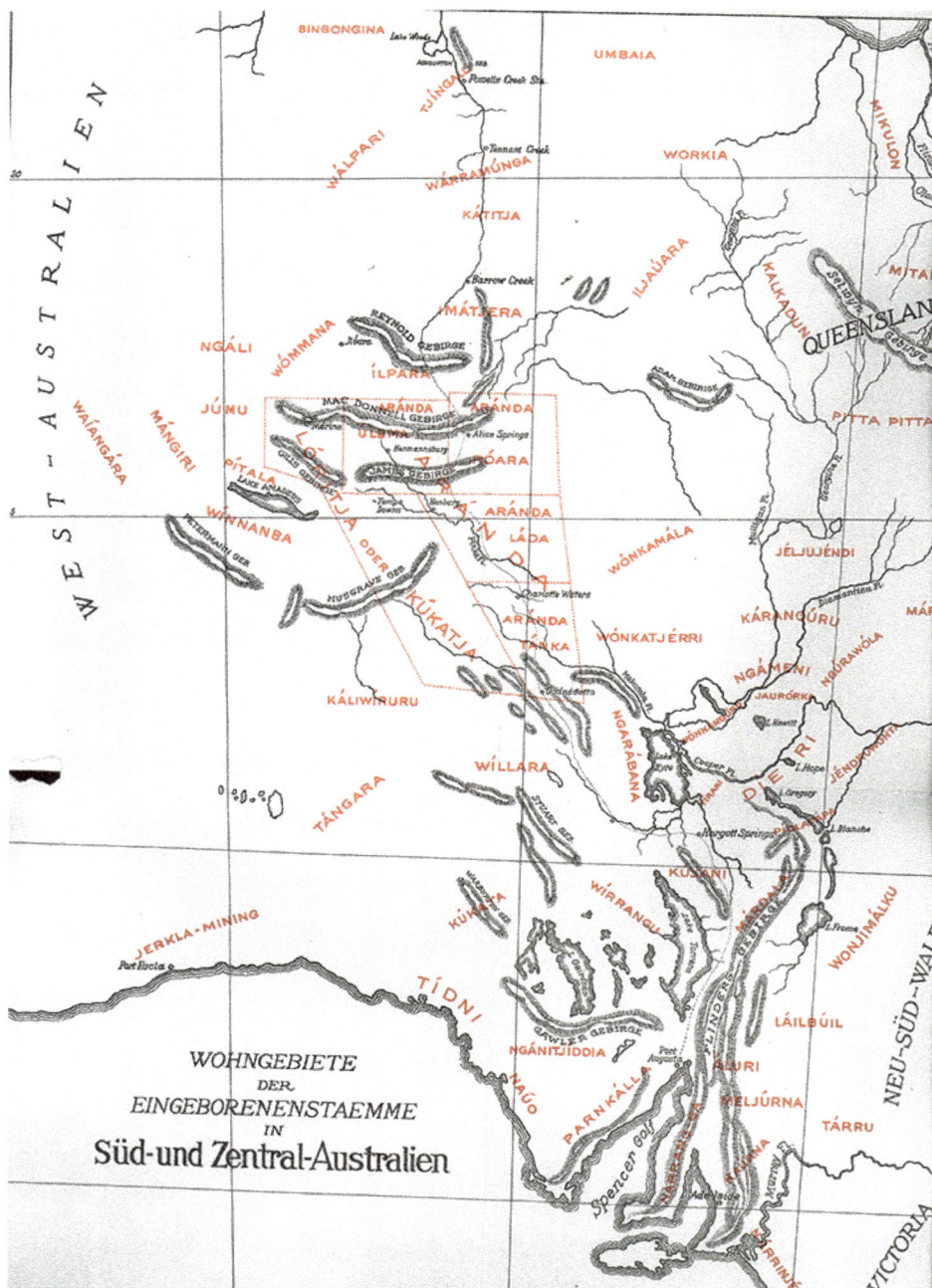

3. Carl Strehlow's map, 1910.

Source: Strehlow Research Centre, Alice Springs.

For the Aranda, first contact with the newcomers occurred in the early 1860s when John McDouall Stuart was trying to find his way to the northern coast of the continent via the inland (Strehlow 1967: 7–8). Owen Springs was central Australia's first pastoral station, and the indigenous people who resided between that station and Ntaria would certainly have encountered the cattlemen and other explorers who passed that way in the early 1870s (Austin-Broos 1994: 131). Ernest Giles, for example, seems to have recorded the first Western Aranda word, 'Larapinta', the name of the Finke River, on the 28 August 1872:

> Soon after we had unpacked and let go our horses, we were accosted by a native on the opposite side of the creek. Our little dog became furious: then two natives appeared. We made an attempt at a long conversation, but signally failed, for neither of us knew many of the words the other was saying. The only bit of information I obtained was their name for the river – as they kept continually pointing to it and repeating the word Larapinta. (Giles [1889] 1995: 8)

The country of the Western Aranda is of a rare beauty, painted by Albert Namatjira (1902–1959), and other artists of the watercolour school of Hermannsburg, who still capture in their art the river systems, magnificent gum trees, gorges, rocky valleys and the creeks that emanate from the aged ranges. The area is one of the best-watered parts of central Australia. This automatically resulted in conflict between the indigenous people and the new settlers.

4. Image of central Australia.

Source: Shane Mulcahy, Desert Vision.

The majority of cattle runs in this region were established between 1876 and 1884, bringing thousands of cattle and horses onto the traditional lands. Naturally the local people reacted, as their waterholes were being destroyed and contaminated by these new animals. A kind of partisan war broke out. The cattle killings were answered by shootings. As the scarce desert resources were fouled by stock, droughts set in and the aggression towards the indigenous population increased, Aranda people drifted to the Hermannsburg Mission that offered easy rations and some safety (see also Morton 1992: 52). Life on the mission was fraught with difficulties for the Aranda. They were crowded into a small area that many of them once would have visited only occasionally, if at all. By the time Carl Strehlow arrived at the mission the Aranda had been largely pacified, although there remained pockets of resistance that annoyed the local police as well as Strehlow. The cattle spearing affected the mission by dragging Strehlow into court to address 'partisans' who lived on the mission lease, or mission cattle speared by these or other groups.[4]

The people living to the immediate west of the Western Aranda called themselves Kukatja or Loritja at the turn of the twentieth century. Today they call themselves Luritja or Kukatja-Luritja when referring to their ancestry and history.[5] The Kukatja may have heard of the newcomers from their eastern and southern neighbours. We cannot know, but at the very latest they would have encountered Europeans when the exploring parties of Ernest Giles in 1872, and William Christie Gosse in 1873, pushed into the Centre and traversed parts of their territory.

The country of the Kukatja-Loritja lies to the west of the Derwent River which marks broadly the language border between them and the Aranda. This language boundary sometimes determines how people perceive their country and often describe the border area as 'mix-up' country, referring to the fact that a number of places have both Loritja and Aranda names and that there is no clear cut border between them. Róheim (1974: 126) called these people 'Lurittya Merino', and noted that they were seen as 'half Aranda'. People who belong to this border area are still today fluent speakers of both Aranda and Loritja and share ancestors as well as traditional laws and customs (Kenny 2010).

Carl Strehlow remarked that the people whom the Aranda called 'Loritja', referred to themselves as 'Kukatja' (Strehlow 1907: 57, Anmerkung 9). According to T.G.H. Strehlow 'Loritja' was the Aranda name applied to all Western speech groups (Strehlow 1947: 177–178). The people themselves refused this designation and used instead 'Kukatja, Pintubi, Ngalia, Ilpara, Andekerinja, etc'. According to Tindale, the name 'Luritja' had a negative connotation with the result that

---

4 Carl Strehlow's letters to his superior Kaibel held at the Lutheran Archives, Adelaide often describe the court dealings and cattle killings which he grudgingly had to tend to. See Vallee (2006) and Nettelbeck and Foster (2007) on frontier conflict in this region.
5 There is a distinct group of people living at Balgo in Western Australia who are also called Kukatja.

Kukatja people asked him to call them 'Kukatja' rather than 'Luritja' (1974: 229). In his monumental *Aboriginal Tribes of Australia* he used Kukatja and placed them 'west of the Gosses Range and Palm Valley on the south of the MacDonnell Ranges; south west to Lake Amadeus, George Gill Range, Cleland Hills (Merandji), Inindi near Mount Forbes, and Thomas Reservoir (Alala): on upper Palmer, Walker, and Rundall creeks' (Tindale 1974: 229).

Over the course of time Luritja has become a linguistic and cultural self-label despite its foreign origin for a number of peoples. By the 1960s people preferred to refer to themselves as 'Luritja' and today 'Luritja' remains a broad term that can be used interchangeably with other Western Desert labels (Smith 2005: 73). 'Kukatja' and 'Mayutjarra', for example, are recognised by middle aged and elderly speakers as being equivalent to the new label, 'Luritja' (Holcombe 1998: 217).

Additional confusion surrounding the language and group label 'Luritja' is a result of migration towards the south by Ngaliya Warlpiri, Pintupi, Jumu or Mayutjarra and Kukatja peoples (see Holcombe 1998: 217). Some of these groups refer to themselves as 'Luritja'. The movements of 'Luritja' groups have been mainly caused by the disruptions of the past 100 years which included epidemics and environmental stress such as drought and starvation. According to Tindale, for example, a group called 'Jumu' or 'Mayutjarra' was decimated by an epidemic in the 1930s. Following their extinction Pintupi and Ngalia Warlpiri people moved into their vacated country (Tindale 1974: 138, 227–228). Smith writes that the Kukatja were on the move to the east and south by the late 1880s (Smith 2005: 1). This chain migration of desert people into the settled districts took several generations to run its course.

During Carl Strehlow's time, Kukatja-Loritja people belonging to the area immediately to the west of Aranda territory moved south-eastwards towards the Hermannsburg Mission (see Leske 1977: 26–27; Smith 2005). When the explorer Winnecke passed through the general area in 1894, he still encountered 'sandhill tribes' living west of Hermannsburg (Winnecke 1897: 37), who were presumably Kukatja. Their eastward migration intensified with the onset of a major decade-long drought in 1895 (Smith 2005: 29) and throughout the 1920s, the Kukatja people moved through the frontier to resume contact with relatives at the mission and on the outlying pastoral properties (Smith 2005: 51; Holcombe 1998: 26). The missionaries were aware of 'a vigorous tribe just west of Hermannsburg' with a large population,[6] and in the late 1920s, plans for Aranda evangelists were made to take their message to these groups.

---

6   *Lutheran Herald,* 26.10.1921: 114.

5. T.G.H. Strehlow's map, 1971.

Source: Strehlow Research Centre, Alice Springs.

The location of the 'Kukatja' area today is understood as being along the western edge of Western Aranda territory.[7] T.G.H. Strehlow has maintained that Kukatja land stretched from the western border of Western Aranda westwards to Mt Liebig and Putati spring (1970: 110). Heffernan describes a current perception of the territory that was owned by Kukatja:

> The Kukatja (as distinct from the people of the same title living at Balgo in Western Australia) lived in the country west of Glen Helen Station (Ungkungka) along the tail of the Western MacDonnell ranges through to Mt Liebig, south to Gosses Bluff, the Gardiner Range and then out to Mt Peculiar and Mt Udor. The country includes such prominent communities as Papunya, Haasts Bluff, Umpangara and Mt Liebig. (Heffernan and Heffernan 2005: 4)

Pre-contact, Kukatja-Loritja culture was strongly influenced by Western Aranda traditional laws and customs and vice versa (Strehlow 1947). When white settlement destabilised desert life, they moved into the Hermannsburg Mission and the Aranda influence on Kukatja ways would have become more intense. Heffernan and Heffernan write about the Kukatja:

> Because these people lived on the fringe of Arrernte country, they moved into Hermannsburg very early on (for reasons that were important to them at the time – easy food is one most frequently given). A good number of their descendants today live in outstations west of Hermannsburg, and in the Papunya region. They instinctively refer to themselves today as Arrernte or Luritja and only as Kukatja on the basis of ancestry. (Heffernan and Heffernan 2005: 4–5)

Today the cultures of Western Aranda and Kukatja-Luritja people have many features in common. This is not surprising, given their close relationships that involve joint ceremonies, intermarriage and an overlapping land tenure system (Strehlow 1908, 1913; T.G.H. Strehlow 1947, 1965, 1970; Kenny 2010) as well as a shared environmental space – the well-watered range system. In more recent times, commonalities have been re-enforced not only at Ntaria but also at other settlements including Haasts Bluff, Mt Liebig and Papunya.

Carl Strehlow's life and work in Australia

Carl Strehlow arrived in Australia in 1892, not long after graduating from the Neuendettelsauer seminary in southern Germany. His first posting was the

---

7 Stirling had noted in 1894 that 'the territory of the Luritchas marches on the western boundary of Aruntas, and comprises the country about Erldunda, Tempe Downs, Gill's Range, Mereenie Bluff and Glen Helen' (Stirling 1896: 11).

Bethesda Mission at Lake Eyre in South Australia. The moment he arrived at the mission, he showed interest in the language of the local people. Within six months he spoke Diyari (Schild 2004a: 55) and by the end of 1894, with J.G. Reuther, he had translated the New Testament into Diyari. It was called *Testamenta marra*, published in 1897.

In October 1894 at the age of 22 he was transferred from Bethesda to Hermannsburg in remote central Australia. He arrived at the abandoned mission station with two fellow missionaries, Reuther and Linke. His first impressions of the Hermannsburg Mission were not favourable because the small congregation had dispersed:

> I was disappointed … It was very hurtful to see the jewels of a mission station, the little church and school, fallen into disrepair … There was not one Christian to welcome us like at Bethesda. Only a few naked heathens looked at us in amusement when we arrived.[8]

6. Carl Strehlow's *'Aussendungsphoto'*, 1892.

Source: Archiv/Mission Eine Welt, Neuendettelsau.

---

8   Carl Strehlow, *Kirchlichen Mitteilungen*, No. 3, 1895: 19.

He stayed for nearly three decades at this place. He ran it as a mission and a cattle and sheep station, providing pastoral care for more than 100 Aboriginal people who became Christians, as well as a large number of their relatives who lived on the fringes of the mission. At the same time he was keeping aggressive pastoralists at bay and dealing with a range of social issues that had been caused by the forcing together of different Aboriginal groups. Some Western Aranda and Kukatja at Hermannsburg, for example, had been enemies for a long time (Strehlow 1947: 62).

These local arrangements were extraordinary. Hermannsburg was the largest settlement in central Australia, bigger than Alice Springs. The people living at the mission were not a group that traditionally would have lived there together for extended periods. The mission created a completely new setting for the indigenous population who were hunters and gatherers. They must have tried to accommodate this situation by activating, reconciling and adapting every imaginable tie to country and kin. It is likely that tensions emerged between the actual local group of Ntaria and other mission inhabitants from neighbouring or far-flung countries. The situation therefore would not have favoured traditional territorial organisation.

Administrative work for both church and state were also a part of Carl Strehlow's duties. He became the postmaster, Justice of the Peace and contributed to the school by developing curricula, translating hymns to the music of Bach, and preparing lessons in Aranda. His work at Hermannsburg would bring him into conflict with pastoralists, the police, governments, the British anthropological establishment and even his own church.

The young man was soon left to his own devices by Reuther and Linke who returned south. Despite the desolate conditions of the mission, Strehlow started rebuilding it with great enthusiasm, not least motivated by the prospect that his young fiancée Friedericke Johanna Henriette Keysser would be arriving within the year. Their courtship is documented in endearing epistles that travelled between central Australia and Germany. The complete correspondence[9] has survived and gives a unique insight into their relationship (Brandauer and Veber 2009: 113–127). From Hermannsburg, Carl wrote to Frieda about every detail that she would encounter. Her future home, the surrounding landscape and the palm garden behind the house – which he considered the 'most beautiful place in the whole of the Northern Territory'[10] – were familiar to her when she arrived at the mission. He wrote:

> My dearest loved Frieda! … Now you may want to know more about Hermannsburg, where, so God will, we shall find our home. The area around the station is prettier than around Bethesda. Transpose yourself

---

9   Held at the Strehlow Research Centre (SRC) in Alice Springs.
10   Carl Strehlow to Frieda Keysser, 10.10.1894.

in your imagination to Hermannsburg standing beside me and looking out of the window. Not far to the north you see a long, high range, with some mountains in its foreground, that is the MacDonnell Range. When you move to the next window with me, looking to the south, you can overlook our gardens that are quite big. You can see the date palms, the peppertrees and some pomegranate trees in bloom now, the red blooms are wonderful. ... There is also a gazebo in which we will be sitting comfortably and chatting intimately in the cool evenings. Beyond the garden lies the Finke River, but no water is flowing in it, only some gumtrees are growing in it. Behind the Finke rise steep and high mountains, which are only sparsely vegetated with grass and flowers.[11]

The young couple had only met once in a three-day encounter during Easter 1892 (Brandauer and Veber 2009: 114), just before Carl had left for his Australian calling. It was love at first sight. Three years would pass until they met again after a long and protracted battle with her guardians. Her letters to him shared his passion and enthusiasm. About their first meeting she writes:

When you looked at me with those blue eyes, I knew, that you loved me. When you had left that day, I just wanted to cry and cry, but I was not permitted to let anyone know... But now you are mine after a long battle. If it were only my decision, I would come sooner to you.[12]

Frieda was looking forward to her new life and adventure in Australia, which her imagination clothed in a romantic haze. In her letters she discussed with her future husband her dowry which included measured curtains for their home. Travelling from Germany, Frieda, 19 years of age, joined Carl in 1895. The voyage to the Centre in the early summer was an ordeal. The heat, the flies and discomfort of the travel were unbearable. In addition she suffered from excruciating toothaches. Her luggage with the curtains for the house arrived months later leaving her without the essentials for her new life.

Despite the inconveniences, Frieda embraced her role as a missionary's wife. She started to learn Aranda, teach the women household skills intended to improve health and elevate living standards, and had six children at the Hermannsburg Mission. Her first child Friedrich was born in 1897, her only daughter Martha in 1899, Rudolf in 1900, Karl in 1902, Hermann in 1905 and her youngest son Theodore, who would later become one of the most controversial figures in Australian anthropology, in 1908. Together Carl and Frieda made Hermannsburg a refuge for the local people and fought for their physical and mental survival. By 1912 the efforts of the Strehlows were obvious. Carl was able to report:

---

11   Carl Strehlow to Frieda Keysser, 12 .11.1894.
12   Frieda Keysser to Carl Strehlow, 22.7.1894.

1. that the number of deaths during the past years has steadily gone down; and therefore 2. the state of health of the blacks on our station has improved and as far as the inhabitants of our station are concerned, 3. the Aranda are not yet thinking of dying out (!). (Strehlow 1913: Preface)

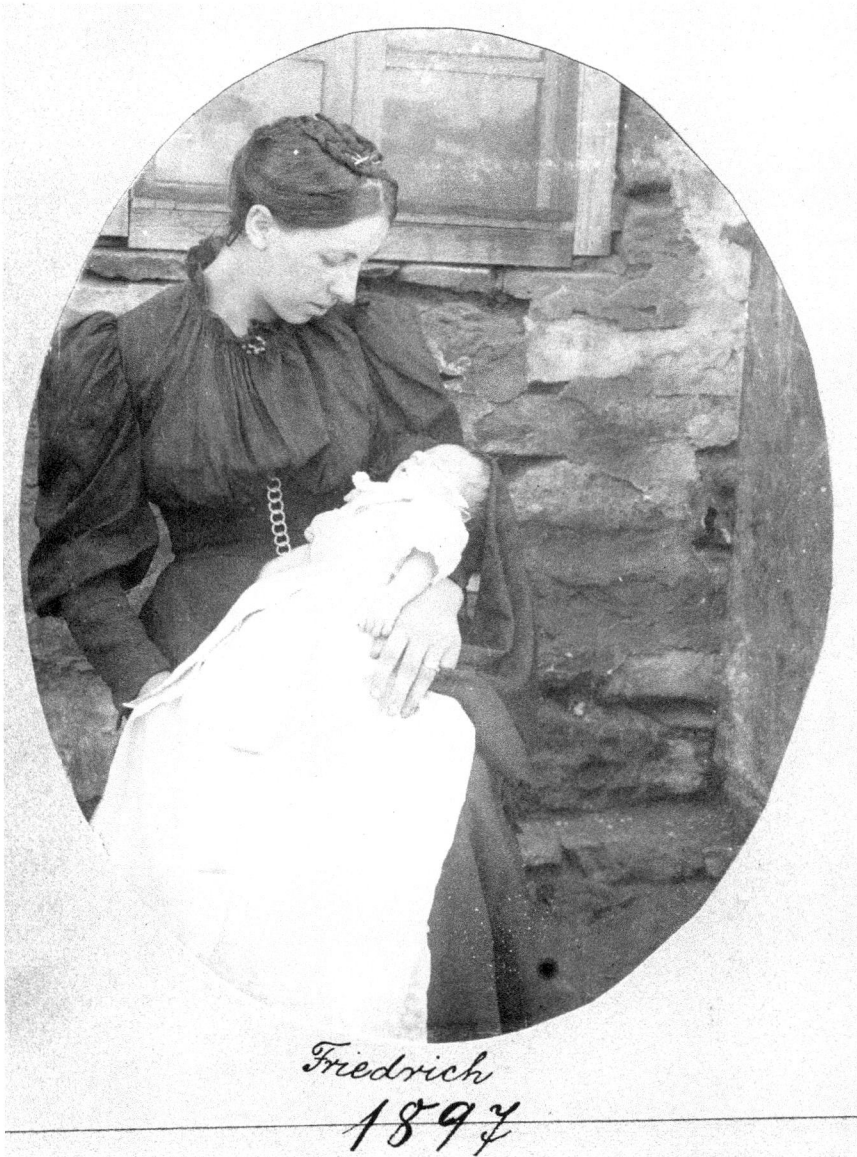

Friedrich
1897

7. Frieda Strehlow and her first child Friedrich, 1897.

Source: Strehlow Research Centre, Alice Springs (SRC 7762).

Frieda was one of the very few European women to know the unforgiving life of the desert frontier, becoming by default one of central Australia's first female ethnographers, predating Daisy Bates and Olive Pink. She was not to know that her married life would include work on her husband's ethnographic masterpiece.

8. Aranda girls with Frieda at Hermannsburg in the 1890s.

Source: Strehlow Research Centre, Alice Springs (SRC 5835).

Carl Strehlow started work on language and translation immediately. His fluency in Diyari and the bible translation facilitated his acquisition of the local languages, Aranda and Loritja. His previous experience is likely to have helped him grasp the intellectual concepts of the Aranda and Loritja at Hermannsburg. He was also able to draw on language materials compiled by his predecessor missionaries, Kempe and Schulze. He became fluent in Aranda within months and preached in the vernacular. In 1896 only two years after his arrival on Aranda territory, Strehlow's Aranda was so good that Gillen, who had been living among Arandic peoples since 1875, used his services as a translator for his anthropological research in Hermannsburg (Mulvaney, Morphy and Petch [1997] 2001: 118–119). In 1899 Strehlow supplied some information on Aranda kinship terms and subsection systems to Otto Siebert and Howitt.[13]

In 1904 Carl Strehlow published an Aranda Service Book, *Galtjindintjamea-Pepa Aranda Wolambarinjaka* which included 100 German hymns translated into Aranda and some of them set to Bach's church music. This work was partially based on that of his predecessor Kempe and the assistance of Aranda

---

13   Otto Siebert to A.W. Howitt, 22.4.1899 (Howitt Collection at Melbourne Museum).

men like Moses Tjalkabota who seemed to have embraced Lutheran teachings (Tjalkabota 2002: 237–300). On the other hand, Tjalkabota was one of the main informants for Strehlow's ethnographic oeuvre and had been initiated. At the end of 1904, Strehlow's future editor, von Leonhardi, who had some queries on religion, offered to publish anything that Carl might write. Although Strehlow had already collected some material on mythology[14] and collated an extensive wordlist of Aranda, Loritja, Diyari and German, his ethnographic research only started seriously in 1905 after von Leonhardi expressed his interest in a publication (Kenny 2005).

9. Loatjira, Pmala, Tjalkabota and Talku, 1906/7.

Source: Strehlow Research Centre, Alice Springs (SRC 6196).

---

14   Carl Strehlow to von Leonhardi, 30.7.1907.

The building blocks were now in place: language fluency, a stable domestic life, growing ease with the people, increasingly engaged informants, a European contact promising publication and, most importantly, intellectual engagement. Carl Strehlow spent the following five years collecting ethnographic data from senior men at Hermannsburg and sending plant, animal and insect specimens as well as material culture[15] to Germany. The specimens were widely distributed by his editor to museums and reputable scientists in Germany for research, classification and display.

Carl Strehlow collected his material mainly from senior men who were not Christians or still immersed in their traditions. From what we know about ownership of dreaming stories and country, he could only have gained his information from the appropriate owners of a certain age group. Four of his main informants, Loatjira, Pmala (Tmala), Moses (Tjalkabota) and Talku, are mentioned by him and his son (Strehlow 1971: xx–xxii).

Loatjira (c.1846–1924)[16] was Carl Strehlow's main informant on Western Aranda culture. He was the most important contributor to *Die Aranda- und Loritja-Stämme in Zentral-Australien*. He was the inkata (ceremonial chief)[17] of Ntaria, 'the grand old man of Hermannsburg', and an important ngankara (healer, doctor), who 'had possessed full knowledge of the dreaded death charms' and had taken part as a young man in avenging parties (Strehlow 1970: 116). He was not resident at the mission and resisted conversion. According to T.G.H. Strehlow, Loatjira was the main upholder of Aranda religion who 'remained strongly opposed to Christianity throughout the lifetime of my father, and in fact came to Hermannsburg very rarely after the completion of my father's book'.[18] Loatjira chose to live outside Hermannsburg near Ellery Creek, which was on the eastern boundary of the mission-lease, and only came permanently into Hermannsburg after Strehlow's death. Carl wrote that 'the old heathen Loatjira' had learnt the commandments despite of his old age and blindness, but left the station with his wife due to a death.[19] That day in 1913, 20 people left the mission in accordance with mourning customs. There must have been lots of coming and going due to the deaths that occurred at Hermannsburg. It is not known if Loatjira returned to the mission before Carl's death.

H.A. Heinrich noted that Loatjira was among a number of persons who had received pre-baptismal instruction from Reverend Strehlow. He was baptised in 1923 and christened Abraham. T.G.H. Strehlow reports that he died a broken

---

15 Von Leonhardi to Carl Strehlow, 2.6.1906. Strehlow sent von Leonhardi a letter on the 8.4.1906, in which he seems to have offered for the first time to send ethnographic objects to Germany.

16 According to T.G.H. Strehlow (1971: 753).

17 T.G.H. Strehlow's gloss for 'inkata [ingkarte]'.

18 T.G.H. Strehlow's *Handbook of Central Australian Genealogies* (1969: 125) and Strehlow (1970: xxi).

19 Carl Strehlow, *Kirchen- und Missions-Zeitung*, No. 5, 1914: 34.

man on 4 October 1924 from Spanish influenza (Strehlow 1970: 116; 1971: xxi, xxxviii, 262–263, 599, 650). In *White Flour, White Power,* Rowse (1998: 82) cites Lohe (1977: 37) who does not quote his sources:

> Quite significantly was the baptism of the old blind Aranda chief and sorcerer, Loatgira (Loatjira), who only three years before has called Christianity 'rubbish'. Already in 1913 as reported above, he had joined Strehlow's class of instruction, but this was disrupted when he left Hermannsburg in 1914, returning only in the early 1920s. With longing joy he announced his desire to be baptised. In answer to the question 'why', he said: I believe that Jesus is my Saviour. Tjurunga (the sacred objects of the Aranda and the ceremonies connected therewith) is of the devil and a lie. I desire with all my heart to become a Christian. I believe that Jesus is able to save even me… (Lohe 1977: 37 cited in Rowse 1998: 82)

I doubt that Loatjira really converted. He wanted to die on his own country. One of the main features of Aranda belief is 'becoming country', going into the country and becoming part of it – all songs end with the ancestors growing tired and longing for their home and returning to their place of origin. Loatjira wanted to die at Ntaria. It was on his father's and father's father's country as well as in the vicinity of his conception site where his spirit-child (called 'ratapa' in Carl Strehlow's work) had come from and where his 'iningukua', his spirit-double, usually dwelt.[20]

Not much is known about Pmala (Tmala), the second person on the photograph of Strehlow's main informants. Pmala (c.1860–1923) was a Western Aranda man with his conception site at Ndata belonging to the euro dreaming, north-west of Glen Helen Gorge (Strehlow 1971: xxi, 599, 760). Pmala married Annie Toa in 1890. He was baptised 'Silas' on the 16 April 1900 by Carl Strehlow. According to T.G.H. Strehlow Silas often chopped firewood for the Strehlow home, and normally brought down on his head the large bread-setting dish with the fat and innards from the killing pen. He died on the 24 June 1923 suddenly of heart failure. He had been blind from youth.[21] He appears on one of Carl Strehlow's genealogies as Ulakararinja (Carl Strehlow 1913). He is known to his descendants as Silas Mpetyane.

Moses Tjalkabota (c.1873–1950) is the best-known contributor to Strehlow's oeuvre. He became a famous evangelist in central Australia, despite his blindness, and thus was well documented by the Finke River Mission. He had been baptised on the 26 December 1890 by A.H. Kempe when he was about 12 or 13, but had been nevertheless initiated. He was married on the 25 January

---

20 Loatjira's conception site was Mbultjigata near Ntarea (Ntaria), belonging to rameia (yellow goanna) dreaming (T.G.H. Strehlow 1971: 753). According to Carl Strehlow loatjira is a synonym for rameia (1907: 80 fn. 3).

21 T.G.H. Strehlow's *Handbook of Central Australian Genealogies* (1969: 125, 157, 211).

1903 to Sofie and had 12 children, only one of whom survived. Interestingly, Moses also had his sons initiated, despite being a staunch Christian. According to his autobiography, he was among the first to shake Carl's hand at his arrival in 1894 and taught Carl Aranda (Tjalkabota 2002: 272).

The fourth man in the picture is Talku (c.1867–1941), Carl Strehlow's main Loritja informant on myth and song (1908, 1911). While he was able to collect a substantial amount of kinship terminology (1913) from him, he was not able to complete Talku's family tree. He remarked:

> Unfortunately, I could not gather sufficient data to complete [the family tree], for my informant, Talku, who also supplied most of the Loritja myths and cult songs, has once more left our station, and his other tribal companions residing here have married local women and have therefore already been included in the family trees of the Aranda.

> The man sitting at the end of the row on the right is Talku. He used to make it his task in life to spear the cattle belonging to the whites. An attempted escape during his arrest resulted in him being shot through the abdomen. He was then brought to the Mission station and remained there until he ran away one day to enjoy his golden freedom. (Strehlow 1913: 85, and note 2)

Talku was also an important informant for his son, T.G.H. Strehlow (1970: 137; 1971: xxi, 768), who knew him as Wapiti, Talku's name in old age. 'Wapiti' means yam. T.G.H. Strehlow made some biographical notes on Talku, aka Wapiti, as well:

> Talku, like Loatjira, was not a resident of Hermannsburg. He was the ceremonial chief of the Kukatja yam centre of Merini. Born about 1867, he organised raids upon cattle belonging to Tempe Downs Station at the beginning of the century. A police party surprised these raiders one day south of Ltalatuma, and fired upon them when they sought to evade capture. Talku was hit by a bullet from a police tracker's rifle which passed through his body and emerged again without apparently injuring any vital organs. His upper thigh bone was, however, shattered. He was carried on the backs of his friends across the ranges to Hermannsburg, a distance of some twenty-five miles. His tough constitution and unconquerable courage carried him through this ordeal. After being nursed back to health at Hermannsburg, he showed his gratitude to my father by providing him with detailed information on Loritja totemic rites, sacred songs, and social organization. And then he disappeared again one day into the free wild life of his own country. (Strehlow 1971: xxi)

Talku must have left the station at the very latest in 1909. By 1929 he was back at the mission. On his research trip to Hermannsburg, Norman Tindale made a data sheet of Wapiti which also confirms his identity. He died at about the age of 70 on the 14 January 1941.

Other informants of Carl Strehlow seem to have included Hezekiel's father, a western quoll man, and Nathaniel Rauwiraka, a main man of Ellery Creek.

Carl Strehlow's methodology was rigorous. He sat with his informants who sang and dictated word by word their songs and myths and described ceremonies and performances. Their dictation allowed verbatim recording of songs along with their accounts of the choreography and meaning of the sacred ceremonies and artefacts used in them. Strehlow's records were not an eyewitness description of performances. His language proficiency allowed detailed, accurate recording of the descriptions, explanations and interpretations that Aranda and Loritja people themselves provided for their ceremonies and cultures.

He seems to have spent as much if not more time between 1905 and 1909 on his ethnographic project than on his missionary duties. The Lutheran hierarchy criticised Strehlow for the amount of time and energy he devoted to his research and writing. As far as his superiors in the Barossa Valley were concerned, he was wasting his time. We can only imagine what kind of impression he made on the Aranda. Certainly it seemed to elicit respect. Strehlow's Aranda informants may have read in their engagements with him a form of exchange they were not unfamiliar with. Here perhaps was a man bent on building a portfolio of knowledge concerning both his own law and the Aranda's (see also Austin-Broos 2004: 61). Of course, the emplacement of Christian knowledge would have been an issue, especially for Loatjira and other custodians for Ntaria. Carl Strehlow had become a form of inkata (ceremonial chief) regarding Christian law and ceremony. In the course of his stay, Carl became the inkata of Altjira (Aranda word used for Christian God; this word was also used around the turn of the century for beings significant in indigenous religion). For the Aranda it appears not to have been difficult to extend these meanings. Strehlow junior also suggests that his father was seen as a form of inkata.[22]

In the last few months of 1909, before leaving central Australia for Germany, Carl Strehlow was working on the conclusion of *Die Aranda- und Loritja-Stämme in Zentral-Australien*, which was concerned with material culture and language including sign language. By the time he left Hermannsburg in mid-1910 also his dictionary was completed.

---

22 The meaning of inkata [ingkarte] has changed significantly over the past century. Today it is used for Lutheran pastor. It is likely that the shift started to occur during Carl Strehlow's period, because he seems to have been their first white inkata.

The trip was intended as a well-deserved break for Carl and Frieda, and to secure an education for the eldest five of their children who had, by all accounts, adopted the ways of the bush. During his stay in Germany his editor von Leonhardi died. After von Leonhardi's death, staff members of the Frankfurt museum, B. Hagen and F.C.H. Sarg, took on the arduous and time-consuming work to complete the publication of *Die Aranda- und Loritja-Stämme in Zentral-Australien*. Von Leonhardi's anthropological library and Strehlow's unpublished material had been bequeathed to the museum. Sarg prepared five family trees out of 20 that Carl Strehlow had sent von Leonhardi for publication and completed the editing of the fifth volume on social life, which had been proof-read by Marcel Mauss (Strehlow 1913: Preface). Mauss was also going to help with the publication of the sixth volume, but he dropped out at the beginning of World War I, keeping some of Strehlow's material in Paris. Mauss had been on friendly terms with von Leonhardi, whom he had visited in Gross Karben, and had taken great interest in Strehlow's work. After von Leonhardi's death, Mauss travelled to Frankfurt specifically to find out what was going to happen with the remaining manuscripts and offered to correspond with Strehlow in place of von Leonhardi.[23]

It is not quite clear who finalised the editing of the sixth volume (Strehlow 1915) as Sarg and the museum had fallen out with each other[24] and further communication with Carl Strehlow or Marcel Mauss was not possible due to World War I. Hagen was involved and possibly Dr Ernst Vatter, a young and talented geographer.[25]

After Hagen's death, the seventh and final volume on material culture was published by Ernst Vatter in 1920, just after World War I. He added an index and wrote in his preface that further research may follow by Carl Strehlow, as his work had raised new questions and aspects, which were of great scientific interest. He expressed the optimistic and enthusiastic hope that Carl would continue his ethnographic investigations, because:

> This comprehensive, indeed in many ways singular, observation and report concerning the Aranda and Loritja constitutes a challenge to further study and scientific preoccupation. The publication of the concluding part from Strehlow's pen will finally open the door to further debate. The Ethnological Museum of Frankfurt intends to devote one of its forthcoming publications to a continuing scientific study of

---

23   F.C.H. Sarg to Carl Strehlow, 20.9.1912 and 18.11.1912.
24   B. Hagen to Carl Strehlow, 10.9.1913.
25   Vatter wrote a book on Australian totemism (1925) and a classic German monograph called *Ata Kiwan* (1932) which pre-empted post-modern ethnography (Kohl 2001: 498). He had to leave Germany in the late 1930s as his wife was Jewish and became a poultry farmer in Chile.

Strehlow's vast material, enriched and enlarged by further inquiries from him, and to make up for lost opportunities due to the war. (Vatter in Strehlow 1920: Preface)

However, Carl Strehlow did not pursue any further ethnographic research. After an extended stay in Germany and placing his five eldest children with relatives and friends, he returned in 1912 to central Australia, with his wife Frieda and only with their youngest son Theodor. Instead, he started the first translation of the New Testament into Aranda with Moses Tjalkabota, Nathaniel Rauwirarka and Jacobus in 1913.[26]

Carl Strehlow's magnum opus

Carl Strehlow's magnum opus *Die Aranda- und Loritja-Stämme in Zentral-Australien* was published in Germany between 1907–1920 in seven instalments by the Ethnological Museum of Frankfurt. It is a very dense and difficult text that presupposes knowledge of the existing literature on indigenous Australians and some ideological standpoints common at the turn of the century. Although the exact transcriptions of indigenous myths and songs in Aranda and Loritja are accompanied by German interlinear and free translations, his unpublished Aranda-German-Loritja dictionary is required to study his work in its full richness.

First and foremost, Strehlow's ethnography documents the mythology and cosmology of the Aranda and Loritja, which occupies volumes one to four. In his letters he employs various terms including *religiösen Anschauungen* (religious views), *Religionen* (religions),[27] *religiösen Ideen und Traditionen* (religious ideas and traditions) and *Religion der Schwarzen* (religion of the blacks) to refer to this corpus.[28] He uses these terms in the style of his time with a range of interconnected references. There is little evidence that he saw religion as a functionally integrated phenomenon of cosmology and ritual practice geared to particular ends. Nonetheless, he and his editor were asking the right questions, such as:

> The Aljeringa half animal, half human [like the Mura-mura of the Dieri] lived before the present human beings and left a large number of ceremonies behind which are still performed. Spencer and Gillen's accounts give no indication of the purpose of these ceremonies; is it a kind of cult?[29]

---

26 *Lutheran Herald,* 16.2.1925: 54; Carl Strehlow's letter to the Mission Friends, 9.1.1920 (Albrecht Collection Acc. No. AA662, South Australian Museum Archives). He writes that he worked on it between 1913 and 1919.
27 Carl Strehlow to von Leonhardi, 2.6.1906 (SH-SP-2-1).
28 Carl Strehlow to N.W. Thomas, 1906 (SH-SP-6-1).
29 Von Leonhardi to Carl Strehlow, 9.9.1905.

Given the times, it is significant that Strehlow and his editor understood these indigenous beliefs as 'religion' whereas Spencer and Gillen did not and Spencer's mentor Sir James Frazer perceived the same system as 'magic'. For Frazer, magic was a 'false science'. In this he followed E.B. Tylor who argued that magic belongs 'to the lowest known stages of civilization, and the lower races', practice based on a false 'Association of Ideas' and the 'antithesis of religion' (see Lawrence 1987: 22–24).

Carl Strehlow's myth collection focuses on the ancestral beings, called in Aranda 'altjirangamitjina' and in Loritja 'tukutita', who created the central Australian landscape and its laws, and play a crucial role in ceremonial life. The stories concerning these mythological ancestral beings are referred to in today's literature as 'dreamings'. It has often been claimed that Carl Strehlow's view of Aranda and Loritja cosmology was flawed, because he was a missionary and ascribed indigenous high gods to them. Despite his data on the supreme or high beings, Altjira and Tukura, he maintained that ancestral beings were the main protagonists in the sacred life of the Aranda and Loritja. As subsequent discussion will reveal, the positioning of high gods in different cosmologies can vary considerably. The subtlety of this ethnographic issue was not grasped by Spencer, or by later anthropologists in Australia (but see Hiatt 1996).

His remaining three volumes (1913, 1915, 1920) describe aspects of social life and material culture. Initially, Strehlow had written a piece called 'Land und Leute' (land and people) that had been intended as an introduction to his work on myth and song.[30] However, in the course of his correspondence with von Leonhardi, aspects of 'social life', i.e. social classification and organisation, became an additional area of interest, especially as they studied relevant English and Australian anthropological works and engaged with contemporary debates and hypotheses. Marriage classes and kinship terminology[31] were topics raised regularly in their correspondence. Von Leonhardi believed that the views of Australian researchers on kindhip topics were still hypothetical.[32]

All volumes of *Die Aranda- und Loritja-Stämme in Zentral-Australien* also contain data relating to language and material culture. The word lists and comments that Strehlow included in his published work were a supplement to the major dictionary and an Aranda grammar that he had compiled. Additionally he collected data on the natural environment, often seen from an Aranda and

---

30 Carl Strehlow to von Leonhardi, 13.12.1906 (SH-SP-7-1).
31 Strehlow's collection of kinship terms, for example, is still current and a take-off point for modern kin-studies. Further detail in his unpublished dictionary (1909) exceeds the supplements of what was published in *Die Aranda- und Loritja-Stämme in Zentral-Australien*.
32 Von Leonhardi to Carl Strehlow, 2.6.1906.

Loritja perspective, and specimens that were classified in Germany by leading scientists of the time. In sum, the project of these two committed scholars came close to being cosmographic.

The original manuscripts

Unlike Strehlow's scientific letters to his editor that have only survived in draft form and shorthand, the original handwritten manuscripts of *Die Aranda-und Loritja-Stämme in Zentral-Australien* have survived. The only previously known manuscripts, destroyed in World War II, were duplicates provided to von Leonhardi. Strehlow had copied his original manuscripts meticulously for his editor, sending it in segments to Germany for publication. The bombing of the Ethnological Museum of Frankfurt buried 47 people sheltering in the vaults. It also destroyed much of Strehlow's research collection and correspondence.

10. Ethnological Museum of Frankfurt, 1943.

Source: Institut für Stadtgeschichte Frankfurt am Main.

The original manuscripts consist of three volumes called *Sagen*, *Cultus* and *Leben* and run to 1224 pages. *Sagen* (myths/legends) contains the Aranda and Loritja myth collections. In *Cultus* (cults) Carl Strehlow collated many sacred songs connected to myths that were sung during ceremonies and describes the choreography and paraphernalia of these rites and ceremonies. *Leben* (life) describes aspects of social life.

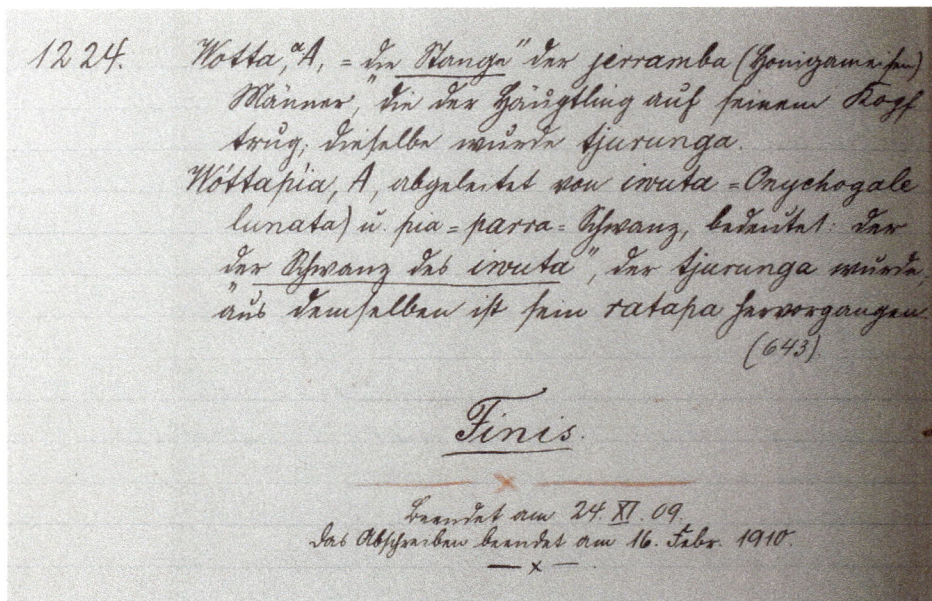

11. Page 1224 of Carl Strehlow's handwritten manuscript, Volume 3, *Leben*.

Source: Strehlow Research Centre, Alice Springs.

These manuscripts had been in the possession of Carl's son, T.G.H. Strehlow. They seem to have sat most of his life on his desk alongside his father's unpublished dictionary. The manuscripts were among the items confiscated from the house of K. Strehlow, T.G.H. Strehlow's second wife, in the 1990s. Their existence was known only to a handful of people. Notes found with these manuscripts and FitzHerbert's letters of the 1930s held at the Strehlow Research Centre and the Special Collection of the Barr Smith library indicate that T.G.H. Strehlow had owned them since the 1930s. In the light of these original manuscripts it is clear that von Leonhardi kept largely to his protégée's original, which refutes Spencer's allegations that an educated editor had changed Carl Strehlow's work.[33] The original is even richer than the published version. Were there ever a republication of the German text, possibly the original manuscript with critical annotations should be considered.

---

33   Spencer to Frazer, 10.3.1908 (Marett and Penniman 1932: 110).

Aranda myths

Carl Strehlow's first publication of 1907 is a collection of Aranda myths labelled *Mythen, Sagen und Märchen* (myths, legends and fairy-tales) and arranged into seven sections. A preface by von Leonhardi contextualises them and their main protagonists, the ancestors:

> In primordial times the "totem gods" (altjirangamitjina) walked this earth and eventually entered the earth, where they are still thought to be living. Their bodies changed into rocks, trees, shrubs or tjurunga made of stone or wood. (Strehlow 1907: Preface)

Following von Leonhardi's short preface, Carl Strehlow's brief account of Altjira, a high god, follows in Section I. Altjira is thought to be 'ngambakala' (eternal) having emu feet, many wives, sons and daughters. They live in the sky which is imagined as an eternal land with permanent water, trees, flora and fauna. Altjira and his family live much like the Aranda, they hunt and gather (1907: 1–2). Here Carl Strehlow makes an important remark on the meaning of the word 'altjira', which pre-empts Róheim and T.G.H. Strehlow:

> The etymology of the word Altjira has not yet been found. The natives associate the word now with the concept of the non-created. Asked about the meaning of the word, the natives repeatedly assured me that Altjira refers to someone who has no beginning, who did not issue from another (erina itha arbmamakala = no one created him). Spencer and Gillen's claim (Northern Tribes of Central Australia p. 745) that "the word alcheri means dream" is incorrect. Altjirerama means "to dream", and it is derived from altjira (god) and rama (to see), in other words, "to see god". The same holds true for the Loritja language. Tukura nangani = "to dream", from turkura (god) and nangani (to see). *It will be demonstrated later that altjira and tukura in this context do not refer to the highest God in the sky but merely to a totem god which the native believes to have seen in a dream.*[34] (Strehlow 1907: 2)

After introducing Altjira, Section II, 'Die Urzeit (Primordial Time)', delivers a general account of the conditions on earth, or more precisely of the territory of the Aranda, in primordial times (Strehlow 1907: 2–8). The earth is described as an eternal presence in which undeveloped humans, who were already divided into moieties, called 'alarinja' and 'kwatjarinja' (of the earth and water respectively), and an eight-class (subsection) system. Here the anthropomorphic ancestors called 'altjirangamitjina' are introduced, emerging in their primeval state from

---

34 My emphasis.

their underground dwellings (Strehlow 1907: 3). The ancestors wandered over the as yet formless land, shaping the landscape as it is still seen today, performing and transforming themselves, establishing the world's structure.

Section III deals with *Putiaputia und andere Lehrer der Aranda* (Putiaputia and other teachers of the Aranda) who came from the north and taught the Aranda about certain institutions such as initiation (Strehlow 1907: 9–11). The 'erintja' (evil beings), and 'rubaruba' and 'wurinja' (bad winds) are mentioned in Section IV (1907: 11–15) and *Die Toteninsel* (The Island of the Dead) (Strehlow 1907: 15–16) is the subject of Section V.

Section VI, the largest, is called *Sagen über die Totem-Vorfahren* (Myths about the Totem Ancestors) (Strehlow 1907: 16–101). It contains 64 narratives of the individual mythical beings, the altjirangamitjina, who populated and created the Aranda landscape and its particular places. They are associated with celestial bodies (sun, moon, evening star, Pleiades), animals, plants and other natural phenomena (including fire and rain). These narratives are roughly arranged in three groups: 'dead objects', animals and plants, and female ancestors.

The myths on the celestial bodies tell about the mythical beings associated with the sun, the moon, Tmálbambaralénana (The Evening Star),[35] Kuralja (Pleiades), and are followed by a water dreaming story linked with the site Kaporilja. The second group concerns the majority of ancestors who are associated with the plant and animal world of the central Australian landscape. He wrote that 'most of their myths are local myths, that belong to particular places'[36] and specific ancestors or 'totem gods are associated with certain places where they have lived and generated their totem animals' (Strehlow 1907: 4). The Aranda myths are concerned with the actions, travels, places, petrifying, going into the landscape, place names, the proper way to do things, interaction with other beings from other places and even from other language backgrounds, as there are place names, words and even songs in languages other than Aranda. Nearly all of these stories end with the ancestors turning into tjurunga or metamorphosing into natural features.

The third group of stories in Section VI are about female ancestors who are usually called alknarintja meaning 'eyes look away'. These narratives tell of women who reject advances of men. They too are connected to particular places on Aranda country and ceremonies. The last Section VII contains four narratives classified as fairy-tales.

---

35 Tmálbambaralénana means Evening Star. A contemporary spelling can not be found, because the etymology is not certain, although Carl Strehlow indicated that tmalba means 'flame'.
36 Carl Strehlow to von Leonhardi, probably 8.4.1906 (SH-SP-1-1).

Loritja myths

Strehlow's collection of Loritja myths is not as extensive as his Aranda collection. While it is organised in a similar fashion, only one myth is reproduced in Loritja, called 'Papa tua, Knulja ntjara (the dogs)' (Strehlow 1908: 12–16), as well as in Aranda. In the fourth volume we are informed that its ceremony is part of Loritja as well as Aranda initiation (Strehlow 1911: 15). Von Leonhardi appended six additional Loritja prose texts (Strehlow 1911: 59–75) to this volume, which Strehlow had recorded during research on Loritja song.

Section I of this volume is called Tukura, after the highest being of the Loritja. Like the account of Altjira, it is rather short. Here I quote the entire passage on Tukura to illustrate how the so called 'high gods' feature only in passing in this work:

> The Loritja call the supreme being Tukura. Linked with Tukura is the concept of the Non-created One, the eternal. I am unable to provide an etymological derivation of the word. One envisages Tukura as a man with a beautiful red skin, long flowing hair and a long beard. The Western Loritja believe that he has emu feet – like the Altjira of the Aranda – but the Southern Loritja accredit him with human feet. Tukura has only one wife, by the name of Inéari (A: tnéera meaning the beautiful), and one child which always remains a child. The latter is called Arátapi (A: ratapa; i.e. offspring). The Western and Southern Loritja agree that Inéari has human feet. Tukura's residence is the sky ilkari (A: alkira). The Milky Way, called merawari, i.e. wide creek, or tukalba, i.e. winding creek, by the Loritja, is lined with gum trees (itára), mulga trees (kurku) and other trees and shrubs. In their branches live parrots and pigeons, while kangaroos (mallu), emus (kalaia) and wild cats (kuninka) roam through Tukura's realm. While Tukura amuses himself in his hunting ground, his wife and son are out gathering edible roots called wapiti (A: latjia) and tasty bulbs (neri), as well as grass seeds which grow there in abundance. Tukura sleeps at night, but during the day he conducts ceremonies to which he calls the young men (nitaii) living nearby. The stars (tjiltjana) are the campfires of Tukura. As is the case with the Aranda, the women and children also know of Tukura's existence. The Loritja imagine the sky, which has existed from eternity (kututu), to be a vault-like firmament, resting on "legs of stone". One fears that some day the vaulted sky could collapse and kill everybody. (Strehlow 1908: 1–2)

The following pages on Loritja myths relate to the scene at the beginning of time when the tukutita, the eternal-uncreated ones, emerged out of the earth that, like the sky, had always been in existence (Strehlow 1908: 2–5).

Section III concerns *Die bösen Wesen* (The evil Beings) and Section IV, *Die Toten-Insel* (The Island of the Dead) (1908: 5–7). Again the largest Section V, *Sagen über die Totem-Vorfahren*, is 'about the Totem Ancestors' (Strehlow 1908: 8–48). It includes 42 narratives about the earth-dwelling ancestors, the tukutita, who are associated with celestial bodies (moon, sun, morning star, Pleiades), and the animal and plant world. The stories of how the travels of the tukutita and the events surrounding them create the landscape and constitute society are prominent in this volume as well.

In his discussion of Loritja myth, Strehlow began to note differences between the Aranda and Loritja (Kukatja) mythologies. The Loritja concept of what it was like at the beginning, that in primordial times the earth 'was not covered by the sea' but was always dry, contrasts with 'the views of the Aranda' (Strehlow 1908: 2). This account of 'primordial times' outline a number of differences between the Aranda and Loritja:

> There is a marked difference between the Aranda and Loritja legends. According to the tradition of the Aranda, most of the meandering altjirangamitjina were changed into tjurunga-woods or stones and only a few became trees or rocks. According to the tradition of the Loritja, however, the reverse is true. The bodies of the tukutita were mostly changed into rocks and trees. Naturally, this results in the lessening of the religious meaning and importance of the tjurunga. Among the Dieri living in the South-East, all the bodies of the Murra-murra are changed into rocks, trees, etc. and the tjurunga do not occur at all. (Strehlow 1908: 3–4)

He also began cross-referencing Loritja myths with each other and with Aranda myths published in volume one, because story lines connected or intersected with each other at particular places and identical songs and terms appeared in two different myths indicating borrowing. Sometimes the Loritja ancestors, the tukutita, interacted with the Aranda ancestor, the altjirangamitjina. The myth of a Loritja wallaby man (Strehlow 1908: 28), for example, is cross-referenced with the Aranda possum myth (Strehlow 1907: 62, Anmerkung 15), because at a place called Tunguma the wallaby ancestor joins some possum ancestors for a ceremony and go together into the ground there creating a water-source. Or a Loritja myth on emus (Strehlow 1908: 18–20) is cross-referenced to the Aranda one on emus (Strehlow 1907: 42–45), because at the end of both myths the emus coming from Aranda and Loritja country end their travels at a place called Kalaia-tarbana, meaning in Loritja 'the emu go in'.

Another emu myth of the Loritja (Strehlow 1908: 32) is also connected to an Aranda myth (Strehlow 1907: 44, Anmerkung 6), because the site Apauuru, north-west of Hermannsburg, features in both narratives. This Loritja dreaming story has a number of interesting 'foreign features' incorporated into its narrative. It begins in Loritja country and travels east. At Iloara, a salt lake on the southern edge of Anmatyerr country, the emu's wife hurts her foot and cannot follow her husband. He sings a threat song which inserts Loritja words into an Ilpara (believed to be today's Warlpiri) song, additionally mentioning Kulurlba, a famous Aranda native cat ancestor, who had thrown a boomerang at his disobedient wife. This treatment of myths went as much towards particularism as refined diffusionism.

In sum, Loritja myths like Aranda myths tell about the ancestors' epic journeys over country visiting places and metamorphosing or going into the landscape. These narratives end with the mythic beings turning into natural features, tjurunga or kuntanka stones and rocks.[37] The last two narratives in Carl Strehlow's Loritja myth collection are designated as fairy-tales.

The second part of volume two deals with the totemic concepts of the Aranda and Loritja (Strehlow 1908: 51–70) and tjurunga (Strehlow 1908: 71–83). Strehlow explains that the belief systems of the Aranda and Loritja were very similar, but that the difference lay in the fact that the myths were 'local myths' and each connected to particular places in the landscape.

Cultus: Songs and ceremonies

The manuscript *Cultus* was published in two instalments in 1910 and 1911, called *Die Totemischen Kulte der Aranda und Loritja Stämme*. It contains songs connected to myths he had recorded in prose as well as sacred ceremonies. Carl Strehlow documented 59 Aranda ceremonies and their associated songs and 21 Loritja ceremonies which included some relating to female ancestors acted out by men. He found that two types of ceremony were performed:

> The Aranda and Loritja today still regularly hold the cult rituals according to the instruction of their altjirangamitjina. However, there is one significant difference. In primordial times one ceremony was intended to serve two purposes, now two distinct performances are held, each with its own name, and each serving a specific purpose. When the young men undergo the various initiation rites, a series of ceremonies are performed for them which are identical to the real cult rituals, except for certain very special and characteristic details, but do not serve the purpose of increasing and enhancing the growth of the respective totem. Their only aim is to show those who are about to become men or have become men how these ceremonies should be

---

37 Like tjurunga, kuntanka is polisemic. Kuntanka describes to a lesser degree a sacred object, but rather particular features of a landscape that represent dreaming beings or parts of them.

performed. In view of their purpose these ceremonies are therefore known as intitjiuma (L. tintinpungañi) i.e. to initiate into something, to show how something is done. However, when the same ceremonies are performed at the particular totem place which an altjirangamitjina called home in primordial times, or where he had spent some time, and if their purpose is to care for the increase and growth of the totem, then this performance is called mbatjalkatiuma (L. kutintjingañi), i.e. to bring about, make fertile, improve the conditions of. (Strehlow 1910: 1–2)

Carl Strehlow also wrote 'that in primordial times the altjirangamitjina travelled about with their novices and that they performed certain ceremonies at their "eternal camps" as well as at other locations during their journeys' (Strehlow 1910: 1). These accounts of songs and ceremonies are accompanied by drawings, descriptions of who performs what, at which places in the Aranda landscape it is performed, how it is performed, what ceremonial artefacts are used and their purposes. The letters between Strehlow and von Leonhardi discuss and analyse these 'cults' in detail whereas the publication is a descriptive and empirical account.

Leben: Social life

The remaining volumes, based on Strehlow's manuscript called *Leben*, are not as well structured and presented as his previous publications, because they were not edited by von Leonhardi. After von Leonhardi's death, staff members of the Frankfurt museum, B. Hagen, F.C.H. Sarg and E. Vatter, completed the publication of *Die Aranda- und Loritja-Stämme in Zentral-Australien*. Volumes five and six describe a number of important facets of Aranda and Loritja life around 1900, some of which are still practised. These volumes cover subjects such as birth, name giving, games, initiation ceremonies, the marriage system, kinship terminology, marriage customs (Strehlow 1913), the political and legal system, death, burial, blood revenge, illnesses, magic, terms for numbers and time, secret language registers of men (Strehlow 1915) and sign language (Strehlow 1915: 54–78).

These instalments include Carl Strehlow's kinship data. It appeared in the fifth volume in 1913, called *The Social Life of the Aranda and Loritja Tribes*. Compared to his four volumes on myth, his kinship material appears deceptively slim. However, he managed to condense into 26 pages an incredible amount of empirical data. He published substantial accounts on the section and subsection systems of people living at Hermannsburg at the time, extensive lists of kinship terms (Strehlow 1913: 62–89), five extensive family trees and a list of all names occurring in the family trees with their linguistic and technical explanations (Strehlow 1920: 15-39).

The chapter 'Birth, Smoking and Name-Giving' in Carl Strehlow's fifth volume is almost certainly based on information collected by his wife, Frieda Strehlow (Strehlow 1913: 1–5). The relevant part in the handwritten manuscripts is in Frieda's hand; it is the only passage in these manuscripts written by her. She may only have copied her husband's notes. However, the topic relates to birth and women's ritual. It is unlikely to be mere chance that this part of the manuscript is in her hand. Only with great difficulty and coercion would Carl Strehlow have been able to obtain this kind of data from women. It could of course be second hand information from Aranda and Loritja men, but this seems unlikely. Another indication of Frieda's involvement in the production of *Die Aranda- und Loritja-Stämme in Zentral-Australien* is a remark by Sarg, one of Strehlow's later editors. He asked Carl to indicate which data his wife had collected, because in his view it was very important to be able to say that 'this I observed' or 'the observation was made by my wife'.[38] However, World War I intervened and communication with Australia broke down.

Both Frieda and Carl had an excellent understanding of indigenous kinship systems. Carl Strehlow had been classified as a Purula (Aranda subsection associated with Ntaria, Hermannsburg and surrounding area) and his children therefore as Kamara.[39] He used his knowledge of indigenous kinship, which determines conduct and obligations towards particular kin, when engaged with his congregation.[40] It is likely that some of the genealogical material was obtained by Frieda, if the current situation can be taken as indicative. During field research in the past 20 years, I have generally found that the majority of central Australian Aboriginal men have a hard time reproducing a significant list of lateral relatives in their own and proximate generations. Aboriginal women tend to be more able to provide a kin universe.[41] A reference to Frank Gillen's method of data collection also provides some insight. Ernest Cowle, a policeman in the 1890s in central Australia, remarked once to Spencer on Gillen's genealogical work with one of Cowle's Aboriginal prisoners:

> Gillen got at him in his den and unfolded a papyrus as long as himself and started to trace his descent through endless aunts, and great great grandfather's mothers he fainted away completely! ... even a Sub-Protector has no right to invent tortures, surpassing those of the Inquisition in general fiendishness... (Mulvaney, Petch and Morphy 2000: 91)

---

38 Sarg to Carl Strehlow, 18.11.1912.
39 According to T.G.H. Strehlow ([1950] 1997: 47), he was classified as a Kamara (Kemarre) by reason of his conception site Ntarea (Ntaria). It is just as likely that T.G.H. Strehlow simply received the right subsection through his father's classification which was probably Purula (Perrurle). (Garry Stoll thought that Ted was a Kemarre (pers. comm.).)
40 Strehlow's letters to Kaibel (1899–1909) held at the Lutheran Archives, Adelaide (LAA).
41 Gillen was probably also asking about people with tabooed names which is likely to have caused some distress.

Frieda may also have contributed to Carl's myth collection. The whirlwind which brings bad spirit-children, or the myths relating to female ancestors, may have been inserted by her. Her letters are often about her work with Aranda women, her close engagement with them in everyday life and indigenous beliefs. She mentions in her letters to family and friends, for example, the infanticide of twins and beliefs about spirit children.[42]

Material culture

Images, descriptions and interpretations of material culture are interspersed throughout Strehlow's work to illustrate and enhance the text. Only the last volume (Strehlow 1920: 8–14) contains a few pages on material culture although the data on his collection could have filled an entire volume.[43] He had sent artefacts and objects of varying quality to his editor in Germany. Interestingly many of these items were commissioned, not originals. Strehlow remarked, for instance, about stone knives: 'I regret, that I cannot send you better stone-knives. These ones are not at all well worked; only steel knives are in use now.'[44]

On his own initiative, Carl Strehlow had started in 1906 to send indigenous artefacts and tjurunga to von Leonhardi as well as samples of flora and fauna. He initially sent material culture to his editor to illustrate his written data and that 'maybe better drawings could be made' because 'I am a bad drawer',[45] but it soon became a separate project. Strehlow may have been inspired by Spencer and Gillen's plates in their publications and by Siebert and Reuther,[46] who had been collecting material culture for their own research on the peoples of the Lake Eyre basin, as well as by Eylemann (1908) who had been in Hermannsburg collecting artefacts and ethnographic data.

Carl Strehlow's collection included well over 1000 sacred objects and mundane artefacts. He sent hundreds of tjurunga,[47] a large number of ceremonial objects,[48] carrying dishes, boomerangs,[49] spears, spear throwers, clubs, shields, hair

---

42   Other letters by women from Hermannsburg make interesting remarks on the life of Aranda women. Maria Bogner for example talks about a women's ceremony one night in the creek in 1896.

43   F.C.H. Sarg (1911) and Vatter (1915) used his collection for their publications.

44   Carl Strehlow to von Leonhardi, probably on 3.12.1906 (SH-SP-8-1).

45   Carl Strehlow to von Leonhardi, probably 8.4.1906 (SH-SP-1-1).

46   Siebert had collected objects by 1904, which the new Völkermuseum of Frankfurt (called Museum der Weltkulturen today) exhibited in the same year at its opening (Nobbs 2006: 12). Reuther collected approximately 1300 artefacts including ceremonial objects, nearly 400 toas and a large collection of ethno-botanical specimens (Nobbs 2005) between 1903 and 1906. Reuther's collection was purchased by the South Australian Museum in 1907 for £400 (Nobbs 2005: 42).

47   Carl Strehlow wrote to von Leonhardi that 'there are nearly no Tj. left in most stonecaves in the vicinity', probably 10.12.1907 (SH-SP-15-1).

48   Carl Strehlow to von Leonhardi, probably 10.12.1907 (SH-SP-15-1).

49   F.C.H. Sarg (1911) described in 'Die Australischen Bumerangs im Städtischen Völkermuseum' some of Strehlow's boomerangs.

strings, stone knives and axes, digging sticks, chains made of native beans, and many other items that he documented in his unpublished dictionary. His collection also included some hybrids: 'As a curiosity without scientific value I include tied up rabbit tails that the blacks have started to make since the rabbit plague has reached the interior of Australia'.[50] His editor in Germany greeted Strehlow's collection with great enthusiasm and became his agent for the distribution of these objects.[51] In fact, von Leonhardi seems to have become nearly addicted to these consignments. Much of Strehlow's collection did not survive the bombing of Frankfurt in World War II.

Strehlow used his collection to illustrate and explain aspects of traditional Aboriginal daily life and sacred ceremonies. He described each artefact's form and function, but does not seem to have recorded the names of the indigenous artisans or suppliers. Information on how the artefacts were made and where they were used and traded among the different groups, make interesting reading:

> Because the natives have no concept of money, they engage in lively trade. Important living places along the borders of befriended tribes are also important trading places, unbunba. At Ingodna on the lower Finke, for example, the Aranda-Tanka barter with the Aranda-Lada and the Aranda-Ulbma; and at Utnádata on the southern border of the Aranda Tanka, they conduct their trade with the Arábana.
>
> The Southern Loritja, as well as the Southern Aranda, bartered with the Aranda-Ulbma here at Hermannsburg. On the other hand, the trading place for the Aranda Ulbma and the Western Loritja is at Apanuru, situated on Loritja territory. The Aranda-Ulbma also trade with the Aranda-Roara at Alice Springs, with the Ilpara at Ilóara in the north, and with the Katitja and Imatjera at Tnimakwatja in the north.
>
> The Aranda trade the following items with other tribes: shields, spears, spearthrowers, small boomerangs ulbarinja lubara, strings ulera, nose-bones lalkara, pitch nobma, stone knives karitja, trays made of para wood, etc. With the northern tribes, however, they trade trays made from ininta, headstrings kanta, necklaces gulatja, breaststrings tmakurka, neck decorations matara, shells takula and sticks wolta; while from the south-eastern tribes they receive the large boomerangs and pubic coverings. (Strehlow 1920: 13)

---

50 Carl Strehlow to von Leonhardi, probably 10.12.1907 (SH-SP-15-1).

51 Bastian's salvage anthropology had trigged an international run on the world's existing indigenous material culture. The German and international collecting frenzy before everything was lost forever seems to have reached every corner of the globe. Strehlow also saw it as a source for some extra income for his ever financially suffering congregation.

After the death of his editor, Strehlow continued to collect for the Cologne[52] and Frankfurt museums,[53] and to distribute artefacts, when he returned from Germany on the 5 April 1912 with his wife and youngest son Ted to central Australia. However, once the Great War (1914–1918) overshadowed international relations, it became impossible to export Aboriginal material culture.

12. Last photograph of the complete Strehlow family, 1910/11.

Source: Archiv/Mission Eine Welt, Neuendettelsau.

When World War I broke out Strehlow suffered greatly for leaving his children in Europe. He had left them in Germany, so they would be properly educated. He was not to see them again. This guilt and loss may have driven him to increase his efforts for the people at Hermannsburg and the bible translation into Aranda; completed in 1919. Although an Australian citizen, he was hounded by the South Australian Government to register as an alien. With the support of Sergeant Robert Stott who was known as the 'Uncrowned King of Central Australia' Carl Strehlow was able to continue his and Frieda's work. However, the mission was permanently threatened by financial ruin. In 1917 Hermannsburg lost its 300 pounds per year government subsidies, largely due to anti-German prejudice, which flourished during the Great War (Rowse 1998: 84).

---

52 Letters between Carl Strehlow and Fritz Graebner between 1912 and 1913, held at the city archives in Cologne.
53 Correspondence between Strehlow and his second editor Sarg. Letters at the Strehlow Research Centre (SRC) in Alice Springs.

With war's end and word that his children had survived, Strehlow attempted to get a replacement so he could leave for Germany to see his children. As he waited at Hermannsburg for his superiors in the Barossa Valley to organise his replacement, he made a last effort on his still unpublished dictionary of over 6000 Aranda and Loritja words that included thousands of derivations.[54] Finalising his linguistic work appears to have been the ultimate proof that indigenous languages can express the gamut of human cognition, including the bible's revelations. However, 30 years of effort had taken their toll on Strehlow. The desert, the battles with state and church bureaucracy and pastoralists as well as his limited success with conversion, had weakened his body and spirit.

Mid 1922 Strehlow was struck down by a mysterious illness which he himself diagnosed from his medical books as dropsy, and for the first time he did not take the service on Sunday. His youngest son wrote in his childhood diary about this service:

> I played the organ because Mum and Dad stayed at home. ... The congregation remained completely silent during the first liturgy, so Herr Heinrich started singing the responses himself fairly in the wrong tune, until some men took over and ended the verse in a strangely off melody.[55]

All attempts to treat him locally proved fruitless and his 'Journey to Horseshoe Bend' began. As he was taken away his Aranda friends sang *Kaarrerrai worlamparinyai*, a hymn he had translated for them to the music of Bach. The journey down the bend was agonising and his youngest son, who accompanied him on this last journey, was to write that 'Horseshoe Bend is a place whose shadows I can never escape'.[56] Carl Strehlow died on the 20 October 1922. Some years after his death the *Lutheran Herald* reported:

> Not long after the death of the late Rev. Strehlow, it was indeed perceptible how a spiritual awakening stirred not only our natives at Hermannsburg, but all Aranda people. All seemed to feel and realise, that by devoting his whole life to it, even laying down his life in the service, there must be something great and true in what Rev. Strehlow taught, to thus enable him to unselfishly work for them, in contrast to most other white folks they knew.[57]

On the 4 November 1923, one year after Strehlow's death, something like a mass-baptism seems to have occurred at Hermannsburg (Strehlow 1969–70: 178–180). Moses Tjalkabota and H.A. Heinrich had continued Strehlow's pre-

---

54 *The Register*, 1921; C. Strehlow's dictionary 1900–1909.
55 T.G.H. Strehlow's childhood Diary III, 30.7.1922. Translated by Lisa Wendtlandt.
56 T.G.H. Strehlow Diary (1960: 155) quoted in Cawthorn and Malbunka (2005: 72).
57 *Lutheran Herald*, 1926: 75.

baptismal instructions that resulted in the baptism of 26 adults and 14 children on that day. Carl Strehlow had baptised only 46 adults at Hermannsburg in nearly three decades.[58] As already mentioned among these converts was Carl Strehlow's main informant Loatjira who had been christened Abraham that day, and died shortly after his 'conversion'. There are no reliable records of Carl Strehlow and Loatjira's state of minds towards the end of their lives. Both men had been devoted to their faiths, but were troubled. They had both reached the edge of knowing and doubted. Loatjira had obviously wavered in his faith, and, according to T.G.H. Strehlow (1969: 174–179), so had Carl.

---

58   Carl Strehlow, *Kirchen- und Missionszeitung*, 9.1.1920.

II. A Certain Inheritance: Nineteenth Century German Anthropology

In the context of Spencer and Gillen's work, and also that of Howitt (1904) for example, two questions should be posed of Carl Strehlow's text. First, how might one explain his lack of engagement with anthropological debates on the origins and evolution of indigenous Australians? Second, what explains Strehlow's quite particular focus on myth and song among the Aranda and Loritja when the work of his contemporaries tends to move, in a British vein, from origins, to social organisation, to rite?

Strehlow, it might be argued, had little contact with his British-Australian contemporaries. Neither Spencer nor Gillen rated the Lutheran Strehlow highly as a colleague or consultant. Gillen's interaction with Strehlow as a scholar was minimal. Spencer's dismissal of Strehlow's scholarship was advertised widely which Strehlow junior answered in his own masterwork, *Songs of Central Australia* (1971: xv, xvi, xx–xxxviii). In addition, Frazer's long list of consultants around Australia makes it clear that he chose Spencer as his Aranda source, not Strehlow. Perhaps then, Strehlow's text was simply the product of an isolated missionary, distant from professional or mainstream scholarship. Again, as a missionary bent on the task of conversion, possibly he was required to maintain a Christian humanism. Concern with the history or evolutionary stage of the lower human ranks could not sit happily with proselytising.

Strehlow was a missionary rather than an academic. However, he received his Christian education within the context of nineteenth century German humanism. Although the Lutherans sustained their own distinctive tradition of scholarship and missionary work, they were also part of a broader German intellectual milieu deeply influenced by historical particularism. The modern culture concept, and its repudiation of rationalist theories of universal human development, had its origins in this setting. In fact for Herder, himself a Lutheran pastor, the plenitude of human culture was also the plenitude of God's creation (see Darcy 1987). The two approaches dovetailed into one consistent humanistic approach. From this viewpoint, the central concerns of Strehlow's magnum opus were not accidental. His correspondence with von Leonhardi contains no suggestion that starting with oral literature was strange. To the contrary, it was natural simply because Strehlow and von Leonhardi shared an intellectual orientation that affirmed the status of language and literature, or oral text, as the key to a culture.

This chapter considers the emergence of nineteenth century German anthropology and its passage to the United States in the hands of Franz Boas.

Boas and Strehlow shared similar intellectual interests and a similar scholarly style. Following this account, I describe Strehlow's own education and the intellectual milieu of the German Lutheran seminary; and unpack the detail of Strehlow's correspondence with von Leonhardi. In their letters, a shared concern with language and empirical observations is evident. These are the three major influences on Strehlow, some quite direct and others more diffuse, that shaped the production of a unique Australian work. However, while this work was unique for its time in British-influenced Australia, it readily finds a place in the tradition of German historical particularism and its foundational role in modern (American) cultural anthropology.

Johann Gottfried Herder's concept of *Volksgeist*

During the nineteenth century, a German tradition of anthropology[1] emerged that paid great attention to specific cultural configurations. According to this tradition, humanity was comprised of distinct cultures (*Kulturen*) and peoples (*Völker*) which were the products of individual histories and environmental milieux. This plenitude or plurality of human culture reflected, most immediately evident in particular languages, the universal creativity of groups and at the same time the unity of humankind.

The 'birth' of German anthropology may be seen in the light of the standoff or tension between two prominent intellectuals of the eighteenth century, Immanuel Kant and Johann Gottfried Herder (Zammito 2002; Gingrich 2005: 65). Kant was a classic representative of the Enlightenment whereas Herder marked the beginning of the Counter Enlightenment in Germany, a movement called Romanticism. Although Kant was the first to use the word anthropology in his work for a new 'science of man', it was ultimately Herder who determined the course of German anthropology. Kant's relativism played a role only insofar as his idea of understanding phenomena on their own terms entered anthropological thought. Consistent with this view, people should be studied not to prove or disprove a theory, but rather because a scholar '[finds] them interesting' (Adams 1998: 296). In this sense Kant contributed to the cultural relativism and particularism of German anthropology (Adams 1998: 276–277). At the same time, Kant had the dubious honour of promoting the concept of race in intellectual life (Zammito 2002; Petermann 2004: 320). When Kant turned from general reflections on human thought and a 'cosmopolitan law' for all peoples to accounts of people and place, scholarship was pushed aside

---

1   The meaning of this term was not well defined at the time. It encompassed what is known as ethnology and ethnography as well as aspects of other disciplines like physical anthropology to which it tended to cross over. In the late eighteenth century it was simply understood as 'the science of man' which was very broad and not well defined.

by other presumptions. As Harvey remarks, 'Kant's *Geography* is nothing short of an intellectual and political embarrassment' (Harvey 2001: 275). He cites the following passage, among others, from the *Geography*:

> In hot countries men mature more quickly in every respect but they do not attain the perfection of the temperate zones. Humanity achieves its greatest perfection with the white race. The yellow Indians have somewhat less talent. The negroes are much inferior... (Harvey 2001: 275)

Herder, who rejected Kant's notion of race, provided instead crucial concepts that would determine the study of cultures. Many of Herder's pioneering concepts including both *Zeitgeist* and *Volksgeist* entered intellectual and anthropological discourse, without users being aware of their Herderian origins (Barnard 2003: 5, 108). Already in 1828, Goethe,[2] both foe and friend to Herder, observed that a number of Herderian ideas had become seminal; absorbed into the mainstream of philosophical and, ultimately, anthropological thought (Marchand 1982: 20).

Among many other disciplines, Johann Gottfried Herder's (1744–1803) complex oeuvre influenced the development of German anthropology in a lasting and profound way. His concept of *Volk*, a cultural group or entity, and *Volksgeist*, the essence of a cultural group that sets it apart from other groups, were the basis of his particularism, which was to become a central principle of nineteenth century German anthropology. He recognised that each culture possessed a moral and intellectual framework that determined its possibilities and its individual development. For Herder, language was the defining element of a cultural group and its identity, as it was in language that a people's *Volksgeist* is expressed (see Barnard 1969: 32).

For Herder there were no people without a culture (Barnard 1969: 24–25; Barnard 2003: 134). In his *Ideas for a Philosophy of the History of Mankind* (1784–91), he used the concept in the plural deliberately (Petermann 2004: 309). He professed to a humanity made up of a multiplicity and therefore rejected the notion of enlightenment as a pervasive developmental stage. Herder's idea that culture was a universal phenomenon was novel at a time when cultured and uncultured peoples were distinguished from each other. In contrast, he maintained that wherever people live together as a group over a period of time there is a culture (Barnard 2003: 134–135). In short, the universal human property he recognised was difference: the propensity of groups to specify themselves through culture.

The principles of the French Enlightenment, in which the universality of human reason across space and time, the subjection of uniform human nature to unchanging natural laws, the steady progress of civilisation through history

---

2   Goethe wrote in his memoirs *Dichtung und Wahrheit* that one of the most significant occurrences in his life was his acquaintance with Herder whom he had met by chance in the Gasthof zum Geist (Goethe 1998: 430).

toward an enlightened state of reason and the laws that governed these codes, were questioned by the Counter Enlightenment (Berlin 1980: 1–25). By rejecting the French dogma of the uniform development of civilisation, Herder argued for the uniqueness of values transmitted throughout history:

> Herder sharply differs from the central thought of the French Enlightenment, and that not only in respects that all his commentators have noted. What is usually stressed is, in the first place, his relativism, his admiration of every authentic culture for being what it is, his insistence that outlooks and civilisations must be understood from within, in terms of their own stages of developments, purposes and outlooks; and in the second place his sharp repudiation of that central strain in Cartesian rationalism which regards only what is universal, eternal, unalterable, governed by rigorously logical relationships – only the subject matter of mathematics, logic, physics and the other natural sciences – as true knowledge. (Berlin 1976: 174)

Herder laid the foundations for German historical particularism, because he was interested in historical difference and in the differences between contemporaneous groups in different places (Adams 1998: 271). In his view, every cultural group was the product of its circumstances and could not be measured by the values of another group. He made it amply clear in his *Letters for the Advancement of Humanity* (1793–97) that European culture was not to be considered superior to any other:

> Least of all must we think of European culture as a universal standard of human values … Only a real misanthrope could regard European culture as the universal condition of our species. The culture of man is not the culture of the European; it manifests itself according to place and time in every people. (Herder cited in Barnard 1969: 24)

Herder attempted to free the assessment of the 'other' from imposed value systems and categories. He urged historical study of a culture and analysis of its own internal relations (Barnard 2003: 137). He projected a history of peoples of the globe in terms of their self-defining values and cultures (Fink 1993: 56). In 1774 he wrote: 'Each man, each nation, each period, has its centre of happiness within itself, just as every sphere has its centre of gravity' (Herder cited in Barnard 1969: 35). Thus, each human group could be understood only as a particular historical configuration. Each one of these in its individuality contributes to humanity as a whole and through language the intricacies of cultures could be understood. Herder wrote that to enter into the spirit of a people, to understand and share its thoughts or deeds:

> ... do not limit your response to a word, but penetrate deeply into this century, this region, this entire history, plunge yourself into it all and feel it all inside yourself – then only will you be in a position to understand; then only will you give up the idea of comparing everything, in general or in particular, with yourself. For it would be manifest stupidity to consider yourself to be the quintessence of all times and all peoples. (Herder 1969a: 182)

Herder's humanistic ideal, his *Humanität* (humanity), is one in which diverse cultures exist side by side (Berlin 1980: 11) and also together exhibit the essence of humanness involved in the potential for creativity and specificity. His concept of humanity was a unifying principle through which to formulate his understanding of human existence in the infinite variety of its configurations (Knoll 1982: 9). It was his universalist principle of *Humanität* that enabled him to fit his pluralist concept of humankind into his view that all humans were equal and had the same origin (homogenetic). He believed that the diversity of peoples had only developed in the course of time, rejecting all claims that man evolved from animal forms (Nisbet 1992: 10–11). From this unity of humanity he concluded that there are no superior cultures and condemned, for instance, colonialism and slavery.

He rejected the concept of race (Mühlmann 1968: 62) and stated that the term 'race' was not fit to be used in relation to humans, as it referred to a posited difference in origins that he repudiated (Barnard 1969: 41). Herder believed in homogenesis and thus saw humanity as a unity. In his *Ideen zur Philosophie der Geschichte der Menschheit* (*Ideas for a Philosophy of the History of Mankind*) (1784–91) he wrote that 'in spite of the vast realm of change and diversity, all mankind is one and the same species upon earth' (Herder 1969b: 283). Herder's view on humanity encompassed the plurality of mankind which made humanity up as a whole. He concluded:

> In short, there are neither four or five races, nor exclusive varieties, on this earth. Complexions run into each other; forms follow the genetic character; and in toto they are, in the final analysis, but different shades of the same great picture which extends through all ages and all parts of the earth. Their study, therefore, properly forms no part of biology or systematic natural history but belongs rather to the anthropological history of man. (Herder 1969b: 284)

This passage was considered by Kant as truly indicative of Herder's intellectual shortcomings (Barnard 2003: 65).

In 1772, Herder published an epoch-making essay on the origin of language called *Über den Ursprung der Sprache (On the Origin of Language)*. This essay had a tremendous influence on his contemporaries. It would also influence the development of anthropological and linguistic thinking (in hindsight marking the beginning of a modern philosophy of language). Although this essay already contained what would become one of Herder's most original contributions, his concept of pluralism evolving out of his thoughts on language (as languages are an expression of humanity's variability and multiplicity), his initial concern was different. His main intention was to counter Süssmilch's assumption that language was a direct gift from God and to deny 'Condillac's and Rousseau's theories which traced the emergence of human speech to animalistic origins' (Barnard 1969: 17). The Lutheran pastor Herder[3] did away with the view that language has a divine origin. Instead he introduced the idea of slow and gradual development of language 'from rude beginnings' (Sapir 1907: 110). Language for Herder was an organic product grown in time, determined by the history of each individual group. Every language was therefore unique, like its speakers. Each language expressed a particular culture in space and time.

Herder argued that language originated and developed from within the individual; that it was not the imitation of nature's sounds or a given act by God. His key concept in accounting for the development of language was 'reflection' – in which individuals arrive at awareness and recognition of the self. Through language the individual becomes at once aware of his selfhood and of his cultural identity (Barnard 1969: 7; see also Fink 1993: 54–55).

In Herder's view, language lies at the basis of being because there is no coherent thought without words. He believed that a people did not have an idea or concept for which there was not a word. Ideas are constituted through language (Frank 1982: 16). There is no thinking outside languages and human beings are historical because there is no language in the abstract detached from human beings. There are only historical languages placed in the real world, with specific characteristics which mutate through time (Burns 2002: 61). This view would be repeated by Boas' student, Edward Sapir. He expressed the view that 'thought is impossible without language, that thought is language' (Darnell 1990: 99) and thereby echoed Vico, Herder, the Humboldts and other German thinking on language.

For Herder the human condition was ever changing, constantly developing and altering in response to diverse historical needs and circumstances. The most important element for Herder in this dynamic process of human historical transformation was language (Whitton 1988: 151). Herder recognised that whether language had been used to write history or not, it constituted a history of a given culture at a given time and place with all its idiosyncrasies. He perceived language as perpetually engaged in the process of generating a new

---

3   Herder held the highest position in the Lutheran Church at the court of Weimar.

self out of the old self (Frank 1982: 18). In Herder we find already the notion of language's constant change or flux.[4] Herder used the metaphor of organic growth to explain the permanent evolving of the nature of language (Marchand 1982: 26). He used 'organic' in the sense that that which is being transformed is assimilated and applied (Whitton 1988: 153). Through the historical transformation of a language, traditional concepts and beliefs are continually synthesised with those of new generations (Whitton 1988: 152).

The empirical investigation of language was for Herder the basis for understanding cultural life, because a people's innermost essence was inherent in their language and literature, including the oral literatures of indigenous peoples (Zammito 2002: 155, 159). The language, mythology and folksong of a people were particularly important because they were the highest form of expression and revealed the essence of a people, the *Volksgeist* – today the term *Geist* is more usual. Thus, indigenous text ranked high on the agenda of German nineteenth century anthropology. Language embodied a people and reflected their *Geist*. A group's *Geist* was manifest in language. Language defined human beings, making them human. For this reason, as Whitton observes:

> As an attribute specific to human beings, language is seen by Herder as the central expression of a uniquely human, reflective consciousness. In developing language, individuals give shape to their inner conscious nature, formulating their ideas and preconceptions through reflections on their experience of the external world. (Whitton 1988: 151)

Herder believed that no greater misfortune could befall a people than to be robbed of their language. With language loss came the loss of their spirit.

Herder's unique particularism which at the same time embraced universalism infused the new nineteenth century science of man. Herder's insights were carried forward by others including the von Humboldts, Waitz, Bastian and Boas. Ultimately they would lead to the plural modern culture concept, and to forms of ethnographic method that privileged language and the text, including indigenous oral literature.

Wilhelm and Alexander von Humboldt

Wilhelm von Humboldt (1767–1835) pursued Herder's thoughts on human cultural diversity and on the relation between language and culture (Barnard 2000: 48; Petermann 2004: 281). From 1791, he began to design and propagate a plan for a comparative anthropology (Mühlmann 1968: 65). In this anthropology,

---

4   Sapir called it 'drift'.

he intended to deploy the methods of natural science, history and philosophy. The three approaches would converge (Reill 1994: 355). More specifically, Wilhelm's interest lay in combining linguistic research and philosophy in an empirical anthropological project (Trabant 1994: 210, 219–229).

His comparative approach in anthropology was built on two foundations: a view that humanity shared a common nature and that this nature was expressed in individual national characters. This range of nation-characters encompassed the entire human species. Documenting these characters was the empirical task of anthropology (Bunzl 1996: 22). Each national character was embodied in a totality of traditions: customs, religion, language and art. These outward manifestations revealed the degree of development in each group or nation. Since these achievements were specific to each national entity, they could not be compared to an external standard. Each deserved an unconditional respect. However, in Wilhelm von Humboldt's view, some nations had realised their potential to a greater degree than others. Not surprisingly Wilhelm's view was that European nations were among the more developed (Bunzl 1996: 22).

Wilhelm von Humboldt also elaborated and refined Herder's thoughts on language. For Humboldt language was the defining element of human life (Bunzl 1996: 29), and the embodiment of each people's soul (Burns 2002: 61). It was through language that a people expressed their worldview (*Weltanschauung*) and *Geist*. In his view, language is the single most important factor that determines human culture – both human beings' capacity for culture and their specific *Geist*. He focused on the different linguistic forms of diverse languages and the relation between language and cognitive structure (Losonsky 1999: ix). He chose language as his focus because in language national character expresses itself most fully. His idea of a comparative linguistic method for the empirical study of diverse languages was to lead to central developments in the study of culture (Bunzl 1996: 29).

At least in part this was due to the fact that he saw clearly that language was both a unifying element of humanity, and also a point of differentiation. He acknowledged the ability of the human mind to acquire different languages, enabling any individual to acquire numerous worldviews (*Weltanschauungen*). Wilhelm believed that different languages embody different types of psychological structures. These structures in turn shaped different views of the world (Bunzl 1996: 34). He regarded all languages as functionally equivalent, as no language had yet been found that was functionally or formally incomplete (Humboldt [1820] 1994: 12). Each and every language in his view was equally capable of expressing any conceivable idea; an opinion that he shared with both Jesuit and Lutheran scholars at the time. Thus, for Humboldt it followed that language is universal to humankind. The urge to speak, to use sound, to designate objects and connect thoughts is the subject of certain general laws that are universal. In this sense, all human beings have the same language though their initial capacities are developed historically in diverse ways (Losonsky 1999: xii, xx; Foertsch 2001: 112–113).

Wilhelm von Humboldt believed that the study of the origins of language could only be 'the object of futile speculation' (Bunzl 1996: 34). His empiricism led him to emphasise that comparative linguistics offered no answers to questions beyond the realm of immediate experience. He rejected explicitly the notion that any known language offered a glimpse into the far past or origins of human communication. No language had been found that lacked grammar or that was so recent as not to be the product of the activities of many generations of speakers. In the spirit of Herder he refused to propose a uniform law for the development of languages.

Alexander von Humboldt (1769–1859), Wilhelm's younger brother, was one of the most influential figures of his time in the field of natural science. In his *Kosmos* he tried to embrace 'all individual phenomena in their totality'. His inclusion of human interpretation in his cosmography though, led him to make an explicit contrast between positivist approaches and his own. He emphasised an empirical approach to a natural world that included cultural phenomena (Bunzl 1996: 39). He believed that both the unity of humanity and the specificity of individual cultures had to be studied empirically. He hoped to reveal 'the law of cosmic harmony' by reducing the multiplicity of forms in the natural world to some general laws of variation (Koepping 1983: 70, 77).

Like his brother, Alexander was furiously opposed to deduction and classification established without empirical observations. Alexander von Humboldt demanded the thorough description of the physical reality of nature as the primary objective of his cosmography (Bunzl 1996: 38). In this task, he included ethnography as a strictly descriptive exercise. The beginning of German ethnography may possibly be traced to the 'prodigious travels and explorations of Alexander von Humboldt between 1799–1829' (Adams 1998: 290) and the Humboldts' joint demands for empirical study of cultural phenomena.

Another crucial figure in the formation of nineteenth century German anthropology was Theodore Waitz (1821–1864), a philologist who maintained that humanity was homogenetic by virtue of the fact that all human beings had similar cultural and moral propensities (Petermann 2004: 429). He sought to integrate both the linguistic and natural science orientations that came from the Humboldts in an all-embracing project. Waitz produced an influential six volume work called *Anthropologie der Naturvölker* (1859–1872), parts of it appeared in English translation as *Introduction to Anthropology* (1863). His study was a response to the polygenist ideas advanced by various mid-nineteenth century writers. To prove homogenesis he confronted evidence provided by physical anthropology with his own ethnological interpretations of culture. Amassing the data available on physical traits among all the world's peoples, 'Waitz demonstrated the constant blurring of purported lines of racial demarcation, asserting that this precluded the existence of truly distinct types – an argument that Alexander von Humboldt had previously made in his *Kosmos'* (Bunzl 1996: 45). Waitz echoed Herder's view in *Ideas for a Philosophy of the History of Mankind* and would be echoed in turn by Boas in the first few decades of the twentieth century.

This psychic unity of humankind proclaimed by Waitz was fundamentally different from the French Enlightenment's universal rationality. Following Herder and the Humboldts, Waitz saw cognitive processes as diverse and always the product or result of particular histories. These forms differed in time and space and could not be reduced simply to a standard repertoire of rational reflection. At the same time, Waitz rejected any innate racial hierarchy in cultural achievement (Bunzl 1996: 46). He was a forerunner of Franz Boas's humanist relativism. Waitz criticised the racist and supremacist worldview of his French contemporary Arthur de Gobineau (a founding father of twentieth-century racism). He was 'the author to establish the monogenetic theory of a unified descent of races in German anthropology, a position on which Rudolph Virchow, Bastian and Boas would be able to build soon thereafter' (Gingrich 2005: 80).

However, Waitz was not without bias towards his own cultural group (Petermann 2004: 429). He assumed that people he identified as Caucasians had attained the highest form of culture, other peoples could also attain this given the right context. According to Streck (2001: 508), his achievement lies in his idea that all humans are encultured and thereby have the same potential to learn and develop.

During this period German philologists of the Romantic Movement, such as Schlegel and Bopp, were studying non-European languages and developing a great admiration for these other languages and cultures. They accompanied these studies with comparable ones focused on Europe's folklore (Gingrich 2005: 77). In this process German philologists began to develop a sense of German linguistic identity (Smith 1991: 61). At the same time, and under the influence of Herder, the Grimm brothers were pursuing systematic studies of folklore by collecting folktales and 'recovering' the essence of German culture, its *Volksgeist*. With these activities grew the view that the essence of a cultural group could be discerned in its mythology, folk tales and song. This interest in the traditional cultures of Europe was transferred to the so-called primitive peoples. Comparative mythology seemed to help trace the diversity in human unity. Myth and ritual as well as song became central to German anthropology.

Prior to these developments, the concept of culture and in particular the traditional philological concept of culture had been reserved for European societies;[5] for places where *Bildung*, the cultivation of a people, was clearly apparent in a written literature. For some time, classicists had been drawn to the study of 'primitives' for the contrasts that could be drawn between these groups and the Greeks and Romans, the 'cultured people' (Whitman 1984: 216). Now this traditional German philology exerted some influence on a nascent German anthropology with its own new interest in primitive life. The classicists were allies in a response to vulgar materialism that tried to apply natural scientific method to all fields of knowledge, and reduce all phenomena, including the cultural, to a single material substrate (Whitman 1984: 215–216). Barnard remarks that 'the development of theoretical ideas in linguistics has throughout the history of that discipline foreshadowed the development of related ideas in social and cultural anthropology' (Barnard 2000: 48).

By the late 1850s when Bastian returned from his first long trip (1850–1858) around the world he found that cultural scientists had opened up a new academic territory, the study of primitive life, and this was exactly the scope for Bastian's new science of man (Whiteman 1984: 224).

Adolf Bastian and Rudolf Virchow: The psychic and physical unity of man

The two most influential figures of nineteenth century German anthropology were Adolf Bastian (1826–1905), who established anthropology as an academic discipline in Germany, and Rudolf Virchow (1821–1902), the leading pathologist and physical anthropologist at the time. Intellectually, they dominated the main institutional sites and ideological tendencies of German anthropology. They maintained that no one race or people was superior to any other and that humanity was based on psychic and physical unity (Evans 2003: 200). With Waitz, Bastian and Virchow ensured that the emerging discipline of anthropology in Germany would be based on the presumption of monogenesis (Streck 2001: 503; Massin 1996: 87).

These representatives of nineteenth century anthropology were opponents of race theory, the attempt to assert the primacy of a biologically defined 'race' in determining the shape of social and historical process. They publicly opposed the biological determinism of social Darwinism or evolutionism.[6] In 1880, for

---

5   China, India and other literate societies were often also included.

6   There are different evolutionist positions: not all of them are based on biological determinism and polygyny. Sociocultural evolutionism, which can be understood as a proto-theory for comparison, has to be distinguished from Darwinian based evolutionism.

example, as the deputy of the Progressive Party in the *Reichstag*, Virchow rejected any kind of racism and challenged Bismarck himself, asking him to explain his position on anti-Semitism (Massin 1996: 89).

Virchow was the most influential and powerful physical anthropologist of nineteenth century German anthropology. He and the majority of his colleagues (Ranke, von Luschen, Kollmann) believed in the unity of the human species and argued that there was no physical evidence that one race was superior to another. Virchow's declared empiricism led him to regard Darwin's biologically-based evolutionist hypotheses as unproven (Massin 1996: 83). He also criticised social-cultural theorising based on biological determinism, pioneered by Herbert Spencer (Stocking 1987: 134–136, 141–142). Virchow made sure that no race theorist ever published a single line in any of the reputable German anthropological journals which he controlled directly or indirectly with Bastian and Ranke (Massin 1996: 93).

Bastian delineated and differentiated the field of anthropology/ethnology from a range of other disciplines. He held the first academic position in German anthropology and championed empirical observation (Koepping 1983: 3, 28). He was the founder of the Royal Museum for Ethnology in Berlin in 1886 and its director until his death in 1905.[7] He was also instrumental in establishing the Berlin Society for Anthropology, along with its journal, *Zeitschrift für Ethnologie*, which became the most prominent German journal in the field (Adams 1998: 291; Penny 2002: 19).[8] To document the diversity of human life, Bastian spent 25 years recording ethnographic data and collecting material culture in the Americas, Asia, Australia and Africa as well as in Europe (von den Steinen 1905: 242). The end result was an oeuvre of unmanageable proportions. Bastian's salvage anthropology was driven by the conviction that most other cultures would vanish in the confrontation with the imperial European powers.

He put great emphasis on the collection of material culture, because in his view artefacts were the embodiment of ideas and the tangible expression of the diversity of humanity (Koepping 1983: 107). Material culture, filtered through European eyes and understanding, was seen as rich in historical significance and of great empirical value that went beyond the limitations of written records (Penny 2002: 26). Bastian's museum project initiated a collection frenzy that took hold of German anthropologists and ethnographers. Through the incredible mass of material culture accumulated from overseas, it was believed that humanity could be represented in museum spaces. These ethnographic museums were meant to be well-ordered institutions, and were intended to function as laboratories for the comparative analysis of human artefacts. It was

---

7   Felix von Luschan succeeded Bastian as the museum's director in Berlin (Lally 2002: 77).
8   From Bastian and Virchow, Boas learned that intellectual influence had to be combined with institutional power.

thought that they would be the foundation of an inductive study of mankind, leading to fundamental truths about human character and development (Penny 1998: 159). Soon, however, museums were overflowing with material, collections became disorganised, and personnel unable to realise Bastian's and others' initial goals (Penny 2002).

The institutional achievements and legacy of Bastian are more obvious than his theoretical and intellectual influence. Although he produced a vast amount of ethnographic data and many publications, his main theoretical framework circled around the attempt to explain the unity of mankind (von den Steinen 1905; Ankermann 1926). At the heart of his theoretical approach lay three main elements: *Elementargedanken* ('elementary ideas' or 'thoughts'), *Völkergedanke* (folk thought or idea) and geographical province (Ankermann 1926: 223, 226; Koepping 1983; Penny 2002: 22–23). Bastian believed that human nature was uniform around the globe despite its ostensible diversity. This unity was captured in elementary forms of thought. These elementary ideas or thoughts, Bastian argued, were common to all human beings due to the psychic unity of mankind: '*Elementargedanken* were thus hidden behind humanity's cultural diversity – a diversity that was historically and geographically contingent. Understanding the unique context in which each culture took shape, Bastian stressed, was thus critical for gaining insight into the universal character of human being' (Penny 2002: 22). However, elementary ideas materialised in the form of unique folk thoughts (*Völkergedanken*) among each cultural group. These were the product of environment and the interactions between a particular people. The third element of Bastian's theory was the 'geographical province' in which a certain *Völkergedanke* was at home. Thus, there are as many *Völkergedanken* as there are geographical provinces (Ankermann 1926: 226).

In sum, every *Völkergedanke* is based on the same elementary thoughts, common to all people. Each *Völkergedanke* though is also dependent on an environment including social practices in concert with what Bastian called a 'geographical province'. Previously Herder, and later German diffusionists understood these factors as historical circumstance and immediate context. It was largely Bastian's interest in identifying these particular contexts in time and space that led Fritz Graebner to credit him with bringing indigenous peoples into history (Penny 2002: 22), although Gustav Klemm had already attributed history to non-European peoples in the first part of the nineteenth century (Rödiger 2001; Gingrich 2005: 79). However, Bastian's influence was certainly significant.

Bastian's view of humankind was closely related to Herder's. His *Völkergedanke* approximates Herder's *Volksgeist* and Wilhelm von Humboldt's national character or *Weltanschauung*. From Herder, Bastian also inherited the 'seminal notion' of language. These ideas were influential in his formulation of *Völkergedanke* (folk idea) or the collective representation(s) of a particular ethnic group (Koepping

1983: 55). He also underlined the issue of ethnography, of recording cultural particularity. This served to stress his view that there is no inherent difference between the thought of primitive and modern men:

> The propensity is the same in both cases, and the elements are the same. The results of these thought processes, in the form of folk ideas or worldview, are diverse, but the formative and structural principles are the same. Bastian emphatically denied the superiority of the European value system or the possibility of measuring one against the other. (Koepping 1983: 54)

Bastian used the notion of psychic unity to explain some of the 'extraordinary similarities' that cultural groups could display even though geographically they were distant from each other. Because he believed that cultures evolved in similar ways due to the nature and workings of the human mind, he argued that independent invention rather than diffusion or direct cultural contact should explain similarity. This seemed the preferable path to positing forms of contact or influence where there was no proven historical record (Adams 1998: 293). Bastian's emphasis on the psychic unity of mankind or the primacy of collective consciousness as the moving principle for endogenous growth led to a controversy between advocates of independent invention and advocates of diffusion (Koepping 1983: 60). Bastian's main opponent was Friedrich Ratzel, a theoretical geographer and diffusionist.

Bastian's anthropology also stood in contrast with trans-Atlantic and Continental anthropology influenced by Lewis Henry Morgan, Herbert Spencer and E.B. Tylor, although he eschewed social evolutionism and as well as progressivism. In German anthropological circles a more general reaction against social Darwinism had emerged. Bastian, Waitz and Virchow opposed the biological presumptions in social Darwinism. These German anthropologists insisted that the development of a people's culture was something that should be understood with reference to their own particular history and environment. Moreover, the study of these specificities should be historically grounded.

Despite his admiration for Darwin's travels, Bastian found Ernest Haeckel's popularisation of Darwin's thought especially offensive (Penny 2002: 21; Streck 2006). Bastian even rejected reflection on the origin of man, maintaining that were the issue to be tackled, this could only occur following exhaustive empirical research and the considered use of induction. The prefix 'Ur-' was highly suspect to him (Petermann 2004: 535). Thus, he and most of his colleagues steered away from Darwinian theorising and distanced themselves from the race debate (Massin 1996). Bastian hoped, rather, to use extensive empirical research to the end of formulating uniform principles for the mental creations of mankind (Koepping 1983: 78). At the same time he warned explicitly of simplification and generalisation resulting from notions of biological determinism in accounts of socio-cultural evolutionism. He drew on induction and empirical observation to avoid the classification of data according to predetermined categories, regarding schemes of classification as works in progress rather than definite models (Penny 2003: 93).

Bastian took human distribution across the earth as a given of natural life (Ankermann 1926: 226). He did not pursue an explanation of how this distribution occurred or of its particular features. This would be the task of the German diffusionist school.

Friedrich Ratzel and Fritz Graebner: German diffusionism

German diffusionism acquired its impetus from Friedrich Ratzel (1844–1904), a German theoretical geographer. He was interested in the relationship between humans and their immediate environment. In 1882 Ratzel published his major work, *Anthropo-Geographie*. It was an attempt to formulate a general theory of the human geography that Alexander von Humboldt had envisioned, and to provide a comprehensive account of the world's various histories of the type that Bastian had in mind (Müller 1993: 210; Petermann 2004: 538). Ratzel tried to develop an approach in which the materials collected could be deployed to explain the multiplicity of humanity in terms of migration and diffusion across the globe (Barnard 2000: 50). He opposed Bastian's idea of independent invention, the explanation of similarities in terms of a psychic unity. Ratzel was not prepared to place that much weight on a shared human creativity. Rather, he argued that cultural similarities were due to diffusion through migration, while differences could be explained with reference to particular environments. Ratzel was peripheral to the dominant anthropological circle and sought ways to have an impact on the establishment in Berlin. Therefore he initially adopted Darwin's idea of natural selection. It seemed to have at least in part an environmental reference in its account of the diversity of species (Smith 1991: 141). However, later he abandoned this position due to the biological determinism and progressivism involved in social Darwinism. Ultimately he believed that mankind was a homogenetic species influenced by history (Petermann 2004: 542).

Ratzel proposed that the object of ethnological study should be historical. It should trace the movements of people and cultural traits across the earth's surface. The patterns of these past movements should be linked with similar phenomena in the present in order to predict the future (Smith 1991: 142). In this fashion, Ratzel thought, one might begin to understand origins as well

(Petermann 2004: 540–541). To study the processes of change in society and culture, the (early) histories of specific peoples had to be investigated and from this research historical laws inferred (Smith 1991: 145). In pursuit of his ideas, Ratzel too emphasised detailed empirical research.

Ratzel's theory was developed into an elaborate *Kulturkreislehre* (theory of culture circles) by German diffusionists who took up his objectives. Initially Leo Frobenius (1873–1938) extended Ratzel's ideas (Barnard 2000: 50; Müller 1993: 203–204). It was only in the 1920s, however, that Frobenius became influential when he returned from his African adventures to formulate his Paideuma-Theory and to found his institution for *Kultur-Morphologie*.[9]

Fritz Graebner (1877–1934) and Pater Wilhelm Schmidt (1868–1954) elaborated on Frobenius' initial theory. Frobenius suggested that the diffusion of ideas occured in successive waves from a few fixed points of special cultural creativity. This position set itself against social Darwinian views because it built on Ratzel's and Bastian's thought. It used ideas of diffusion and human creativity in concert. At the turn of the century, the *Kulturkreislehre* was emerging as the main anthropological theory in Germany. It found its footing in November 1904 when Graebner and Ankermann presented ground-breaking papers at a meeting of the Berlin Anthropological Society. Subsequently, the papers were published in the *Zeitschrift für Ethnologie*. This meeting is often said to be the birth place of the *Kulturhistorische Methode*, although only in the 1910s did the first major works appear (Hahn 2001: 137).

In the first decade of the twentieth century most theorising on the *Kulturkreise* and *-schichten* (culture circles and -layers) was undertaken in private letters or at anthropological gatherings. The leading theorists of the new school, Graebner and Schmidt, were still refining their ideas (Lowie 1937: 177), and others who would publish later on the subject were developing their methodological approaches or collecting data and material culture in the field. Only occasionally short contributions – works in progress – appeared in anthropological journals such as *Globus*, *Petermann's Mitteilungen*, *Anthropos* or *Zeitschrift für Ethnologie*.

Work on migration waves and subsequent cultural 'layering' as well as culture circles took initially as its focus material culture, religion and marriage rules. Language appeared later in these studies, because comprehensive language studies barely existed, especially for Australia. Graebner focused on material culture in Oceania, including Australia; across the world he only compared cultures that seemed to be closely historically related.

---

9   On Frobenius see Heinrich 1998 and Petermann 2004.

The first brief linguistic contribution on Australian language to support the *Kulturkreislehre* was written by Pater W. Schmidt in 1908.[10] He had began his comparative study of Oceanic languages in 1899. His research seemed to indicate diffusion of language through Oceania that was carried by waves of migration. Comparative linguistics at the time was accustomed to relating languages historically and then locating their speakers on time-lines of cultural development. The comparison and classification of language was believed to give insight into ethnic origins, migrations and prehistory (Hoenigswald 1974: 348). Interestingly, Schmidt had been in contact with Carl Strehlow's mentor, von Leonhardi, but not with Strehlow himself. Based on his linguistic evidence Schmidt declared, that the Aranda were not 'primitive'[11] and their culture was not an inferior early form as social Darwinists of the British Isles wanted to see them.

For Schmidt as well as Graebner and Foy,[12] the population of Australia was not homogeneous, but consisted of a number of layers of peoples and cultures who had migrated and partially amalgamated. Graebner (1905, 1911) speculated that cultures emerged from different places of origin and spread in phases over the globe. Graebner was proposing three layers.[13] His work was not based on empirical observation and he did not outline the limitations of his sources. Paradoxically he advocated meticulous and critical research and empirisim. His view on Australia was that the oldest layer of culture had come from Tasmania and then had spread across the entire continent. Von Leonhardi, who was abreast of all emerging theories in anthropology, communicated to Strehlow that it was believed that at least two further layers of culture had spread over this Tasmanite layer and had brought new cultural elements like totemism, the boomerang and the spear thrower to mainland Australia.[14] Schmidt (1908b: 869) suggested that a fourth layer originated in New Guinea that had covered large parts of Northern Australia including areas where Aranda was spoken. Schmidt believed that he had found evidence for this fourth layer in his study of language.

One obvious trait of a culture circle was language or a language group that helped to distinguish one circle from another, or suggested overlay and mixing. Language presented itself as a central medium for tracing a people's historical development and cultural connections. However, these directions in anthropological thought were in their infancy (Kluckhohn 1936). The theory of the emerging *Kulturkreislehre* was still very hypothetical and most details

---

10   The first major work on the *Kulturkreislehre* and linguistics was Pater Schmidt's Die *Gliederung der Australischen Sprachen* published between 1912 and 1918 in his journal *Anthropos*, which he used scrupulously as his vehicle during his long academic life.

11   Schmidt (1908b: 866–901).

12   Dr. W. Foy was the director of the Cologne Ethnological Museum and Graebner's editor.

13   Von Leonhardi to Carl Strehlow, 2.3.1909.

14   Von Leonhardi to Carl Strehlow, 2.3.1909.

quite unclear at the end of the first decade of the twentieth century. Where Australia was concerned, for instance, the source of the two layers and waves of migration thought to overlay the Tasmanite stratum remained something of a mystery.[15] It was not even clear what particular features or 'traits' needed to be present in a culture circle to define it (Kluckhohn 1936: 138–139). This and other problems remained unresolved although Schmidt (1911: 1013) wrote in 1911 that his language studies corroborated Graebner's views on the composition and distribution of Oceanic culture circles. In general terms, diffusionism described some apparent patterns rather than presenting a coherent theory (Smith 1991: 151). The approaches of the main theorists of the *Kulturkreislehre*, like Ankermann, Graebner, Schmidt, Frobenius, Foy, Thomas and von Leonhardi were too diverse.

In 1911 Graebner's classic *Methode der Ethnologie* was published, as well as Boas' seminal works *The Mind of Primitive Man* and his introduction to the *Handbook of American Indian Languages*. These works were milestones in the history of anthropology. They synthesised important aspects of an historical and language-based approach to research in the first decade of the twentieth century. This was also the year in which W.H.R. Rivers declared his conversion to diffusionism, though his writing was not yet directed towards a critique of the social evolutionism of his time (Langham 1981: 118–121). Later Rivers would make the first serious attack on nineteenth century evolutionism in England, leading rapidly to the emergence of English functionalism (Langness 1975: 51).

Graebner's diffusionism was based on deduction and suggested a general history of humankind. Notwithstanding his own recommendations, his work was not empirically grounded. In his crisp review of Graebner's work, Boas pointed this deficency out and stated that concepts of diffusion and cultural transmission could not be applied to distances that spanned continents (Boas 1940: 295–304). Shortly after the publication of his book, on the eve of World War I, Graebner set sail for fieldwork in Australia, but on arrival he was interned in an Australian war camp (Petermann 2004). Although Graebner would be forgotten after the war in the rising tide of Nazism,[16] his futile trip to Australia into Strehlow's proximity draws attention to the intellectual milieu in which Carl Strehlow worked.

Strehlow in the mission and Boas in the academy

An overview of nineteenth century developments in German anthropology almost immediately allows Carl Strehlow's magnum opus to fall into place. No anthropological theorist himself, he was kept to the empirical task by his editor

---

15 Von Leonhardi to Carl Strehlow, 2.3.1909.
16 Only surviving in P.W. Schmidt's work.

Baron von Leonhardi's constant queries, Strehlow's work makes sense within the context of his German predecessors and particularly his contemporary, Boas, who, unlike Strehlow, became a professional in the academy in the United States.

In the first instance, Strehlow's respect for Aranda and Loritja people, his certainty that their intellects equalled his own, was in accord both with his theological training and with the presumptions of German historical particularism. Although a clear formulation of a plural culture concept would await the emergence of Boasian anthropology in the United States, Strehlow showed respect for another technologically limited culture and carried the nascent assumption of plural cultures across the globe; the same nascent concept that resided in the work of Herder, Wilhelm von Humboldt and Bastian. Consistent with this position, Strehlow simply assumed a homogenetic humankind. Certainly, his theology promoted the view, also endorsed by Humboldt, that any culture and language could express any conceivable idea. Although he laboured in his task of Christian conversion, Strehlow reported high god beliefs among the Aranda and Loritja. In an ironic way perhaps, and one that Spencer would not have understood, this aspect of Strehlow's ethnography reflected his commitment to plural cultures. Central Australian cultures like European ones were, in his view, open to the full range of human possibility. Both Herder and Strehlow used a theory of plenitude to explain a multiplicity of cultures rather than polygenetic theory. Boas would later begin the task of supplying this theory of plenitude with a basis in symbolic imagination rather than theology. Contemporaneous multiplicity would be explained not by spurious biology, or appeals to God's creation, but rather in terms of the multiple forms of representation that human beings can create – mainly through language.

Noting the impact that Herder had on the Grimm brothers, and the central role of studies in myth and language in an evolving German tradition, Strehlow's initial focus is also not surprising. He collected assiduously and carefully translated numerous examples of Aranda and Loritja myth and song. He tried to classify this material according to the Grimms' categories – *Mythen, Sagen und Märchen* (myths, legends and fairy-tales). Clearly inadequate to the task of a modern anthropological interpretation of myth, it nevertheless shows Strehlow's engagement with a genre of nineteenth century German thought that saw the key to a culture in oral text. Almost without reflection perhaps, Strehlow sought to record phenomena that would provide most ready access to a *Volkgeist* (Herder) or a *Weltanschauung* (Humboldt). The fact that this German tradition saw language study as a *sine qua non* of the empirical focus that they recommended, may possibly explain the role that Strehlow's Aranda and Loritja dictionary had in his own research. This extraordinary compilation that grew to vast proportions only to remain unpublished was perhaps evidence of the missionary's serious scientific intent. Consistent with both the German and Lutheran humanistic tradition from which he came, this compilation of language would be the ultimate and definitive route to central Australian cultures.

Finally, Herder's view that the greatest misfortune for a people would be to lose their language also throws interesting light on Strehlow's German-to-Western Aranda translations. His initial translation of the bible was an unusual achievement. Also interesting though, was his Aranda primer written for school children. *Pepa Aragulinja: Aranda Katjirberaka* was published posthumously in 1928. It contained the elements of Aranda literacy along with a small collection of bible stories and Lutheran hymns in Western Aranda.[17] Strehlow quite literally grasped Aranda culture in the act of translation. There could be no greater testimony to the importance of language study than his pioneering work.

There is little evidence in Strehlow's work of great engagement with Graebner's and Schmidt's ideas about multiple cultural layering. However, Wilhelm Schmidt's exchange of letters with von Leonhardi brought Strehlow into contact with diffusionist thought. Like Boas, Strehlow was interested in small-scale regional diffusion. It is possible that he chose to record both Aranda and Loritja myth noting differences in theme engendered by natural environment under the influence of the German diffusionists. His observations on geography also seem to recall Ratzel, and make an interesting link with T.G.H. Strehlow's observations on environment and social structure in different regions of arid Australia (Strehlow 1965). Carl Strehlow certainly had a sense of regional cultures. It is notable that as W.H.R. Rivers moved through diffusionism and towards functionalism in his studies of kinship terminology, Strehlow was developing a sense of culture area studies that had a resonance both with Graebner and Boas. Strehlow also collected material culture, in which he may have been responding indirectly to the priorities set by Bastian which seem to have reached every corner of the globe. Governed by their own tenets of empiricism, there was undoubtedly a view that in some sense or other the material object carried truth – something eternally retrievable for further research and also the counterpoint to a central focus on language.

Strehlow's major text was in one sense the product of a lonely missionary scholar in remote Australia. Placed in the intellectual tradition from which both Strehlow and his mentor came, however, his magnum opus mirrors in a striking way the anthropological concerns in the Germany of his time.

Thus, another way in which to position Carl Strehlow's intellectual endeavours is to juxtapose them with his contemporary, Franz Boas (1858–1942). Boas migrated from Germany to the United States and would become the founder of North

---

17   The work was published by the Finke River Mission in Adelaide with the co-operation of Auricht's Printing Office, Tanunda, South Australia.

American cultural anthropology. Initially he studied physics and geography, taking his doctorate in 1881 from the Kiel University in Germany. He began to travel between Germany and the United States, developing a lifelong interest in west coast Native American groups and especially in the Indian groups of British Columbia. By 1886, Boas had an appointment in geography at the University of Berlin and maintained an association with Bastian's Museum of Ethnology. His later interests in museums, collecting and in the human unconscious in culture likely stemmed from this association. Silverman writes that Boas 'transposed the notions of Bastian and Rudolph Virchow to his treatment of culture in the American context' (Silverman 2005: 260). In 1892, Boas was instrumental in the founding of Chicago's famous Field Museum and from there moved on to the Museum of Natural History in New York (Bohansan and Glazer 1988: 82). At this time, he also delivered lectures at Columbia University. This would be a lifelong association; a base from which Boas would train numerous prominent anthropologists including Alfred Kroeber, Ruth Benedict, Magaret Mead and Edward Sapir. Carl Strehlow's affinities both with a nineteenth century German tradition, and with the anthropology that Boas would develop are clear. The following account focuses on three central areas: Boas' field-based anti-evolutionism, his focus on language as a key to culture and, finally, his use of culture-area studies, a refined and empirically focused diffusionism.

Although this discussion juxtaposes Strehlow's immersion in the field to Boas' engagement with the academy, Boas was also an assiduous fieldworker. The injunctions of Bastian, Graebner and others to a disciplined empiricism were realised in Boas' professional practice. As Stocking proposes, Boas was the person who, in the United States, founded a modern fieldwork discipline. He was deeply rooted 'in the intellectual traditions of his homeland' (Stocking 2001: 26) and transformed 'a museum and government-based inquiry into an academic discipline in which "culture" replaced "evolution" as a dominant paradigm' (Stocking 2001: 1). Boas' anthropology was well informed by his predecessors in the German tradition. The cosmographic approach of Alexander von Humboldt is evident in his writings as well as Wilhelm von Humboldt's language project (Boas 1940: 639–647; Bunzl 1996). He had a good understanding of Herder, Kant and other classic German thinkers through his education at a German gymnasium (Liss 1996: 155–184; Cole 1999: 280). Like his colleagues of the *Kulturkreislehre*, he did not believe in racial or biological determinism or linear development of societies in which peoples could be arranged according to evolutionistic sequences.

During his sojourn in Berlin, Boas also formed a lifelong friendship with Virchow. From him Boas learned quantitative method and also became an expert in physical anthropology amassing anthropometric data to prove that no grounds existed to discriminate against any group of people on the basis of physical difference (Boas 1940; Petermann 2004; Synnott and Howes 1992: 154). In his work he approached the question of races from diverse angles, each time reaching the conclusion that there was no conclusive evidence regarding physical traits to establish a diversity of race. Boas found that 'differences were not great enough to allow living men to be placed on different evolutionary stages' (Stocking 1968: 220).

Empiricism and quantitative method initially determined his approaches to the new discipline. However, the fieldwork experience itself seems to have been the crucial one for Boas. According to Lévi-Strauss, he 'became aware of his anthropological vocation during the course of his first field work, as a result of a flash of insight into the originality, uniqueness, and spontaneity of social life in each human group'. Thus, while Boas sought to apply to the subjective world the 'rigorous methodology that he had learned in the natural sciences, he recognized the infinite variety of historical processes which shapes [the subjective] in each case' (Lévi-Strauss 1963: 8). As Boas proceeded in his work, language and history became increasingly important in his interpretation of human multiplicity. In the late 1880s, Boas wrote that his method was to inquire into the peculiarities of single tribes through a thorough comparison of language, customs, and folklore. His historical analyses were focused on issues of inheritance and borrowing. In his view, it was crucial to evaluate and distinguish what was original and what was borrowed in customs and folklore as well as in language (Stocking 1968: 206). Cultures were the product of numerous elements coming together from a range of factors in a region. Therefore, they could never be a simple matter of linear progression from one stage to the next.

Because his work was empirical with a small area focus, Boas was led to the view that each culture has its own 'logic', and its own particularity. Ultimately, his view was relativistic and a product of the tradition from which he came. In an interesting comment, that bears on Carl Strehlow's work as well, Darnell remarks that 'Boas' emphasis on descriptive ethnology in a historical context, later criticized as atheoretical, was itself part of a consistent methodology based on an explicit theoretical commitment' (Darnell 1998: 290). For example, in his descriptive work on *Primitive Art* published in 1927, Boas weaves the repudiation of speculative theory regarding origins into his comments on style:

> I doubt very much that it will ever be possible to give a satisfactory explanation of the origin of these styles, just as little we can discover all the psychological and historical conditions that determine the development of language, social structure, mythology or religion. All these are so exceedingly complex in their growth that even at best we can do no more than hope to unravel some of the threads that are woven

into the present fabric and determine some of the lines of behaviour that may help us to realize what is happening in the minds of the people. (Boas [1927] 1955: 155)

This developing fieldwork method fed into Boas' rejection of nineteenth century evolutionism and its notions of sequenced developmental stages. Boas criticised the premature classification of superficially similar phenomena that may be the product of quite different regional histories (Stocking 1968: 205). It was these concerns that produced one of his most famous essays, written in 1896, *The Limitations of the Comparative Method in Anthropology* (Boas 1940: 270–280). By 'comparative method' he meant 'the specific procedures followed by the evolutionists' (Silverman 2005: 261). In this essay he denounced the evolutionary assumptions that dominated the English-speaking world. By noting that ostensibly similar phenomena are not always due to the same cause, Boas was undermining the approach of independent invention and evolutionary sequencing.[18] In this famous article, a nascent sense of the modern culture concept began to emerge. In criticising 'the comparative method' as it was understood within evolutionism, Boas was pointing not simply to particularism but also to contextual specification; to the variable meaning or significance of a thing or practice within varying historical contexts (Sahlins 1976: 67; Bohansen and Glazer 1988: 84). He argued that the same phenomenon, a mask for example, does not always have the same meaning and may well have developed out of very different contexts (Sahlins 1976: 68).

According to Stocking, 'what was actually at issue was not simply the general evolution of culture but the extrapolation of evolutionary stages in every area of cultural life – the presumed sequences of art forms, of marriage forms, of stages in the development of myth, religion, and so forth' (1968: 211). Boas focused on the fundamental historicity of cultural phenomena, and on the ability of cultures to assimilate and also innovate with newly acquired material. In this he stood in marked contrast to the evolutionists who tried to arrange all peoples of the world in stages of a linear development according to predictable laws with a predictable outcome. Once again, the very different views that Baldwin Spencer and Carl Strehlow held on Aranda people conform with this divergence. Where Spencer saw inevitable decline, Strehlow as missionary and nascent historicist, saw innovation and a future.

Boas' critique of evolutionism rested on his German historical particularism; on an appreciation of the historically conditioned plurality of human cultures. This position also allowed him to engage other ideas concerning notions of *Volksgeist* and, most importantly, the centrality of language in culture. Language

---

18   At the basis of the critique of independent invention were his view of causality and classification (see Stocking 2001).

was central in Boas' work for a number of reasons. Like other early German anthropologists, he believed that language was something that belonged to every human group. There were no inferior languages. He saw language as one of the routes to unravelling the history of indigenous peoples and traditional worldviews, because 'the history of language reflects the history of culture' (Boas 1940: 631). In the introduction to his *Handbook of American Indian Languages* (1911), Boas stated clearly that it was paramount for the student of American Indian cultures to know the language of the people studied, to be able to grasp the essence of that particular culture (see also Stocking 2001: 72), although he acknowledged that 'the practical difficulties in the way of acquiring languages are almost insuperable':

> Nevertheless, we must insist that a command of the language is an indispensable means of obtaining accurate and thorough knowledge, because much information can be gained by listening to conversations of the natives and by taking part in their daily life, which, to the observer who has no command of the language, will remain entirely inaccessible. (Boas 1911: 60)

In view of these remarks, one cannot but summon the image of Carl Strehlow's more than 20 years in 'the field'. In addition, Boas argued that text collection in original languages was essential for ethnography and a foundation for further research. Boas wrote that 'no translation can possibly be considered as an adequate substitute for the original' because:

> The form of rhythm, the treatment of the language, the adjustment of text to music, the imagery, the use of metaphors, and all the numerous problems involved in any thorough investigation of the style of poetry, can be interpreted only by the investigator who has equal command of the ethnographical traits of the tribe and of their language. (Boas 1911: 62)

Language knowledge was the pre-condition for meaningful ethnographical research, but at the same time language was also in itself an ethnological phenomenon (Boas 1911: 63). Just as language mirrors a culture, 'the peculiar characteristics of languages are clearly reflected in the views and customs of the peoples of the world' (Boas 1911: 73).

Boas was particularly interested in folklore, meaning the body of customs and traditions of a society that were largely stored in mythology, and thereby in the language and texts of a people. It was this complex that determined culture rather than biology or race. Language and mythology were possible sources of data on migrations. They revealed customs which were often hidden or extinct and provided a way to trace the history of a people. Most important though, the folklore of a people reflected their *Volksgeist* or *Weltanschauung* (Stocking

1968: 223). The mythology of a people provided the best material for evaluating beliefs and practice as well as the ethical and aesthetical values of a culture. Folklore and mythology were the key to a people's particularity.

Text or oral literature (myths and tales as well as related traditional laws and customs) were therefore immensely important to Boas. Developing his argument against racially-based mental differences, Boas suggested that the minds of humans shared similar powers of abstraction, inhibition and choice. Their particular manifestation, however, was shaped by the body of custom and traditional material that was transmitted from one generation to the next. Much of this was unconscious, like the hidden complex morphological or grammatical categories and structures of language. The behaviour of all humans was the result of a body of habitual behavioural patterns of the particular culture in which they live (Stocking 1968: 220–222).

Lévi-Strauss wrote that Boas must be given credit for defining more lucidly than ever before the unconscious nature of cultural phenomena. By comparing cultural phenomena to language in this regard, Boas anticipated both the subsequent development of linguistic theory and a future for anthropology. He showed that the structure of a language remains unknown to the speaker until the introduction of scientific grammar (Lévi-Strauss 1963: 19). Boas wrote:

> It would seem that the essential difference between linguistic phenomena and other ethnological phenomena is, that the linguistic classifications never rise to the consciousness, while in other ethnological phenomena, although the same unconscious origin prevails, these often rise into consciousness, and thus give rise to secondary reasoning and to reinterpretation. (Boas 1911: 67)

These were Boas' primary and secondary rationalisations that pointed to the taken-for-granted in culture and juxtaposed it to conscious elaborations of meaning; different dimensions of culture with different degrees of stability (see also Ogden and Richards 1946).

Boas accepted diffusion but not the grand patterns of Graebner's approach (Adams 1998: 294). In Boas' view, diffusionist accounts were useful only when applied to small areas where empirical research was possible and allowed comparison. Only detailed studies of phenomena would be able to shed light on how cultures evolved through time. The thorough study of local phenomena in a well-defined, small geographical area would bring the histories of individual cultures alive. Boas offered a critique of generalising approaches in his essay, 'Review of Graebner, "Methode der Ethnologie"' which he included in *Race,*

Language and Culture (Boas 1940: 295–304). He emphatically rejected Graebner's method because, ultimately, Graebner fell back on generalised notions of historical development. Boas concluded:

> Thus it seems to me that the methods of Mr Graebner are subject to the same strictures as those of the other schools, and the "Ferninterpretation" (remote interpretation), "Kulturkreise" and "Kulturschichten" must be considered as no less hypothetical that the "Stufenbau" of Breysig or the sequences of Lamprecht (Boas 1940: 303).

Boas' views on diffusionism were influenced by his studies of myth. He had gained a detailed sense of the ways in which culture contact within a region could result in forms of borrowing that re-shaped myth (Darnell 1998: 279). Therefore, in Boas' view, it is never easy to arrive at origins, to discern how 'foreign material [is] taken up by a people and modified by pre-existing ideas and customs' (cited in Stocking 1968: 207). Myths were the result of complex historical growth combining elements from various sources, thus a product of diffusion and amalgamation. For Boas, human creativity was expressed in the imaginative manipulation and reinterpretation of elements provided by a tradition, or borrowed from proximate others (Stocking 1968: 226).

The Boasian style of analysis therefore stressed territorial contiguity and the reshaping of traits within a limited historical area over time (Darnell 1998: 188). Comparison was only possible in a small area in which the elements were comparable. Sometimes recent borrowing could not be distinguished from a common origin, but neither 'stages' of development nor 'layers' of culture had much explanatory value for Boas (see also Darnell 1998: 217). He thought it very unlikely that whole culture blocs would travel over vast areas virtually unchanged, which was the prevalent belief of German diffusionists of the *Kulturkreislehre*. His diffusionism is sometimes termed, *der verfeinerte Diffusionismus*, 'the refined diffusionism' (Szalay 1983: 33).

Boas' position seems consistent with Strehlow's approach to his research with Western Aranda and Loritja people. It seems likely that the convergence in style of these two transitional anthropologists in the German tradition came mainly through a diffuse humanistic tradition, an interest in history and language, and in a shared admiration for diligent empiricism. Strehlow, missionary in the field, and Boas, doyen of the American academy, had a similar style.

Concluding remarks

In summary, nineteenth century German anthropology and ethnology was a humanistic endeavour that tried to understand different peoples and cultures in their own right without comparing them with others. As a result the theoretical and ideological orientation of German anthropology was monogenetic, anti-racist, particularist and historical (viz. focused on area studies and small-scale diffusion). In the hands of scholars including Boas and Strehlow, this meant that their ethnographic work was more often than not descriptive and did not present explicit and developed general theoretical insights. Owing to his place in the academy, Boas, however, drew out the implications of his position in considerable detail and also provided his reasons for rejecting other positions.

German nineteenth century anthropologists challenged eighteenth century progressivism that proposed a linear succession for humanity in time and space from one stage of development to the next, culminating in enlightenment. They were also opposed to nineteenth century evolutionistic thought that was based on biological determinism and which arranged peoples on a scale of different stages of mental and social development. Social Darwinism was seen as highly speculative and hypothetical, based on vulgar forms of deduction. German historical particularism also carried with it an emphasis on empirical research which encouraged the study of language. Especially with Boas, language rather than biology became the crucible of human difference. Thus, contrary to common perception, nineteenth century German anthropology was anti-racialist and monogenetic nearly to the eve of World War I. The majority of German anthropologists rejected any kind of human difference based on race and professed the unity of humankind. This was the diffuse formative milieu in which both Boas, and Strehlow (guided by von Leonhardi), pursued their respective works.

Carl Strehlow was conducting his research in the first decade of the twentieth century, before Boas and Graebner published their seminal works in 1911. Strehlow concluded his research in 1909 which means that his study of language and myth was pursued in a 'pre-modern anthropological' framework phase of modern anthropology – at a time when Boas was still trying to detail his position. Carl Strehlow could not have read Boas' *Handbook of American Indian Languages,* for instance, prior to the publication of his own work. Strehlow shared with Boas and his circle, the nineteenth century German tradition: a commitment to empirical research, a strong focus on language and myth and an interest in small-scale diffusion as well as an aversion to evolutionism involving biological determinism. This is the intellectual milieu into which Strehlow's *Die Aranda- und Loritja-Stämme in Zentral-Australien* fits. Both Boas and Strehlow were drawn to language and myth, and produced dense records of field material. Strehlow's *Die Aranda- und Loritja-Stämme in Zentral-Australien* is descriptive ethnography that, in Sahlins' terms, allowed indigenous Australians to 'speak for themselves' (Sahlins 1976: 76). With this in mind, Strehlow was almost certainly 'interested in ethnography as an end in itself' (Adams 1998: 295).

Nevertheless, it seems that Strehlow, and his German contemporaries, had a good sense of the cultural multiplicity that would be the focal interest of a modern, professional anthropology. The making of a 'plural culture concept' is foreshadowed throughout the German tradition. The plural of the term culture appears in North America with regularity only in the first generation of Boas' students around 1910 (Stocking 1968: 203). Boas did not arrive at the point where he could finally show, despite his massive detailed research on the particularity of individual cultures, patterns and structures that allowed a society/culture consistency over time. Boas did not go beyond the plural of culture; patterns and structures of cultures would be left to his students. Kroeber would develop a concept of the superorganic, Ruth Benedict would write *Patterns of Culture* and Lévi-Strauss would tackle structures of the unconscious, for example. Boas' programme exceeded a lifetime, like the Humboldts or Bastian, he would not be able to conclude his project.

Surveying the conceptual genealogy of nineteenth century anthropology, it seems that Herder's *Volksgeist*, Humboldt's national character and *Weltanschauung,* and Bastian's *Völkergedanken* are only variations on a theme that echoes Herder's concept of *Humanität* and his idea of cultural diversity and pluralism.

The theology of Carl Strehlow finds a curious precedent in Herder's thought. Darcy observed, that Herder had adopted the Platonist concept of the Great Chain of Being, 'an imaginary link starting with God and descending through the angels to man and onto the animal world' (Darcy 1987: 7). In fact, Darcy writes:

> Herder expanded the chain to include a "chain of cultivation". Humankind became a differentiated totality of cultures all equally attached to the Godhead. The potential in such a philosophical system is clear: once the links to the Godhead were removed, Herder's intellectual system would become simply an apprehension of the multiplicity of human cultures. (Darcy 1987: 10)

Boas was ensconced in the academy while Strehlow remained in the church. Both, however, were grounded in the German tradition: a unique combination of universalism and particularism with the desire for empirical research and the acceptance of human diversity.

III. From Missionary to Frontier Scholar

Carl Strehlow is principally known to us through remarks by his son, T.G.H. Strehlow, in *Journey to Horseshoe Bend* (1969) and *Songs of Central Australia* (1971), and recently also by his grandson, John Strehlow, in *The Tale of Frieda Keysser* (2011). In *Journey to Horseshoe Bend*, T.G.H. Strehlow records the loyalty of the Aranda and Loritja people to the ailing man and the apparent disloyalty of the Finke River Mission board as it responded in a cumbersome way to his father's suffering. He also evokes the image of an overwhelming missionary-father. The son's ambivalence towards the father is readily apparent in the former's corpus. In *Songs of Central Australia*, T.G.H. Strehlow defends his father intellectually from the glib but damaging critiques mainly of Baldwin Spencer. His defence of his father involves revealing the limitations in Spencer and Gillen's consultations with their indigenous informants due to their lack of language competence. Yet, he provides only a sparse sketch of his father either as missionary or scholar-intellectual which is strangely devoid of emotion, although he writes in his diary (Strehlow 1960: 155) that 'Horseshoe Bend is a place whose shadows I can never escape' (cited in Cawthorn and Malbunka 2005: 71). The man who peers out with a calm intensity from his best-known portrait, taken with his wife, Frieda Keysser, in 1895, remains a relative stranger.

Accounts by Phillip Scherer (1994), Walter Veit (1991, 1994, 2004a,b), Benedikt Liebermeister (1998), Harriett Völker (2001), Paul Albrecht (2002, 2006), Maurice Schild (2004a), Barry Hill (2002), and, Carl's grandson, John Strehlow (2004a,b, 2011), provide additional biographical, historical as well as anecdotal detail, and further aspects that were formative of Carl Strehlow's scholarly development, though they also oscillate between the two poles set by the son. These accounts about Carl Strehlow as a missionary and scholar explain aspects of his potential, but are still not sufficient to understand how a seemingly stern and at times self-righteous man could have dealt in the same serious way with two very different cosmologies and ontologies. In many ways his Lutheran world that he tried to replicate in central Australia and the indigenous world of that place were and still are so different, although the two worlds have since converged and produced a particular kind of Aranda Lutherism and narratives (see Austin-Broos 1994).

Carl Strehlow's grandson John Strehlow (2011) has written an epic biography of the first part of his grandmother Frieda Keysser's life naturally incorporating a narrative on his grandfather. Trying to reappraise Carl Strehlow's legacy, he has largely followed in the vein of his father, T.G.H. Strehlow, defending and justifying his grandfather against Spencer. Veit (2004b: 92–110) also chose to write about this opposition. He contrasts Carl Strehlow's 'cultural anthropology' with Spencer's 'social anthropology'. While this opposition indicates correctly that different ideologies motivated the two investigators, it must be remembered that modern anthropology as 'social' or 'cultural' did not exist yet at the beginning of the twentieth century. As already discussed, different poles generated the tension: one was based on evolutionism and the other on eighteenth and nineteenth century German philosophy and philology. However, Veit (2004b) remarks correctly that Carl Strehlow's work reflects a tradition that derives from German humanistic thinking.

13. Frieda and Carl Strehlow, 1895.

Source: Strehlow Research Centre, Alice Springs (SRC 7104).

Thus, Veit as well as Schild (2004a) have portrayed Carl Strehlow's intellectual background through his mission training at Neuendettelsau, trying to explain how this education may have made it possible for a missionary to record the cultures of other peoples in their own right. They write that Neuendettelsau instilled in Strehlow a humanistic approach towards others and encouraged language studies. Veit (2004a) indicates also that at the turn of the century the discussion in Lutheran theological mission circles on how to accommodate different religions became increasingly explicit.

In the following discussion, I pull the threads together and show how his missionary and German intellectual heritage had elements in common. It was not one or the other that made his ethnography possible, but underlying common premises and the right encouragement from an unexpected source. Three different experiences shaped the scholar that Carl Strehlow became: his youthful education at the Neuendettelsau Mission Seminary and the German Lutheran approach to language as it was reflected in the Australian practice of Lutheran missionaries; his field encounters with indigenous Australians, the Diyari, Aranda and Loritja; and finally, his correspondence with Moritz von Leonhardi, his German editor. Each engagement brought something specific to his work and mediated the final product in particular ways. Furthermore, negative encounters, especially attitudes of some Lutheran superiors in Australia to ethnographic work were countered by others – in this case, his keen engagement with indigenous peoples and von Leonhardi's seminal intellectual influence, support and companionship.

Training at the Neuendettelsau Seminary under Johannes Deinzer

The education at the Neuendettelsauer Missionsanstalt (Neuendettelsau Mission Seminary), at the time run by Dr Johannes Deinzer, was formative for Carl Strehlow's development and the *Menschenbild* ('the view of man') he took into the field. The seminary's mission-theology was based on the views of Wilhelm Löhe as interpreted by Deinzer. The latter was particularly interested in the 'outer mission' and ethics; not the 'inner mission' that catered for existing and lapsed Lutherans but rather the out-reach to those who remained unconverted. Language was emphasised. Greek, Latin and Hebrew were rigorously taught at the Neuendettelsau Seminary to prepare the missionaries for their language tasks. The German Lutheran linguistic tradition, based on Luther's view that the gospel was to be preached in vernaculars and translated into the mother tongues of peoples (Wendt 2001: 8), heavily influenced the seminary's approach towards indigenous peoples. It went without saying that the knowledge of indigenous vernaculars was the prerequisite for successful mission work. Thus, potential missionaries were encouraged, through linguistic work, to learn about other people's cultures. The serious study of indigenous languages lead some missionaries towards an interest in the *Weltanschauung* and mythology of a particular people. Neuendettelsau's style made a major impression on the enthusiastic teenage Carl.

At the age of 16 in early 1888, Carl Strehlow was one of the youngest students to be educated and trained at the Neuendettelsau Seminary for mission work. In 1923, Ziemer remarked in Carl Strehlow's obituary that Carl had entered with reluctant paternal consent, because his father did not wish his son, one of seven children, to be a cleric or have a higher education (Liebermeister 1998: 16). He felt that it was not appropriate for a child of such modest station to reach beyond the means of a village teacher. Carl Strehlow's family was not in the position to finance any kind of further education for any of their children beyond that offered in the public system – at the time, a meagre training. For talented young people without any means, the only venue for further education and amelioration of social status was often the path within the church and even that left Carl's father anxious.

The village pastor of Strehlow's birthplace Fredersdorf Carl Seidel recognised the outstanding talents and potential of the child and sparked his interest in myth and song. With great dedication and effort, Seidel prepared his protégée for entry into a seminary. After Strehlow had been refused at the Leipzig Seminary, due to his young age, Seidel wrote to the Neuendettelsau Mission Seminary. He proposed that it would be 'generally beneficial for the whole development of the child to be removed from the narrow circumstances in Fredersdorf' and promised to try to raise as much money as he could to pay Carl's school fees (Liebermeister 1998: 17–18). As late as 1899, seven years after he had left Neuendettelsau, Carl Strehlow voluntarily tried to pay off some of his outstanding fees from his modest missionary income in central Australia, 'so other impecunious students may benefit from this'.[1]

Seidel taught Strehlow the basics of classical languages, mathematics, geography, world history and correct German syntax and orthography. Carl needed these in order to compete with other applicants who mainly came from Gymnasiums, academically demanding secondary schools, which provided their students with a classical education (Pilhofer 1967: 29). When Carl Strehlow joined the seminary, he was also familiar with the Romantics. His early teacher and mentor, Carl Seidel, was interested in the work of the Grimm brothers and folklore generally (John Strehlow 2004a) and had an understanding of the importance

---

1   Carl Strehlow to Inspector Deinzer of the Neuendettelsau Seminary, 20.1.1899 (Neuendettelsauer Missionswerk).

and meaning of mythology, in which he saw moral teaching embedded.[2] These influences and the German philological tradition which emphasised the classics and comparative language studies in educated German circles gave some bearings to his inclination towards language.

The selection process at Neuendettelsau was rigorous (Koller 1924; Pilhofer 1967). The criteria for successful applicants included a high level of secondary education, as well as a strong personality and excellent health. The intense course lasted three years with a very demanding and dense curriculum. The expectations and the pressure were immense, both imposed by the seminary as well as by the students themselves. Nervous breakdowns, it seems, were not unusual (Pilhofer 1967: 29).

The classical orientation of the Neuendettelsau curriculum gave their students a solid basis to recognise structures of foreign languages, which facilitated the writing of grammars and dictionaries – essential for the translation of the Holy Scripture,[3] and mission preaching and schooling. Clearly language studies were encouraged if not expected from the graduates once they proceeded to their postings. In addition to classical languages, correct German style and orthography was taught along with basic English. It was assumed that the latter would quickly improve once graduates took up posts in America and Australia. German essay and speech writing were also taught.[4] Another subject that held a prominent position was music, in the tradition of Luther's own deep engagement. Finally, even physical education was integral to an individual's training.

Ethnographic approaches or methodology do not appear to have been part of the curriculum; anthropological study came mainly through language study. There do not seem to be any texts that were used at the Neuendettelsau Seminary that explicitly encouraged students to learn about the cultures of the peoples they were to live with. In 1929 Carl Strehlow's brother-in-law, Christian Keysser,[5] finally introduced anthropological subjects into the curriculum (Pilhofer 1967: 32) and explicitly articulated the mission approach to ethnography (Veit 1994; Liebermeister 1998: 127) when he became a teacher at Neuendettelsau after returning from his posting in New Guinea.

The focus on language prepared Carl Strehlow well for his calling. Not all institutions that trained missionaries had Neuendettelsau's classical orientation. In the field, missionaries from other seminaries often rued their inadequate

---

2 Carl Seidel to Carl Strehlow, 12.9.1908 (SH 1908-2-1).

3 House tradition of the Neuendettelsau seminary was to use the Greek source for translation (Dr Hauenstein of the Neuendettelsauer Missionswerk, Neuendettelsau, pers. comm., August 2005).

4 This can be gleaned from the handwritten chronicles held at Neuendettelsau's archives.

5 Christian Keysser published a number of ethnographic works.

linguistic training. In 1877 Kempe and Schulze, the first missionaries at Ntaria, for instance, felt their lack of knowledge of Latin and language learning skills and tools. However, they still managed to learn and write Aranda (Kneebone 2001: 149).

Neuendettelsau had its own style of mission theology which was based on Wilhelm Löhe's view of the *innere und äussere Mission* (inner and outer mission). This particular approach did not have a mission to indigenous peoples as its pre-eminent goal.[6] The inner mission, according to Löhe, was to hold the Lutheran congregation together through general pastoral care that would keep them from flagging in their commitment. The outer mission had the task of finding people to be baptised, which included Germans and indigenous peoples. Once baptism was accomplished, the outer mission led automatically back into the inner mission which saw its role not only in collecting sheep, but also in caring for the congregation. This included education, and holding and sustaining pastoral assistance (Weber 1996: 353, 360), which were viewed as a responsibility of the mission. The mission then was an ongoing commitment that stretched well beyond conversion.

Wilhelm Löhe (1808–1872) seems to have originally founded the seminary with an emphasis on the inner mission. Missionaries were sent out to take care of existing Lutherans and their communities in North America where, it was thought, communities readily lost faith due to the lack of Lutheran clerics. Löhe was principally concerned with the care of German diaspora communities (Koller 1924; Pilhofer 1967). From North America, disturbing, even shocking reports had reached Löhe and other Lutheran clerics regarding perfectly good Christian parents who had up to 11 unbaptised children due to the absence of qualified clergy. The German migrants were growing up 'like the Indians'. The dispersion and spiritual 'decrepitude' proved initially to be far greater than anticipated in America, so that the inner mission amongst Germans took precedence (Weber 1996: 346). However, Löhe could mention Indian and German heathen parents in the same breath indicating that the agenda was set (Weber 1996: 346). The broader pastures of North America were soon beckoning. By 1888 'the society for the inner mission' added 'outer' to its name (Schlichting 1998: 5). The *Gesellschaft für die Innere (und Äussere) Mission* still exists today and has turned its attention inwards again.[7]

For Löhe, the inner and outer mission were parts of the same issue and church (Weber 1996: 343). Hence, missionaries and pastors received the same education

---

6   Wilhelm Löhe is seen today as one of the fathers of World Lutherism. He also made significant contributions to social development and education, at a time when the state was not much engaged in social amelioration and this was left to the church's care. See Schild 2004b; Weber 1996: 15; Schlichting 1998: 7; Farnbacher and Weber 2004.

7   For more information see: <http://www.gesellschaft-fuer-mission.de> (accessed 31.5.2013).

at Neuendettelsau. The concepts relating to the inner mission would have been transferred immediately into the indigenous context where, after the outer mission had recruited new members, they would quickly become a Lutheran community with the potential for an inner mission. Therefore, the members of such a community (the result of the outer mission) were treated like any other member of a Lutheran community, regardless of their colour or culture.

Löhe's mission theology was taught to the students of the Neuendettelsau institution by Friedrich Bauer and later on by the Deinzer brothers, university graduates, who integrated this theology into their broader academic programme. Bauer had gained fame by writing an excellent grammar of the German language which was republished 14 times alone during his life (Pilhofer 1967: 11) and became the base of the DUDEN, a standard work for correct German syntax today. Bauer also drafted the two basic manuscripts *Entwurf einer christlichen Dogmatik auf lutherischer Grundlage* and *Entwurf einer christlichen Ethik auf lutherischer Grundlage* pertaining to theological studies in Lutheran dogmatics and ethics. The style was much influenced by Löhe, but also included Bauer's own views on education as the route to individual freedom and *Bedürfnislosigkeit* (lack of needs) (Pilhofer 1967: 18–19). These were regarded as general forms of ethical value that pertained equally to the inner and the outer mission. Free will and individual choice were of paramount importance in the education at Neuendettelsau and a key element in its mission theology. During a six-month probation period, recruits had to prove that they were absolutely certain of their calling.

In Carl Strehlow's mission approach, individual 'free choice' was a formative concept. He perceived the indigenous people at Hermannsburg as individual human beings who could make free choices regarding their circumstances. Strehlow only accepted converts when he believed that they were firmly convinced of their step to conversion, or they were able to convince him of their sincerity. Conversion and confirmation allowed indigenous people to participate at Hermannsburg as full members of the Lutheran community. Paradoxically, Löhe's doctrine of the inner and outer mission, and Bauer's emphasis on freedom (from desire) may have had an unexpected consequence in the lonely and isolated setting of Hermannsburg in central Australia. Strehlow's outer mission became his inner mission, so that the missionary became the inkata ('ceremonial chief' in Aranda) of, in his view, freely baptised Christians. Löhe's Lutheran doctrines, with their inward gaze that may have signified a sect more than a broad church, became for Strehlow the basis for an unusual Christian community (Kenny 2009a: 104).

Johannes Deinzer's particular concern led Carl Strehlow in this direction. As the main teacher and director at Neuendettelsau until 1897, Deinzer expanded interest in the outer mission to encompass Australia, Papua New Guinea and

East Africa. It was under him that the first graduates of Neuendettelsau were sent to Australia. By 1914 about 40 had gone to Australia, the majority as pastors for the German immigrants to Australia (Pilhofer 1967: 22; see also Koller (1924) on Deinzer). Deinzer had another interest that may have influenced Carl: ethics. He placed a heavy emphasis on ethics in his classes and favoured students who could follow his intellectual path (Pilhofer 1967: 23). He considered ethics as more important than dogmatics, because it allowed interpretation according to (historical) context. Deinzer's interest in ethics, encouraged among his students, may have directed their missionary task to human engagement with others; an interest in the other person as much as in pietistic formulae. It is likely that Strehlow's propensity to acknowledge the human dignity of others, including indigenous Australians, was encouraged by Deinzer's classes.

Neuendettelsau was less conservative and pietistic than other mission training institutions such as Hermannsburg in Germany or the Basler Mission in Switzerland, for instance. It gave its students a broad education in humanities (relative to their time of course) (Moore 2003: 23). The whole education was geared towards the development of strong personalities who would be fit for the demanding tasks and challenges that awaited them at their overseas postings. The hard training was to equip the students with self-discipline, endurance and an inner, spiritual (*geistige*) strength that would carry them through hardships and environments that would push them to their limits. The teachers at Neuendettelsau were painfully aware of the realities that the young people had to face once out in the field (Koller 1924; Pilhofer 1967). At the same time, community shaped by patriarchal structure was emphasised to give the individual a context and to provide fraternal support and ultimately helped to underline the natural shift from outer to inner mission within a newly formed community. These diverse ideas and influences in intellectual life, theology and human social ethics all emerged to some degree in the very different and remote context of Carl Strehlow's Finke River Mission at Hermannsburg in central Australia. It gave its community some unusual features of humanistic engagement (along with the missionisation) hardly known in other Australian frontier settlements.

Carl Strehlow graduated with a '*gut plus*' (good plus) in 1891[8] and was sent to his first posting in April 1892 (Liebermeister 1998: 19). He had just turned 20 when he was on his way to Bethesda in remote and arid Australia to join J.G. Reuther (1861–1914) who had left the Neuendettelsau Seminary four years earlier.

The second major formative factor in Carl Strehlow's experience was his engagement with Diyari, Aranda and Loritja people. He learnt firsthand that the different Aboriginal peoples each had a particular language and mythology. His

---

8   Zeugniss der Neuendettelsauer Missionsanstalt, 17.4.1892.

close relationships with people of completely different cultural backgrounds for nearly three decades, and his intense efforts in language learning, enabled him to appreciate, collect and translate the oral literature of the Aranda and Loritja. Through the thorough knowledge of language and its oral forms, he gained a deep appreciation and understanding of their worldviews.

Language, ethnography and the Lutheran tradition in Australia

The milieu that Strehlow entered when he came to Australia would be both a help and a hindrance when it came to his subsequent anthropological studies. German missionaries in Australia brought their linguistic tradition with them. Among the missionaries, it went without saying that it was paramount to learn the language of the people they were working with and sent to serve. It had been a crucial part of Luther's reformation to spread the gospel in German rather than in Latin or even a German rendition of the Vulgate. Luther preached that the word of God was to be taught in vernacular and translated into a people's mother tongue (Wendt 2001: 8). As a consequence, in the nineteenth century it was characteristic of German Protestant mission theology and practice to pay special attention to a people's language and its implications for idiom and other dimensions of culture (Schild 2004: 54).

It was clear to German missionaries that it was essential to know a people's language to be able to convey and persuade them of Christianity, as conversion was to be by free will and choice. Already in the late 1830s the missionaries Teichelmann and Schürmann, who had been trained at the Dresden Mission Society, started documenting the Kaurna language of South Australia (Leske 1996: 30, 92–94). Within 18 months they produced the only existing grammar of this language and a dictionary with 2000 words. Their work has allowed the partial recreation and revitalisation of Kaurna today (Amery 2004: 9–12). At least sometimes, not surprisingly, a by-product of these studies of indigenous languages was not only grammars and dictionaries but also collections of myth and other traditional laws and customs.

In the 1860s with a stream of Protestant missionaries arriving at Bethesda (Killalpaninna) and Kopperamanna in the Lake Eyre region the Diyari language and culture received a great deal of attention. One of the first missionaries at Killalpaninna Mission, Carl Schoknecht, wrote a simple Diyari grammar and a wordlist (Schoknecht 1997: 16, 80). His successors continued to collect data on the Diyari language and culture until the mission was closed in 1917. The Lutheran ethnographers of this region are well-known today. J.G. Reuther produced a monumental 13-volume manuscript on the Diyari and Otto Siebert collected a great amount of data for A.W. Howitt that was incorporated into the latter's classic *The Native Tribes of South-East Australia* (Howitt 1904). The first Hermannsburg missionaries, Kempe and Schulze, studied the language and culture of the people they met at Ntaria on the upper Finke River in order to develop effective communication for their transmission of the gospel to the local population. In the course of learning about them they published linguistic as well as some ethnographic data.

Upon arrival in 1892 at Bethesda Mission near Lake Eyre, Carl Strehlow immediately started to study the language of the Diyari. According to Otto Siebert and Reuther's son, the linguistic achievements at the mission were Strehlow's rather than Reuther's who was 'lame at languages'. Even for the Diyari grammar Strehlow is said to have been 'the mainspring of the work'.[9] In Reuther's defence, it has to be remarked, that the comment 'lame at languages' was made in comparison to Carl Strehlow, who was an outstanding linguist, as well as a competent musician (Lohe 1965: 5), and to Otto Siebert, who was particularly interested in languages and ethnography for mission purposes (Nobbs 2005).

At Hermannsburg, Strehlow became fluent in Aranda and preached in vernacular within months of his arrival in 1894 (Schild 2004; Eylmann 1908). In 1896, two years later, Gillen (Mulvaney, Morphy and Petch 2001: 118–119) remarked in a letter to Spencer that 'Revd Mr Strehlow' spoke the language of the Finke very well and used his services as a translator for his anthropological research in Hermannsburg. Strehlow published in 1904 a Service Book called *Galtjindintjamea-Pepa Aranda Wolambarinjaka* which included 100 German hymns translated into Aranda. This work was partially based on the work of his predecessors, in particular Kempe's catechism.[10] After he had completed the compilation of Aboriginal mythology and cosmology he translated the New Testament into Aranda between 1913 and 1919.[11] Parts of it were published after his death (Hebart 1938: 317) as *Ewangelia Lukaka* (1925) and *Ewangelia Taramatara* (1928), without mentioning his role as translator.

As soon as Lutheran missionaries at Bethesda and Hermannsburg had managed to acquire a moderate proficiency in the vernacular, they used indigenous languages in church services and schools. Lessons were also held in German and English (Moore 2003: 24). This ready and constant deployment of languages meant that the missionaries were constantly developing their proficiency moving

---

9   Tindale interviewed Siebert and Reuther's son in the 1930s. Tindale Collection Acc. No. 1538, South Australian Museum.

10   Carl Strehlow's letters to Kaibel (1899–1909) held at the LAA. Strehlow had been able to draw on published and unpublished Aranda language material (Schild 2004a; John Strehlow 2004: 83). The SRC and LAA hold unpublished material by Kempe produced between 1877 and 1891.

11   Carl Strehlow's letter to the Mission Friends on the 9.1.1920, Albrecht Collection Acc. No. AA662, South Australian Museum.

towards that time when their skills would be sufficiently developed to begin the translation task. The latter required familiarity with idiom and generally this came only through immersion and through trial and error.

John Strehlow (2004b: 82) suggests that his grandfather began his anthropological research not long after his arrival in Australia. In 1893, with the translation of the New Testament into Diyari, Carl Strehlow spent much time with senior Aboriginal men evaluating terms and concepts which would be appropriate for the translation. This early research, though, was not geared towards anthropology, but towards his linguistic mission task. Early ethnographic research by Carl Strehlow is documented in letters by Gillen to Spencer in 1896 and by Otto Siebert who forwarded information and charts on Aranda marriage rules and subsection systems collected by Carl Strehlow to A.W. Howitt in 1899.[12] On the 14 July 1896 Gillen wrote to Spencer that he had 'Mr Strehlow on the job and he, having a fair knowledge of the Arunta language, should be able to learn something shortly' (Mulvaney, Morphy and Petch 1997: 130). Other loose notes in Gillen's notebook of the 1890s, mention Strehlow in connection with research on particular ceremonies, called Inkura in Carl Strehlow's work and Engwura in Spencer and Gillen's. One of the notes is labelled 'to Strehlow', dated '26/8/96' and a remark reads: 'Have the old men any tradition as to the origin of "Rev C Strehlow" Engwura did it originate with altjirra Knaribata?'[13] This intriguing note is part of a longer piece, but unfortunately the rest appears to be missing.[14] Finally, Strehlow's personal interest in Aboriginal mythology is evident in occasional remarks in letters published in the *Kirchlichen Mitteilungen*.[15]

Strehlow's first report on Hermannsburg, written at the end of 1894, for example, shows his interest in myth. He describes briefly how the palms at Palm Valley (then called Palm Creek), were created according to the beliefs of the 'Aldolinga tribe'. He wrote: 'According to the old heathen beliefs the gods from the high north brought the seeds to this place.'[16] He would later collect a detailed story and its associated songs (Strehlow 1907:88–90; 1910: 129–132) about Mt Rubuntja and the fire ancestors who came from the north to Palm Valley; this is still a well known myth among Arandic people. It was one of these in passing observations that drew in 1901 Baron von Leonhardi's attention to Strehlow.

---

12   Otto Siebert to A.W. Howitt, 22.4.1899 (Howitt Collection at Melbourne Museum).

13   Loose pages in Gillen's Field-diary 1896 (Barr Smith Special Collection).

14   Did Gillen forget to reference a crucial informant on Engwura? And who is this altjirra Knaribata [old man altjirra]?

15   The *Kirchlichen Mitteilungen* was a monthly church newspaper about mission work in North America, Australia and New Guinea that had been publishing since 1868. It also published letters and sometimes even brief accounts on indigenous languages, beliefs and customs. It was edited by the university-educated mission inspector Deinzer, the head of the Neuendettelsau Seminary where Carl Strehlow had been educated and prepared for his calling.

16   Carl Strehlow, *Kirchen- und Missions-Zeitung* 3, 1895: 20.

In Australia, Strehlow had access to Warneck's *Allgemeine Missionszeitschrift*[17] as well as to the *Kirchlichen Mitteilungen,* the monthly newsletter of the Neuendettelsau Seminary and *Kirchen- und Missions Zeitung* of the evangelic-Lutheran church of Australia, published in Tanunda South Australia. These monthly publications were not only parish and community announcements, but also included numerous ethnographic reports on different countries and their cultures, including religion, mythology and cosmology. Through this reading, Strehlow was well aware of other cultures and religious belief systems. In his letters to Baron von Leonhardi, for example, he makes comparison between Aranda and West African beliefs[18] and Aranda and Chinese ancestral worship.[19] Neither, he maintains, are comparable to the Arandic perception of ancestors.

Like other theologians, clerics and missionaries, Dr Gustav Warneck, Professor at the Halle University, emphasised the importance of learning local languages for missionaries to transmit God's word (Wendt 2001: 8; Veit 2004a). He was one of the main Lutheran scholars of mission studies and well known in German nineteenth century missionary circles through his prolific writing on relevant topics. In 1874, he founded the *Allgemeine Missionszeitschrift*, and was its editor for decades (Lueker 1954: 1120). This journal published ethnographic material from all over the world as well as theological and other theoretical treatises. Warneck's main thoughts on missionising were synthesised in *Evangelische Missionslehre. Ein missionstheoretischer Versuch* (1897). His chapter on the justification of ethnographic work for mission purposes gives some insights into how and why missionaries could become interested in ethnography (Warneck 1897: 278–304).

The nucleus of Warneck's thinking was that Christianity had the universal capacity to adapt to all peoples and thus could assimilate its teachings to all ethnic, social, cultural and state forms (Warneck 1897: 279). In his view, all humans in all times, climates and cultures had religion and language (Warneck 1897: 285).[20] He maintained that since there were no peoples in the world that were speechless, there also could be no people that were without religion. This was evident in the fact that the gospel could be preached in all languages and all languages were suited for bible translation.

Warneck's arguments on humanity's spiritual unity reflected his homogenetic outlook which stemmed from his reading of the Old and New Testament. He used current German anthropological literature of the time by eminent scholars like Waitz, Ratzel and Müller to support his theological views, maintaining that 'Humanity is a unity, despite of its multitude' (Warneck 1897: 285) and that

---

17 Carl Strehlow to von Leonhardi, 23.10.1907 (SH-SP-14-1).
18 Carl Strehlow to von Leonhardi, 23.10.1907 (SH-SP-14-1).
19 Carl Strehlow to von Leonhardi, 2.6.1906 (SH-SP-2-1).
20 Warneck uses the plural: *Kulturen* (cultures).

the unity of mankind was an ethnological fact. His views were consistent with those of Herder and the Humboldts. He too postulated that humanity's spiritual and intellectual unity was particularly manifest in languages which were a common feature among all humankind. He was of the view that each language is a masterpiece of *Geist* (Warneck 1897: 286) and that there were no peoples with an inferior language and that the word of God (due to its universality) could be translated into any language and transmitted in any language. For many missionaries this was a fact because the bible had been translated into all known languages. Among Jesuit missionaries and scholars, and there were many, this had been common knowledge for a long time (Foertsch 2001). Protestant clerics had made a similar experience by translating the bible into a variety of mother-tongues in Europe and overseas since Luther's Reformation.

Owing to this universality of a spiritual propensity to Christianity, in Warneck's view it was never necessary to destroy a culture in order for its people to become Christian converts (Warneck 1897: 282). Rather, the object was to learn about them so Christian thinking could be culturally and linguistically appropriately conveyed. Although it is not clear that Strehlow was taught Warneck's principles on language and religion (or ethnography) at the Neuendettelsau Seminary, Veit writes that it is reasonable to assume that he was at least familiar with some of these Warneckian thoughts about the 'foreign and the familiar' (Veit 2004a: 146). Strehlow's approach to language and culture at his two Australian postings and his anthropological work are consistent with Warneck's approach.

Carl Strehlow's keen interest in mythology is thus the result of a number of factors including his education in the classics at the Neuendettelsau seminary and earlier by Seidel who also emphasised German folklore. He was probably from the outset open to the oral literatures and worldviews of the Aboriginal people he met, because he may have felt that the ancient worlds of the Old and New Testaments as well as Greek mythology which he knew from language studies of Greek and Hebrew, had affinities. Such a view seems to appear in a statement he made towards the end of his life:

> The well-constructed language of the Aranda remind one of the old Greek language; in fact, it has more moods than the last mentioned. It possesses an indicative, conditional, optative, minative, and imperative, it has not only the usual tempora, present, imperfect, perfect and future, but also three aorist forms, aoristus remotus, aoristus remotior, and a remotissimus; besides, it has dual for all three persons. In the declination of the noun there are not only a double nominative (transitive and intransitive) and a genitive, dative, and accusative, as in other old languages, but also a vocative, ablative, a double locative, an instrumentative, a causative, &c. The derivations and compounds are often quite marvellous. Then the great number of words! It is difficult

to count them on account of the many derivations and dialectical forms but, the latter included I estimate, that the Aranda language possess not less that 6000 words.[21]

Carl Strehlow was a scholar, with a positive and intimate appreciation of the ancient biblical and classical worlds which were older and different to his own; in Australia he came in contact with another different world, which seemed to him in some ways analogous to these remote worlds. This new world opened itself up to him through his intensive study of its languages and his personal interest in myth and song, and allowed him to enter the world of Aboriginal mythology which gave him a glimpse of the worldviews of the Aranda and Loritja.

Language went hand in hand with culture and its particular intellectual concepts, it was not a big step to ethnographic and other scientific research (Wendt 2001: 9). Strehlow's predecessors Kempe and Schulze had already compiled some ethnographic data published in the 1880s and early 1890s. Schulze had even communicated with Howitt on aspects of Aboriginal culture – it goes without saying that this data included 'marriage rules' – between 1887 and 1889.[22] Thus, precedence for ethnography as a by-product of language studies in the mission context existed at Ntaria.

Yet missionary Siebert's experience shows that on the local Australian scene, ethnographic pursuits – as opposed to linguistic ones – were viewed with more ambivalence, if not suspicion, by the Lutheran church. In the course of his anthropological research, his superiors alleged that he was neglecting his calling for the sake of this scientific work. In a brilliantly argued letter of 28 March 1900 to the Lutheran committee at Point Pass, Siebert rejected these allegations. He made a strong case for the use and application of ethnography in evangelism (Siebert 2005: 46–53). His letter reads like a manifesto for ethnographic research in the name of God and the mission, and convinced the pietistic Point Pass committee to concede, albeit grudgingly. They allowed Siebert to pursue his scientific research as long as it did not interfere with his mission duties (Nobbs 2005: 39).

Strehlow knew about this dispute between Siebert and the Lutheran committee.[23] It may have led him to heightened circumspection regarding his own research. Strehlow's letters to friends, family and superiors are devoid of any indication that he was conducting a major ethnographic research project between 1901–1909. He only made passing references to his anthropological endeavours to his brother-in-law, Christian Keysser,[24] and to Carl Seidel in this period. His communications on ethnography were all directed to his editor,

---

21 Carl Strehlow, *The Register*, 7.12.1921.
22 Schulze's letters to Howitt, 1887–1889 (State Library of Victoria, Howitt Papers MF 459, Box 1051/Icc).
23 Bogner to Carl Strehlow, Bethesda, 8.5.1900 (SRC 1900-21-2).
24 Christian Keysser to Carl Strehlow, 4.9.1905 (SRC 1905/26(a)).

von Leonhardi.[25] This reflects more about Strehlow's mission board in Adelaide than it does about his own interests or aspirations. It is likely that he thought that his ethnographic research would meet the same kind of resistance as did Siebert's and later on Reuther's work with his superiors in the Barossa Valley. J.M. Bogner[26] had written to Strehlow that Siebert had wasted his time trying to explain his endeavours to their superiors in the Barossa Valley, because 'they would not understand it'.[27] In 1904, Reuther had send some Diyari myths from his collection to his superior Kaibel who was not impressed:

> If instead of the big piles of legends and fables you have collected, which are of no use to anyone – who would anyway finance their publication? – you would send us brief monthly reports, you would be fulfilling your duty, satisfying us and be doing something useful.[28]

Carl Strehlow's circumspection about his anthropological work would prove justified. Kaibel's reaction to the first volume of *Die Aranda- und Loritja-Stämme in Zentral-Australien* in 1908 surpassed the one to Reuther's work:

> My heartfelt thanks for sending me your work on the Aranda. It is a beautiful monument of German diligence. In any case, the material is the most worthless one can think of which has been brought into written language. Almost all is chaff with hardly a kernel of moral value here and there. It certainly needs not a little self-denial on your part to have recorded those thoughtless legends in which only an ethnographer could be interested in.[29]

Left solely to this barren field, the seed of Strehlow's interest would surely have withered and died in the isolation of central Australia. Lutherans in Germany had furnished Strehlow with linguistic skills, social and ethical dispositions and even a theology that could nurture his budding interest in ethnography. However, in the Australian milieu, this came with a pietistic parochialism and anti-intellectualism that could have been his undoing. While his superiors in the Barossa Valley of South Australia supported linguistic studies that had a tangible use in spreading the gospel, ethnography was seen as an indulgence and possibly to a certain degree as blasphemy. This made the contribution and support of another and different type of mentor and friend absolutely crucial for Carl Strehlow's ethnography.

---

25   However, Seidel's reaction to the first volume in 1908 suggests that Strehlow may have written about his research. Seidel organised public talks on Aboriginal culture for Carl when he was in Germany in 1910.

26   J.M. Bogner was a co-missionary of Carl Strehlow between 1895 and 1900 at Hermannsburg. He too was a graduate from the Neuendettelsau Seminary.

27   Bogner to Carl Strehlow, 8.5.1900 (1900-21-2).

28   Kaibel to Reuther, 18.2.1904 (LAA). Hercus and McCaul (2004: 36) have also translated this passage. I am not sure if their interpretation of *Lügenden* as 'liar legends', is correct. The spelling of this word may also be due to Kaibel's particular German dialect and not a Freudian slip.

29   Kaibel to Carl Strehlow, 6.8.1908 (LAA). Also quoted in Veit (2004b: 95).

Baron von Leonhardi's anthropological influence

Without doubt, Baron Moritz Wilhelm Georg von Leonhardi (1856–1910) was an important and direct influence on Strehlow's development as an anthropologist. He was a man representative of the nineteenth century German anthropological tradition, and turned Carl's use of language towards an ethnographic method. He furthered Strehlow's anthropological training by posing research tasks, thereby pursuing empirical research with him.

He was born on the 9 March 1856 in Frankfurt am Main, the son of a wealthy, aristocratic family of the principality of Hessen. Moritz attended the Darmstadt Gymnasium (Secondary School) receiving a classic German humanistic education. He matriculated in 1876 and took up law in Heidelberg (Völker 2001: 176). However, he was soon forced to terminate his law studies due to ill health. After recovering from illness, he turned his attention to the subjects of natural science and philosophy. Although he was the Archducal Chamberlain of Hessen and a member of the Upper House between 1892–1910, Baron von Leonhardi spent much of his time studying on his country retreat in Gross Karben.

Von Leonhardi was a contemporary of nineteenth century German writers and thinkers such as Bastian, Virchow, Ratzel, Frobenius, Graebner, Schmidt and Boas. He was familiar with the current trends of the cultural sciences and had a close understanding of their main intellectual ancestors like Herder, Kant and the Humboldt brothers. His letters to Carl Strehlow show an interest in the Humboldtian ideas of the unity of man and the project of languages, Herder's concept of *Volksgeist*, Bastian's belief in independent invention due to the psychic unity of mankind and the emerging diffusionist *Kulturkreislehre* (theory of culture circles).

In the last decade of von Leonhardi's life, anthropology moved into the centre of his interests. He became a classical armchair anthropologist, corresponding and debating from his study with a number of well-known scientists in Europe like A. Lang, N.W. Thomas, P.W. Schmidt, H. Klaatsch, F. von Luschan and numerous representatives of the natural sciences,[30] and reading everything on anthropology available to him. According to Dr Bernhard Hagen (Strehlow 1911), the director of the Frankfurt ethnological museum, von Leonhardi had a close to complete anthropological library, including books not readily available in Germany (Völker 2001: 178). His library held not only books but also most anthropological journals published in America, Britain, France and the German-speaking world. He subscribed to all major journals on anthropology including the *Zeitschrift für Ethnologie*; *Man, Folklore, American Anthropologist* and *Anthropos*. He was also

---

30   Von Leonhardi also corresponded with missionaries Reuther and Siebert in Australia (see Völker 2001: 173-218).

an occasional contributor to the German weekly journal *Globus*. His library[31] and his letters to Carl Strehlow, document what von Leonhardi had read and make it possible to gauge what his methodological and theoretical position had been. A number of comments and comparisons by von Leonhardi on American, African, Australian and Melanesian indigenous peoples, Asian 'high cultures' and theories by Frazer, Lang, Schmidt, Graebner, Foy, Fison, Howitt and Roth, indicate his broad knowledge of nineteenth century international anthropology. In several letters to Carl Strehlow he refers to anthropological hypotheses and debates of the day, which he asks him to test, so they could deflate some of the current 'fairy-tales' such as 'group marriage of primeval times'[32] or 'a disaster ... like the one of Spencer and Gillen's reincarnation theory'[33] or 'A sun cult, which exists without doubt amongst the North American Indians, but does not seem likely to me in Australia'.[34]

In line with the *Zeitgeist* of nineteenth century German anthropology, von Leonhardi believed that thorough empirical research had to be conducted before universal laws pertaining to humankind and ideas of origin could be approached and generated. The evolutionistic position of the English anthropological establishment seemed highly speculative to him. Although he did not subscribe to an evolutionary proposition, due to his grounding in a humanistic tradition which paid tribute to the plurality and particularity of human kind, like most European cultural scientists, he believed that the indigenous cultures of the colonised world were doomed.

In this context, religion was one of the most discussed and written about topics around the turn of the century. Central Australian Aboriginal people, the Aranda in particular, occupied the centre of this anthropological discourse. Through Spencer and Gillen's work they had attained collective celebrity on the international anthropological stage (Morton 1992). The Horn Expedition report and *The Native Tribes of Central Australia* (Spencer and Gillen 1899) had intrigued and fascinated von Leonhardi like the rest of the anthropological world. Indigenous Australian religion became particularly worthy of study. Von Leonhardi perceived the need for further empirical research among the Aranda. The existing material, in particular on mythology and language, was not sufficient or adequate to give an idea of the *Geist* of the Aranda or any other central Australian people. Still, mid 1908 von Leonhardi complained to Strehlow about the low standard of available linguistic materials:

---

31   Baron von Leonhardi's library survived World War II. It is still in Gross-Karben. However, the ethnological publications were integrated into the library of the Frobenius Institute in Frankfurt which holds a large amount of early anthropological publications.

32   Von Leonhardi to Carl Strehlow, 10.4.1907.

33   Von Leonhardi to Carl Strehlow, 15.12.1907.

34   Von Leonhardi to Carl Strehlow, 7.8.1906.

I did not think that you would be satisfied with Basedow's work.[35] Our periodicals always accept such work; because – with incredibly few exceptions – we have no other vocabularies. The vocabularies in the 3-volume work of Curr are not much better and yet we have to work with them. And that is really depressing. In regard to phonetics, there are no correctly recorded Australian languages at all in the existing literature, even Threlkeld, Günther, Meyer are inadequate.[36]

This German intellectual background and its conditioning determined how von Leonhardi guided Carl Strehlow's ethnographic research and formed their methodological and theoretical approaches. His comments on methodology to Strehlow reveal his commitment and desire to see indigenous peoples described in their own right without considering any theories and making hasty inferences. This intention is clearly reflected in the style of *Die Aranda- und Loritja-Stämme in Zentral-Australien*. Carl Strehlow's monograph is pre-eminently descriptive and factual rather than theoretical, thus belonging to the tradition of German ethnography which was interested in source material rather than premature theoretical insights.

Von Leonhardi's dedication and persistency kept Strehlow to the task and provided him with the intellectual support and recognition he needed to sustain his research into the cultures and oral literatures of the Aranda and Loritja of central Australia.

When Carl Strehlow began to work with von Leonhardi, the conditions for successful research were in place: he had lived with the Aranda and Loritja for over ten years and fluent in their languages. He had also gathered some ethnographic data with a publication in mind,[37] including myths and songs.[38] By April 1906[39] Strehlow had collected over 50 Aranda myths and investigated the concept of tjurunga as well as recorded '300 Tjurunga'[40] songs.[41] A few months later he informed N.W. Thomas that he had 500 songs.[42] These numbers are somewhat ambiguous, because his published collection of Aranda songs amount to 59 and Loritja songs to about 20. This count may relate to verses rather than

---

35   Basedow published in 1908 a vocabulary of Arunta in the German journal *Zeitschrift für Ethnologie*.
36   Von Leonhardi to Carl Strehlow, 29.8.1908. The vexed question of Western Aranda/Arrernte/Arrarnta orthography has not been solved to this day (see Kenny and Mitchell 2005: 5; Breen 2005: 93-102).
37   Carl Strehlow to Kaibel, 30.8.1904 (LAA).
38   Carl Strehlow to von Leonhardi, 30.7.1907 (SH-SP-17-1).
39   Carl Strehlow to von Leonhardi, probably 8.4.1906 (SH-SP-1-1).
40   Tywerrenge (modern spelling), usually means today 'sacred object' and is not often spoken about (Breen 2000: 60). The term tjurunga (Carl and T.G.H. Strehlow's spelling) is a very complex term that can mean songs, stories, dances, paraphernalia or sacred objects associated with ancestral beings (see Appendix 2). Here it does not refer to the objects.
41   Carl Strehlow to von Leonhardi, 2.6.1906 (SH-SP-2-1).
42   Carl Strehlow to N.W. Thomas, mid to end of 1906 (SH-SP-6-1). The end of this quote echoes his editor's language programme, articulated in 1905.

to songs. While his interest in indigenous language and through language in culture was not unusual for a German missionary in Australia or at any other overseas posting, his interest in ethnography and in particular in mythology was reinforced and encouraged by von Leonhardi. On the 9 September 1905 von Leonhardi explicitly articulated what would become their linguistic agenda which included the collection of indigenous text and made Carl Strehlow's work unique for its time in Australia:

> Myths in the Aranda language with interlinear translations would be of great value; and a dictionary and a grammar would provide the key to them. A dictionary outlining the meaning of words as well as short explanations of the meaning of individual objects, characters in the myths etc., is highly valued in science.[43]

Von Leonhardi's suggestion is reminiscent of Wilhelm von Humboldt's view that there were two steps in language research which needed to be undertaken to be able to make statements about a people's culture and language. The first step was to describe the structure of a language (grammar and dictionary) and then its use (*Gebrauch*) (Humboldt 1994: 16), with which he meant oral literary text (Foertsch 2001: 113). He repeated this view, again in reversed order, after he had read a transcription of an Aboriginal song by R.H. Mathews (Martin 2007: 127):

> We are still lacking good texts in the original language with interlinear translation; of course the texts would have to have been recorded with the greatest precision. Such texts, though, would be more pertinent at the moment than grammars and vocabularies, which the scholar in the end – if the texts are only somewhat extensive – could derive from them himself.[44]

Nevertheless, von Leonhardi repeatedly emphasised the importance of a publication of a comprehensive grammar and comparative dictionary of Aranda, Loritja and Diyari. According to Carl Strehlow,[45] the dictionary was going to be part of the publication on Aranda and Loritja cultures, literatures and languages. The language study had been planned as a separate publication, which von Leonhardi thought would be the culmination of Strehlow's ethnographic work:

> As the coronation of the total work, you must finally write a language study of Aranda and Loritja.[46]

---

43   Von Leonhardi to Carl Strehlow, 9.9.1905.
44   Von Leonhardi to R.H. Mathews, 9.6.1908 (Thomas 2007: 247). Translated by C. Winter.
45   Carl Strehlow to N.W. Thomas, mid to end of 1906 (SH-SP-6-1).
46   Von Leonhardi to Carl Strehlow, 23.12.1908.

This language study would be the last piece to unlock the inner thoughts of the Aranda and Loritja. By the time the first volume of the *Die Aranda- und Loritja-Stämme in Zentral-Australien* was published at the end of 1907, Strehlow had collected over 6000 Aranda and Loritja (Kukatja) words and derivations as well as hundreds of Diyari words. His dictionary contains extensive references to kinship terms, ceremonial vocabulary, mythology and material culture, as well as historical incidents. The 'coronation' of his masterpiece never came to be. It is still an unpublished handwritten manuscript, bound and sewn together by hand, based on work commenced during the 1890s. It probably represents the largest and most comprehensive dictionary of indigenous Australian languages compiled around the turn of the century and possibly to date. It is a unique documentary record in Australia.

Strehlow's linguistic and philological communications on language and indigenous text were very detailed. They ranged from pronunciation[47] and grammatical, etymological to semantic interpretations of key terms like Altjira – aljeringa reflecting his intimate knowledge of Aranda and Loritja intellectual life. He also tried to systematically and consistently employ (Breen 2005: 94) an orthography of the indigenous languages he was documenting at a time when spelling systems and the study of language were not well developed in Australia (Moore 2003). He remarked on his system:

> When you compare my work with Spencer and Gillen's, you will see immediately that our orthographies are completely different, because the two gentlemen choose the English spelling, I in contrast use the continental one. It is a pity that Spencer and Gillen did not use the latter as well, which Mr. Spencer as professor in Melbourne must have known.[48]

Initially their approaches to language seemed to differ. Strehlow's studies of language and culture were used in applied ways for bible translation, education and ultimately for conversion. For von Leonhardi ethnography and language studies had a wider scope. They were primarily to further human knowledge about the world. Language was not only a research tool, it also had a crucial philosophical dimension; it showed how other people thought and different modes of perception. It gave insight into people's worldviews and their true spirit and intellect. Language also had an historical dimension in von Leonhardi's methodological and theoretical framework, which he discussed with Strehlow. He was exploring the use of comprehensive descriptions and documentations of languages to help explain some hypotheses of the infant theory *'Kulturkreislehre'* of the German-speaking world. Von Leonhardi's understanding of language in

---

47 Von Leonhardi to Carl Strehlow, 23.9.1909.
48 Carl Strehlow to von Leonhardi, 13.12.1906 (SH-SP-7-1).

the *Kulturkreislehre* was informed by close reading of the limited amount of existing material in the first decade of the century and his correspondence with P.W. Schmidt. Von Leonhardi makes first explicit mention of the *Kulturkreislehre* in relation to language to Strehlow in early 1908. At the time a number of very basic wordlists and grammars of Aranda, Loritja and Diyari were being published and Schmidt was studying and comparing Australian languages.

Von Leonhardi viewed language as the embodiment of a people's mind and spirit. Language and culture could not be separated. Language was method and phenomenon. His language project echoed in many ways German linguistic traditions and often sounded Boasian. Text collection was paramount in Boas' ethnography; it was part of the methodological foundation. Boas understood the study of language and its literature as an aid to unravel the history of indigenous peoples and traditional worldviews. Through language, phenomena like myths and social institutions as well as material culture that seemed similar, related or identical, could be established as specific within their own cultural and linguistic context. Carl Strehlow's Lutheran tradition and von Leonhardi's nineteenth century German anthropological tradition both emphasised the significance of language for understanding other peoples' particularity and saw languages as the embodiment of peoples *Geist*; this view had been part of mainstream intellectual life in Germany for over 100 years. A number of principles of these traditions overlapped. They were based on some of the main thoughts on language emanating from Herderian and Humboldtian philosophy, which were explicitly expressed by Bastian, Virchow and their anthropological circle, and by Boas in North America.

Clearly Strehlow's ethnographic oeuvre stands in the German fin de siècle anthropological tradition that was language based and through language, which implied understanding, tried to document cultures in their own right, avoiding deduction and preconceived theories. Ultimately language was not only method for him, but final evidence that the Aranda were part of the universal plurality of one humanity. After 27 years studying the Aranda language and culture, the Lutheran pastor Carl Strehlow made this clear in his last published remark in regard to Aboriginal people on the 7 December 1921 in Adelaide's newspaper *The Register*:

> If you see in the present type of the aborigines the missing link, you require 11 more links from the present type of the aborigine to the common ancestor of man and ape, because the greatest difference between an ape and an aborigine is not the bodily structure, but the wonderfully structured language of the aborigines, and their religious beliefs.

IV. The Making of a Masterpiece

The publication of *Die Aranda- und Loritja-Stämme in Zentral-Australien* was the result of the collaboration between Carl Strehlow and his editor and friend, Moritz von Leonhardi.[1] Although his editor understated his contribution in the making of this masterpiece, his contemporaries N.W. Thomas (1909), P.W. Schmidt (1908), Émile Durkheim and Marcel Mauss[2] were aware of his involvement. Durkheim remarked that it would be 'proper to add to Strehlow's name that of von Leonhardi, who played an important role in the publication. Not only was he responsible for editing Strehlow's manuscripts, but also, by judicious questions on more than one point, he led Strehlow to specify some of his observations' (Durkheim 1995: 89, fn. 21 quoted in Kreinath 2012: 408). Von Leonhardi carefully studied Carl Strehlow's manuscript, compared it with all other literature available on the subject, compiled long lists of questions, added references, had Australian animals, insects and plants classified, inserted their Latin names into the text and, finally, went yet again through the arduous work of reading the proofs. But most importantly he never tired emphasising empiricism and displaying scepticism when Strehlow's field results seemed inconsistent. The research at Hermannsburg was driven by von Leonhardi's never-ending desire for empirical data and the precise questioning of what it really was that Strehlow encountered daily at his mission station. Armchair-researching the cultures of central Australian Aboriginal people in Germany, he had noticed gaps, contradictions and broad generalisations in the existing material. He wanted to know what the different researchers had exactly observed in different parts of the continent and why their research yielded different results. Thus, he was keen on further field investigation to verify or reject the existing assumptions on Australian indigenous cultures.

Through his editor's persistent interest in empirical observations, Carl Strehlow wrote his seven volume monograph in a five year period, an impressive achievement considering his many other duties and difficulties he faced on his lonely mission in central Australia. Although he had been side-lined in the English-speaking anthropological world even before he had written the first volume of his monograph (Marett and Penniman 1932: 95–97; Veit 1991, 2004b; John Strehlow 2004b, 2011), in Germany the research was driven forward and elsewhere read and celebrated (Preuss 1908; van Gennep 1908; Schmidt 1911; Mauss 1913).

---

1   Other classics of this era were also collaborations (Jones 2005: 6-25; Nobbs 2005: 26-45).
2   F.C.H. Sarg to Carl Strehlow, 20.9.1912.

Sehr geehrter Herr Strehlow!

On the 10 of September 1901, with Spencer and Gillen in mind, Baron Moritz von Leonhardi was sitting at his desk in his country retreat, writing to Pastor Carl Strehlow at the central Australian Hermannsburg Mission, who was at this stage unknown to him. Von Leonhardi had by chance read, during his extensive research into the religion of the Australian peoples, a letter written by the missionary in the church newspaper *Kirchlichen Mitteilungen* of the 15 May of the same year. He had been struck by a sentence in it, namely 'Their God is not at all concerned about human beings, just as they are not with him.' This remark induced him to write:

Gross-Karben, d. 10/IX 1901.

Grossherzogthum Hessen.

Esteemed Sir!

In Mission Inspector Deinzer's *Kirchlichen Mitteilungen* of the 15 May of this year I saw a letter by you,[3] which described the situation on your mission and also contained a few remarks relating to the natives of your station. I read in it: "Their God is not at all concerned about human beings, just as they are not with him." This indicates that some kind of concept of a divine being exists among the natives. As I have studied for many years the religion of primitive people, I have of course endeavoured to collect everything I could find on the religious-ethical views of the Australian peoples. The information on the natives in the vicinity of your mission – they are called Arunta by researchers; is this name correct? –, is scanty, although, as you may be aware, in the past years two large and very important publications on the natives of your area and its surroundings have been published. I am referring to Horn's Scientific Expedition to Central Australia Vol. IV Anthropology and Gillen and Spencer's[4] *Native Tribes of Central Australia.*[5] Both publications are densely packed with information, in particular on initiation ceremonies and mythology of the tribes studied; however, the material also raises a number of questions. For example, little or nothing can be gathered on the existence of one or more divine beings or spirits who created the world and human beings, and taught them the sacred ceremonies (circumcision, male youth's and men's initiation etc.) from these publications. However, I suspect, in analogy to other tribes of

---

3   Carl Strehlow's letter had been written on the 8 January 1901.
4   Von Leonhardi's order.
5   *Report on the work of the Horn Scientific Expedition to Central Australia* Vol. IV (1896); Spencer and Gillen's *The Native Tribes of Central Australia* (1899).

the continent, that such a concept cannot be completely absent. Your remark referred to above as well as a statement ("Children are a gift of Altjira (God)"[6]) in an older scientific journal by one of your predecessors, missionary Kempe,[7] confirm my inference and leads me to ask you for a great favour, if you had the energy and time. I would be very thankful if you could answer a few questions.[8]

Von Leonhardi was addressing an empirical problem. It seemed to him that there were gaps in the existing literature caused by lack of attention to particularities. His queries related mainly to the concepts of Ulthana,[9] Twanyirika,[10] and 'two beings who were Ungambikula (out of nothing, self existing)' and had come 'to Earth in the oldest Alcheringa time' (Spencer and Gillen 1899: 388), but he also remarked that 'It goes without saying that I would be very thankful for any other information about the natives, their lives and intellectual concepts'.[11] The letter travelled overland from Gross Karben to Frankfurt and then north to one of the ports in Germany (Bremerhaven or Hamburg) to embark on a ship to one of the remotest areas of the known world. About six weeks later the letter arrived in Port Adelaide, where it was loaded on a train going north to Marree (Herrgott Springs) and Oodnadatta in remote Australia. At Oodnadatta the railway ended. Cargo and mail going any further into the inhospitable interior of this still largely unknown part of the Australian continent was transferred with much needed food supplies and other essentials onto camel caravans led by Muslim camel drivers or a mail buggy, which would trek for weeks northwards through central Australian desert regions.

On the 20 December 1901, Carl Strehlow answered the German aristocrat's queries about his little Aranda congregation. Only extracts of Strehlow's letter, copied by others, have survived in a number of archives in Australia and England.[12] Strehlow answered and explained the concepts of 'Twanyirika' and 'Ulthana', and wrote that 'according to the view of the Aranda there is a being of the highest order called Altjira or Altjira mara' and that they did not know anything about 'reincarnation'. He also mentioned some other indigenous beliefs at Hermannsburg which deviated from Spencer and Gillen's recordings. However, what really made Strehlow's work controversial was that he discussed the semantics of ngambakala ('surely the Ungambikula of Gillen-Spencer') and

---

6   Kempe (1883: 53).
7   Kempe was one of the missionaries who established Hermannsburg in 1877. He wrote in 1883 *Zur Sittenkunde der Centralaustralischen Schwarzen* and in 1891 *A grammar and vocabulary of the language spoken by the Aborigines of the MacDonnell Ranges*.
8   Von Leonhardi to Carl Strehlow, 10.9.1901.
9   Spirit being documented by Gillen (1896: 183).
10   Spirit being documented by Spencer and Gillen (1899: 264, 654).
11   Von Leonhardi to Carl Strehlow, 10.9.1901.
12   Rowan Private Collection (Melbourne), W.B. Spencer Papers (Melbourne Museum) and E.B. Tylor Papers (Pitt Rivers Museum).

altjira, which did not 'agree' with Spencer and Gillen's concept of Alcheringa, and explained that they had not understood some key concepts due to the lack of language skills.[13] They maintained, for instance, that Alcheringa meant 'Dream-times' (Spencer 1896: 111).[14] According to Strehlow, this was a linguistic misinterpretation of the term (Strehlow 1907: 2).[15]

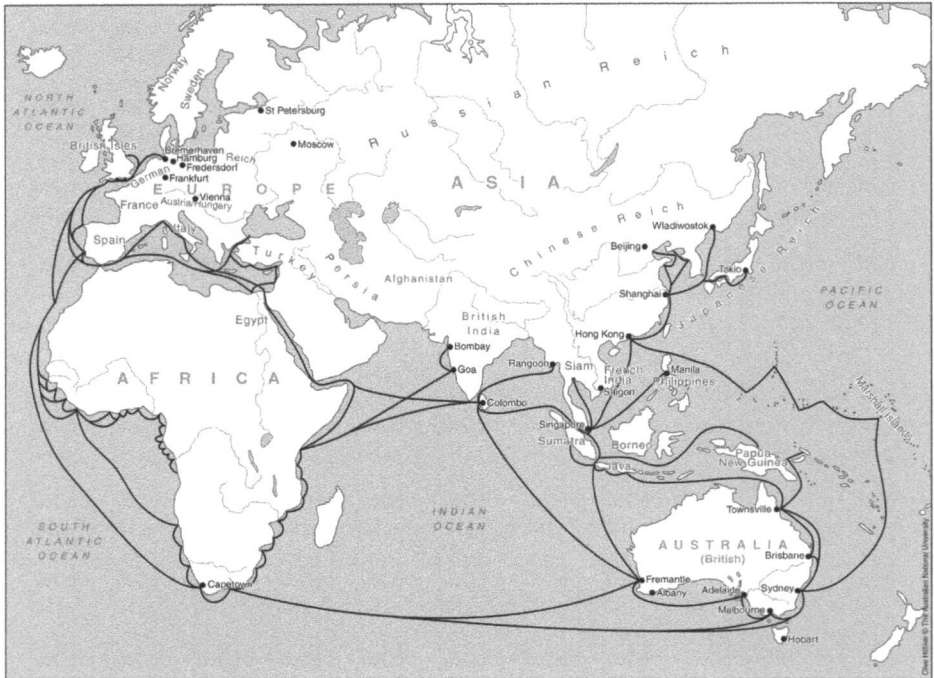

14. Map of postal routes between Germany and Australia.

Source: Clivie Hilliker, The Australian National University; adapted from *Kleiner Deutscher Kolonialatlas* 1904.

Carl Strehlow's reply reached von Leonhardi sometime in early 1902; and what he read was pleasing. Strehlow's comments were sent to none other than Andrew Lang in England, who had set himself against the whole tendency of Tylorian anthropology (Stocking 1995: 60; Hiatt 1996: 103). Lang received Strehlow's findings on a superior divine being amongst the Aranda in late 1903. They were a welcome contribution in the controversy surrounding high gods, which Lang seemed to be losing.

The high god debate that began in the mid 1800s (Swain 1985: 34) was about the emerging view that evidence of primeval or early forms of monotheism

---

13   Excerpts of Carl Strehlow letter to von Leonhardi, 20.12.1901 (Rowan collection). Spencer the recipient.
14   See Chapter V.
15   Strehlow to von Leonhardi, 2.6.1906 (SH-SP-2-1).

existed in indigenous beliefs. The reports from Australia even threatened to place 'the blackfellow on a par with his white supplanters' (Hiatt 1996: 100). Although, according to E.B. Tylor, religion was universal to humans, he defined religion simply as 'the beliefs in spiritual beings' (Morris 1987: 100).[16] Tylor and his circle could not accept a high being or monotheism among Aborigines because it would place them on a higher level in their evolutionistic schema that moved from animism to monotheism and would have thrown their theory into disarray. Frazer, whose evolutionistic chain of events did not even allow religion among Aboriginal people, also opposed people such as Lang, who postulated the existence of a supreme being amongst indigenous people, which in Frazerian terms proved that Aborigines had religion. For people like Lang and Frazer having religion was tantamount to having a high god (Swain 1985: 94, 96). There was a shared assumption embedded in their thought, namely that having a high god had a uniform significance throughout all religions – which it clearly did and does not. This made Strehlow's observations particularly acute.

Thus, Lang showed Strehlow's notes to Tylor and wondered if Spencer knew the indigenous language, as *Native Tribes of Central Australia* did not have 'philology in it'.[17] In letters to Tylor he remarked that 'I had my suspicions of Twanyirika', although Spencer and Gillen 'are excellent',[18] and that:

> I hold it also not only for possible, but in the highest degree for probable, that the myths and legends of the arunta should by different persons differently reported. The accounts according to Spencer and Gillen make quite too much the impression of a universal widespread determined metaphysical system … I hope certainly further communications on the Arunta through the German missionary to receive [Lang's wording].[19]

Lang could not resist, and sent 'the original German to Prof Spencer in Melbourne'.[20] Lang's main motivation in spreading word on Strehlow's highest being was to back his thesis that high gods and thus an early form of religion existed among indigenous Australians that many of his colleagues rejected.

Therefore, there was a difference between Lang and von Leonhardi's understanding of the underlying issues. Lang's assumption of a universal widespread system (i.e. proving the origin of religion) stood in contrast with German empiricism and particularism as well as diffusionism that were an alternative to evolutionistic theory (Swain 1985: 105). Von Leonhardi had simply been making the point that field observations could contradict theories, and

---

16 See also Lawrence (1987: 18–34) on Tylor and Frazer.
17 A. Lang to E.B. Tylor, 19.10.1903 in E.B. Tylor Papers, Box 6 (2), Pitt River Museum.
18 A. Lang to E.B. Tylor, 28.10.1903 in E.B. Tylor Papers, Box 6 (2), Pitt River Museum.
19 A. Lang to E.B. Tylor, 2.11.1903 in E.B. Tylor Papers, Box 6 (2), Pitt River Museum.
20 A. Lang to E.B. Tylor, 19.10.1903 in E.B. Tylor Papers, Box 6 (2), Pitt River Museum.

deviate or complement other field observations. However, he was well aware of the 'controversy' and is likely to have tried to show that even in English theorising the Aranda had 'religion' and hence might undermine evolutionism.

'Temper and bias have set in like a flood'

The impact of Carl Strehlow's first letter dated 20 December 1901 on the British anthropological establishment and Baldwin Spencer has been discussed a number of times in contributions by Mulvaney and Calaby (1985), Veit (1991, 2004b) and John Strehlow (2004, 2011). The exact events and dates of the ensuing 'controversy' are still not quite clear. What really transpired between Australia and England after Strehlow's letter had been circulated amongst important members of the anthropological scene is hard to say. However, a number of letters give a flavour of what might have transpired. Without doubt, Spencer felt troubled by Strehlow's research and set out to side-line him.

After Carl Strehlow's information on a supreme being or a 'high god' amongst the Aranda had been handed around to key players of the British anthropological establishment, Spencer, who was just about to publish another volume on the Aborigines of central Australia, wrote angry and to some degree defamatory letters to Lang and Frazer about Strehlow's observations.

Spencer wrote to Frazer, who was proof reading his and Gillen's forthcoming book *The Northern Tribes of Central Australia,* on the 9 December 1903, that he had to write a long letter to Lang in reply to 'a short paper by a Lutheran missionary named Strehlow' that had 'more utter misleading nonsense packed into a small space that I recollect having come across before' and 'remarks (hostile in tone to Gillen and myself) are appended by some one' (Marett and Penniman 1932: 96). Von Leonhardi seems to have added these remarks, and they could hardly have been called 'hostile'. For example, one stated in regard to 'Altjiramara':

> Here again one finds the influence of the missionaries or imagines it, unjustly as I believe. In mode of expression one may trace Christian influence. "He is the creator of the world & the ruler of mankind" – such an expression is taken from "the almighty creator of heaven and earth" of the Apostles' Creed. But in actual fact there is no need to attribute anything to Christian influence. As early as 1882 a case was noticed by Miss. Kempe in his report.[21]

---

21 Excerpts of C. Strehlow's first letter with von Leonhardi comments, Rowan Private Collection (Melbourne).

Spencer furiously pointed out that the early missionaries had been teaching the 'poor natives that Altjira means "God"' and that Strehlow had seized upon this doing the same and now was making the claim that his informants were telling him that Altjira meant 'God'. He told Frazer that Strehlow's linguistic explanations of the word Altjira and its compounds were naïve and that 'Strehlow is talking rubbish when he speaks of Twanyirika as the leader of the ceremonies'. He had to tell 'Lang that, after spending months watching the natives preparing for and performing their ceremonies, to meet with this rubbish from a man who not only has never seen a ceremony, but spends a good part of his time telling the few natives who frequent the station that all their ceremonies are wicked, is rather too much of a good thing' (Marett and Penniman 1932: 95–97). Lang reported Spencer's reaction to Strehlow's notes on the 13 January 1904 to Tylor:

> Dear Tylor,
>
> … Today comes a long tirade of Spencer against Strehlow. Is it proper to send it to you? If you think so, I will add, typed, my reply, which, at all events, I may send, and from it you would gather what Spencer said.
>
> It comes to this, Strehlow is a beast of a missionary, not admitted to ceremonies, and would not go if he got a ticket. But Spencer adds that he and Gillen have not worked Strehlow's district at all, so how can they know what he found there? He does not explain why Gillen in Horn Expedition (IV 182, I think)[22] has "a great being of the heavens", with an emu foot, as in Strehlow. Any being with a wife and child, (as Zeus, Apollo) is borrowed from missionaries.
>
> I understand that Howitt recants his remarks on great beings, but how the deuce was I to know that, and why, 20 years after date, does he recant what he published in initiation. He never told me, though I think I sent him my book.
>
> Spencer thinks Strehlow wants to discredit him, whereas he only answered inquiries. I sent you what he said. Temper and bias have set in like a flood, and if Howitt and Gillen disclaim their published words, how can we trust any body's reports … Of course I shall not print a line on Strehlow just now. I enclose Strehlow, which please return.[23]

Frazer raised Carl Strehlow once more with Spencer in 1908 after he had read the first volume of *Die Aranda- und Loritja-Stämme in Zentral-Australien* (Strehlow 1907): 'I wish you would tell me what you think of it and of Mr. Strehlow

---

22 *Report on the work of the Horn Scientific Expedition to Central Australia* Vol. IV (1896).
23 A. Lang to E.B. Tylor, 13.1.1904 in E.B. Tylor's Collection, Box 6 (2), Pitt River Museum. Transcription held at the SRC.

as an anthropologist' (Marett and Penniman 1932: 106). Spencer replied with indignation, 'I don't know what to do in regard to Strehlow. He is so uneducated that he can't write publishable German' (Marett and Penniman 1932: 109). He again made similar dismissive remarks on Strehlow's understanding of 'Altjira' and his biases as a missionary that disqualified him as a reliable source (Marett and Penniman 1932: 110–111).

On the 19 April 1908, Frazer responded to Spencer's assessment of Strehlow and also mentioned his 'new book on Totemism' in which he was intending 'to describe all the principal facts of totemism so far as they are known at present in geographical or ethnographical order' beginning with 'Central and North Central Australia, drawing my materials, of course, exclusively from you and Gillen; then I take up south-east Australia, using chiefly Howitt's facts. … So you see I am making the "Geographical Survey" pretty full' (Marett and Penniman 1932: 116). Then he turned to the missionary living in central Australia:

> From what you tell me about Strehlow, it seems to me that I cannot safely use his evidence; so I intend to make no use of it. I wish you would publish your reason for distrusting his evidence, such as you have stated them to me, so that I could refer to them. The shakiness of Strehlow's facts ought to be known here in Europe. (Marett and Penniman 1932: 116)

Spencer did not publish his views on Strehlow until 1927, well after the missionary's death, and incorporated linguistic explanations of some key terms that are conspicuously reminiscent of Strehlow's material. Nevertheless, Frazer ignored Carl Strehlow's research in his *Totemism and Exogamy* of 1910 on the grounds that he was a missionary and therefore, biased. The Director of the Frankfurt museum, Bernhard Hagen, remarked in von Leonhardi's obituary (Strehlow 1911: I): 'Unfortunately, an intended preface, in which Frazer's critique was going to be rejected, remained unfinished.' While von Leonhardi had managed to edit the fourth volume of Strehlow's work (1911) before he died, he did not get around to writing the preface intended to respond to Frazer's allegations that missionary Strehlow's sources and information were 'deeply tainted' (Frazer 1910: 186–187), and thus, not scientifically reliable sources. Instead, Pater Wilhelm Schmidt launched an attack on Frazer in his journal *Anthropos* (1911: 430–431). He criticised Frazer for dismissing information provided by missionaries and in particular by Carl Strehlow, who had collected ethnographic and linguistic material for 'scientific' discourse despite of his Christian mission context. Strehlow mentions, for example, the work of missionary Spieht among the Eweer in Africa.[24] Although Spieht's article relates to bible translation, Strehlow extracted the ethnographic data on how the Eweer personify the celestial elements and how this correlates with Aranda views of

---

24   Carl Strehlow to von Leonhardi, 23.10.1907 (SH-SP-14-1).

Altjira and the sky. Schmidt pointed out that Frazer had used the information of at least 46 missionaries if not more in *Totemism and Exogamy*;[25] and that there was no reason to believe missionaries any less than agnostic 'professionals' (Marchand 2003: 297). Frazer's treatment of Carl Strehlow also met with disapproval from Haddon (Veit 1991: 114) and other Cambridge scholars,[26] and from the French quarter. Marcel Mauss and Émile Durkheim (1913: 101–104) wrote in *L'Année sociologique* that Frazer's and Spencer's resistance to Strehlow's work was not justified.

What was problematic about the high gods amongst central Australians was that they did not fit into Frazer's sequencing of evolutionistic events. They were not a problem *per se*. The existence of Strehlow's 'highest being' Altjira meant that the Aranda had 'religion' in Frazer's evolutionistic framework. He rejected this, because he classified Aranda beliefs as 'magic'. It stood in opposition to Frazer's view that belief systems moved from magic to religion and then to science (Morris 1987: 104; Hiatt 1996; Frazer 1922). While he had taken Tylor's idea of uniform progress in human religious development up, he had reduced Tylor's parameters 'animism, polydaemonism, polytheism and monotheism' (Tylor 1871). Spencer and Gillen followed Frazer's lead integrating central Australian Aboriginal people at the beginning of a simple line of development. Thus, they were exemplary for the lowest stage on this linear development:

> Frazer believed that magic precedes religion in the social evolution of mankind. In his view the Aranda were proof of this because they were obviously the most primitive people in existence and their totemic ceremonies were magical fertility rites. (Peterson 1972: 15)

A final note on high gods

In this context it seems necessary to comment briefly on the 'high god' debate of the turn of the century, because its ongoing discussion in Mulvaney and Calaby (1985), Veit (1991, 2004), Hill (2002) and John Strehlow (2004b, 2011) still evokes the impression that Carl Strehlow gave prominence to a high god amongst the Aranda and Loritja and participated in this controversy, which he did not.

---

25   Frazer had not been able to abstain completely from Carl Strehlow's work, he uses it in his fourth volume of *Totemism and Exogamy* (1910: 59) in a footnote. He also relied heavily on information of missionary Christian Keysser, Carl Strehlow's brother-in-law, in his *The Belief in Immortality*. He wrote in his section on New Guinea: 'Mr. Ch. Keysser, who has laboured among them for more than eleven years and has given us an excellent description of their customs and beliefs' (Frazer 1913: 262).
26   F.C.H. Sarg to Carl Strehlow, 20.9.1912.

For the German researchers the debate was not about the existence or non-existence of a high god that would prove 'religion'. The Aranda, according to Strehlow and von Leonhardi, had religion regardless of whether or not they had a high god. It was about empirical observation. Von Leonhardi had noticed that the generalisations in Spencer and Gillen's publications did not seem uniformly applicable to all Arandic peoples. Clearly Strehlow's observations suggested that the Western Aranda at the Hermannsburg Mission had different or at least additional views and outlooks. And for that matter even Spencer and Gillen (1904: 498–500) had found a 'high god' among the Kaitish (Kaytetye), a northern Arandic group.[27]

Von Leonhardi did not believe in high gods in the same way as Pater W. Schmidt, who was trying to prove that monotheism existed among all peoples in one way or another. During his long academic life, the Austrian scholar Pater Schmidt was bent on proving the primeval revelation amongst indigenous people around the world. The theory in question was his theological diffusionism, which suggested that hunters and gatherers would 'remember' god's creations in their own belief system, i.e. the primeval revelation or Ur-monotheism (see Conte 1987). In the debate about the existence of 'high gods' amongst indigenous people Andrew Lang was seen by the Schmidt school as their British ally (Marchand 2003: 294), although the reasons why Lang wanted indigenous people to have high gods was different to the Austrian school's views. There were serious efforts under way to instrumentalise empirical data, including Strehlow's, for underpinning Schimdt's theory of 'primeval revelation' that would be almost as racist as some forms of evolutionism. However, Strehlow's data and views were not suited to fit Schmidt's theory of primeval monotheism, which emphasises the merits of Strehlow's achievements that have survived the passage of time, while Schmidt's attempts at best provoke a tired shrug (Conte 1987: 262). Thus, von Leonhardi stated to Strehlow that he was 'not of the opinion that these [high gods] represent calls from a primeval revelation'[28] but rather that high gods or supreme beings were a common feature of Australian belief systems (see also Ridley 1875: 136; Howitt 1884: 459; Parker 1905: 6). On the 28 August 1904 von Leonhardi wrote:

> Most tribes in the South East of the continent have such a belief: A big/large with supernatural powers endowed Black lives in the sky now, previously he also lived on earth. He is immortal, created people and everything else, taught customs and ceremonies (Kult) (sometimes also morals); he is good. However, no one is troubled by him, only at the initiation of young men does he play a role, women and children do not know about him etc. (Baiame of the Kamilaroi or Munganjaur of the Kurnai, for example). This concept may also exist amongst the Aranda

---

27 Kaytetye is an Arandic language spoken to the north of Alice Springs.
28 Von Leonhardi to Carl Strehlow, 28.8.1904.

and according to you, it exists untouched by white people's beliefs. Further examination would be at any rate very desirable. Possibly the old men do still know more about it. For instance, is thunder, the voice of Altjira mara? Further I would like to point out that Spencer and Gillen — I am sure you will soon get hold of it yourself — found a Kaitish myth on a supreme being, but do not comment on it (p. 498). It is exactly these kinds of myths that I suspect to exist everywhere in various modifications.[29]

In my view, von Leonhardi was only provoking the English establishment. He used the 'high gods' to make a point against unwarranted generalisations and selectiveness of material to justify evolutionistic sequencing in culture development (see also Swain 1985: 93). He remarked later on to Strehlow:

> I share your impression that Howitt is completely under the influence of Spencer and in many ways it is not a good one; in any case it is biased. That Howitt does not mention Mura in the sky, although missionary Reuther certainly told him about it, is not acceptable. He should have expressed his doubts, as he was not entitled to simply suppress the matter. The Dieri — and for that matter the Aranda too — in contrast to the natives of SE Australia, are to be classified at all costs on the lowest stage of development. Thus, certain views and beliefs are not allowed to be found! A further reason for classifying the Dieri, Urabanna etc as representatives of the lowest stage of development is the supposition that they practice group marriage of primeval times (analogy to the Piranguru relationship?). Hopefully this fairytale will soon be laid to rest; even in England, no one less than Mr N.W. Thomas is fighting against it. For most English and in particular Australian scientists group marriage of the Dieri is still a dogma.[30]

N.W. Thomas, who briefly corresponded with Carl Strehlow and participated as a proponent of the 'high god' in the debate, wrote that it was naive to get the Christian god and indigenous 'high god' mixed up, because it was evident in Strehlow's description that he had emu feet and many wives that could only qualify him as an indigenous god. He even made a cynical remark that one could see if one wanted to elements of Mohammedan beliefs in Altjira's description (Thomas 1905a). Ironically this may not have been an absurd idea. After all, Muslim cameleers had been present in remote Australia since the 1860s, servicing the mission and the pastoral settlement. They had not only interacted

---

29 Von Leonhardi to Carl Strehlow, 28.8.1904.
30 Von Leonhardi to Carl Strehlow, 10.4.1907.

with the new settlers, they had also formed relationships with the indigenous population (Kenny 2009b). The Aranda at Hermannsburg called them *Apagana* or *Matawalpala* and even had a hand sign for them (Strehlow 1915: 58).

N.W. Thomas made the first published comment in *Folklore* on Strehlow's work and description of Altjira and his many wives:

> Immortal virgins, it is true, are hardly a savage conception; but it seems hardly likely that such an idea would be derived from a Lutheran missionary; if anything they rather recall the houris of Mohammedanism than any Christian idea. (Thomas 1905a: 431)

High beings are not unusual in indigenous Australian religion. Independent reports on the 'high god' phenomenon have been present in the anthropological literature since material on Aboriginal religion has been recorded (Swain 1985). Hiatt (1996: 100–119) has shown that high being beliefs did exist in Australian indigenous religion and are not necessarily an import of Christian provenience. Many peoples have had 'high gods' positioned, though, quite differently from Judeo-Christian or Islamic schemes. They often do not figure as the major creators or as an ultimate source of a moral order. Indigenous Australian high gods were, rather, beings with more power and significance who coexisted with the rest of the ancestral beings, and assumed prominence due to variable circumstances in particular context and ceremony. Hiatt indicates that Aboriginal beliefs were far more resilient than many researchers have maintained and remarks in a footnote that 'No modern Australianist, to the best of my knowledge, denies change as a fact of history, but we do affirm the existence of a pre-contact structure of cult belief and practice strong enough to survive the immediate impact of colonization' (Hiatt 1996: 199).

Neither Carl Strehlow nor missionary Reuther, a Lutheran ethnographer at Lake Eyre and Strehlow's contemporary, attributed overwhelming importance to a 'high god' or a supreme being among Aboriginal people.[31] Only the first one and a half pages of the first volume of Strehlow's publication *Die Aranda- und Loritja-Stämme in Zentral-Australien* contains a brief account of a supreme being called Altjira or *der Unerschaffene/Ewige* (the unmade/eternal one) and the remaining hundreds of pages of the work deals with the mythological ancestral beings, the altjirangamitjina, in contemporary literature referred to as dreamings or dreaming beings. Also the second volume on Loritja myths dwells only in the opening page on the so called 'high god' Tukura.

Carl Strehlow's perception of Aranda, Loritja and Diyari high gods and other indigenous religious concepts was complex and differentiated. The high gods

---

31 Reuther maintained that among the Diyari the ancestral beings, called muramura, played a prominent role in cosmology and not Mura (the high being).

he called Altjira, Tukura and Mura were only a part of indigenous cosmology and indeed they were not the main creators of the world. Strehlow wrote that 'highest beings' and the dreaming ancestors co-existed:

> The Loritja also know of a highest being in the sky, called Tukura; which is differentiated from the Tukutita, the totem gods, like the Altjirangamitjina of the Aranda, they turned into trees and cliffs, or into Tjurunga. This view seems to be quite common amongst Australian peoples, the Dieri have a similar tradition. Among the peoples mentioned the totem gods are differentiated from the highest god. The Dieri call their highest being Mura and the totem gods or divinities, Muramura; the Aranda call the highest being Altjira, the Totem Gods Altjirangamitjina (the eternal unmade ones; Altjira: unmade, ngamitjina: the eternal) or Inkara, the immortals (the ones who never die). The Loritja call the highest being Tukura (the unmade one), the Totem Gods, Tukutita (from Tuku: unmade and tita: the eternal one).[32]

Although Carl Strehlow found that a 'high god' called Altjira, existed in the cosmology of the Aranda as well as of the Loritja, called Tukura, and Mura among the Diyari, he maintained that the ancestors, called altjirangamitjina, tukutita and muramura had overriding importance in indigenous mythology and were the ones that determined the belief system and the shape of the world. He understood this supreme being as existing beside the ancestors and not as an overarching powerful being that brought about a biblical genesis. Indeed, as his research into indigenous cosmology progressed he qualified and amended the concept of this supreme being.

Strehlow had doubts about the high god concept, because he had realised that it had no similarity with the concept of a Christian God and monotheism. He wrote to his editor that 'the blacks do not think of their God as an absolutely sacred, sinless being, not even as the creator of the universe'.[33] He nevertheless published the Altjira and Tukura accounts, because his senior informants reassured him that this being in the sky existed and they believed in him. In one of his footnotes some reluctance is discernable:

> Although I have to accept as certain that the Aranda and Loritja believe in the Highest Being in the sky and that they held this belief prior to their contact with whites, it is nevertheless beyond question that the traditions pertaining to it are far less important than the myths concerning the totem ancestors. (Strehlow 1908: 2)

---

32   Carl Strehlow to von Leonhardi, 19.9.1906 (SH-SP-3-1).
33   Carl Strehlow to von Leonhardi, 2.6.1906 (SH-SP-2-1).

It only remains to be mentioned here that at the end of his career, Spencer went full circle. When he republished his and Gillen's data in *The Arunta* (1927: 355–372), he added an extensive section on 'the supreme ancestor, overshadowing all others' known as Numbakulla, but did not feel the need to correct any earlier impression he may have given' (Hiatt 1996: 106). Numbakulla[34] was conspicuously similar to Carl Strehlow's Altjira as well as to Gillen's early account of Ulthana, a powerful being in the sky, in the Horn report *Anthropology* (Gillen 1896: 183). At the time Carl remarked in a footnote:

> In the 'Report of the Horn Expedition' IV. p. 183, Gillen states this about the Arunta [Aranda], "The sky is said to be inhabited by three persons – a gigantic man with an immense foot shaped like that of the emu, a woman, and a child who never develops beyond childhood." Obviously, what he is referring to is Tukura and his wife and child, and I suspect that Gillen obtained his story from a Loritja and not an Aranda. (Strehlow 1908: 1)

With this discussion, I hope the high god debate in connection with Carl Strehlow has been sufficiently conceptualised and for the moment can be laid to rest. Three factors seem especially pertinent: (i) the relation between pre-contact indigenous knowledge and that of newcomers, Central Asian as well as European; (ii) the role of 'high gods' in critiques of nineteenth century evolutionism; and finally, (iii) the challenge that empirical methods face in the context of competing theories, institutions and nations.[35] This said, discussion of Strehlow's masterpiece on the earth-dwelling and place-bound ancestral beings can finally move beyond the first pages of his volumes.

'Our publication of your manuscript'

Although Strehlow's first letter of 1901 made a significant impression on its recipients, the German collaboration began after Spencer and Gillen's second book *The Northern Tribes of Central Australia* had been published in mid 1904. It triggered, nearly three years later, von Leonhardi's second letter to Carl Strehlow because he had again detected inconsistencies, over-systematisations and generalisations in Spencer and Gillen's publication. He wrote to Strehlow:

> The big mistake of the books by these two researchers, seems to me, is that they systemise too much and try too hard to show universal views existing in a large area, where there may be no more than individual

---

34 See also Spencer and Gillen (1899: 388–390). This being appears later as Ungambikula (Spencer and Gillen 1927).

35 In this light it is not at all a mystery that Frazer ignored Strehlow. He could not have missed that the German's work was outstanding, himself being a classicist and knowing a number of languages including German.

myths, local views and customs etc. and not a coherent, well-ordered system of mythology and custom. Only by providing individual stories and customs is it possible to tease out by comparison general aspects, this however needs to be done in the study.[36]

The critique of the attempt to systematise and generalise social and religious frameworks of indigenous peoples lies at the heart of von Leonhardi's inquiries. As with the high gods he was not interested in proving any kind of theory but wanted to know what was really said on the ground and what were the particularities. Towards the end of his ethnographic research, Strehlow would also express this view:

> I believe that Spencer and Gillen commit the same error in this case as they have in others, in my opinion they do it often, by generalising information and observations of individual culture traits and then by imputing the deduction to the blacks, or perhaps to have it confirmed by them, something that natives are quite willing to do. (Strehlow 1910: 7–8)

Von Leonhardi was convinced that different Aboriginal groups could not possibly have such a homogenous culture as Spencer and Gillen were proposing again in their new book. Thus, at the end of his second letter he offered to have everything printed that Strehlow would write. Strehlow immediately accepted the challenge; he had been contemplating a scientific publication on central Australian indigenous culture,[37] and had begun collecting ethnographic material. He had just published the Aranda service book *Galtjindintjamea-Pepa Aranda Wolambarinjaka*, and was in need of a new intellectual challenge. He sent a copy of this service book to von Leonhardi on the 9 February 1905[38] as well as some answers to his queries.[39]

During this letter exchange a remarkable friendship gradually developed between two men from diametrically opposed backgrounds. This intellectual friendship brought von Leonhardi, a wealthy aristocrat with poor health and an insatiable curiosity, as close as one could ever get in an armchair to a vastly different place and people's *Geistesleben* (spirit and mind) compared to his own. Beside the detailed ethnography of the Western Aranda and Loritja peoples, von Leonhardi would receive over the years plants, animals, insects, photographs and objects from his collaborator in central Australia. In his private hothouse in Gross Karben he created his own central Australian landscape from seeds Strehlow had sent him. Von Leonhardi dedicated the last years of his life to Carl Strehlow's research and 'our publication of your manuscript'.[40]

---

36   Von Leonhardi to Carl Strehlow, 28.8.1904.
37   Carl Strehlow to Kaibel, 30.8.1904 (LAA).
38   Excerpts of this letter were published in *Globus* in 1907.
39   Von Leonhardi to Carl Strehlow, 28.8.1904.
40   Von Leonhardi to Carl Strehlow, 23.4.1907.

Carl Strehlow's motivation to embark on this time-consuming intellectual journey is far more difficult to comprehend. A number of reasons spring to mind for his immediate willingness to collect 'for science invaluable data'.[41] Firstly, the Neuendettelsau Seminary, where he had been prepared for his mission, encouraged their students to pursue linguistic and to a certain degree ethnographical studies to understand the peoples with whom they were involved (Veit 2004a) and to be able to spread God's Word in vernacular. Secondly it was a way to contribute knowledge to his homeland, *Heimat*. The significance of *Heimat* should not be underestimated as Strehlow's motivation to form an intellectual relationship with von Leonhardi. *Heimat* as a concept is both emotionally highly loaded and essential to a German sense of belonging.[42] Thirdly, von Leonhardi's offer was compelling as an outlet for his intellect. Not only was it an escape from the isolation of Hermannsburg and a link to the outside world, but the recognition and respect of a very well situated and educated man must have been enticing. His editor's interest did not wane once during their entire correspondence.

Carl Strehlow's empiricism

Although all observations have some implicit theory, researchers can reduce their assumptions by striving for awareness of their own limitations. So while all observation is theory laden to a degree, there are differences in the extent to which an investigator's assumptions flow into a work, depending on how constantly they examine and question their records. *Die Aranda- und Loritja-Stämme in Zentral-Australien* was understood as source material. The ethnography was Herderian and Humboldtian, particularistic and linguistic, and through von Leonhardi's attempts to explain Graebnerian *Kulturkreislehre* (diffusionism) with Boasian ethnographic source material on language and literature and refined diffusionism, historical. Therefore, von Leonhardi and Strehlow's aspiration, simply to observe and record, could never be entirely realised as such, but it did guard against premature generalisation and systematisation. Their approach was far from an explicit and systemised theory that late nineteenth century evolutionism had become. As it was, von Leonhardi would constantly remind Strehlow and himself, that the current theories were all still 'problematic', 'hypothetical' and 'speculative'.[43]

41　Von Leonhardi to Carl Strehlow, 28.8.1904.
42　See Applegate (1990) for an extensive treatment of the concept *Heimat*.
43　This is not to say that types of 'theory' involving evolution or world-wide diffusionism has generated no useful 'middle-range' theories in modern anthropology.

Von Leonhardi sent many key questions to Strehlow, which gave the research project at Hermannsburg its general bearings. Religious beliefs were the centre of his inquiries, thus questions on totemism, ceremonies, ritual paraphernalia, spirit concepts and individual myths dominated his letters and questionnaires.[44] He sent precise questions on 'Altjira', 'Twanyirika', 'guruna and ltana' and of course wanted to know exactly what the tjurunga concept was all about and requested lists of totems, and exact descriptions of flora and fauna. Queries on Altjira, a divine being, and its possible influence were of initial interest, but soon the earth-dwelling ancestors moved centre stage, as it became clear that 'the word Altjira would not only be a proper name, but would also be used for the totem ancestors'.[45] This research also raised questions indirectly related to land tenure because subjects such as mother's dreaming, the possible collective symbol of mother filiation through the wonniga and conception sites affiliation emerged.[46] The initial interest in high beings broadened and scepticism was always close. Even when he was very pleased to hear that Strehlow's research was progressing well, and fine results were obtained, he never seemed to be completely convinced or satisfied:

> The discovery of the relationship of each person to the maternal totem beside the one received through conception, is a very fine result. Thus, the Aranda can clearly inherit a totem and for that matter from the maternal side. This result places the totemism of this tribe among other known totemic relationships and takes it out of its previous isolation. Possibly, the totem acquired through conception is secondary and came into existence only in the course of the development of the tribe; or emerging from the personal totem (called Nagual in America; also shown to exist in Australia)? I will have to consider the issue further and wait for your upcoming reports before I form a final opinion. I cannot quite follow your deduction of tmara altjira from Altja. It seems to me that here too altjira equals 'divine being'. The totem is altjira because it is connected to the ancestors who are worshipped as gods. However, for the moment this is only an assumption. Linguistically I cannot make a judgement on whether altjira may be derived from altja.[47]

The Aranda concepts of soul and spirit, ltana and guruna, and what happens with these entities caused von Leonhardi lots of 'headaches'. He struggled over

---

44   Most questionnaires are missing (Strehlow inserted the answers and sent them back); they are believed to have been lost in World War II.
45   Von Leonhardi to Carl Strehlow, 7.8.1906.
46   Carl Strehlow to von Leonhardi, n.d. possibly 6.4.1907 (SH-SP-11-1, SH-SP-12-1).
47   Von Leonhardi to Carl Strehlow, 26.11.1906.

a long period with the 'ltana and guruna' concepts and the beliefs connected with them.[48] Answering yet again an inquiry about the soul, Carl Strehlow wrote:

> Personally I agree with you, that the guruna is the 'Körperseele' (body's soul?) and the ltana could be called the 'Geist'. However, I do not want to impose these interpretations of the words on the blacks, because they surely would simply agree with me. The question is what becomes of the guruna when the ltana has left the body? Does it stay forever at the grave? Not according to the natives. They think that the ltana (ghost) stays at the grave until … And then it goes north, after it has picked-up its tooth at its tmara altjira which had been knocked out in his youth. This stuff I got to know about, when I was investigating the custom of knocking out teeth. I will continue to investigate the relationship of guruna and ltana.[49]

It was enormously difficult for the researchers to grasp these concepts that were new to them. They sometimes tried to find related concepts to be able to understand and articulate these indigenous ideas adequately. Von Leonhardi pursued for years the concept of tjurunga and other issues of their research project. He repeatedly asked Strehlow to reinvestigate subjects surrounding tjurunga:

> The nature of tjurunga is still not quite clear to me. You think, it is not the seat of the second soul, (called soul box by English ethnographers), but a second body. Is it possible that a person's life is in the tjurunga? This would be similar to a commonly held belief found in German and Nordic fairy tales. A person's life is magically connected with a particular object and has to die, when it is destroyed. However, the latter does not seem to apply to the tjurunga. Or is it a misfortune for the Aranda when a person's tjurunga is stolen or destroyed? Your statements about the relationship between the tjurunga and the bullroarer meet my expectations. One idea is dependent upon the other.[50]

Strehlow matched von Leonhardi's inquisitiveness and rarely seemed to be satisfied with his initial impressions. In 1907, for example, he was still sceptical about his understanding of the underlying concepts of the tjurunga. And when he finally thought that he had understood it, he only discovered that there was more to it and his inquires led into new areas:

---

48   See von Leonhardi to Carl Strehlow, 5.9.1907; Strehlow (1908: 77); Kenny (2004a).
49   Carl Strehlow to von Leonhardi, 23.10.1907 (SH-SP-14-1). Carl Strehlow's data on ltana and guruna deviates from contemporary perceptions of these concepts (see Kenny 2004a,b).
50   Von Leonhardi to Carl Strehlow, 26.11.1906.

However, this investigation had rather the benefit, that it clarified the relationship of an individual to his totem ancestor. The totem ancestor is seen as the guardian, 'the second I',...[51]

The research seemed never ending, results had to be adjusted, reconceptualised and rearticulated. The investigations went ever deeper as their understanding broadened and the questions became more relevant and detailed. While von Leonhardi was impressed by Strehlow's initial research, he thought that observations should be continued, as Spencer and Gillen had certainly left some open questions. He seems to have pushed, in particular, questions relating to terms and concepts that were obvious to Strehlow or taken for granted by him. Strehlow may have been immersed in Aranda and Loritja life in such a way, that some issues not at all obvious to von Leonhardi or any other outsider, were completely clear to him. In such instances his editor typically sent new queries, hints and reminders to 'delve deeper' into matters:

> I assume that you will record the detailed myth of the Rukuta men, which I consider as very important. What does Rukuta and Tuanjiraka mean? It appears that the small bull-roarers are the bodies of novices. Is the bullroarer, given to a certain young man, the body of an Iticua[52] of the same totem as the young man? It would be important to establish this. ... And now to tnantantja (nurtunja Sp. and G.). It seems clear that the kauaua is the feather-plume on the tnantantja. It is, or rather, it represents the bundle of spears of a particular "totem god". Is it therefore not the representation of the "totem god" itself?

> As the taking down of this pole seems to be particularly diligently performed and all the other proceedings associated with this ceremony (the totem images on the bodies) are different to the ones already described, it may be justified to ask about the special and particular meaning of this event.

> It always seemed unlikely to me that this could be a sun cult, however, Foy stays with it and has based a whole theory on it. That's how theories come into being![53]

Very pleased to have been able to deflate yet again a theory, as the conclusion was that the ceremonial object represented objects of ancestors or ancestors, and was not a sun cult (Strehlow 1910: 23, fn. 2), von Leonhardi rounded his letter off with 'By the way what is actually the proper name of the Engwura?' As the

---

51 Carl Strehlow to von Leonhardi, possibly 6.4.1907 (SH-SP-11-1). 'the second I' is the spirit-double of a person, called by Carl Strehlow 'iningukua' and by his son, 'atua naltja'.

52 Possibly he meant 'iningukua'.

53 Von Leonhardi to Carl Strehlow, 10.4.1907.

religious concepts took shape, marriage-order and kin terminology, which was generally the focus of turn of the century research into classificatory kinship,[54] began to emerge in connection with myths, songs and ceremonies, and became increasingly an important subject of discussion. Carl Strehlow recorded, for example, that only certain kin could perform in particular ceremonies held by particular individuals (see Strehlow 1910, 1911). By late 1907, they regularly discussed the 'marriage-order', 'marriage classes', descent and how the subsection system locks into the kinship system.[55] During the research into social classification and marriage order, von Leonhardi again emphasised that 'What is of real importance is how the natives group the classes; everything else is marginal in comparison'.[56] Right to the end of their research he continued to point inconsistencies out,[57] and usually Strehlow reinvestigated and if necessary adjusted his conclusions.

With his editor's *'Fingerzeiger'*[58] (indications) Carl Strehlow's field research became anthropological, as far as that was possible at a time when in Australia all researchers who pursued anthropology were from other disciplines. In this sense they were all amateurs. As Strehlow was conducting fieldwork he was also reading all Australian anthropological literature he could get hold of which included Spencer and Gillen, Stirling, Howitt, Taplin, Roth, Kempe, Schulze, Schmidt, and Mathews.[59]

Von Leonhardi's main methodological advice was to consult the old men and record what they say. He never tired to ask, implore and repeat 'to reinvestigate with the old men',[60] 'In general old magicians would be the best informants'[61] and to emphasise to ignore theories. Even in his second last letter to Carl Strehlow on the 16 November 1909, he repeated to 'have the old men dictate the texts to you'.[62] Von Leonhardi was not interested in the opinions or interpretations of European researchers of foreign cultures. He wanted to know about the views of people of particular cultures, what they say about their customs and if they make conscious reflections on their traditions. He had a particular aversion to theories that isolated cultural elements pressing them into preconceived categories, such as Foy's sun cult projected on to the Inkura ceremony[63] due to analogies found in a North American ceremony that 'are quite striking'[64] (see above).

---

54   See Chapter VI.
55   Von Leonhardi to Carl Strehlow, 5.9.1907; Carl Strehlow to von Leonhardi (SH-SP-12-1, SH-SP-13-1, SH-SP-14-1).
56   Von Leonhardi to Carl Strehlow, 26.2.1909.
57   Von Leonhardi to Carl Strehlow, 26.2.1909.
58   Carl Strehlow to von Leonhardi, probably 8.4.1906 (SH-SP-1-1).
59   References to these works can be found in Carl Strehlow's letters, von Leonhardi's letters and footnotes in Strehlow's handwritten manuscripts.
60   Von Leonhardi to Carl Strehlow, 28.8.1904.
61   Von Leonhardi to Carl Strehlow, 9.9.1905.
62   Von Leonhardi to Carl Strehlow, 16.11.1909.
63   Inkura in Carl Strehlow's work and Engwura in Spencer and Gillen.
64   Von Leonhardi to Carl Strehlow, 7.8.1906.

Strehlow's editor guided the research project in central Australia towards a form that went beyond philology and mission ethnography; he impressed on Strehlow the importance of the production of primary source material based on solid empirical research, sometimes by citing examples of misleading or rash inferences by armchair anthropologists or even by himself. With von Leonhardi the work went towards an inductive research project, which had the purpose to document the languages and cultures of the Aranda and Loritja in their own right, attempting to avoid Christian and other theoretical biases. Without von Leonhardi's guidance Carl Strehlow may very possibly have been drawn to making unwelcome parallels with Greek mythology or other ancient worlds known to him.[65]

In the third volume on Aranda song and ceremony, the German researchers addressed explicitly the methodology of their ethnographic project and noted its limitations, especially due to the fact that the missionary did not attend ceremonies believing it would jeopardise his credibility as a Christian evangelist (Strehlow 1910). They had a commitment to transparency which they thought was not apparent in Spencer and Gillen's publications.[66] Thus, Strehlow's missionary context had to be made apparent and explained. Von Leonhardi wrote to him:

> I think we will have to make a few comments on how you conducted your research on the tjurunga songs and performances. What do you think? We will have to say that you, due to mission work, have never actually taken part or have been present at performances, i.e. that you therefore describe the performances only from what the men have told you about them, but that you wrote down the songs after their recitation, exactly as the men performed them for you. I believe it is necessary to make such a statement so it does not appear as if you withheld anything, which might be of interest for the assessment of the material provided.[67]

Baron von Leonhardi had discovered through R.H. Mathews that Spencer and Gillen had set up a depot of food in Alice Springs and invited 'the natives promising them all these lovely things if, in return, they would perform ceremonies'.[68] He asked Strehlow if he had heard about this and commented:

> It is possible, that these days this is the only way to see ceremonies — similar approaches have been taken in other countries — but in these

---

65 His youngest son's *Songs of Central Australia*, in contrast, became impregnated with references to European mythologies. This is likely to have been an influence of his father's instructions in his childhood and later reading of his father's work as well as his literary background. Maybe it was also a reflection of how he, his father and the German tradition valued other cultures, like their own.

66 Von Leonhardi to Carl Strehlow, 18.8.1909; von Leonhardi (Strehlow 1910: v-ix).

67 Von Leonhardi to Carl Strehlow, 26.2.1909.

68 Von Leonhardi to Carl Strehlow, 24.9.1908.

instances researchers have mentioned this fact quite openly and indeed have a scientific obligation to do so. Spencer and Gillen, however, give the impression that the performances were being performed as they were arriving; that is dishonest! The scientific value of such performances on demand is of course of less value; the use of data and photographs has to be far more cautious.[69]

Von Leonhardi was aware that Spencer and Gillen had created an artificial context for the performance of ceremonies in 1896 and that the photographic equipment had interfered with the usual process of performing ceremonies in Alice Springs.[70] He in contrast had asked Strehlow nearly two years earlier, before he had uncovered what he perceived as fraud, to describe the contemporary circumstances of Aboriginal life in central Australia:

> If I may express a further request for the manuscript, it would be a brief history of the mission work among the Aranda, as well as of the white settlement of the area. It would be lovely if photographs of the area (mission station) and of the natives, maybe of your main informants, could be included in this chapter.[71]

According to Middendorf (2006: 22–34), Spencer and Gillen's photographic representation of their indigenous informants was the one of the Australian Aborigines as doomed 'gothic figures' (Middendorf 2006: 26). While it is likely that Spencer was trying to create a remote and ancient time in his photography, it was rather an earlier evolutionistic stage of human development that he was attempting to evoke, or the 'alcheringa' that became Spencer and Gillen's famous 'Dreamtime'. Jones (2005: 14–17) remarks that Spencer employed an ahistorical style in the text of *Native Tribes of Central Australia* where historical incidents in Gillen's original text had been edited out; a similar process occurred with the published images in which shadows of the photographers (Gillen and Spencer) were retouched. Kreinath (2012) proposes that the use of photography created the illusion that an armchair anthropologist could participate at such ritual events. He makes a careful analysis of Durkheim's use of Spencer and Gillen's images.

Von Leonhardi was not so much bothered by the fact that the Aranda were not in 'their natural state', because he acknowledged it might have been the only way to see ceremonies,[72] but that Spencer and Gillen were trying to make their presentation seem more authentic by withholding the context. He asked Strehlow to point this fact out:

---

69 Von Leonhardi to Carl Strehlow, 24.9.1908.
70 Von Leonhardi to Carl Strehlow, 24.9.1908.
71 Von Leonhardi to Carl Strehlow, 7.8.1906.
72 Von Leonhardi to Carl Strehlow, 24.9.1908.

Somewhere you should also mention the fact that Spencer and Gillen asked the aboriginals to come together and that without artificial feeding it would just be impossible for a larger gathering of Aboriginals to stay together in Central Australia for weeks, or even months. Also the misconception of Spencer and Gillen's absolute credibility will need to be addressed publicly.[73]

Strehlow's approach differed from Spencer and Gillen's and seemed less authentic. He had never been present at ceremonies, because he believed that it would have compromised his position as a missionary (Strehlow 1910) and possibly his authority. However, while he chose not to participate actively at ceremonies, he inevitably saw and heard them. Ceremonies were performed only a stone's throw away from the mission boundary in the dry riverbed of the Finke from where the chanting must have been occasionally audible at the mission precinct. In 1896, for example, he came upon an emu ceremony.[74] Years later, he wrote that 'Aranda and Loritja today still regularly hold the cult rituals according to the instruction of their altjirangamitjina' (Strehlow 1910: 1) around Hermannsburg (Albrecht 2002: 347). Today, Western Aranda people still perform initiation ceremonies during the hot months of the year.

Strehlow's great advantage over the English researchers was his intricate knowledge of the Aranda and Loritja languages (including the secret-sacred language registers) as well as Diyari and his long residency at Hermannsburg. This enabled him to collect myths and songs in vernacular. He took the exact dictations from his Aboriginal informants and discovered that they were well aware of the meaning of their myths and songs. In contrast, Spencer and Gillen (1904: xiv) had contended that they were not understood by their performers. Strehlow remarked after he had recorded hundreds of verses that they had meaning and were understood, in particular by the old men, the 'knaribata'.[75] He wrote:

> The old Tjurunga-songs, I have already collected over 300, provide the desired clues on their religious views. I will try to make a literal translation of them in German and in footnotes I will indicate as far as I can when the meaning of words deviate from current language use. In some of the songs there are words from other dialects, which the blacks are not quite sure about. Thus, I cannot guarantee their correctness. While the meaning of most words are completely clear, it is sometimes the translation that is very difficult, as the natives think and express themselves very differently to a European.[76]

---

73 Von Leonhardi to Carl Strehlow, 26.2.1909. Von Leonhardi's comment is not accurate. Although large-scale ceremonies that lasted some months were rare, they did occur. T.G.H. Strehlow (1970: 102) remarked that while each group had to stage at some point the complete ceremonial cycle, these were rare occasions.
74 Carl Strehlow to Kaibel, 10.7.1896 (LAA).
75 Carl Strehlow to N.W. Thomas, mid to end of 1906 (SH-SP-6-1).
76 Carl Strehlow to von Leonhardi, 2.6.1906 (SH-SP-2-1).

Carl Strehlow's informants dictated and sang word for word their myths and songs in Aranda and Loritja prose and verse to him in countless sessions. They described and explained to him the choreography and meaning of the sacred ceremonies, and the material culture used on these occasions in their own languages and words. Von Leonhardi emphasised that it was a very wearing methodological process 'not only on Strehlow's part, but also on the part of the blacks' (von Leonhardi in Strehlow 1910: iii). Thus, Carl recorded the descriptions, explanations and interpretations of Aranda and Loritja people of their own cosmology. It was not an eyewitness description of a monolingual English observer who saw 'naked, howling savages' who were 'chanting songs of which they do not know the meaning' (Spencer and Gillen 1899: xiv). Carl Strehlow's method, transcribing over years in indigenous languages the reports of the actual performers of the events, stood in contrast to eyewitness reports of people who did not understand the languages of the performers and observed for only a few weeks.[77]

Róheim made in his article 'The Psycho-Analysis of Primitive Cultural Types' (1932: 19–20) a comparative assessment of Spencer and Gillen's ethnographic methodology with that of Carl Strehlow. He called Spencer a 'behaviourist' and said that Strehlow Senior had a 'lifeless study-method', because he refused to attend ceremonial activity. Strehlow Junior appears to have been on Róheim's side on this one (Strehlow 1971: xvi). (Needless to mention that Róheim maintains that his own psychoanalytic method got it just right.) It appears, however, that despite of Strehlow Senior's failings, e.g. not attending ceremonies, he nevertheless brought 'life' to 'culture' where Spencer and Gillen perhaps did not. The Aranda and Loritja myth and song collections were after all made from the direct dictations of their owners.

Problems in the field

Strehlow's ethnographic research was stretched over a long period of time. He often carefully revisited subjects he had already discussed a number of times with his informants so he would not be left with any doubts. Von Leonhardi, on his part, kept on asking new questions as well as posing old questions over and over again, to find further details and push Strehlow to delve ever deeper into the Aranda's world. The questions on the same subjects changed over time. The departure points were sometimes abandoned, as they had to adjust to the

---

77 His son, T.G.H. Strehlow, as well as other researchers critiqued his approach. T.G.H. Strehlow had decades later the advantage of hindsight, and was able to combine knowledge of language and eyewitness report in his work.

results that the field yielded. Observations raised new questions and he was constantly reminded to pay great attention to what elements were 'original' and what elements imported. In 1904 his editor had written:

> I assume that these beliefs, just like amongst other peoples, are determined by very uncertain or even contradictory ideas; often a more recent concept has covered an older one, without completely replacing the older one. This generates a great confusion of ideas which, however, does not disturb the peoples themselves in the slightest. Local variations may also play a role.[78]

Carl discovered that there were 'newer' views and mythological features woven into the fabrics of myth complexes as well as variations of myths.[79] He even observed that Christian beliefs seemed to have influenced some Aranda beliefs and concepts;[80] Christian teachings of his predecessors had after only 15 years made an impact.[81] In some instances he had to make detailed and persistent inquiries and argued with his indigenous informants trying to convince them that Christian beliefs had made their way into their cosmology:

> I read in Kempe that God created humanity by dropping a Tju.-Stone on earth during a visit which some Christians who grew up on the station confirmed. This is definitely a skewing of biblical[82] and heathen beliefs; for this reason I retreat from this view. In the meantime, after consulting heathens, who have grown up in heathenism and have been in influential positions (one of them is a famous Zauber-Doctor),[83] I had to concede that Kempe's view is wrong.[84]

Another problem Strehlow faced was that he suspected that his informants deliberately made their cosmology appear Christian to appease him and his missionary zeal. He wrote:

> Here it means to check and recheck. Towards a missionary the blacks like to show themselves in a better light and thus give their myths a Christian tinge. In this regard missionary Kempe was not careful enough; I thought initially, that I was able to follow his lead on Altjira, as some of the Christian blacks had confirmed, that Altjira had created everything, even the totems. However, on further investigation with some heathens and Christians who have not absorbed Christianity completely, I found

---

78 Von Leonhardi to Carl Strehlow, 28.8.1904.
79 Carl Strehlow to N.W. Thomas, 1906 (SH-SP-6-1).
80 Carl Strehlow to von Leonhardi, possibly 8.4.1906 (SH-SP-1-1).
81 Carl Strehlow to L. Kaibel, 30.8.1904 (Lutheran Archives, Adelaide).
82 Although the word is not quite readable, the context makes clear that it is 'biblical'.
83 This was almost certainly Loatjira.
84 Carl Strehlow to von Leonhardi, possibly 8.4.1906 (SH-SP-1-1).

a lot different. A researcher can simply not develop his own view and then ask a black: is it like this. ... The right question is: What did the old people say about this story?[85]

He was cautious about what he collected, often remarking, that he was unsure and needed more time for further investigation, or that he did not want to push an issue as he may not receive the right answer and 'they would agree with my view'.[86] For example, he wrote about his efforts to get to the bottom of the high god concept in Aranda and Loritja belief:

> In order to clarify this issue I have put some precise questions to the old men of both tribes. They emphatically assure me that they themselves believe in the existence of the Highest Being and that they teach the young men the concepts related to it as truth. They maintained this assertion even though I told them that I would rather correct an error in order to learn the truth than to write down something that was false. (Strehlow 1908: 2)

What kind of impression did it make on his informants, who appear in his genealogies with their 'totem affiliation', when he was trying to explain to them that Christian teaching had affected their cosmological beliefs? He may have compromised his mission and the conversion of the indigenous people at Hermannsburg with his intense study of their cultures. According to his own accounts, his overall success rate of Christianisation was modest.[87] He had only baptised 46 adults by 1920.[88] He seems to have spent as much time talking with senior Aranda men about their own beliefs as he was about the gospel. The recording of the myth, song and language data was extremely time consuming, as were the interlinear and free translations and annotations,[89] and required long consultations and discussions on semantics. Through his thorough studies of indigenous cultures he developed a deep appreciation of their human achievements. Many missionaries who had been sent around the globe developed a relativistic worldview (Veit 1991: 129–130), including the Protestant pastor and missionary Maurice Leenhardt (1878–1954) who became the chair after Lucien Lévy-Bruhl at the École des Hautes Études en Sciences Sociales (Clifford 1980).[90] Jesuits, for instance, sometimes refused to translate their

---

85   Carl Strehlow to von Leonhardi, 2.6.1906 (SH-SP-2-1).

86   Carl Strehlow to von Leonhardi, 23.10.1907 (SH-SP-14-1). See also SH-SP-2-1.

87   It is interesting to note that during a survey Carl Strehlow compiled for the census authorities in 1921 from the grand total of 176 Aboriginal adults at Hermannsburg, 66 were labelled as 'Lutherans', the rest clinging to their own religion. From these 29 were men and 37 women (Strehlow's Handbook of Central Australian Genealogies 1969-70: 119-150). It would be his successor Albrecht who would have a breakthrough.

88   *Kirchen und Missionszeitung*, 9.1.1920.

89   Carl Strehlow, Hermannsburg, 19.9.1906 (SH-SP-3-1).

90   Maurice Leenhardt had studied for decades myth, kin and language on New Caledonia, similar to Carl in Australia. Leenhardt became a relativist by the end of his ethnographic studies. His career ended very differently to Strehlow's; he became a professor at a secular institution.

Christian materials back into the original languages, as too many unpredictable surprises could have emerged (Foertsch 2001: 93–94). Carl Strehlow's behaviour must have appeared to the very least ambiguous to his informants.

The Aranda's pepa

So what was the motivation of the senior Aboriginal men to go to so much trouble and effort to tell Strehlow their stories in such detail and to spend countless hours teaching and explaining to him their myths, songs and ceremonies? It has been suggested that it may have been a religious exchange (Gent 2001: 463; John Strehlow 2011) and the men felt that they had to preserve this knowledge for the future because there were no young worthy men to give it to (T.G.H. Strehlow 1971; Völker 2001). Although these reasons may have been part of their motivation, none of these seem forceful enough to have facilitated this extraordinary transmission of indigenous knowledge to a single non-Aboriginal person. It is, for example, nearly impossible to imagine what Loatjira's motivation could possibly have been to tell Carl Strehlow, who, as an inkata (ceremonial chief), had taken his dreaming place Ntaria over.

While this transmission was linked to exchange there was another crucial factor that made it possible. Austin-Broos (2003b) makes an important observation which may explain why the senior men worked so hard with Carl Strehlow. She discusses 'pepa', a new Aranda word, used for everything connected to Christian belief and which assumed a related meaning to tjurunga:

> This rendering of God's law as a form of Western Arrernte [Aranda] law was known as pepe [pepa], the Arrernte word for "paper" and one that is deployed with a range of references similar to the Arrernte term tywerrenge, used for the sacred boards or stones that carry men's ritual designs. Just as the latter refers not simply to the boards or stones but all paraphernalia and practices involved in Western Arrernte rite, so pepe refers to the bible but also to the Lutheran liturgy generally – to all the books, buildings, calls to prayer and services that are part of Lutheran practice. This similar naming of different laws is indicative of the way in which the Arrernte became Christian by rendering Christianity in an Arrernte way. (Austin-Broos 2003b: 312)

It seems that Carl Strehlow's senior informants 'hoped that this form of inscription might be more enduring than their revered tywerrenge [tjurunga], which were abused by settlers and some of their own, and then de-legitimised by missionaries' (Austin Broos 2003b: 314) and were making a new type of tjurunga called pepa with him. By transferring their cosmology into this new medium, which the bible used, they may have hoped to give their own beliefs new power. Aranda people were literate in their own language by the 1890s. They wrote letters, postcards and short essays. Literacy took hold at Hermannsburg and its people had an understanding what the medium of the written word could achieve (Kral 2000).[91] They laboured with the missionaries over the translation of biblical myth and must have been at least to some degree aware of the power of codification.

A remarkable incident occurred in the 1890s that may have demonstrated the power of 'pepa' in the Lake Eyre region and is likely to have been known at Hermannsburg, because a fair amount of traffic occurred between the two Lutheran inland missions. Pastor Reuther had barged into a meeting and started to argue in Diyari with an Aboriginal man who finally asked him if he was armed. Reuther had kept one arm in his pocket and slowly withdrew his hand and produced not a firearm, but a pocket bible. With the suspense of the situation he managed to sit everyone down in front of him and read a text from the bible (Stevens 1994: 125).

While the use of the new word 'pepa' was probably at the beginning of the century metaphorical – its semantic connotations and syntactical use fluid – in the course of the twentieth century its meaning seems to have solidified, relating to Christian 'tjurunga'. Nevertheless, the agency of the Aranda in the making of this masterpiece should not be underestimated.

Towards refined diffusionism

Carl Strehlow's *Die Aranda- und Loritja-Stämme in Zentral-Australien* is practically devoid of theory. This is mainly due to von Leonhardi's constant probing and scepticism. He had never ceased to emphasise to Strehlow the need to avoid preconceived ideas, to ignore theories and to describe as faithfully as possible the old men's information. This did not stop them, however, from privately discussing theoretical approaches to their new data that they largely managed to keep out of the publication itself.

Strehlow's myth collection seemed to be a perfect case study to test diffusion and borrowing of myth elements and language, because some of his material related to the territorial and linguistic boundary area of the Aranda and Loritja peoples. His work detailed differences (i.e. language affiliation) as well as communalities in spiritual beliefs and social structure between these cultures. Von Leonhardi was very keen to establish links or their lack thereof between them, based on language and myth comparison,[92] which seemed to show evidence of small-scale diffusion.

---

91 See Kral (2000) generally on Arrernte literacy between 1879 and the present.
92 Von Leonhardi to Carl Strehlow, 12.2.1909.

Von Leonhardi's approach to diffusionism was a combination of Boasian 'refined diffusionism' and Graebner's *Kuturkreislehre*, a theory on general large-scale diffusion across continents. He was testing with this Boasian small-scale approach Greabner's desk-top theory and suggested diffusion and the incorporation of borrowed elements into local myths. His approach indicates that he is likely to have read Boas in *American Anthropologist* and other journals he subscribed to. In a footnote, for example, he made a comment on particular elements of the Loritja myth 'The rainman and the rainbow':

> Many motives ... of this very strange myth remind of the Jonas-myth, which is dispersed over the whole world. This wandering tale *(Wandermärchen)* is also known in Melanesia, Polynesia, on the islands of the Torres Straits and has been recorded in North Queensland by W.E. Roth in a particular variation. L. Frobenius (Zeitalter des Sonnengottes 1 pag. 16) claims to see this myth also in New South Wales and Tasmania, which seems to me rather doubtful. In this case, if one wants to admit a connection at all, one has to assume that this wandering myth has fused with a genuinely Central Australian rain totem myth and the view of the dangerous water-snake, which is distributed Australia-wide. (Strehlow 1908: 10)

Although his analysis was carefully formulated and tentative, von Leonhardi seemed to consider this myth to be the result of diffusion and borrowing in a Boasian vain. At the same time he may also have been playing with a Frazerian approach to myth, and hinting at a universal, human mythical theme or even independent invention. Strehlow's editor had a tendency to test all theories and methods of interpretation on the material he had available.

Language was also understood to give clues about cultural change and history. Like Pater W. Schmidt, who wrote extensively about Oceanic and Australian languages to bolster his version of diffusionism (*Kulturkreislehre*), von Leonhardi was interested in linguistics. The comparison of vocabulary, he speculated, would possibly indicate from where the central Australian Aboriginal peoples had come from:

> Thank you for completing the word-glossary. I expected a greater correlation between Loritja and Dieri. Thus, Loritja belongs to the Western Australian languages. The isolation of the Aranda vocabulary [and surely also their grammar] – or more precisely – their isolation in regard to other Australian languages and link to the northern tribes and possibly to New Guinea languages and cultures, which we assumed, shows up quite clearly.[93]

---

93   Von Leonhardi to Carl Strehlow, 12.2.1909.

To be able to make further supporting statements on this issue he needed further empirical evidence. He asked Strehlow for additional Loritja texts so they could be compared with the Aranda texts, because 'It would be of great importance to establish if the Loritja and Aranda languages are distinct in structure and vocabulary'.[94] Von Leonhardi wanted to know if there were any correlations between the language and culture of the Centre and the South Coast of Australia. He understood some of the linguistic material as possible proof or evidence that the Aranda had come from the north (New Guinea) and that the Loritja seemed to belong to an earlier cultural layer of people from the south due to their affiliation to Western Desert languages. This approach was reminiscent of an early view held by Boas in 1888:

> The analysis of dialect enables us to follow the history of words and of concepts through long periods of time and over distant areas. The introduction of new inventions and migration into distant countries are often indicated by the appearance of new words the origins of which may be ascertained. (Boas 1940: 631)

As Boas developed his understanding of cultures, he limited this possibility to small-scale diffusion, because diffusion could only be empirically observed in small areas, which were not necessarily applicable to other areas where the same phenomenon appeared but caused by other events. Although it seemed to von Leonhardi that Strehlow's material showed a certain degree of diffusion and exchange of cultural elements between two distinct groups, he remained sceptical because he believed that 'analogies deceive only too often'.[95]

Von Leonhardi further speculated that very ancient elements of culture may have been preserved on the southern coasts of Australia where apparently no boomerangs, shields, marriage classes and no real totemism existed and it 'would be the very oldest population of Australia, probably the Tasmanian one, which may have been pushed by migration waves with a slightly higher culture and differing language to the south and south east and possibly to the south west coast where they seem to have survived'. However, he concluded, 'this is all still very problematic'.[96]

Along with evolutionism, diffusionism would be abandoned and never became an unquestioned paradigm. Diffusionism had been used to critique evolutionism but was soon supplanted by functionalism (Swain 1985: 101–105). It had not been possible to define individual culture circles precisely. Particularities and language border areas made it impossible to make conclusive judgements on the cultural and linguistic make-up or denominators of a 'culture' area. In the

---

94   Von Leonhardi to Carl Strehlow, 3.4.1909.
95   Von Leonhardi to Carl Strehlow, 15.12.1907.
96   Von Leonhardi to Carl Strehlow, 12.2.1909.

border area of Kukatja-Loritja and Aranda, for instance, the Kukatja belong linguistically to the Western Desert peoples, but their traditional laws and customs in relation to their land tenure system, connects them clearly to their Arandic neighbours to their east. T.G.H. Strehlow (1965: 143; 1970: 99–100, 109–110) wrote some years later that although these groups spoke different languages, due to communalities in their religious beliefs and close kin ties, they shared 'a local group system'. He wrote that the Kukatja, often called Western Loritja by his father, were not a typical Western Desert group and that the cultural boundary occurred further to the west, where the landscape became more arid, and, thus the land tenure model fluid.

The exact description of language and transcription of original indigenous text had various uses. It was believed to give insight into peoples' worldviews and their true spirits, and possible clues to the history of migration. Indeed, the collection of indigenous literature was one of von Leonhardi's earliest requests from his Australian colleague,[97] and without doubt the linguistic publication, a comparative grammar and dictionary of Aranda and Loritja would have followed had it not been for von Leonhardi's premature death.

Von Leonhardi's health was failing by the end of 1909, when he wrote his last letters to Strehlow in central Australia. He was desperately working on the third and fourth volume of 'our publication of your manuscripts' as well as on the remaining parts on the social life of the Aranda and Loritja. Although sometimes unable to work, he still wrote to Strehlow and sent lists of questions, because Carl Strehlow was about to leave Hermannsburg with his family to visit Germany and it was not clear if he would return. Von Leonhardi not only asked for clarification of some issues in the manuscript, he also sent a long wish list of objects, tools, animals and plants. One desperate question, demand and request after the other poured out of the ailing scholar. Thus, in the last few months of 1909 Carl Strehlow was working frantically on the conclusion of his oeuvre. After five years of intensive research he finished his ethnographic inquiries on the 24 November 1909 and copied the last pages for von Leonhardi on the 16 February 1910.[98]

On the 11 December 1909 von Leonhardi sent his last Christmas and New Year's wishes. In it he thanked Carl Strehlow for the continuation of the manuscript and expressed his delight that six additional Loritja myths had been recorded. It is the last letter to Strehlow in Australia, who was due to leave Hermannsburg

---

97   Von Leonhardi to Carl Strehlow, 9.9.1905.
98   Strehlow's handwritten manuscript has 1224 pages. By December 1909 von Leonhardi had 1104 pages. It is not clear if in the course of 1910 he received the remaining 120 pages on sign language. Von Leonhardi mentions in May 1910, that he had received all material for volumes five and six on Aranda and Loritja social life and material culture (Strehlow 1910: xvii).

mid 1910 to visit his homeland. In his luggage to Germany Strehlow took many of the requested items with him including an emu egg and a kangaroo skin which were going to be his personal presents for von Leonhardi.[99]

However, just before Carl Strehlow was to visit Gross Karben his editor's health gave way. Baron Moritz von Leonhardi died from a stroke late in October 1910, only days before Carl Strehlow was to visit him, a meeting he had for years been hoping for. They never met.

---

99 From a letter by Auguste or Hugo von Leonhardi to Carl Strehlow we know that Carl gave these items to his siblings (Letter 1910 by Auguste or Hugo von Leonhardi.) Moritz did not marry or have any descendants (Peter von Leonhardi, grandson of Hugo von Leonhardi, Moritz's brother, pers. comm., 6.5.2004).

Part II

V. *Geist* through Myth: Revealing an Aboriginal Ontology

It is a given of contemporary Australian anthropology that at the heart of Aboriginal ontology lies the person-land-ancestral inter-relationship (Rumsey 2001: 19), and that this system of belief, glossed in English as 'the dreaming', encompasses all dimensions of life (Stanner 2011; Berndt 1970). These elements of Aboriginal cosmology and ontology are taken for granted. Most land claim or native title claim reports, for instance, dedicate a chapter or a substantial section to the dreaming, outlining its main features and key terms, such as altjira, tnankara (tnengkarre/tnangkarra) or tjurunga (tywerrenge), and their translations.[1] They summarise how the landscape was created and imbued with meaning by ancestral beings and how, at the same time, this landscape represents ancestral connections to the land and the mythical beings that created it, as well as furnishing central narratives, including travelling and local dreaming stories. Further sections of such reports outline how land described in these myths are held or owned by certain people or groups of people thereby conferring on those owners rights, responsibilities and duties.

Today the Western Aranda term tnankara,[2] in Luritja tjukurrpa,[3] encapsulate this key concept. It explains how the world came into being and is the source of traditional laws and customs that provide codes by which people abide. Western Aranda people translate this term often with the word 'dreaming' which is a polysemic expression. Dreaming can mean mythological ancestors, the travels and actions of the ancestral beings and their deeds, or their marks and physical representation in the landscape (trees, rocks, etc.). It can be used to connote spiritual power, religious laws and objects, ritual, design and songs and ceremonies although there are other indigenous terms that describe these concepts more accurately. 'The dreaming' can also refer to a past era in which the supernatural ancestral beings created the physical and spiritual world of people living today.

Yet what we take for granted in rehearsing this Aboriginal ontology is the product of a long process. It led to an understanding of the dreaming only after decades of ethnographic writing. Carl Strehlow stood at the beginning of this process and he came surprisingly close to understanding its unusual particularity. His approach to Aboriginal mythology still contributes to our empirical knowledge of the Aranda and Loritja's engagement with the land and

---

1 These are Western Aranda terms.
2 In other Arandic languages and dialects altyerre is used for this concept.
3 Tjukurrpa is also used in Pintupi and Pitjantjatjara and Jukurrpa in Warlpiri.

its natural species. In this chapter I propose to show how Carl Strehlow's study of myth, although characterised by European assumptions and some distance from approaches of professional anthropology in the mid-twentieth century, realised a Boasian ideal: to pursue the *Geist* or logic of a people's culture through attention to their myth. To understand what Carl Strehlow achieved through his empirical approach, I will draw on insights from Lévi-Strauss regarding 'savage' thought and 'primitive classification'. It was his recording of the intimate relation between nature and social-cultural life among Aranda and Loritja people that would lay the ground for T.G.H. Strehlow's work. Although Carl Strehlow's corpus of myth lacked a modern sense of symbolism, or comparison beyond its region, it allowed his son to conceptualise the person-land relationship which led to a contemporary view of an Aboriginal ontology.

My point is different from the one made by Hiatt who calls Stanner's approach to myth 'ontological' (Hiatt 1975: 10–13). He described Stanner's approach in terms of isolating, through the study of myth and rite, a certain structured (and moral) order that Stanner describes as 'good-with-suffering' or 'order-with tragedy'. It is grounded in the social world of kinship, sexuality and rite. Instead, I have chosen the human specifying view and experience of environment (person-land and -species relations) that were constituted through Australian hunter-gatherer life. The focus here relates more closely to Heidegger's observations on nature: that far from being a given, the 'Things of Nature' are always constituted through a particular practice of life and in turn confer on that life particular forms of experience, a particular 'World' (see Heidegger 2002: 288–289). For this reason, Lévi-Strauss's *The Savage Mind* rather than his structural analyses of myth as such is useful here (cf. Hiatt 1975: 12–13). These ideas are more at home with contemporary phenomenology in Australian anthropology than with the work to which Hiatt refers. This contemporary writing was foreshadowed by Strehlow (1947, 1970) and Munn (1970). It is of some interest that, in his 1975 discussion of myth and ontology, Hiatt did not judge either T.G.H. Strehlow's magnum opus, *Songs of Central Australia* (1971) or his essay on the 'totemic landscape' (1970) worthy of direct discussion. The former is cited only for its view on Róheim, the latter, not at all.

This chapter's main focus is the substantial record of a cultural logic that Carl Strehlow produced in his studies of central Australian myth and song. The value of his work lies here rather than in his framework which I contextualise briefly at the outset. I then show how a particular sense of Aboriginal ontology grew as Carl recorded in extraordinary detail an indigenous engagement with environment, with species and the land itself. T.G.H. Strehlow in turn connected these data with issues of identity, authority, sentiment and ownership, issues that were further explored by Róheim, Munn, Peterson, Myers and Morton to produce a contemporary account of indigenous ontology.

Frameworks for studying myth: Modernist approaches and Carl Strehlow's

Four methods which may be designated as functional, structural, social symbolic and psychoanalytic help position Carl Strehlow's early twentieth century study of myth among Aranda and Loritja people. To a greater or lesser extent, these approaches allow comparison between the myth-complexes of different cultures, and also some degree of specification. Comments from Hiatt's discussion of approaches to Australian myth will link these four general categories to the world of Australian ethnography.

Malinowski was the most explicit about a 'functional' approach to the analysis of myths that counted them as charters for ritual and social life. Speaking of the rites and myths that informed the Kula, he remarked that 'myth possesses the normative power' to fix custom, to sanction modes of behaviour and to give 'dignity and importance to an institution'. He wrote:

> The Kula receives from these ancient stories its stamp of extreme importance and value. The rules of commercial honour, of generosity and punctiliousness in all its operations, acquire through this their binding force. This is what we could call the normative influence of myth on custom. (Malinowski 1979: 237)

Malinowski comments further that a role of myth is to present in idealised form, the practices and realised aims of the living. Its message is that 'the best of all possible worlds' is attainable. These ideas are made more real by the fact that myths and the ancestral heroes that they describe are owned by particular 'members of a sub-clan, or a local unit', who 'can claim a mythical hero as their direct ancestor, and members of a clan can boast of him as of a clansman'. He observed:

> Indeed, myths, like songs and fairy stories, are "owned" by certain sub-clans. This does not mean that other people would abstain from telling them, but members of the sub-clan are supposed to possess the most intimate knowledge of the mythical events, and to be an authority in interpreting them. (Malinowski 1979: 238)

Likewise Ronald and Catherine Berndt have maintained that Australian myth acts as a charter for moral behaviour. Their proposal is that frequently wrong behaviour is punished in myth or singled out for moral comment by narrators or an audience in the process of performance (cited in Hiatt 1975: 6). The repertoire of Aranda myth recorded by both Strehlows, renders this proposal somewhat implausible. Murders of fathers by their sons and vice versa occur without the orderly moral accounting that the Berndts imply. As Hiatt observes, the quite high incidence of 'bad examples' in Australian myth suggests that it acted 'to undermine morality as much as to safeguard it' (Hiatt 1975: 7).

This approach to myth was revolutionised by structuralism. Lévi-Strauss shifted the focus of the analysis of myth from the domain of explicit rule to the implicit and rational unconscious. He argued that the myths of a region, and indeed around the world, should be seen as (logical) transformations of each other. Far from relating mainly to the contingent present or to an imagined past, myth or rather its 'specific pattern' is timeless; 'it explains the present and the past as well as the future' (Lévi-Strauss 1963: 209).

Among the human minds ('primitive' as much as the 'modern') around the globe, Lévi-Strauss sought to demonstrate 'the invariant human mind coping with variant environments and trying to reduce them to manageable systems' (Maranda 1972: 12). Through forms of transformation and inversion, the cognitive oppositions of the mind work to define the problems of existence and especially those that devolve on the distinction between nature and culture, including the getting of fire, the problem of incest and humankind's distance from the sky. Lévi-Strauss's view of myth was closely related to his view of totemism and received heavy criticism from Australianists (see Hiatt 1969; Peterson 1972). Even Maddock, who saw some virtue in structuralism, was tempered in his use of Lévi-Strauss's ideas when it came to myth (Maddock 1982: 137–138). Nevertheless, the impact of Lévi-Strauss's abstract and cognitive approach was to stimulate other forms of symbolic analysis, grounded in social life, the social treated as text, or in intra-familial relations interpreted through psychoanalysis (see for instance Turner 1968: 13–24).

The social symbolic in Australia soon became a particular genre of phenomenology – the type of account of subject-object transformations that in Munn's work spoke equally about belief, semantics, environment and experience. Influenced by the Africanist, Victor Turner, Munn sought to address a symbolic experiential world in which ancestors and their descendants were embedded in the landscape. She wrote:

> The purpose of this paper is to push our attempts to understand transformation beyond the artificial boundaries of "mythology" into the domain of socialization or, more generally, the problem of the relationship between the individual and the collectivity as mediated by the object world. (Munn 1970: 141)

She took as her focus the travels of people and mythic heroes across the land, and transformations that were not cognitive and abstract but, rather, embodied – as subjects went into the land, imprinted the land, or else drew objects from their bodies to be transformed as they lodged in the landscape. These intimate and transforming subject-object relations were foreshadowed by T.G.H. Strehlow (1947) and in 'Geography and the Totemic Landscape in Central Australia' he wrote:

> In a land where the supernatural beings revered and honoured by their human reincarnations were living, not in the sky, but at clearly marked sites in the mountains, the springs, the sandhills and the plains, religious acts had an immediate personal intimacy … The human reincarnations turned into living symbols during the impersonations of the supernatural beings at the sacred sites. The visible totemic landscape was considered to be an integral part of reality of eternity. … each major sacred site was the geographic fountain of authority for the territory that surrounded it. (Strehlow 1970: 133–134)

Like Munn, T.G.H. Strehlow emphasised that the makers of this myth-rite complex were people who travelled across the land. Contemporaneous with Strehlow junior, and just prior to Munn, Géza Róheim established a psychoanalytic rendering of these travels (1925, 1945). Guided by Freud's *Totem and Taboo*, Róheim, as Hiatt observes, formulated at least three different positions, concerned at the outset with an historically or personally encountered 'primal scene', the father in coitus with the mother, and later with the 'separation anxiety' for which travel and return to the land become the master symbol. Hiatt summarises Róheim's intent:

> The central theme of *The Eternal Ones of the Dream* is that Australian religion acts both to widen the gap created naturally by parturition and to compensate the offspring for the loss of his mother. Within this general scheme, myths play three important functions. First, by celebrating phallic heroes and libidinising the countryside that they created and wandered over, myths counteract the deprivation felt by maturing youths … Second, myths help to effect an eventual transfer of libido from the mother to the father (or, in social terms, the removal of the boy from the domestic group into the all-male cult group) by offering a heroic and supernaturally conceived dual unity of Father and Son in place of the natural dual unity of mother and son. Finally, myths keep alive the dream of an eternal union with the mother. (Hiatt 1975: 9)

Both Hiatt (1975) and Morton, in his discussion for instance of the symbolic significance of the native cat hero (western quoll), 'a provocative image of prolific reproduction through loss' (Morton 1985: 224), provide accounts of the manner in which indigenous myth and rite re-genders parturition and creates a solidarity among men. In his treatment of mainly Aranda and Loritja myth, Morton (1985) integrates these symbolic insights with an analysis of opposition, fragmentation and reconstitution between earth and sky marrying Lacan to Lévi-Strauss. Later, as I show below, he uses this approach not only to libidinise Munn's indigenous landscape, but also to place within it active male agents driven by desire.

In this ontology, Morton would synthesise Freud, Lévi-Strauss and the Dukheimian tradition foreshadowed by Hiatt (1975) in his discussion of Stanner and Róheim. These Australianists sought to integrate analyses in ways advocated by others. One was Robin Fox who argued that the sociological and psychological in the study of myth and rite can be used to complement each other without resort to reductionism (Fox 1967b). Similarly, Turner described Ndembu rite and myth as stretched between two poles, the one referencing social norms, the other, 'organic and physiological phenomena' (Turner 1968: 18). Turner remarked, 'it would seem that the needs of the individual biopsychical organism and the needs of society, in many respects opposed, come to terms with one another in the master-symbols of Ndembu society' (Turner 1968: 19).

These various insights on myth drawn from different types of approach, not always mutually exclusive, were one of modern twentieth century anthropology's significant achievements. What made these approaches different from those that had preceded them is that they were based on direct observation of the manner in which peoples used myth as genres of knowledge and ritual performance. The 'present' of myth, as Lévi-Strauss described it, was directly apprehended. However, most myth, including Aboriginal Australian myth refers to a distant past which led many nineteenth century interpreters to render it either within the domain of history as legend, or in that of imagination as fable or fairy-tale. As Hiatt relates, even Ronald and Catherine Berndt in their early formulations classified Aboriginal myth in terms of types of history either factual or imagined. Based on their 1958 account, Hiatt constructed the following diagram.

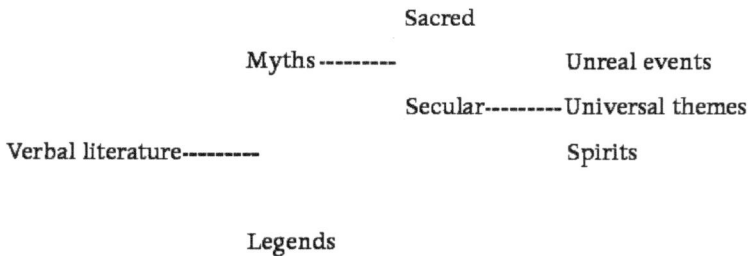

<pre>
                              Sacred

              Myths---------   Unreal events

                              Secular---------Universal themes

Verbal literature---------   Spirits

              Legends
</pre>

15. R. and C. Berndt's early myth classification.

Source: Hiatt (1975: 2).

Legends and myths that were sacred or secular involved a classification that was not too distant from Carl Strehlow's own categories, myths (*Mythen*), legends (*Sagen*) and fairy-tales (*Märchen*). The important feature of Strehlow's work is the juxtaposition of a European perspective on types of oral literature that clearly pre-dates modern anthropology, and a fieldwork-like empirical record of people's accounts of ancestral life and its natural environment. Carl Strehlow was transitional not simply for the lack of modern theory, but also for the way in which his empiricism made his approach feasible.

Carl Strehlow's framework in context

Strehlow's framework for the study of myth, evident in the structure of his published myth collections, derived from German intellectual life. It was a common form of classification in nineteenth century German anthropology and ethnography, invoking the German Romantic Movement and its orientation towards folklore and philology. Originally a ethnologist and folklorist (Morton 1988: viii), Róheim too was grounded in similar European traditions and adopted similar Grimmian terms to classify Aboriginal stories – see for instance *Children of the Desert II* (Róheim 1988).

Well-known representatives of this genre, the Grimm brothers, coined the terms *Mythen, Sagen und Märchen* (myths, legends and fairy-tales).[4] They established myth as a form of story told in traditional oral societies and distinguished by its reference to matters of 'collective, usually sacred, importance' (Von Hendy 2002: xiii). The Grimm brothers developed their triple distinction over a generation. A brief sketch of its generic criteria appears in Jacob Grimm's preface to the 1844 edition of *Deutsche Mythologie*:

> Looser, less fettered than legend, the Fairy-tale lacks that local habitation, which hampers legend, but makes it more home-like. The Fairy-tale flies, the legend walks; the one can draw freely out of the fullness of poetry, the other has almost the authority of history. … The ancient mythus, however, combines to some extent the qualities of fairy-tale and legend; untrammelled in its flight, it can yet settle down to a local home. (Grimm 1883, vol. 3: xv in Von Hendy 2002: 63)

According to the Grimm dictionary, *Mythen* (myths) are narratives of sacred events that are held to be true by their tellers, and may have features of both *Sagen* and *Märchen*. The term is usually applied to the myths of ancient Greece

---

4   The German terms do not correlate exactly with their English translations. The English term legend, for instance, does not correspond precisely with the German *Sage* or *Legende*. Thus, *Sagen* can be translated as myths or legends.

or Rome. *Sagen* are a genre of stories that are locally rooted in true events; typically used for Nordic myths. *Märchen* (fairy-tales) are narratives that are not bound to a specific landscape, place or true events. Their content can draw from fiction and imagination. The Grimms saw it also as a 'sunken myth' (Schweikle and Schweikle 1990: 292).[5]

Strehlow was aware that the brothers Grimm's three-fold classification *Mythen, Sagen und Märchen* did not describe Aranda and Loritja cosmology adequately. In his handwritten manuscript titled *Sagen* he used 'traditions' to label the different types of stories he had collected. The two main categories of Aranda myths were 'The oldest traditions of the Aranda' and 'The specific traditions of the Aranda'. The second category was split into four sub-categories: 'Traditions about celestial bodies and natural phenomena', 'Traditions about the most ancient time', 'Traditions about totem-gods, who travelled in animal shape' and 'Traditions about totem-gods who travelled usually in human shape'. He also used the word 'traditions' to describe Loritja myths, trying new categories and headings like 'The highest being (Tukura)', 'The Tukutita, the first people' and so forth.

On the title page of *Die Aranda- und Loritja-Stämme in Zentral-Australien*, however, the classification *Mythen, Sagen und Märchen* appeared. It is not clear if this was Strehlow's or von Leonhardi's decision. Possibly it was an editorial decision to make the content obvious to potential buyers. Within the publication the classification was not consistently followed; it is not explicit which narratives are to be understood as *Mythen* or *Sagen*, and only a small number of stories are clearly labelled, namely those called *Märchen*. Carl Strehlow made a comment on the difference between fairy-tales and myths:

> The difference between these Märchen and the Sagen is that the latter may only be told to people who have been accepted by the men as members of their society, and who accept the veracity of these stories. The Märchen, however, may be told to women and children. They serve to divert from the secrets of the men (see the Märchen of Tuanjiraka) or to instil into the women and children a fear of the pursuits of the evil beings (bankalanga). Other Märchen, like the one concerning the arinjamboninja, are simply told for entertainment. (Strehlow 1907: 101)

The last two narratives in Carl Strehlow's Loritja myth collection are also labelled as fairy-tales. It is hard to see why he called these narratives fairy-tales, other than to differentiate them from restricted stories.[6] The distinction foreshadows the Berndts' effort at distinguishing sacred and secular myth (Hiatt 1975: 1–2).

---

5 This Grimmian model is still an accepted taxonomy in folklore studies and often taken for granted.
6 Today unrestricted stories are sometimes referred to as 'children's stories'. In Strehlow's view, this might have made them 'fairy stories' as well.

Yet both categories draw their content from the happenings in a mythological past, which blurs the boundaries between the sacred and the mundane – a typical feature in traditional Aboriginal Australia (Berndt 1970: 216).

The classification of indigenous narratives was an issue for von Leonhardi. In a response to a critical remark on Strehlow's categories made by W. Foy, the director of the museum in Cologne, in the *Kölnische Zeitung* in 1908,[7] he discussed in a letter to Carl the terminology and classification of indigenous narratives and proposed that in volume two a justification was required. He remarked in a preface:

> The critic in the Cologne newspaper further regrets the term "Märchen" used for some of the stories told. He is of the opinion that "they represent serious concepts of belief, also for men." I do not wish to debate the word "Märchen". It does not stem from me, but from the author. I completely agree with the meaning it conveys. There is indeed a great difference between the sacred Sagen, known only to the men, and these "Märchen". The stories that are found on p.101–104 of the first instalment count on the women and children's fear of ghosts; though it must be admitted that the men themselves believe in the bankalanga and their evil deeds. In this way they are not Märchen in the true sense of the word. (Strehlow 1908: Preface)

Although von Leonhardi did not like Carl Strehlow's narrative classification, as well as the terminology used to describe the mythical ancestors, namely 'gods' and 'totem gods', he did not change them when he edited the manuscripts. He maintained that the meaning was clear. He seemed to accept that to a degree, classification and terminology were arbitrary affairs, and that a precise 'fit' for a narrative corpus could not be found. In the same period, in 1906, Arnold van Gennep commented that European classification of mythological narrative was not adequate for indigenous mythology and admitted that he used 'mythes' and 'légendes' interchangeably (Hiatt 1975: 185) and 'that each of the assumed classes overlaps the others' (van Gennep [1906] 1975: 193). In his *Songs of Central Australia* (1971), T.G.H. Strehlow resolved the classification issue by defining how he used 'song' and 'poem' in the central Australian context. He made it explicit that they were place bound and pertained to cosmology.

Today the narratives that Strehlow called *Mythen*, *Sagen* and *Märchen* are generally labelled in English as 'myths', some restricted to gender or age.[8]

---

7   *Kölnische Zeitung*, 26.4.1908.

8   Aboriginal people in Central Australia often label today their stories in Aboriginal English: Olden time stories, bush tucker stories, dreaming stories ('proper', 'true' story). Within the category of dreaming stories, Western Aranda people distinguish 'inside' and 'open' stories. The general public, including children, may hear outside or open stories, which are often public versions of restricted dreaming stories.

Many of Strehlow's myths were male versions of particular stories. All of his main informants were men and in Aboriginal society this type of knowledge is gender specific. He does not seem to have made a remark on the existence or non-existence of women's-only myth, to which he is unlikely to have had direct access.[9] Nevertheless, there is some suggestion of women's sacra in his collection. These narratives may be a public version of women's myth in the event told by men (Malbanka 2004: 14) or are a male version of a restricted women's dreaming. An example is the Loritja myth of the Pleiades:

> The Pleiades are many girls (okarála) who once resided in the west at Okaralji [place of girls], a place to the north of Gosse's Range, where they lived on the fruit of a climbing plant (ngokuta = (A) lankua). Some time later they ascended to the sky and, after many journeys, returned to Okaralji, where they once more gathered ngokuta-fruit and performed the women's dance (untiñi = (A) ntaperama). During this time the Pleiades are not visible in the sky. (Strehlow 1908: 9)

Just as he used the categories *Mythen*, *Sagen* and *Märchen*, to organise his data, which denoted in a German intellectual context particular genres, Carl Strehlow was also drawn to compare Aranda and Loritja myth with the European corpus:

> But as in the Greek mythology, the Supreme God Zeus receded in the background, and the greatest interest, was bestowed on the semi-gods just the same thing happened in the religious traditions of the Australian aborigines. They neglected the Supreme Being, and turned their main interest to the demigods, half-animals and half-men, and endowed them with supernatural powers. The Aranda call these demi-gods Altjira-ngamitjma (the eternal uncreated); the Loritja, Tukutita; the Dieri, Muramura ... These semi-gods wandered from place to place, instructed their novices and performed ceremonies by which the Totem animals or plants were produced.[10]

The structure of his myth accounts seems to indicate that he tried to present indigenous mythology as a whole, internally connected, like Greek or Nordic mythology or like biblical myth. These corpuses unfold in a well-defined realm in which the protagonists interact and events intertwine. These myth collections start usually with setting the general scene and describing what was at the beginning of time and where the protagonists dwelt: Olympia and Hades, Asgard, Midgart and Jötenheim, or Heaven and Earth.

---

9   Much detail of mythology and ceremony belonging to Aranda women has vanished in the course of the last century mainly due to mission life. The basic story lines as well as place names, however, are often still known, and some song and dance is still held by Aranda women who have close ties to Pertame and Luritja women. These ceremonies relate to some of the female ancestors as well as to other stories which have a 'woman's side'. Other beliefs in spirits have survived in modified forms (see Kenny 2004a,b).
10   Carl Strehlow, *The Register*, 7.12.1921.

Both Aranda and Loritja myth collections begin with general descriptions of 'primordial times'; where the ancestral figures would live, travel, interact and end their journeys. These introductions are summaries of the narratives Strehlow collected from a number of people which usually begin with particular ancestors emerging out of the earth or commencing a journey. Read together they are indeed connected, because the same places and ancestors appear often in a number of narratives; and the main motives and themes in these myths are the travels, petrifying, naming, actions, and interacting of ancestors. They can create the impression that the mythic whole was shared knowledge in Aboriginal societies.

However, knowledge about myths was and is not evenly distributed. The transmission of knowledge generally, and in particular about country, was and is gradual. The entire body of information about a particular site or story is never conveyed all at one time. Learning about traditional laws and customs was a long process that could last a lifetime. Dreaming stories involve layers of knowledge, and the sum of these layers may be transmitted over several decades. In the case of male initiation, which took place between ten and 30 years of age, Morton (1987: 110) writes, 'Throughout the cycle of initiation, perhaps lasting as long as twenty years, a youth constantly absorb[ed] knowledge and ancestral powers into his body'. No single Aranda or Loritja person would have known the entire body of mythology pertaining to Aranda and Loritja countries, because myths played and still play a very important role in land ownership. Therefore, considering a myth complex from different ownership positions gives it a different orientation. Rights and interests in land in central Australia were and are usually articulated through knowledge of particular dreaming stories, segments of dreaming tracks, songs, ceremonies, and sacred designs that describe the country and places created by the ancestors of a landholding group (Pink 1936; Strehlow 1965; Morton 1997a,b; Kenny 2010).

As a result of presenting Aboriginal mythology like European mythology and organising the myths in terms of a creation story, and a descent from the heavens to the earth, the modus operandi of Aranda and Loritja myth was masked. These European preconceptions made it difficult, even for von Leonhardi, to address why the Grimm brothers' classification seemed only partly to fit. At the same time, and in the spirit of Herder and Boas, these ill-wrought tools of a transitional anthropology allowed Carl Strehlow to make a start. He embarked on the collection of raw material, which left his corpus open to subsequent interpretation because he tried to document the myths in their own right – notwithstanding his presuppositions. This type of work contrasts with attempts like Frazer's monumental *The Golden Bough*, which looks for universal myth themes and rules applicable around the world. Owing to Carl's reluctance to analyse, it is difficult to evaluate what he derived from his investigations. It seems however fair to say that his research led him towards an understanding of the normative order he saw reflected in Aboriginal religion. In this his views were both like and unlike the Berndts. In addition, indigenous knowledge of the natural environment became a matter which he recorded assiduously. Finally, as his attention turned to the Loritja he also gained a sense of regional fine grain diffusion and borrowing.

What Strehlow saw: Normative order, natural history and regional diffusion

In 1906 Strehlow wrote to N.W. Thomas that the tjurunga songs he collected gave 'valuable clues on the religion of the blacks, because they tell of the wanderings and the deeds of the ancestors, their totems'[11] and to von Leonhardi that these songs give insight into the Aranda's 'religious beliefs'.[12] Berndt's remark that in Aboriginal Australia 'Morality and religion are not conceived of as being separate spheres of experience' (Berndt 1970: 219) is likely to approximate Carl Strehlow's view. Christianity is a moral religion, and in German intellectual life mythology was understood as reflecting normative aspects of a people's culture. This position on issues of the social-moral order in myth may be seen as a harbinger of the later functionalist view 'that the narratives constitute a conservative, socialising force' and a 'normative influence ... on custom' (Hiatt 1975: 5; Malinowski 1979: 237). The lives of the ancestors reflect issues of everyday life and '[i]n the majority of situations it is taken for granted that the majority of people will follow the socio-cultural patterns laid down in the creative era' (Berndt 1970: 219).

The myths of the earth-dwelling beings and their activities explain how the world was created and reflect many aspects of Aranda life. Strehlow believed that they represented the indigenous understanding of the world and their perception of how the laws of life came into being. This interest is evident in the first sections of his myth collections (see for example Strehlow 1907: 8, 9–11) in which he chose to call some of the ancestral beings 'teachers' ('*Lehrer*') who establish and pass on 'laws' ('*Gesetze*'). On the 12 September 1908, his life-long friend and mentor Seidel wrote:

---

11   Carl Strehlow to N.W. Thomas, mid to end of 1906 (SH-SP-6-1).
12   Carl Strehlow to von Leonhardi, 2.6.1906 (SH-SP-2-1).

It was a great pleasure to receive your book and letter, – thank you very
much – I was particularly pleased about the book. I have not read it yet
cover to cover, but I can glean already now, that the myths contain what
one can call the religion or the teachings of the natives.[13]

The conundrum of myth as charter – how to regard bad examples – is evident
in Strehlow's work. The following myth presents an obvious case that a wrong
doing, theft, has major consequences for the perpetrator:

> Soon after this, the inhabitants of Mulati went off to avenge the theft.
> They travelled via Arambara, Tnolbutankama, Taraia, Jinbaragoltulta,
> Ruékana and Ratata to Iwopataka. When the inhabitants of the latter
> camp saw the approaching group of avengers, they said to the ngapa-
> chief, "You have stolen the latjia, that is why the inhabitants of Mulati
> are coming here." When the group of avengers had come close to the
> camp, the inhabitants of Iwopataka said to them, "Here is the man who
> stole your latjia. Kill him with your sticks (tnauia)." Although the raven-
> man took flight, the latjia men threw their tnauia at his neck and he
> fell down dead. Then all the raven-men and latjia-men entered the local
> stone cave and everyone, including the gathered latjia-roots and the
> thief, became tjurunga. (Strehlow 1907: 76–77)

However, moral statements in Aranda and Loritja myths are usually less explicit.
An example is provided in a mythic trespassing incident concerning the ancestral
native cats, who are important both to the Aranda and Loritja (Strehlow 1907;
1908: 24–26). Loritja native cats, coming from the south, were stopped from
proceeding into Aranda country as they arrived at a place just south of Gilbert
Springs, a main Aranda native cat place, where the chief Malbunka was residing.
Malbunka was angry to see them there and furiously uttered an Aranda spell on
them which inflicted blindness on the Loritja native cats which stopped them
from continuing their journey. Instead they metamorphosed into trees and cliffs.

There are also more mundane and prosaic instructions on how to prepare or
do certain things, such as cooking game and distributing it correctly to kin, in
Strehlow's myth collections. The following are some common examples on the
subject of cooking:

> Lakalia, who had meanwhile come near, lifted big grey kangaroo
> Lurknalurkna with ease and laid it on the coals. After it had roasted a
> little, he took it from the fire, scraped off the singed fur and with a stone
> knife lopped off the legs and the tail, which he kept for himself, while
> giving the legs to the young fellows. Then he laid the rest of the meat
> back on the coals. When this had roasted sufficiently, he spread tree

---

13   Carl Seidel to Carl Strehlow, 12.9.1908 (SH 1908-2-1).

branches on the ground, cut up the meat and laid the individual pieces on the cushion of branches. While leaving most of the meat for the young fellows, he took for himself the spine of the kangaroo (toppalenba), the tail and the fat, and returned to Irtjoata, where he sat down near a stone cave. (Strehlow 1907: 42)

This typical myth, on how to do things the 'proper way', often includes how particular laws and customs came about. For example, in the beginning, two 'indatoa' (handsome men) lived with their blind aunt, Kaiala, at Umbañi, a place in the far south-west. Every day the men went hunting in a different direction, killing emus and cooking them in a particular way. They gave their blind aunt enough meat, but very little fat. Fat is still highly valued in central Australian Aboriginal societies. One day they accidentally gave her a very fat female emu and she noticed that they had not done the right thing by her. As punishment she gave eyesight to all emus. The myth goes:

> Every day the two indatoa went hunting in a different direction, killing many emus with their sticks, digging pits in the ground and roasting the emus in them. After they had first eaten the entrails, they plucked (bailkiuka) an emu, broke its legs (lupara mbakaka) and spine (urba ultakaka), placed the cooked meat on green twigs and consumed it. The remaining emus they tied together, put a circular cushion made of woven grass (nama ntjama) on their heads and carried their prey home on it. They gave Kaiala sufficient meat, but very little fat. One day they were delayed while hunting and returned home after night had fallen. They accidentally (balba) gave the goddess a very fat female emu. After she had eaten the meat, the goddess went away from the camp but returned very soon because she had poked a twig into her blind eye, causing it to water a great deal (alknolja = tears). She rubbed the fat into her eyes and – she regained her sight. When she saw all the fat emus in the camp she said to the two men, "You have always withheld the fat emus from me, therefore all the emus will receive their sight from now on." (Strehlow 1907: 30–31)

Aboriginal people in central Australia today still say that any activity in their landscape should be carried out in the 'proper way' or 'right way', implying that it is done according to the rules set down by their ancestors. These activities can apply to virtually anything: cooking traditional food, hunting, approaching a sacred site or performing a ritual or ceremony. As Berndt noted, 'Aboriginal religion was, and is, intimately associated with social living, especially in relation to the natural environment and its economic resources' (Berndt 1970: 219). His remark echoes Herder's view that 'the mythology of every people is an expression of the particular mode in which they viewed nature' (Herder cited in Von Hendy 2002: 20).

Carl Strehlow understood myths not only as reflecting normative order, but also as reflecting an indigenous engagement with environment, a key element of their ontology. Aranda and Loritja mythology represented for him indigenous natural history, 'as the totems of the Aranda belong usually to the animal and plant world, reflecting their knowledge of the natural world; thus, they contain the popular natural history of the blacks.'[14] He wrote:

> The tjurunga-songs in their totality therefore present the blacks, who grew up without education, with a fine popular study of nature. They frequently show a transition from the narration of the exploits of the altjirangamitjina to a description of the totem animals or plants. Even the actors who perform the cult rituals are mentioned in them. (Strehlow 1910: 5)

With great enthusiasm, he recorded in detail the flora and fauna of central Australia as perceived by Aranda and Loritja people. While doing so, he admired their empirical knowledge of species and land. He not only collected the precise description of species and their behaviour in myth, he also collected additional practical information on them. In 1906 he started to send animal and plant specimens to his editor who distributed them to leading German scientists for classification. Von Leonhardi, who loved to cultivate these exotic plants in his hothouse at his country retreat in Gross Karben, had as many classified as he could and inserted these new data in their publications. As a result, descriptions of animal and plant behaviour abound in the prefaces, and footnotes throughout the text. To a certain degree their research became a cosmographic project. Von Leonhardi remarked how often 'the fine nature observation of the various bird species' in the 'Tjurunga songs' amazed him.[15] In this way, Strehlow's data testified to the Aranda and Loritja's intimate relations with their natural environment. What his data also show is the manner in which the life of the species in this environment became the medium for narratives that concerned human normative order. The mythical ancestors were part as were flora and fauna of the environment, each of these with their attributes specified meticulously. A section of an Aranda fish myth exemplifies these features:

> During a great flood, which had begun at Tnenjara a tributary of Ellery Creek situated in the northern part of the McDonnell Ranges, a great shoal of fish came swimming down the Ellery Creek. All types of fish were among them. These fish were being pursued by a crayfish (iltjenma) who kept driving them onward, while a cormorant (nkebara)-totem god stood at the banks and speared some of the passing fish with a short spear (inta). He threw them on the banks, roasted them on coals and ate them. When the fish had swum past him, the cormorant ran ahead of the

---

14   Carl Strehlow to N.W. Thomas, mid to end of 1906 (SH-SP-6-1).
15   Von Leonhardi to Carl Strehlow, 31.10.1909.

> flood and came to the place Tolera. There he threw a big heap of grass into the water in order to detain the fish. However, he could only catch the small fish, for the big fish pushed the barrier aside. After he had devoured the captured fish and spent the night at this place, he again ran ahead of the flood on the following morning. He positioned himself at a particularly narrow spot, threw a large amount of grass into the oncoming water and speared a few fish. (Strehlow 1907: 46–47)

Predators of the fish, and their strategies, are described in equal detail with the strategies, technologies and practices of humans. The passage of a flood, its impact on a waterway as well as the detailed features of that waterway that may help both human and animal ancestors, are all described. Parallels are drawn between the techniques of a species and ancestor whom fish may avoid in similar ways. In the myths, human and animal experiences can merge in a shared space. They interact and respond to a topography in both practical and moral ways. Along with these extended accounts come a multitude of singular details and specificity:

> A big grey kangaroo, named Lurknalurkna [sinewy one], used to live a long time ago at Irtjoata, a place to the north-west of the Finke Gorge. It ate the stems of the porcupine grass (juta wolja) and slept in a cave (intia) at night. (Strehlow 1907: 40)

Listening to these forms of myth, Carl Strehlow was able to compile a list of Aranda and Loritja totems containing 442 totems, of which 411 were animal and plant totems (Strehlow 1908: 61–74); of these 312 were used as food or as stimulants. Additionally he listed 20 plants and animals that were not totems for various reasons, remarking that this was not a comprehensive list. In the following issue on songs and ceremonies, he presented a list that showed which totems had friendly relationships to each other (Strehlow 1910: xiii–xvii). In a number of cases, animals are paired with other species that are their food or shelter. The relationships are usually immediate. The species which have been filled with significance 'are seen as exhibiting a certain affinity with man' (Lévi-Strauss 1966: 37).

Carl Strehlow's text conveys an appreciation of this 'World' that anticipates Lévi-Strauss's enthusiastic account of the concrete logics and classifications of indigenous people. In *The Savage Mind* (1966) Lévi-Strauss cited case after case of early ethnographic accounts of the intimate relations between indigenous people and their environments including examples from Strehlow senior. On Hawaii 'the acute faculties of the native folk' was noted, as they described 'with exactitude the generic characteristics of all species of terrestrial and marine life and the subtlest variations of natural phenomena such as winds, light and colour, ruffling the water'. On the Philippines it was observed that the Hanunóo 'classify all forms of the local avifauna into seventy-five categories', 'distinguish about a dozen kinds of snakes', 'sixty-odd types of fish' and 'more than a dozen … types of fresh and salt water crustaceans' (Lévi-Strauss 1966: 3–5); and about a people of the Tyukyu archipelago it was observed that:

> Even a child can frequently identify the kind of tree from which a tiny wood fragment has come and, furthermore, the sex of that tree, as defined by Kbiran notions of plant sex, by observing the appearance of its wood and bark, its smell, its hardness and similar characteristics. (Lévi-Strauss 1966: 5)

Lévi-Strauss famously concluded that 'Examples like these could be drawn from all parts of the world and one may readily conclude that animals and plants are not known as a result of their usefulness: they are deemed to be useful or interesting because they are first of all known' (Lévi-Strauss 1966: 9). From this he drew conclusions about the rational propensities of peoples and the logic of their concreteness. For Strehlow, and his interpretation of Australian religion, the impact was more specific. This intimacy both with the animal and plant world as well as with place contextualised the propensity of 'totem gods' to become earth bound either as tjurunga or as natural features in the landscape. As I discuss below, Strehlow would remark that 'These totem gods are associated with certain localities where they had lived and generated their totem animals' (Strehlow 1907: 4).

Strehlow's interest in myth as shaping normative order, and reflecting the species and landscape of an Aboriginal world, was also marked by his interest in particularity. As he collected terms and myth from two different cultures, naturally both similarities and differences emerged. His initial impression was that the belief systems of Arandic groups were similar, although he had observed differences, obvious in individual myths, which were 'local-myths that refer to particular places'.[16] He made a related remark again when he started research on Loritja mythology:

> I am now researching and recording the traditions of the Loritja and have discovered that the views of the Loritja are in their basic structure similar to the ones of the Aranda, however, the individual myths are very different.[17]

The mythologies of the different Arandic groups and Loritja were specific, despite some basic common features. In his Loritja account of 'primordial times',

---

16   Carl Strehlow to von Leonhardi, possibly on the 6.4.1906 (SH-SP-1-1).
17   Carl Strehlow to von Leonhardi, 19.9.1906 (SH-SP-3-1).

for example, he points to a number of differences between the groups. Aranda ancestors tended to change more often into tjurunga, and Loritja ancestors into natural features, such as rocks and trees (Strehlow 1908: 3–4).

The main marker of difference was language and dialect variation; his comments on these particularities showed that he had a sense of the changing nature of cultures.[18] He cross-referenced differences, changes and similarities. He documented the incorporation of myth motives and expressions as well as whole sentences or verses in foreign languages (such as Warlpiri, Anmatyerr, etc.). His data collection show that the interaction between different cultural and linguistic groups resulted in 'borrowings'. In Loritja myths one finds Arandic words, sites and dreaming beings as well as Warlpiri words and sentences woven through the narratives (Strehlow 1908: 32–33). He collected evidence of amalgamation and assimilation of foreign cultural elements which produced variations.[19] He and his editor were aware that cultures influenced each other and changes took place. He discovered similar motifs in myths of different cultural and linguistic groups and evidence of language change in myths that contained expressions and 'speech' not found in the vernacular and were clearly dated (see Strehlow 1910: 6). This was one of the reasons he was 'intending to write a short grammar and a dictionary of the local language, so anyone can independently translate the Tj-songs, and see, in how far the older language deviates from the current vernacular'.[20]

Although his comparative work indicated small-scale diffusion, he did not articulate this point explicitly. He simply remarked on the import of cultural elements from other regions into his study area, while von Leonhardi appears to have been testing 'refined diffusionism' in a Boasian style. Most of Strehlow's examples and comments relate to the Western Aranda-Loritja border area. His precise recording showed particularities which defied generalisations. At the same time, it showed similarities that were understood to be diffusion through close and immediate interaction between peoples of different cultures. His son, T.G.H. Strehlow, remarked in the 1930s that these communalities were the result of the 'constant intercourse between the two tribes' and that 'Western [Aranda] religion has been deeply influenced in many respects by Matuntara and Kukatja [Loritja] ideas; and Aranda beliefs, in turn, have set their stamp unmistakably upon Loritja traditions' (Strehlow 1947: 66). He observed that 'in Western Aranda ceremonial chants, a great percentage of the verses are composed in the Loritja language'. About half of the verses of the native cat dreaming of the Ltalultuma (Lthalaltweme) landholding group, for instance, were borrowed from the Loritja songs (Strehlow 1947: 66–67). His father had already observed

---

18 See Strehlow (1910: 6); Carl Strehlow to N.W. Thomas, mid to end of 1906 (SH-SP-6-1).
19 See, for example, Strehlow (1907: 79, fn. 9).
20 Carl Strehlow to N.W. Thomas, mid to end of 1906 (SH-SP-6-1).

a similar situation and wrote that in the Loritja songs a large amount of Aranda existed (Strehlow 1910). His son also maintained that shared dreaming tracks, that link people, had similar features due to 'diffusion' or close interaction. The dreaming of the Dancing Women, for example, traverses a number of countries:

> One of the Western Desert mythical tracks that go across the Aranda-speaking area is delineated in the myth of the Dancing Women of Amunurknga. This trail begins in the country west of Mount Liebig; and I have traced it eastward as far as Love's Creek Station, near Arltunga, in the Eastern Aranda area; but the trail goes even further. (Strehlow 1965: 128–129)

T.G.H. Strehlow found that these affinities expressed themselves in a number of ways 'particularly where the animals and plants form ceremonial totems' (Strehlow 1947: 66). Based on his father's material he estimated that about 60 per cent of the terms of dreamings were shared between neighbouring Aranda and Loritja (Kukatja) peoples. He wrote on Tuesday 12 April 1932:

> From my father's A[randa] dictionary I compiled today as complete a list of Aranda names of plants and animals as possible together with their Kukatja equivalents. The result was very interesting:

	Total	Common terms	Separate terms
Names of animals:	300	= 167 (=56%)	133 (44%)
Names of plants:	220	= 147 (=67%)	73 (33%)*

* T.G.H. Strehlow's Diary I (1932: 2).

Premonitions of ontology

The type of mythological material Carl Strehlow collected is the core of Aboriginal belief systems and what today is referred to as the dreaming in English. Strehlow's material contains most elements that allowed – in hindsight – a concept of the dreaming. It supplies excellent source material and empirical evidence. He did not have the tools of modern anthropology and linguistics at his disposal to formulate this concept, and did not experience the intimate relationship first hand that Aboriginal people have to their land. He did not have the opportunity to travel with his informants over their country. Nevertheless his work and data were suggestive of the 'subject into object' transformation (Munn 1970; Morton 1987) and to a certain degree the person-land relationship in indigenous Australian cultures (Strehlow 1947; Myers [1986] 1991). It would certainly help his son conceptualise and articulate it.

The conceptualisation of 'subject into object' was latent in his data collection. Ever recurring motives are the vast travels and the transformations of the ancestral beings into natural features or tjurunga or kuntanka (objects) in both Aranda and Loritja myths. He realised that these journeys and transformations, described in 'their religious traditions' and 'their sacred songs (tjurunga songs)' recited by the old men during ceremonies, were essential features of Aboriginal cosmology.[21]

He remarked that nearly all Aranda songs end with the ancestors returning to their home (*Heimat*)[22] very tired from their long wanderings, and usually turned into tjurunga.[23] The issues of growing tired, going to sleep or 'going in', and actually becoming part of the land, are implicitly all speaking about a particular way that landscape and species are linked to ancestors. The ancestors would 'altjamaltjerama', which means 'become a hidden body, i.e. to assume a different *Gestalt*' (Strehlow 1907: 5), at particular named places or 'tjurungeraka' (meaning 'change into wood or stone') at the end of their activities:

> For not only the whole body of the totem ancestor but also individual parts of it were tjurungeraka, i.e. changed into wood or stone, e.g. the fat of a totem snake (apma andara), the kidney of a possum ancestor (imora topparka), the heart of an emu (ilia tukuta), etc. Indeed, even some of the sticks belonging to the totem ancestors are regarded as tjurunga, etc. (Strehlow 1908: 77)

There are countless examples of this process of becoming country, or being lodged in the country. In a Loritja myth 'The two brothers Neki and Wapiti on the mountain Mulati' (Strehlow 1908: 10) the ancestors Neki and Wapiti (synonyms for a type of edible root) end the story by turning into two cliffs on a mountain called Mulati, meaning twins. The events of this myth take place not far from Merini, a mountain also mentioned in Aranda mythology. In 'Papa tuta. Knulja ntjara' (reproduced in Loritja, Aranda, a German interlinear translation and a German free translation) the dog ancestors change into tjurunga at Rotna, a site on Aranda territory. 'Katuwara', a short Loritja myth about two eagles (Strehlow 1908: 20), tells of an excursion of the eagles to a mountain called in Aranda Eritjakwata (meaning eagle egg/s) and their flights to the north. Like most ancestors, they petrify at their place of departure, Kalbi (meaning eagle feather) west of Tempe Downs. At the end of some of the songs he notes where the ceremony and rites were performed. For example, the Arandic red

---

21 Carl Strehlow to von Leonhardi, 2.6.1906 (SH-SP-2-1). See also Carl Strehlow to N.W. Thomas, mid to end of 1906 (SH-SP-6-1).
22 The German *Heimat* carries strong notions of emotional attachment to landscape. Meggitt ([1962] 1986: 67) chose in his *DesertPeople* the notion of *die Heimat* to describe 'the affection that a man feels for his wider community and its country'.
23 Carl Strehlow to von Leonhardi, 2.6.1906 (SH-SP-2-1).

kangaroo ceremony takes place at Ulamba (Strehlow 1910: 10–13) and the large tawny frogmouth ceremony of the Loritja is held at Kumbuli in the north-west of Hermannsburg (Strehlow 1911: 19). He wrote that the 'mbatjalkatiuma' ceremonies are performed at sites which are in one way or another connected to the relevant ancestor, because they are believed to be hidden at these places in rocks or underground and that they emerge when the old men let their blood flow on these sites during the performance of ceremonies (Strehlow 1910: 8).

The transformations are a main feature of Aboriginal ontology as ancestors externalise themselves in their environment. Carl Strehlow wrote to von Leonhardi, not quite sure what to make of the phenomenon of place names and their creation:

> Esteemed Sir!
>
> With this mail I send you again some myths. I have placed red brackets around the ones that are not worth publishing, because they only contain names that are important to the blacks and for science they seem rather of minor value. However, you are completely free to publish an extract from these as well as from the others I have sent you. The myth of the 'fish totem ancestor', for example, is quite uninteresting, as it contains many fish totem places, and yet I do not want to miss them entirely. They show how the natives imagine the creation of the fish totem places.[24]

Naming, making and marking of places are important features of the creation process. Names such as Rubuntja (Mt Hay), Irbmankara (Running Waters), Aroalirbaka (2 Mile in the Finke) and many others are prominent in all mythological accounts. He wrote about the 'altjirangamitjina' (dreaming ancestors):

> These totem gods are associated with certain localities where they had lived and generated their totem animals. Such localities are mostly found in the vicinity of a high mountain, a spring or a gorge where the totem animals that bear their names usually gather in larger numbers. For example, there is a lizard totem place near Hermannsburg, at Manángananga, where there are many lizards. Fish totem places can be found only in places where there is much water, e.g. in the Ellery Creek. Some of the totem gods remained in their original habitations; these are referred to as atua kutata, i.e. the men who always live in one place. Other altjirangamitjina, however, went on extended journeys and returned home in the company of several young men. (Strehlow 1907: 4)

---

24 Carl Strehlow to von Leonhardi, probably mid 1906 (SH–SP-9-1). See Strehlow (1907: 46–48) on fish dreaming.

All narratives Carl Strehlow collected belong to particular localities of Aranda or Loritja territory and take place during a mythological creation era. He wrote that Aranda myths are local-myths that refer to particular places.[25] As early as 1894 missionary Reuther explained in the *Kirchlichen Mitteilungen* that the muramura (dreaming ancestors) had created the land:

> There are many Muramura. Each one of them established something good, and created the earth; however, because there are so many of them, each made only a part of the land of which he is the patron guardian.[26]

As a result of his empiricism and maybe an intuitive understanding of the significance of place for Aranda and Loritja people, Strehlow collected and recorded hundreds of site names. He had grasped to a certain degree the importance of naming and metamorphosing, writing that their journeys ended with the ancestral beings fossilised or petrified into the landscape, from which spirits rose (Strehlow 1907: 2). He even wrote to his editor that it was unlawful to change or damage natural features of the landscape.[27] But he did not get to the specific subject-into-object ontology as described by Munn (1970), expanded by Myers ([1986] 1991) and elaborated by Morton (1987) and Redmond (2001). Still, he came close:

> The totem, the totem ancestor and the totem descendant, i.e. the actor, appear in the tjurunga-songs as a single entity. Some of the tjurunga-songs are simply beyond understanding unless one bears in mind the inseparable unity between the totem, the altjirangamitjina and the ratapa.[28] (Strehlow 1910: 5)

It was T.G.H. Strehlow who would travel on camel back with Aranda men over their country mapping the exact places of events that had taken place in the mythological past. T.G.H. Strehlow understood the overwhelming significance of land as well as the emotional attachment of indigenous people to ancestral figures in place, as well as to their travels and acts as represented in performance.

'and it was an eye-opener for me'

Ten years after his father's last journey to Horseshoe Bend, T.G.H. Strehlow returned to Hermannsburg on the 5 April 1932. In his baggage he carried his father's publication *Die Aranda- und Loritja-Stämme in Zentral-Australien* and

---

25 Carl Strehlow to von Leonhardi, possibly written on the 6.4.1906 (SH-SP-1-1).
26 Reuther (1894: 57) in *Kirchlichen Mitteilungen*.
27 Carl Strehlow to von Leonhardi, 2.6.1906 (SH-SP-2-1).
28 Among other things 'ratapa' means in Carl Strehlow's work spirit-child that enters a mother to be and gives a person a soul.

unpublished dictionary. He was 23, only one year older than his father had been when he first arrived at the mission in 1894. Hill (2002) describes Ted's feelings and his motives for returning to his birthplace; they were fraught with ambivalence. Yet he was very keen to learn everything he could about central Australia. Once he had familiarised himself again with Hermannsburg and its people, he started studying and checking his father's data and brushing up his Aranda with old friends of his father.[29] Ted found it difficult to get back into the language of his childhood, although he had an enormous head start and was equipped with his father's myth collection and unpublished dictionary, that contained thousands of Aranda and Loritja words.

Within a few weeks he was tracking the bush on camel back in the company of Tom Ljoṇa, an Aranda man, collecting data for his thesis on Aboriginal language. His fourth trip in November and December of 1932 took him onto his 'father's country', Tjoritja (Tyurretye) country, the country that features prominently in *Die Aranda- und Loritja-Stämme in Zentral-Australien*. When he got back to Hermannsburg he wrote that 'The long-dreaded trip is over at last' and 'Now I am home.'[30] After this trip – it had been an important one despite not having collected much linguistic data – he wrote to his supervisor, Professor J.A. FitzHerbert in Adelaide:

> On my last trip I did not find many natives, except at Hamilton Downs and Napperby: since my July trip one of the Western stations has closed down, and the numerous natives have all dispersed, mainly to Hermannsburg. My own camel boy, however, had his original home in these parts. Accordingly, I had a splendid opportunity of getting an insight into the former life of this Aranda group – how their wandering depended on the seasons of the year and the failing or replenishment of their water supplies. I was shown many ceremonial sites and a sacred cave (Ulamba) with the last few tjurunga in it; and *it was an eye-opener for me to see how the old legends fit in with the general geography of the tribal territory*.[31] It is only after a trip such as this that the old legends – which are usually told in an extremely terse style, an intimate knowledge of the locality described on the part of the listeners being presupposed by the story teller – really begin to live in one's mind.[32]

This trip in late 1932 made him realise how intimate the relationship between person, species and the land is. Hill (2002: 175–176) writes that it is surprising that he had not realised the close connection of natural environment and

---

29 T.G.H. Strehlow's Diary I (1932: 1–11).
30 T.G.H. Strehlow's Diary I (1932: 130).
31 Emphasis added.
32 T.G.H. Strehlow to Professor J.A. FitzHerbert, 5.1.1933 (SRC Correspondence 60/32).

people, and that it was only taking shape now, despite his language skills and childhood milieu. However, this is not at all astonishing because the specificity of an Aboriginal ontology, as we understand it today, had yet to be articulated.[33]

T.G.H. Strehlow was struggling with many aspects of central Australia. He was relearning Aranda, acquainting himself with the indigenous and non-indigenous population of the Centre, acquiring survival skills and grappling with geography. It was hard going. An entry for Wednesday the 9 November 1932, camped near Ulamba on Tom Ljoŋa's father's and father's father's country, illustrates his difficulties, which were met on many other days as well:

> A warm day. We spent another morning, tjurunga hunting, and then had to give it up as all likely places had been exhausted. There is only one vague chance that the caves may be right at the Western extremity of Eritjakwata; but its no use messing around any more. For I discovered, when taking the camels down to the waterhole this afternoon that it will be quite dry in a day's time or so after that we'd have to carry the water down to the camels a long distance. Besides, Tom, instead of getting me a wallaby, went out in quest of kangaroos; "the wind reared around in all directions". And Tom returned late – without anything. He threw his own remaining bit of euro away as well because it had gone maggoty. He also informs me tonight that "Baby" is developing a tender left forefoot on the stones. Old "Ranji" is still limping and only this morning I had to pull out some more little splinters and spikes from the open sore on his sole. Such is life, and yes people would "give anything" to have my job – "it must be so fascinating the insight it gives you into the souls of such an interesting people". I climbed the mountain straight North from here today in desperation, in order to reconnoitre the leg of the country. I took angles galore, but nothing corresponds with any of the maps I have – which is a good thing. I got a splendid view right around – all high peaks of the McDonnell and all the ranges North, and the sandhills and plains and salt lakes between [only Karinjarra was hidden by another formation]; but everything was shrouded in haze unfortunately. This made it impossible to gauge distances, and I am still quite in a muddle as to which peaks are Mt Chapple, Heughlin, Zeil and Razorback.[34] – Well here's another moon-light night. I suppose, I'll have to shift tomorrow owing to lack of water – no rest for the wicked.[35]

---

33 This remark reveals that the impression that Ted evokes in his award wining *Journey to Horseshoe Bend* that he was aware of the significance of landscape on his father's death journey is to a certain degree fiction. He may have been unconsciously aware of this fact.

34 Later he plotted these sites on a map as Eritjakwata, Emalgna, Ulatarka and Latjima (Strehlow 1971).

35 T.G.H. Strehlow's Diary I (1932: 121).

Two years after this crucial fourth trip,[36] he wrote three seminal essays in 1934 that would be published as *Aranda Traditions* in 1947; they are the beginning of the arduous work of conceptualising the Aboriginal ontology. Significantly the first essay starts with a fictional visit of the owners to Ulamba. This description is based on his visit to Ulamba with Tom Ljoŋa and was much influenced by the feelings of his 'camel boy', a man in his fifties who was disillusioned and deeply saddened by the loss of his country and the fate of his people. T.G.H. Strehlow (1947: 30–33) captured what Ulamba meant emotionally to Tom. These feelings towards country, he also consciously noted when he was checking his father's version of Tom's 'Atua Arintja from Ulamba'[37] with Angus, Jonathan and Moses in January 1933 back in Hermannsburg:

> I first gave the three men my father's version of the legend, with which they agreed: according to Moses, Loatjira had been the original narrator. Angus could not tell, why the cult was ever performed – the erilkngibata had not given any explanation for it any more. ...

> Strangely enough, in those fragments of the song which are remembered by Angus, Jonathan and Moses and also in those which are recorded in my father's works, the whole stress is laid not on the horrible cannibalism of the atua erintja, but on his longing for home, for his own green Ulamba, and on his sorrow at finding that birds have desecrated his own cave at Ulamba. It sounds almost like an Aranda version of the lost son.[38]

T.G.H. Strehlow was able to formulate the relationship and feelings of Aboriginal people towards country and what the stories of species-ancestors mean in these first essays, because he had experienced it first hand. He saw the parallels between the people's relationship to land/place and the ancestors 'Longing for home' which is the motif that 'lead[s] most of the weary ancestors of legend back to the place whence they originated' (Strehlow 1947: 32). Nearly 40 years later he still wrote about feelings connected to country and 'that in the days of the totemic ancestors the landscape itself reciprocated these feelings of affection' (Strehlow 1971: 584). In the course of his long career T.G.H. Strehlow would gradually articulate explicitly the specific ontology of the Aranda.

---

36   T.G.H. Strehlow's Diary I (1932: 118–130).

37   In his father's work simply called 'Atua arintja, der böse Mann' (Carl Strehlow 1907: 90–92). Ted added 'from Ulamba' and nearly 40 years later it appears in his *Songs of Central Australia* as 'The Arintja Song of Ulamba' (1971: 577–584). Ulamba is also connected to an herre (kangaroo) dreaming (Carl Strehlow 1910: 10–13) where its ceremony is performed.

38   T.G.H. Strehlow's Diary I (1932/33: 145–146).

Conceptualising the dreaming

Unable to travel the Aranda landscape for research, or avail himself of early models of local organisation, Carl Strehlow would not articulate explicitly his informants' intimate relationship to country. Thus, while he had rigorously documented what his informants told him about their dreaming ancestors emerging out of the earth, travelling over its surface during the creation period and metamorphosing into natural features or objects, his son T.G.H. Strehlow would be able to formulate explicitly what these procreational movements and transformations meant. He would pull the threads together that would connect ancestor-person-land with each other. Already in *Aranda Traditions* (1947) T.G.H. Strehlow touched on what would lead in the following decades to an understanding of the essence of Aboriginal religion by himself and other eminent anthropologists, such as the Berndts, Stanner, Munn and Myers. T.G.H. Strehlow writes about the significance of ancestral foundational acts and transformations, the person-land relationship, and also about the libidinal and procreational aspects of myth and rite that have been extensively discussed by Róheim, Hiatt and Morton. Finally, this sense of place and sentiment in Aboriginal culture would lead Hiatt (1969) and Peterson (1972) to reject the juggernaut of Lévi-Straussian rationalism. Morton (1985) would in turn temper the latter's insights with those of Lacan and the emotional struggle against fragmentation, both in the landscape and within the self.

The foundational acts, the travels and actions of these ancestral figures that brought the world into being have been discussed numerous times. For central Australia, T.G.H. Strehlow (1947, 1964, 1971), Munn (1970) and Myers (1976, [1986] 1991) are the outstanding accounts. They describe the significance of ancestral singing, marking and naming places, embodying ancestral figures in performance, and transforming parts of themselves into natural features or sacred objects. They explain what the metamorphosing into the landscape at the end of their journeys, where they are still believed to be resting or sleeping as part of the land, means to Aboriginal people and how the landscape is the symbol of the truth of this time and its system of order. In 1964 T.G.H. Strehlow emphasised again:

> After emerging from their eternal slumbering places, these supernatural beings, commonly labelled "totemic ancestors", moved about on the surface of the earth. Their actions and their wanderings brought into being all the physical features of the central Australian landscape. Mountains, sandhills, swamps, plains, springs, and soakages, all arose to mark the deeds of the roving totemic ancestors and ancestresses. (Strehlow [1964] 1978: 16)

T.G.H. Strehlow (1947: 25–28) made his first attempts in the 1930s to convey how Aboriginal people perceive and understand the dreaming (although he does not use this term). For example, many features of the MacDonnell Ranges are attributed to the blows of ceremonial poles:

> The terrible blows of these smiting poles have left their marks in countless valleys and chasms and gorges in every portion of the MacDonnell Ranges and elsewhere. They cleft gaps in otherwise inaccessible bluff slopes; they fashioned many mountain passes for the feet of wandering hordes at the beginning of time. (Strehlow 1947: 25)

Sometimes simply by camping at a place and eating, hunting, gathering or making tools, behaving and acting as their descendants would, the ancestors gave meaning to the landscape and a code for the people who followed to live by, because 'all occupations originated with the totemic ancestors' (Strehlow 1947: 35). He clearly stated that the dreaming encompasses all aspects of Aranda life, which was also observed by Munn (1970) among Warlpiri and Pitjantjatjara and by Myers (1976: 158–160) among the Pintupi who see the tjukurrpa 'as the ground of all being'. Other activities of course included the performance of ritual and ceremonial dances and songs (which Stanner seems to have rated as more sacred).

The exploits of the ancestral beings were vast and complex. As they created on their wanderings the land and everything on it – water, animals and plants – they also populated the land with spirits and thus 'throughout the Aranda-speaking area it was believed that the totemic ancestors and ancestresses had left a trail of "life" behind them', a constituted world (Strehlow [1964] 1978: 20). Spirits emerged from those parts of the ancestral beings, and the sacred objects representing them, which they left embedded in the land. Some of these spirits were child-spirits, who enter a woman and give human-beings their 'soul', and thus humans owe their existence to the dreaming (see also Morton 1985: 118). People's attachments to country are thus indestructible because they are derived from the 'life-giving properties' left behind by the ancestors at the beginning of time (Strehlow 1947: 88). In this way, they are part of the land and the ancestors who created the land and the people. T.G.H. Strehlow described the significance of the landscape for Aboriginal people:

> A Central Australian Aboriginal community was thus made up of men and women for whom the whole landscape in which they lived represented the work of supernatural beings who had become reincarnated in their own persons and in those of living and dead forbearers, relatives, and friends. (Strehlow [1964] 1978: 39)

Thus, land and things are imbued with notions of person. At the centre of Munn's discussion lies the relationship between the subject and the (inanimate or non-sentient) object world. The objectification of the ancestors in land through transformation symbolises the relationship that people have to land, because they originate from the ancestors who are still in their transformation features of the natural world present in country and objects. Generally, anything created in any way or left behind by an ancestor is thought to contain something of this being. Munn (1970: 143) writes that 'country is the fundamental object system external to the conscious subject within which consciousness and identity are anchored.' Thus, human beings have unbreakable bonds with particular parts of the country (Munn 1970: 145), because their spirits come from these transformations in the landscape. People treat the landscape like a relative, because it also represents their kin (Strehlow 1947; Myers [1986] 1991). Carl Strehlow, for example, wrote that the species-ancestor associated with a man is perceived to be his big brother and treated with great respect (Strehlow 1908).

As Munn (1970) remarked the transformations of subject into object involves a disappearance linked with a new appearance, in most cases parts of the landscape. It is thus the land that can tell about the noumenal world beyond immediate perception. Myers ([1986] 1991) writes that for the Pintupi the land reveals aspects of that past era that bear on the present and can explain phenomena in the lived experience of the everyday. The living are obliged to sustain this inheritance because these traditions are the basis for the continuation of life. Drought and illness may be thought to be a consequence of deviations. T.G.H. Strehlow wrote:

> For in Australia the operation of the concept of the totemic landscape ensured that such things as the stability of tribal boundaries and of linguistic groups, the distribution of interlocking and intermarrying subgroups, and the firm establishment of authority − and hence of the agencies of social control, and of law and order − were all based on the geographic environment. (Strehlow 1970: 92)

T.G.H. Strehlow, Munn and Myers' work on the specificity of Australian indigenous ontology can be juxtaposed with the way in which both Róheim and Morton adapt universal themes drawn from psychoanalysis to the specificity of dreaming myth. In the process, they seek to link central Australian issues of sentiment and desire to themes that might be judged universal, just as Lévi-Strauss sought to establish a cognitive unity for humankind that linked his 'primitive' naturalists with 'modern' minds.

Based on field-research in the late 1920s at Hermannsburg, Róheim championed the psychoanalytical approach to Aboriginal religion by seeking general human dream patterns and wish dreams in Aranda myth. His records include not only references to myth but also many dreams and mundane stories recounted by Aranda people a few years after Carl Strehlow died. Some of these provide matter of fact corroborating evidence for the details of daily life that Carl recorded through his study of myth (see Róheim 1974, 1988). However, Róheim's main concerns were the celebration of the phallic hero, male transition from child to adult and, finally, reparation of separation from the mother in a return to the land (Hiatt 1975: 9). In *The Eternal Ones of the Dream*, Róheim wrote that myth represents repressed wish dreams, particularly day-dreams that 'hide a real difficulty, and offer a consolation. Instead of the mental picture of struggle for daily food or wandering on the scorching sand, the myth describes a state of perpetual erection, a perpetual state of lust' (Róheim [1945] 1971: 10). This means ancestral is 'necessarily' libidinised, i.e., 'as if it were a sexual act' (Róheim [1945] 1971: 9). Hence, foot, tail and making tracks are all seen as euphemisms for sexual intents and acts.

In his work post-1985, Morton, like Munn, carried the study of myth into an analysis of how (male) agents filled with desire created a libidinised landscape (Morton 1985, 1987). In *Singing Subjects and Sacred Objects* he develops the theme of mythic 'procreation' events as the substance of ancestral travels (1987: 100–117). Morton focuses on 'naming' and 'marking' up, complex ancestral performances that are related 'to ancestral singing as the creative outpouring of names' (Morton 1987: 110) that bring the world into being. He also notes Munn's account of how women 'lose' boards. Morton argues for a double transformation:

> Thus men, at initiation, take corporal bodies from women and ultimately transform them into tjurunga bodies, [while] women appear to take tjurunga bodies from men and turn them into fleshy beings. It is these analogous, but also opposed, transformations which I believe to lie behind Munn's discernment of a correspondence between the ancestral surrender of tjurunga and the giving up of boys by women at initiation. (Morton 1987: 115)

He suggests 'that the notion of alienation from The Dreaming's depths during the course of childhood growth may also be general' (Morton 1987: 116), and that male children (at least) are taken from mothers to bring them back to the dreaming, guarantee of the human condition. As Victor Turner remarked, in this myth and rite the needs of 'biopsychical' beings (the boys) might here be reconciled with 'the needs of society' notwithstanding their apparent opposition (Turner 1968: 19).

Other contemporary views by Myers ([1986] 1991) and Redmond (2001), for example, take closer account of the *Lebenswelt* (lifeworld) of Pintupi and

Ngarinyin people. They describe how land constitutes and reveals the world by being able to 'speak' and 'explain' itself, and how people are active in interpreting these experiences.

Altjira and tnankara

It is clear from the foregoing discussion that many rounds of observation, and myth interpretation, were required to specify a central Australian ontology. It was beyond Carl Strehlow's time and conceptual method to grasp the essence of an Aboriginal world. Nevertheless, I would like to end this discussion by returning once more to the word 'altjira' and its semantics. The trajectory of the word's interpretations shows, in condensed form, the power of Carl Strehlow's work on myth.

The term has a certain magnetism, being continuously revisited over time and stimulating many discussions on its meanings (Spencer and Gillen 1927; Róheim 1945; T.G.H. Strehlow 1971; Morton 1985; Veit 1991; Hill 2002; Austin-Broos 2010; John Strehlow 2011; Green 2012). It was, for example, one of the first concepts that T.G.H. Strehlow checked with his father's informants when he arrived back at the mission after ten years absence, in April 1932.[39]

Carl Strehlow was aware of the multiple uses and meanings of the term altjira. The pivotal remark for subsequent debate was published at the beginning of his masterpiece (Strehlow 1907: 2; see quotation in Chapters I and VII). Yet he also wrote to his editor about the term after he had completed his collection of Aranda myths:

> You will note in the section on Altjira, that I had to retreat from a number of points I had made earlier, because it does not hold together after further investigation. ... What I say on page 2 about the derivation/ etymology of "Altjira" = (altja era), is my opinion of course, which I cannot prove, but is an obvious and logical explanation which seems very likely. ... However, the natives are very definite, that the current meaning of the word Altjira is the 'uncreated one', 'the not-made one' who has no beginning. Already Schulze (in Royal society etc. page 242) wrote 15 years ago that the meaning of altjira is 'not made'.[40]

This ambiguity led him to discuss a possible etymology of 'altjira'. He wrote that according to his Aranda informants the concept of the 'non-created' was central and that Spencer and Gillen's (1904: 745) view that the word 'alcheri means

---

39 T.G.H. Strehlow's Diary I (1932: 2–8); Hill 2002.
40 Carl Strehlow to von Leonhardi, 13.12.1906 (SH-SP-7-1).

dream' was incorrect, because 'altjirerama' means 'to dream', and it is derived from altjira (god) and rama (see), in other words, 'to see god'. Concurrently, he indicates that altjira and tukura can also refer to any mythical ancestor seen in a dream. Spencer and Gillen's explanation and translation of 'Alcheringa', as 'dream times' (Spencer 1896: 111; Spencer and Gillen 1904: 745), Carl Strehlow considered as a misunderstanding of the concept:

> The Aranda language does not render the word dream with alcheri but rather with altjirerinja, though this word is rarely used. The normal expression of the blacks is, "ta altjireraka"="I have dreamed". The word "alcheringa", which according to Spencer and Gillen is supposed to mean "dreamtime", is obviously a corruption of altjirerinja. The native knows nothing of a "dreamtime" as a designation of a certain prior in their history. What this expression refers to is the time when the Altjiranga mitjina traversed this earth. (Strehlow 1907: 2)

With the help of his editor, Strehlow became sensitive to the term's polysemy. His editor had realised before Strehlow had that the expression 'altjira' had a wide semantic field and could denote a multiplicity. This was reflected in one of his early remarks. He expressed surprise that Strehlow would use 'Altjira' for God in his service book, *Galtjindintjamea-Pepa Aranda Wolambarinjaka* (1904):

> Today I finally get around to answer your letter and thank you for the book in Aranda. Your letter was very interesting; with the text, however, I unfortunately cannot do much, as long as a grammar and a dictionary are not available, – the only thing I could discern was that you translate God with Altjira; intriguing, that you after all think that this term contains sufficient meaning to convey the biblical concept of God.[41]

A few months later he asked Carl Strehlow to further investigate the underlying concepts of the word 'Altjira':

> Dream is altjirerinja (obviously Spencer and Gillen's Alteringa). You wrote to me that no term exists for the abstract concept of dream. This needs clarification. I ask you to pay the outmost attention to any words related to the concept of Altjira; all are very important. Can the word Altjira also be used as an adjective?[42]

Von Leonhardi's reaction to Carl Strehlow's subsequent discussion of the semantics of Altjira was enthusiastic and begged for further research. He commented in August 1906:

---

41 Von Leonhardi to Carl Strehlow, 9.9.1905.
42 Von Leonhardi to Carl Strehlow, 17.3.1906.

Your explanation of the word altjirerama with the help of the corresponding term in Loritja appealed very much to me. Thus, the Loritja's tukura means 'god'. Hopefully you will have something to tell us about Tukura? In that case Spencer and Gillen's Alcheringa = Altjira-ringa means "belonging to the gods", "the divinities". Therefore the word Altjira would not only be a proper name, but would also be used for the totem ancestors? Have I understood you correctly in this matter? Are the totem ancestors Altjira = gods as well? This is not an unimportant matter.[43]

Strehlow continued to investigate 'the different uses of the word Altjira and tmara and deba altjira'.[44] Gradually, he grasped the term's polysemy and tried to conceptualise his new insights. By the time he published, he had noted and explained that altjira is connected to mother's conception dreaming and place (Strehlow 1908: 57; 1910: 2). Von Leonhardi had alerted him to this aspect of the word by directing his attention to Schulze's work (1891). Strehlow also found that 'altjira' could mean 'the totem god who reveals the people's future in dreams and inkaiama = to set up' (Strehlow 1913: 6; see also Strehlow 1907: 2). Thus, he came to use the word in a number of different contexts. One attempt to solve the polysemy of 'altjira' was to use upper and lower cases, i.e. Altjira and altjira. Upper case 'Altjira' was used for Aranda supreme being or high god; and in the Christian context of the mission, for 'God'. In lower case, 'altjira' was used in a vast array of contexts, assuming meanings in indigenous use and standing in stark contrast to the new meaning the missionaries had tried to impress on it. Spencer noted the use of Altjira upper and altjira lower case, but could not understand the intention of this use (Marett and Penniman 1932: 110).

Carl Strehlow also recorded a synonym for Altjira/altjira – tnankara (tnengkarre). In his entire published work the word tnankara appears only twice (Strehlow 1913: 29; 1915: 48), for a very obvious reason. In his time, tnankara was the synonym for altjira used in 'the secret language that is taught to a rukuta, a novice or young circumcised man' (Strehlow 1913: 29). Róheim ([1945] 1971: 211) too observed that 'Another Aranda word for dream, ancestor, and story, is tnankara. It is not often used, and as far as I could see it means exactly the same as altjira'.

Róheim typically emphasised altjira's meaning 'dream' which is crucial for a psychoanalysis based on dreams. In *The Eternal Ones of the Dream*, Róheim claims that altjira does not mean god or ancestor as Strehlow maintained, but that its meaning covers 'dream, beings seen in a dream and a narrative with a happy ending' (Róheim [1945] 1971: 210–211). He believed 'that Strehlow, from

---

43   Von Leonhardi to Carl Strehlow, 7.8.1906.
44   Carl Strehlow to von Leonhardi, 19.9.1906 (SH-SP-3-1).

the preoccupation with Altjira (God) in the Aranda bible, managed to miss the real meaning of the word, which is known to every Aranda both at the mission and elsewhere'. Róheim also remarked that 'in the Luritja group of languages tukurpa is the universal word which, like the Aranda altjira, covers several meanings of dream, story and also of the oracle game' (Róheim [1945] 1971: 211). Therefore he missed, in turn, that Strehlow also proposed that the term refers in a certain context to 'a totem god which the native believes to have seen in a dream' and that 'every person is also connected with another particular totem which is called altjira. This is the totem of his mother. ... This altjira appears to the blacks in dreams and warns them of danger, just as he speaks of them to friends while they are sleeping' (Strehlow 1908: 57).

T.G.H. Strehlow discusses the term 'Altjira' and his father's view on it in *Songs of Central Australia* (Strehlow 1971: 614–615). He wrote that 'altjira' is a rare word 'whose root meaning appears to be "eternal, uncreated, sprung out of itself"; and it occurs only in certain traditional phrases and collocations'. Part of T.G.H. Strehlow's examination of Altjira/altjira is reminiscent of a note his father wrote to von Leonhardi:

> The word Altjira is a noun. By adding the suffix –erama to a noun a verb can be made denoting 'to become' in Aranda. ... Thus, it is grammatically correct to perceive the verb 'altjiererama' as 'become God'. Rama however, also means: to see; Altjire-rama = see God (in dreams God reveals secrets to them). That this is the meaning of altjiererama = dream follows clearly from the comparison of the Aranda words with the Loritja (neighbouring tribe of the Aranda, who refer to themselves as Kukatja) ones; in this language too 'to dream' is: tukura nangani; tukura = god (altjira) and nangani = to see. Therefore to compose grammatically correct the word 'dream' (the natives very rarely do this and do not say: I had a dream, but I dreamed (altjireraka); thus, 'dream' is altjirérinja. So what does Gillen and Sp. Alcheringa mean?[45]

It is clear now that altjira covered a very complex issue and that its semantic field and syntactic range were vast. Without doubt 'dream' was part of altjira's polysemy (Green 2012: 166, 171–172). The altjira discussion also indicates that language changes over time. Thus, Strehlow's corpus of myth allows some tracing of the history of key concepts and terms. This term has undergone in the course of the past century some major semantic shifts. Carl Strehlow and von Leonhardi had observed a wide semantic field for the term altjira and Carl had discovered a secret synonym of the word – tnankara. In his time, T.G.H. Strehlow (1971: 614) found that 'altjira' was rarely used. Decades earlier Róheim ([1945] 1971: 211) had noted a synonym for altjira 'tnankara' that 'is not often

---

45   Carl Strehlow to von Leonhardi, 2.6.1906 (SH-SP-2-1). Compare with T.G.H. Strehlow (1971: 614–615).

used'. Today in Western Aranda areas the term altjira is used to denote the Christian God and tnankara (tnengkarre) for concepts relating to indigenous spiritual beliefs (Kenny 2003, 2004a, 2010).[46]

'Altjira', and the initial debate about it, distils in one instance the journey of interpretation through which Carl Strehlow's corpus of Aranda and Loritja myth has passed. Transitional or pre-modern in his ethnography, Carl Strehlow's scholarly pursuit of cultures, propelled forward by von Leonhardi, opened doors to contemporary research on indigenous 'Worlds'. In the process, within Australia, the study of myth became an account of a unique Aboriginal ontology.

---

46 Green (1999/2004: n.p.) has observed a similar development for the Anmatyerr words altyerr and anengkerr, that used to be synonyms.

VI. The 'Marriage Order' and Social Classification

Strehlow's editor remarked in 1906 that 'The views of Spencer and Gillen, as well as of other Australian researchers, on the meaning of kinship terms, as well as of the marriage classes, seem still hypothetical.'[1] At the turn of the century the inclination towards evolutionistic theory was prevalent in Australian kinship studies. Reflected in the work of Fison and Howitt, Roth, and Spencer and Gillen, it led to a focus on 'marriage order' and kinship terminology. Questions about group marriage, primitive promiscuity, the transition from a four (section) to an eight (subsection) class system, and the origin of human society, were central in anthropological debate.

The Lutheran missionary Louis Schulze, who had arrived in Hermannsburg in the late 1870s, appears to be the first to report on the subsection system in this region (Schulze 1891: 223–227). However, it was through Spencer and Gillen that their forms of social classification became a seminal case. In particular, the eight-class system, today called the 'subsection-system', was much discussed. Radcliffe-Brown even named the system and its attendant kinship 'Arandic' after them. Frazer understood these aspects of indigenous Australian culture as survivals of a past stage in human social development, from a distant past, like other facets of Aboriginal life.

L.H. Morgan had put the classificatory kinship systems of indigenous societies on to the anthropological agenda, but his aim was to fit the kinship systems of the world into an evolutionary chain. Fox remarks:

> At least half the anthropological literature on kinship has been largely concerned with the terms various systems employed in addressing and referring to kinsfolk and affines. Morgan saw in the study of terminology the royal road to the understanding of kinship systems. He was the first to see that the terminology was a method of classification, and that what it told us was how various systems classified 'kin'. If we could understand this, we could understand the system. 'Understanding' for Morgan, however, meant understanding the evolution of kinship systems, and what the terminology held for him was the clue to the past state of the system. (Fox 1967a: 240)

The study of kinship as social organisation in indigenous society was only slowly emerging at the turn of the century. W.H.R. Rivers had given it an

---

1   Von Leonhardi to Carl Strehlow, 2.6.1906.

impetus with his genealogical method which proceeded from the 'concrete to the abstract' (Langham 1981; Stocking 1983: 85–89). Rivers' method involved collecting genealogies – a genealogical grid – and on it imposing the particular terms, or social classifications, of a particular people. The grid was constructed by requesting the personal names of a person's 'mother', 'father', 'children' and the like and then the 'native' terms for these relatives were listed. Rivers recommended multiple sources as a methodological check. The same set of relatives with their personal names and kin term could be elicited from a range of linked individuals. Through this method, Rivers 'rediscovered' the phenomenon of kinship 'classification' common in Australia whereby parallel cousins, for instance, are designated by the same term, 'sister' and 'brother', and by their children as 'mother' and 'father', just as reciprocally these children refer to each other and are referred to as 'sister' and 'brother'. Rivers, however, took a further step of seeing in the genealogical method a means for studying 'society'. The codes for conduct (see Schneider 1968: 29) or social rules attached to these terms provided a portrait of social order, or 'social structure' as Radcliffe-Brown would term it. According to Fox, 'Radcliffe-Brown – also turning his back on evolution, but retaining the interest in terminology, produced a new and elegant comparative approach to kinship which sought to make generalizations about kinship systems, comparable to the "laws" of natural science' (Fox 1967a: 21).

Carl Strehlow's research lacked a framework that would have led him towards such a study of social structure. He did not integrate his data into a theory of how a society 'functions' as, afterall, the study of kinship as social organisation was just emerging. His collection provides, however, a starting point for the analysis of indigenous kinship systems, because it shows how people name their kinship universe and the manner in which they use kin terms as terms of address. What he did not do, in the fashion of Rivers, was superimpose his recording of kin terms on the genealogies that he collected. Therefore his grasp of a kinship terminology as classificatory, and its implications for a marriage rule for instance, remained somewhat tenuous. Neither was he able to superimpose the Western Aranda's subsection system over the kinship system in its entirety.

What he did do was to use his genealogical material, or family trees, as frameworks on which to record data concerning personal attributes of individuals – their 'totems' and their skin or subsection names. He also looked at family trees in tandem, interpreting the multiple relations between affines across a number of generations. He thereby gave a sense of what it was to address a small-scale society through kinship and in this task von Leonhardi posed a series of scholarly questions. I will discuss three different aspects of Strehlow's data on Aranda and Loritja kinship and individuals: the subsection system, kin terminology and genealogies. Although he did not employ his genealogies as Rivers and his followers would, his use of them had far-reaching implications for Aranda and Loritja people at Hermannsburg, and for subsequent anthropologists.

Carl Strehlow's data on social classification

Without doubt Carl Strehlow's main contribution to Australian anthropology was his myth collections and his language studies. Yet his ethnographic work includes some useful and important data on social classification. He collected a vast number of kinship terms that are still in use today. His collection provides a starting point for the analysis of indigenous kinship systems, because it shows how people classify their kinship universe and 'when we want to understand the kinship rules and behaviour of any people we must ask how they classify kin and on what basis they make distinctions' (Fox 1967a: 262).

Through his long residence at Hermannsburg, Carl Strehlow developed a sense of specifying different forms of Western Aranda and Loritja social relations. He saw that they had a particular form of social life and moral arrangements. He documented this in regard to the class system (section and subsection systems) and by compiling impressive lists of kin terms that showed how Aranda and Loritja people classified their kin in a kin universe, as well as how these systems connected with each other.

His kinship data were based on research he had conducted since 1892 with Diyari, Aranda and Loritja people, and by living and participating in everyday life of Aboriginal people at Hermannsburg and Bethesda. Letters by Gillen (1896),[2] Siebert (1899)[3] and Mathews (1906/7)[4] indicate that Carl Strehlow had systematically collected kinship terms and data on the subsection systems of the Aranda and Loritja at least since 1896. Strehlow approached social classification initially through collecting section, subsection and kin terms, and seems only to have started to collect family trees in 1907 or 1908.[5] Von Leonhardi sent some samples of family trees from Germany showing how they were best recorded from an individual's point of view.[6] His editor may have known the 'genealogical method', as he read Rivers, and this may have prompted his request. Carl Strehlow used these genealogies to illustrate how subsection systems categorised people into groups whose members could or could not be marriage partners.

The following discussion is based on a chapter called *The Marriage Order* in volume five (Strehlow 1913: 62–89) which explores not only 'marriage rules', but also the moiety division, section and subsection systems, classificatory kinship and family trees. At the time it was believed that at the core of indigenous kinship lay the function of marriage regulation and indeed the section system 'used to be called [a] "marriage-class system" and was believed to regulate marriage'

---

2   F. Gillen to B. Spencer, 14.7.1896 (Mulvaney, Morphy and Petch 2001: 130).
3   O. Siebert to A. Howitt, 22.8.1899 (Melbourne Museum).
4   Carl Strehlow to R.H. Mathews, 1906–1907 (NLA 8006/2/4).
5   On the 18.8.1909 von Leonhardi confirmed in a letter to Carl Strehlow the receipt of 20 family trees.
6   Von Leonhardi to Carl Strehlow, 8.12.1907.

(Fox 1967: 188). However, the section and subsection systems are not the basis of marriage rules (Dousset 2005: 15) and marriage calculations are not their only function. These systems are mainly intra- and inter-language group devices to facilitate interaction and communication – often at ceremonial events. Nor is a kinship system a marriage system. Rather, such a system contains a marriage rule. Carl Strehlow did not distinguish clearly between a kinship system, a marriage rule that complements the kinship system, and a subsection system which classifies people according to kinship categories but is not a kinship system or a marriage rule in itself.

The subsection system

Carl Strehlow's account of the 'marriage order' starts with the basic division that organises Aranda society into two groups: exogamous moieties. These patrimoieties were called 'Nákarakia' (our kindred or people)[7] and 'Etnákarakia' (those people or that kindred) or 'Maljanuka' (my friends) by the Aranda. These terms were not names for one or the other moiety but were reciprocally used by both groups (Strehlow 1913: 62). Today Arandic people still refer – from an egocentric point of view – to such groupings that are maljanuka or malyenweke and nákarakia or ilakekeye. Malyenweke means 'them' or 'our in-laws' while ilakekeye means 'us'. In one's own patrimoiety, that is ilakekeye, are one's actual and classificatory fathers and their siblings, father's fathers and son's children, and also one's mother's mother's patriline which is part of ilakekeye, 'us'. In the opposite moiety, malyenweke, in addition to one's spouse and brothers-in-law there are one's actual and classificatory mothers, mother's brothers and mother's fathers and also one's father's mother. Like the Aranda, the Kukatja-Loritja used particular terms for the members of these groups reciprocally. All relatives of an ego's group (own patrimoiety) were called 'Ngananukarpitina' meaning 'all of us'; and all relatives of the opposite moiety were called 'Tananukarpitina' meaning 'all of them' (Strehlow 1913: 79). In societies organised in this way one should always marry someone from the opposite moiety.

Strong kinship ties exist between these two social groups. Some people in the opposite moiety, for example, play a crucial role in ceremonial matters relating to land. They create relationships which serve to articulate ownership of land such that the 'patrimoiety division broadly correlates with complementary roles associated with rights and responsibilities associated with country, sites and ceremonies' (Green 1998: 11). The most important partners in matters of land management and ceremony, are usually recruited from the opposite moiety, and preferably, also from a particular patricouple.

---

7   See Strehlow (1913: 62, fn. 5) for an elaborate attempt on the possible etymology of these reciprocal terms.

The two exogamous groups are further divided into two or four classes, called sections and subsections today. Carl Strehlow recorded that the Southern Aranda had a '4-class system' and the Aranda 'living north of latitude 24 degrees possess 4 marriage classes in each moiety, they have thus, a 8-class system' (Strehlow 1913: 62). He wrote that according to Aranda tradition these divisions were established in a mythological past:

> This division of the people into different marriage-classes is regarded as being of very ancient origin and is already hinted at in the legends concerning the people of primordial times. Even before Mangarkunjerkunja had formed the people, the undeveloped rella manerinja were divided into two strictly separated groups. While the members of one group lived on dry land and were therefore known as alarinja, the members of the other group, having long hair and feeding on raw meat, lived in water and were therefore called kwatjarinja. (Strehlow 1913: 62)

According to Aranda mythology the moiety called 'alarinja' was divided into Purula (Pwerrerle), Kamara (Kemarre), Ngala (Ngale) and Mbitjana (Mpetyane); and the other moiety 'kwatjarinja' into Pananka (Penangke), Paltara (Peltharre), Knuraia (Kngwarreye) and Bangata (Pengarte). In the Southern Aranda myth on the section-system, the alarinja group was composed of Purula (Pwerrerle) and Kamara (Kemarre), while the kwatjarinja group was comprised of Pananka (Penangke) and Paltara (Peltharre).

	Northern/Eastern/(Western) Aranda	Southern Aranda
	(Subsections)	(Sections)
Alarinja:	Purula-Kamara, Ngale-Mbitjana	Purula-Kamara
Kwatjarinja:	Pananka-Bangata, Paltara-Knuraia	Pananka-Paltara

16. Alarinja and Kwatjarinja of the Aranda.

Source: Strehlow 1913.

Each moiety includes two generational pairs in father-child relationships. These pairs are called patricouples and in Aranda 'njinaŋa' (nyenhenge) (T.G.H. Strehlow 1947, 1965). The patricouples Kamara-Purula and Ngala-Mbitjana form one moiety and Paltara-Knuraia and Bangata-Pananka the other. Aranda marriage rules prescribe that Kamara marries Paltara, Purula marries Pananka, Ngala marries Knuraia and Mbitjana marries Bangata. Carl Strehlow (1913: 63) shows this pattern in the following way, A and B are parents and C their children:

A.		B.		C.
Purula m.	+	Pananka f. :		Kamara
Kamara m.	+	Paltara f. :		Purula
Ngala m.	+	Knuraia f. :		Mbitjana
Mbitjana m.	+	Bangata f. :		Ngala
B.		A.		C.
Pananka m.	+	Purula f. :		Bangata
Paltara m.	+	Kamara f. :		Knuraia
Knuraia m.	+	Ngala f. :		Paltara
Bangata m.	+	Mbitjana f. :		Pananka

17. Aranda 'marriage rules'.

Source: Strehlow 1913.

This system, called by Aboriginal people in central Australia 'skin', has been chartered by the Institute of Aboriginal Development in the following way:

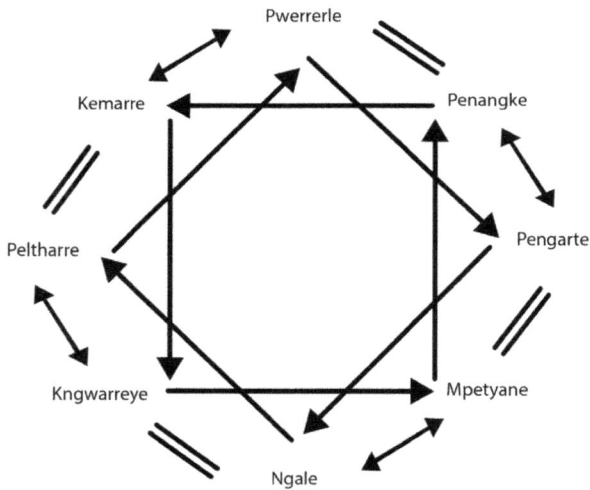

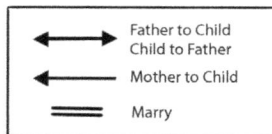

18. Arandic skin chart.

Source: Henderson and Dobson 1994.

Strehlow wrote that the Western Loritja, i.e. the Kukatja-Loritja, had a 'marriage order' identical to the one of the Aranda. They too divided their society into two exogamous groups and into subsections. He made a brief remark on the Southern Loritja, observing that they did not have a section or subsection system. Nevertheless, they did use the reciprocal terms 'Ngananu-karpitina and Tananukarpitina' for patrimoieties, Western Loritja kin terms and the same basic marriage regulation of the Aranda and Loritja, i.e. the grandchildren of different sex siblings, or the children of cross-cousins were preferred marriage partners (Strehlow 1913: 87).

Further, Strehlow described how the sections of the Aranda-Lada and Aranda-Tanka in the south and the sub-section system of Western Aranda could interlock, and that Loritja subsections are compatible with the ones of the Aranda. To him the Loritja subsection terms seemed to have been originally based on the Aranda terms, with the addition of the prefix 'Ta'[8] to indicate a male subsection name and 'Na' a female subsection name. Thus, the Loritja have differentiating subsection terms for their male and female members, which the Aranda do not have.

Eastern/Central Arrernte[i]	Western Aranda[ii]	Loritja[iii]
Angale	Ngala	Ta/Nangala
Ampetyane	Mbitjana	Ta/Nambitjinba
Peltharre	Paltara	Ta/Napaltara
Kngwarreye	Knuraia	T/Nungaraiï
Kemarre	Kamara	Ta/Nakamara
Perrurle	Purula	Ta/Napurula
Pengarte	Bangata	Ta/Nabangati
Penangke	Pananka	Ta/Napananka

i. Reproduced from Henderson and Dobson (1994: 42).

ii. Carl Strehlow's Aranda spelling of subsections.

iii. Carl Strehlow's Loritja spelling of subsections. For a modern spelling of the Luritja terms see the Pintupi-Luritja kinship learning material (Institute of Linguistics 1979).

These observations on how the section and subsection systems interlocked, how people were shifted into different categories and from which areas they came as well as the time frame when this data was collected (1896–1909), are particularly interesting when placed in the context of comments on the diffusion of section and subsection systems and names across Australia. Among others Spencer and Gillen (1899, 1927), T.G.H. Strehlow (1947, 1971, 1999), McConvell (1985) and Dousset (2005), have observed that these systems diffused into the desert areas of Australia. McConvell (1985) suggests that the systems

---

8   Today 'Tja' is used.

of the Aranda had come from the Pilbara; it had diffused fanlike to the east and south-east as far as Southern Aranda territory. Dousset (2005: 40) maintains that the section names Kemarre and Penangke of the Southern Aranda had come from the Pilbara. As the western section system met in the north-east with a section system in the Victoria River Downs (VRD) area, it created a subsection system that facilitated marriage arrangements and probably ritual and social interaction. This subsection system then made its way south towards Aranda country (McConvell 1985).

In 1896 Spencer and Gillen (1899: 72; 1927: 42; T.G.H. Strehlow 1947: 72) recorded that the Central Aranda had originally only a section system and that the additional terms for a subsection system had been a recent borrowing:

> This division into eight has been adopted (or rather the names for the four new divisions have been), in recent times by the Arunta tribe from the Ilpirra tribe which adjoins the former on the north, and the use of them is, at the present time spreading southwards. At the Engwura ceremony which we witnessed men of the Ilpirra tribe were present, as well as a large number of others from the southern part of the Arunta amongst whom the four new names are not yet in use. (Spencer and Gillen 1899: 72)

It is believed that the subsection system is a relatively recent borrowing or innovation in Arandic cultures. The cosmologies of the Western Aranda and Loritja, however, may indicate that the subsection system is an institution of 'ancient origins' (relatively speaking) in Carl Strehlow's study area (Strehlow 1907, 1908, 1913). His data support Spencer and Gillen's and McConvell's hypothesis of the southwards movement of the subsection system, in so far as he described in detail how one system locks into the other and that it had been spreading southwards. At the same time the narratives about Mangarkunjerkunja ancestors (Strehlow 1907: 6–8), suggest that the subsection system had been for quite some time in use on Western Aranda and Kukatja-Loritja territory when Spencer and Gillen were studying the 'Arunta' at Alice Springs in 1896.

Strehlow's myth data may indicate that the systems had possibly fallen into disrepair and had been 're-established' (Strehlow 1907: 6–9). At different times, 'Mangarkunjerkunja' ancestors came from the north teaching the subsection system and the 'marriage-rule', and even later on a third ancestor called Katukunkara had to reinforce the system that had been abandoned. What this really means is impossible to know. It may indicate that at different times in the past, regional meetings of people occurred that introduced new concepts or reinforced communication modes that had not been used for a while. The subsection system is very likely to have been one of them that cross-cut linguistic and social boundaries. He remarks that it is noteworthy that in Aranda traditions all good laws come from the north and the bad spread from the south (Strehlow 1907: 8).

On a more practical note, T.G.H. Strehlow's material, recorded in the 1930s, suggests that the diffusion was not a simple process. Difficulties were encountered to fit one system into the other. He recorded a scathing remark about the subsection system from the north that the Southern Aranda felt was being forced upon them:

> The four-class system is the better of the two for us Southerners; we cannot understand the eight-class system. It is mad and purposeless, and only fit for such crazy men as the Northern Aranda are; we did not inherit such a stupid tradition from our fathers. (Strehlow 1947: 72)

Still decades later in the early 1980s Ray Wood, a consultant anthropologist, recalls his senior Pertame (Southern Aranda) informants complaining about the subsection system:

> The older Pertame generation I worked with in the 1980s told me that there was still only a 4-section system when they were young, and the 8-subsection system has been coming in since then. They said its introduction made for all sorts of complications, even splitting descent groups and sometimes siblings into different patricouples, due to e.g. different mothers, marriages, and/or its differing introduction at different places in the Pertame region, like Horseshoe Bend versus Orange Creek.

> I often noticed that they themselves still struggled with the 8 system quite a bit, and sometimes told me a given apical figure was of this subsection, only to later revise it to another, told me it would be x if you figured it out through Maryvale or through certain of their kin, but y if you figured it out another way etc.[9]

Today most Pertame use the subsection system in inter-group dealings and will readily supply the information of the existence of eight skin names. However, it seems that intra-group dealings may not rely entirely on the subsection system and may be the reason for the oversight of two subsection names that did not appear in a recent Pertame wordlist (Swan and Cousen 1993). T.G.H. Strehlow made another interesting observation on the transition from one into the other system in his family tree FT I. 28, which is based on his father's family tree F.T.

---

9   Ray Wood, email, 14.8.2006.

XXVIII (see also T.G.H. Strehlow 1999). He remarked that 'C.S.'s class-names have been preserved throughout, so as to show the continual wavering and hesitation of his informants when assigning class names to the people in this F.T'.[10]

Today, it is clear that the function of the subsection system is to facilitate group interaction, ritual-exchange and marriage (Elkin 1932; Myers [1986] 1991; T.G.H. Strehlow 1999; Dousset 2005: 78–80). They are convenient social labels and propose global categories for ranges of behaviour that are especially useful in inter-group gatherings and communication. Dousset writes that the section system is 'convenient in the context of contact' and 'that contact is indeed their vehicle for diffusion' (Dousset 2005: 82). What Dousset says about the section system may also be said about the application of the subsection system of the Aranda and Loritja today:

> Such contacts were either traditional – based on networks linking neighbouring groups for ceremonial, economic and marital exchanges and relations – or they were "new", resulting from colonisation's and settlement's increasing effect on inter-group relations and modes of communication. In every case, sections are a lingua franca of kinship, which in turn propose a formal framework for interaction among humans. (Dousset 2005: 82–83)

At Hermannsburg where people were forced together, the compatibility of Aranda and Loritja subsections would have been of invaluable use, because many people were concentrated at the mission who under other circumstances would not have had to interact with the same intensity. It is likely that in this period the compatibility of Aranda and Loritja 'skins' became firmly established, as they had to accommodate and reconcile the new living conditions at the Lutheran mission settlement.

Aranda and Loritja kin terminology

Carl Strehlow made a significant contribution in the area of kinship studies by collecting a vast number of kinship terms (Strehlow 1913: 66–69, 81–85). He described the kinship system as encompassing the whole society. Aranda and Loritja kinship terms could be used for all members of the society without taking 'blood' ties into consideration, although there were ways to describe closeness of relatedness. He observed that every child is born into a particular subsection and thus enters into a certain kin relationship to all other subsections, regardless of whether or not blood ties exist. On the Loritja terminology he remarked that 'The relationships between a member of a certain subsection and the members

---

10   T.G.H. Strehlow's FT I. 28.

of all the other subsections is expressed in kinship terms in Loritja society, regardless of existing blood relationship or the lack of it' (Strehlow 1913: 79). In daily life, the presence or absence of known genealogical connections are not distinguished (Strehlow 1913: 63), and each person stands in a set of relations to others described in kin terms. On both these counts this system differs from a European one.

In a classificatory system, certain kin terms are used to cover a wide range of relatives who are regarded as equivalents of one's father, mother, brother, sister and so forth. For example, in Western Aranda, kata (karte), the term for father, covers all father's brothers, who in English would be called uncles. The term for mother, maia (meye), is used for all mother's sisters, who in English we would call aunties. Maia also includes daughter-in-law, from a man's point of view. Wanna (wenhe), the term for aunt, is applied to father's sisters as well as mother's brother's wife, and from a woman's point of view, it can also include her mother-in-law. The term for uncle, kamuna (kamerne), includes mother's brothers and father's sister's husband. From this it can be seen that the classificatory kinship system not only incorporates consanguineal, but also affinal relatives. Loritja classify their kinsfolk, including affines, in a similar way, although there are differences.

Where some relatives whom Europeans distinguish are classified together in the Aranda system, others who bear the same European term, are distinguished by Aranda speakers. For example, Western Aranda used and still use four different terms for one's grandparents. The terms are aranga (arrenge) for father's father, tjimia (tyemeye) for mother's father, palla (perle) for father's mother and ebmanna (ipmenhe) for mother's mother. The grandparental terms are also used to cover one's grandparents' siblings as well as one's grandchildren on a reciprocal basis. The term for one's father's father, aranga, for example, includes father's father's brothers and sisters and son's sons and daughters. Relationships with grandparents are of particular importance to the question of land-ownership. Carl Strehlow's Loritja kin data records also four grandparental terms (Strehlow 1913: 81–82), but today only two seem to be in use: tjamu for grandfathers (father's father and mother's father) and kami for grandmothers (father's mother and mother's mother) (Sackett 1994: 31; Vaarzon-Morel and Sackett 1997: 36). However, there are ways to express which grandfather is spoken of, in particular when reference is made to land-ownership (Sackett 1994: 31–32).

Strehlow explains the kinship classification of the Aranda and Loritja via the subsection system which locks into the kinship system. He uses as an example of how a Purula man not only calls his natural brothers kalia (older brother) or itia (younger brother) but also calls all other Purula belonging to the same generation as himself brother or sister. At the same time he calls all Purula in the generation above or below him aranga, which is the term for his father's father as well as his natural (and classificatory) son's son, who are both Purula.

As an Aranda person, who has been born into a subsection, can be placed into three connections to the other subsections — on an equal, higher or lower generational level — it follows that just 24 classificatory kin-terms would be required. However, gender and age (whether older or younger than the person speaking), also bear on the kin terms used making for a larger number of terms (Strehlow 1913: 63). To illustrate this point, Strehlow compiled an extensive list of the terms used for classificatory and 'blood' relatives which show how close and distant kin are labelled (Strehlow 1913: 66–70).

Typical for his time Carl Strehlow presented kinship terms at a distance from social life. He did not indicate that they may imply 'codes for conduct' which include avoidance and respect rules, obligations and rights, but for a brief remark in a section called *Marriage Customs* (Strehlow 1913: 89–94) on obligations and behaviour of spouses towards their in-laws:

> The husband is obliged to continue to furnish his father-in-law, whom he calls antara tualtja, with food, particularly with meat. Should he kill a kangaroo, for example, then he has to give a large piece of it to his father-in-law. ... He is further required to give his shorn-off hair to his father-in-law, who will make strings etc. out of it. At the death of his father-in-law he will let his shoulder be scratched with a stone knife (unangarala kalama, from unangara = shoulder, and kalama = to cut oneself) until the blood flows, as a sign of sorrow. Were he to omit this, he might conceivably be clubbed to death by his own relatives. Following the death of his father-in-law, he gives his own shorn-off hair to a brother of the latter.

> The husband is not allowed to speak to his mother-in-law marra tualtja while she resides in the camp. Indeed, he may not even approach her. Should he encounter her outside the camp, he may communicate with her from a distance by means of the common secret language ankatja kerintja, or in the sign language to be described at a later stage. ... The mother-in-law on her part must avoid the hut of her son-in-law and is obliged to give him the hair shorn off her head, so that he can make himself a belt or other strings from it. At his death, the mother-in-law punctures her head with a stone so that blood gushes out of it. (Strehlow 1913: 90–91)

Later, the study of kin terms developed into a study of social terms of address and inter-relations. Green's account of the use of kinship terminology in Arandic languages, for example, demonstrates how the terms work in their social context and how kinship relationships contain behavioural patterns (Green 1998; see also Institute of Linguistics 1979; Centre for Indigenous Development Education and Research 1996). While Carl Strehlow described the regular use of kin terms, Green (1998) explores their actual and pragmatic application taking social context into account which determines their use and may appear as an irregular use of terminology. Also T.G.H. Strehlow (1999) shows that in reality irregularities were not out of the order. There was and is flexibility in a classificatory kin universe that allows variations.

Finally, following the explanation of how section and subsection systems interlock, how they related to a kinship system, and how kin terms are used in relation to close and distant relatives, Carl Strehlow addressed the Aranda's marriage rule. In their system it is the rule to marry one's second cross cousin: a mother's mother's brother's daughter's daughter or MMBDD (Scheffler 1978: 42) who is also a father's mother's brother's son's daughter or FMBSD (Fox 1967: 196). Carl Strehlow's investigation puts great emphasis on the fact of this preferential rule:

> Its most important principle is found in the rule that the pallukua, the grand-children of brothers and sisters (it is immaterial whether they are real brothers and sisters or regarded as siblings according to their class), should marry each other, and that according to their class they are in a relationship of noa = spouse to each other already from birth. The following two tables should demonstrate that this will often lead to the marriage of the grand-children of two natural siblings, and many more examples could be given. (Strehlow 1913: 70)

He included here a discussion on patrilineal descent, although he considered that Spencer and Gillen's work had sufficiently demonstrated that the Aranda and other peoples in central Australia traced descent through the patriline and that subsection names were inherited through fathers or more correctly from father's fathers in alternating generations. The discussion of patrilineal descent and that the subsection is inherited from father's father, one's aranga (Strehlow 1913: 71–72), was motivated by his disagreement with R.H. Mathews who was using material supplied by him[11] without quoting him and arranging it arbitrarily to support his theory that descent is traced matrilineally amongst Aranda people and their subsections are allocated through their mothers (Mathews 1908). Von Leonhardi assured Strehlow that 'Mathews does not understand the marriage laws and classes, not that he would be the only one.'[12]

---

11 Carl Strehlow to R.H. Mathews, 1906–1907 (NLA 8006/2/4).
12 Von Leonhardi to Carl Strehlow, 2.6.1907 and 26.2.1909.

In Aranda society, Strehlow as well as his son maintained, that it is the father's fathers who always give their grandsons their subsection, whether the mother is from the correct subsection or not, the children always belong to the subsection of their father's father (Strehlow 1913: 71–72; Strehlow 1999: 23, 29). To this day, Western Aranda people generally allocate subsections according to father and father's father's subsections.

Carl Strehlow's genealogies

Although Carl Strehlow had recorded all births, deaths and Christian marriages at Hermannsburg since 1894, he seems only to have started to collect family trees when researching social classification with von Leonhardi. He compiled 28 family trees[13] of Aranda families incorporating Loritja people who were living at the Hermannsburg Mission and had Aranda spouses (Strehlow 1913: 85). Only a small portion of his genealogical material was published to illustrate the 'marriage-order' of the Aranda and one 'imaginary family tree of a Loritja belonging to the Takamara class', because he believed that 'one would have had to live among the Loritja for several years and have gained sufficient knowledge of the individuals in order to draw up a really reliable family tree' (Strehlow 1913: 85). His genealogies were supplemented in 1920 with a remarkable index of all indigenous names of the people appearing on them and what they mean (Strehlow 1920: 15–39).

At the beginning of the twentieth century it was not clear in anthropology what 'kinship' should really mean, hence, sociocultural and biological aspects were not carefully distinguished or recognised. European notions of what constituted a family and marriage, what descent and kin terms like father, mother, and so on meant, were taken for granted or at least not well defined (see Schneider 1984: 97–112). To make this point Schneider maintained that 'anthropology's whole enterprise of treating kinship as a genealogical grid laid over the assumed facts of biology was misguided; instead, it was the "core symbols" that defined what kinship was for a given culture' (Silverman 2005: 289). During the 1970s he even rejected the anthropological concept of kinship itself, 'claiming it was nothing more than anthropologists turning their own, Western symbolic system into a universal theory' (Silverman 2005: 320).

Clearly, the European concept of 'family tree' was for Strehlow's study of indigenous kinship inadequate. The notions of consanguinity, apical ancestors and bias towards patrilineal descent attached to a European family tree[14] were

---

13 T.G.H. Strehlow's FT I. 28 and Book of XVII, p. 118a bottom.
14 European traditions tend to have a patrilineal bias for inheritance of surnames and property or accession to a throne, for example. It is nevertheless bilateral and/or cognatic in general character. These sorts of

not sufficient to describe the complexities of classificatory kinship systems, that, for instance, included affines to a much larger degree and categorised close and distant kin not by the sole criteria of 'blood ties'. A European family tree represents a particular universe of biological facts (ideally) which includes the same range of relatives that can be theoretically traced in every society. Descent is commonly understood as consanguine and patrilineal, which suggests ancestry many generations deep with apical ancestors. Aranda and Loritja people did not think of themselves and their relatives, or relatedness, in this way. In Aboriginal societies these links are often assumed, putative and classificatory, and can include 'consanguinity' under certain (ethno-scientific) aspects. The kin universe of indigenous people was vertically shallow, but horizontally very differentiated and wide. The main direction of reckoning kinship was and still is within two descending and ascending generational levels. For instance, the descendants of older and younger brothers and sisters would have been of importance, not an apical ancestor who had lived before their time, and a large number of affines would be included.

The fact that Aboriginal people generally do not remember the names of their great-grandparents, although there are ways to address them if they are still alive (Green 1998: 29), and that the names of deceased people in central Australian cultures were (Strehlow 1915: 17; Meggitt 1966: 5) and are taboo (see also Sansom 2006: 156–157), indicates that a European mode of genealogy-taking could not and would not capture Aranda and Loritja kinship adequately. In addition, it was and is inappropriate in many situations to make inquires about the deceased.[15]

Aranda people today, for example, use the word Kwementyaye (Breen 2000: 27) in place of the name of a deceased person or try to replace the name of a living person altogether finding a synonym. Only after an adequate amount of time has elapsed, is a name put back into circulation and will be associated with a living person. Hamilton (1998: 102) remarked that 'the taboo on the names of deceased persons, and the desire to erase their memory as soon as possible, ensures that no precise genealogical knowledge can be maintained.' Also Meggitt ([1962] 1986: 194) observed that Warlpiri 'men were rarely sure of details of genealogy in their grandparents' generation-level' and Peterson adds that 'young children often do not remember their genitor and this, combined with the prohibition on the mentioning of the names of the dead and the dependence of children on

---

differences also apply in Aboriginal Australia, not least in relation to distinctions between 'actual' relatives as opposed to more nominal ones.

15   Often researchers have to describe 'in a round about way' a person who has a tabooed name and has to ask if it is allowed to say that name. In June 2006, for example, I was asked not to use the Luritja word tjala (honeyant), it had been temporarily taken out of circulation in this particular family due to a recent death. On this occasion I was also informed that the word apme (snake) had been replaced by arnerenye (belonging to the earth/ground or living in the earth/ground) in the Hermannsburg area.

their mothers who are therefore likely to be the main teacher of the terminology, emphasises the tracing of social links through women' (Peterson 1969: 29). Sansom (2006: 153; 2007) makes a strong point that in Aboriginal cultures there are mechanisms specifically to support 'forgetting'.

It is rather unusual to find an Aboriginal person even today who can reproduce their genealogical links beyond their grandparents without the help of archival records. In some cases the answer, when seeking names of great-grandparents, may be jukurrpa or tjukurrpa by Warlpiri and Luritja people – referring to the dreaming. I have, however, not heard this reply from Western Aranda people. This may be the result of their sustained exposure to Lutheran culture and a 'family tree tradition', as well as their relative early sedentarisation at Hermannsburg. Aboriginal people did not have a tradition like the Pashtuns of Afghanistan, or Hawaiians, who incorporated their genealogies into oral traditions (Sansom 2006: 153, 158).

Despite the limited notions of European family trees, Carl Strehlow's genealogies contain valuable data. He did not present ego's descent as strictly patrilineal in his published family trees. He included a number of ancestors whose descendants had intermarried and shows their relatedness, rather than unilinear descent from one apical ancestor. His published family trees illustrate multi-lateral descent of a particular individual and his spouse. The couples Ipitarintja and Laramananka (1,1a), Loatjira and Ilbaltalaka (2,2a), Nguaperaka and Lakarinja (3,3a) and Erenkeraka and Kaputatjalka (4,4a) were placed in the centre of his published genealogies (Strehlow 1913: Stammbäume). His unpublished family trees, in contrast, traced patrilineal descent from an apical ancestor, which were the model that his son and the Finke River Mission would adopt.

The obvious data on Carl Strehlow's genealogies include personal Aboriginal and sometimes European names, if they had been baptised at birth or had converted,[16] subsection affiliations and 'consanguine' relatedness; this data has assisted in land and native title claims to identify appropriate claimants. He also included the 'ratapa' and 'altjira' of most people appearing in his family trees. Both terms are polysemic expressions. In the context of his family trees, 'ratapa' means the conception dreaming of a person, which could be acquired in three ways. Von Leonhardi summarised how this dreaming association could be acquired:

> Either an embryo (ratapa), living in the metamorphosed body of an altjirangamitjina, enters the body of a woman passing by, in which case the child would be born with a narrow face, or a "totem ancestor" emerges from the earth and throws a small bullroarer at a woman, in whose body

---

16   At the mission generally only the Christians had European names.

the bullroarer turns into a child which would then be born with a broad face. Apart from these two methods of conceiving a child some of the blacks also report rare cases of an altjirangamitjina entering a woman and thus being reincarnated. The old men, too, eventually admitted this. Such a reincarnation is possible only once. (Strehlow 1907: Preface)

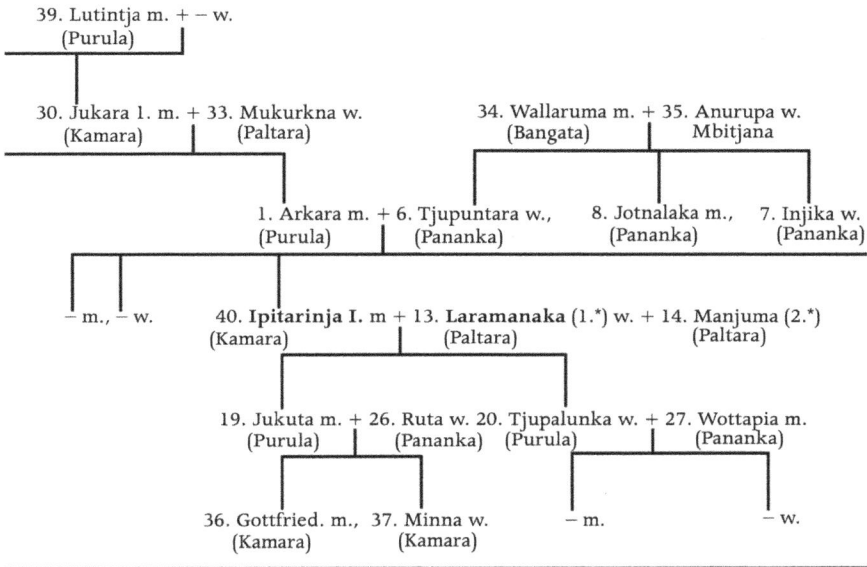

```
39. Lutintja m. + − w.
    (Purula)

30. Jukara 1. m. + 33. Mukurkna w.          34. Wallaruma m. + 35. Anurupa w.
    (Kamara)       (Paltara)                    (Bangata)        Mbitjana

        1. Arkara m. + 6. Tjupuntara w.,    8. Jotnalaka m.,   7. Injika w.
           (Purula)      (Pananka)             (Pananka)         (Pananka)

− m., − w.     40. Ipitarinja I. m + 13. Laramanaka (1.*) w. + 14. Manjuma (2.*)
                   (Kamara)          (Paltara)                     (Paltara)

        19. Jukuta m. + 26. Ruta w. 20. Tjupalunka w. + 27. Wottapia m.
            (Purula)      (Pananka)    (Purula)           (Pananka)

        36. Gottfried. m.,  37. Minna w.    − m.              − w.
            (Kamara)            (Kamara)
```

	Ratapa:	Altjira:
39. Lutintjia	putaia (Wallay, spec.)	lupa (?) Akacie (spec.)
30. Jukara I.	rakara (Vogelart)	ibiljakua (Ente)
33. Mukurkna I.	ara (rotes Känguruh)	tjunba (Varanus giganteus)
1. Arkara	arkara (Vogelart)	ara (rotes Känguruh)
6. Tjupuntara	ilia (Emu)	?
40. Ipitarinja I.	jerramba (Honigameise)	ilia (Emu)
13. Laramanaka	ara (rotes Känguruh)	tjurka (Feige)
19. Jukuta	rukuta (junger Mann)	ara (rotes Känguruh)
26. Ruta	ratapa (Kinderkeim)	tijlpa (Beutelmarder)
20. Tjupalunka	tjilpa (Beutelmarder)	ara (rotes Känguruh)
27. Wottapia	iwuta (Onychogale)	ilia (Emu)
36. Gottfried	ratapa (Kinderkeim)	ratapa (Kinderkeim)
37. Minna	ratapa (Kinderkeim)	ratapa (Kinderkeim)

*) 1. Frau, 2. Frau

19. Genealogy of Ipitarintja and Laramanaka.

Source: Strehlow 1913: I.

In Carl Strehlow's work the word 'ratapa' is not only used as a synonym for 'totem', but also for 'spirit child' or 'child-seeds (*Kinderkeime*)'. He wrote that this word derived from the verb 'ratana' meaning 'coming from, originating'. These spirit children were said to be invisible, but fully developed children with reddish skin colour (Strehlow 1908: 52).[17] He writes that as soon as a woman knows that she is pregnant, i.e. that a spirit child has entered her, the paternal or maternal grandfather carves a small tjurunga with the designs of the ancestor from whom it emerged and stores it in the rock cave where all the other objects are stored. When the baby is crying, it is said to be crying for the tjurunga that is lost when entering into the mother. The tjurunga is called in the presence of women and children 'papa'. To calm the child the relevant tjurunga is taken from the cave, wrapped with strings, to prevent women from seeing it, and laid in the wooden baby carrying tray where it emanates secret powers into the child that makes it grow quickly (Strehlow 1908: 80).

The word 'altjira' in this context[18] references yet again another spirit entity. It is used for mother's conception dreaming. Carl Strehlow describes the relationship that a person has generally to mother's conception dreaming as follows:

> However, every person is also connected with another particular totem which is called altjira. This is the totem of his mother. Every native sees this as the animal or plant, whichever might be the case, that belongs to him, and therefore calls it his garra altjira or deba altjira. The Aranda permit the consumption of these maternal totem animals or totem plants respectively. Although all the children of one family, i.e. of one mother, may each belong to a different totem (ratapa), they nevertheless share another totem (altjira). (Strehlow 1908: 57)

There are a number of remarks which indicate that also other words could be used to denote personal and mother's conception dreaming. He noted, for example, that 'A person's specific altjirangamitjina is called iningukua; the altjirangamitjina of one's mother is simply called altjira' (Strehlow 1907: 3). The word 'iningukua' means 'spirit double' and does not seem to be in use anymore. Western Aranda people call this type of spirit 'pmere kwetethe' (Kenny 2004a,b). Thus, altjira can also mean spirit double of one's mother; and one's own spirit double is called 'iningukua'. However, in a more general context von Leonhardi remarked that 'iningukua' was an alternative name for 'altjirangamitjina' (Strehlow 1910: 7), which means dreaming ancestor. He explains that 'the specific altjirangamitjina, from whose metamorphosed body the ratapa emerges, is described as the iningukua of the person concerned' (Strehlow 1908: 53).

---

17   T.G.H. Strehlow maintained that only the spirit children of Ntaria were called ratapa (Strehlow [1964] 1978).
18   See Chapter VI for discussion on altjira's semantic field.

Carl Strehlow does not mention in his entire work that a dreaming could be patrilineally inherited. This is rather intriguing, in view of later emphasis on patrilineal connections to dreamings in Australian anthropological literature, including his son's work and among the Western Aranda themselves. I will discuss this issue in the following chapter.

Carl and T.G.H. Strehlow's family trees in the present

Carl Strehlow did not use family trees as an instrument of social analysis. He used them as a matrix to show classification of kin, and as a vehicle for collating data on individuals. Nevertheless, they have influenced the family documentation of Western Aranda people. His family trees have determined in two main ways the perception and development of family documentation in Arandic society. They provided a starting point for his son, T.G.H. Strehlow, and they seem to have initiated a practice of recording genealogical data at the Finke River Mission that went beyond the usual practice of the Lutheran church to record birth, marriage and death. It continued for the better part of a century and has to some degree impressed onto the Western Aranda themselves a concept of 'families' with apical ancestors and may have strengthened patrilineal emphasis.

T.G.H. Strehlow was in possession of his father's family trees when he produced his own genealogies nearly 50 years later. During his own research he was often only able to gather data reaching back to the grandparental generation of his informants. He incorporated his father's groundwork, only occasionally referencing it. He compiled 150 genealogies, which usually begin with an 'apical ancestor' and his wife. About 50 of these family trees are based on his father's work and thus, can be dated back to circa 1800, and further, and 'from which all authentic facts can be extracted to substantiate theories of aboriginal land rights and law'.[19]

The information on T.G.H. Strehlow's family trees is very rich, but it can only be understood in its particular theoretical and ethnographic context, which is not immediately apparent. The genealogical data are not clearly defined, as he may have assumed that anyone interested in his family trees would have read his extensive oeuvre and would be able to contextualise them. Like his father's work, his data presupposed an enormous amount of knowledge. Carl Strehlow, for example, included the 'ratapa' and 'altjira' of most people appearing in his family trees published in volume five (Strehlow 1913). It is not clear without having read volume two (Strehlow 1908) what the terms 'ratapa' or 'altjira' describe on these family trees.

---

19   T.G.H. Strehlow F.T. I. 6.

Obvious data on T.G.H. Strehlow's family trees include personal names, subsections and relatedness through apical ancestors, which evokes patrilineal descent and physical kinship. He also included labels such as 'half caste' (H.C.) or 'full-blood', which he colour coded, and sometimes supplemented with fractions, i.e. 7/8. This coding made the notions of descent and blood ties unmistakably clear. Nearly every person on these family trees has a footnote that is often cross-referenced to his diaries or to other family trees. These footnotes contain an immense variety of historical, cultural, social, geographical (location of sites, sometimes the description is in Aranda) and additional kin information as well as gossip.

The conception sites, called 'pmara kŋanintja' in T.G.H. Strehlow's work (1971: 596) and the conception 'totem', 'kŋanintja',[20] of most people can be found on his family trees. However, he does not explain these terms and abbreviations or include an explicit key or legend. The reader is left to his or her own devices to interpret, for example, 'from Emalkna; imora kŋ.' Thus, it is not surprising that many (mis)-interpretations and -understandings occur. The information on a personal conception site is often interpreted by descendants of a particular individual that this place is also associated with them and that they have traditional rights to own it. Sometimes it is even understood as the name of a traditional country or estate. The abbreviation 'kŋ.' stands for kŋanintja and 'from' refers to the place where the spirit-child entered the mother to be, i.e. the conception site of an individual, it is not a patrilineally owned place as wrongly assumed by many Aboriginal people. The example above therefore shows only that a particular person's conception site is 'Emalkna' (Mt Heuglin in the Western MacDonnell Ranges) associated with 'possum dreaming'. See also Morgan and Wilmot (2010) who have made similar observations on these matters.

According to T.G.H. Strehlow, a conception site was the place where a pregnant woman felt for the first time her baby move in her womb, and theoretically could have been on any estate where a woman had the right to forage. At these places the spirit part of a person – left behind in the landscape by the ancestral dreaming beings – entered the mother (Carl Strehlow 1908: 53, 56; T.G.H. Strehlow 1947: 87). The human soul begins its existence when the 'spirit-child' enters a pregnant woman giving the embryo a soul (Strehlow 1908: 52–56; Strehlow 1971, [1964] 1978). T.G.H. Strehlow wrote that these spirits were part of the trails of 'life', left behind throughout the landscape by the ancestral dreaming beings ([1964] 1978: 20, 22). Human children could come into being at all places situated along these trails. In *Aranda Traditions* (1947: 88), he used the word 'ŋantja' for spirit child. He also called them 'life cell' or 'life giving property', which entered a woman and developed into a human being. Pink

---

20 Unpublished dictionary K: 92; see also Strehlow 1947.

(1936: 288–290) wrote that baby-spirits gave the spirit part to human beings when entering the mother. Her Northern Aranda informants maintained that baby-spirits were left behind by a dreamtime ancestor who had left some tjurunga in the landscape.

While, according to T.G.H. Strehlow, the conception site of an individual was of great importance and prominent in an individual's life, it did not confer automatically landholding rights to any of his or her descendants, but they had the right to learn about it, if they were prepared to do so, which required engagement and effort. A conception site was associated with a particular person, unlike the dreaming places or country claimed through father and father's father which would belong to a well defined group of persons.

T.G.H. Strehlow's genealogies usually represent njinaŋa (patricouple) groups with a male apical ancestor; to a degree these genealogies were understood by him as one of the instruments for the analysis of land ownership. To most users of T.G.H. Strehlow's family trees it is not clear that they are dealing with what he called a patrilineal 'totemic clan', i.e. a njinaŋa section. He wrote in *Aranda Traditions* that he had 'attempted to introduce the term njinaŋa section to denote a group of men forming a local totemic clan' (Strehlow 1947: 143). Only the people of this group, who are patrilineally affiliated, belong to the main dreaming associated with a particular place (pmara kutata[21] in T.G.H. Strehlow's terminology) of the male apical ancestors on that particular family tree which may or may not be his conception site.

The lack of an explicit key to the Strehlow genealogies has caused much confusion and misunderstanding of what they represent. In particular when Aboriginal people access T.G.H. Strehlow's genealogical material at the Strehlow Research Centre in Alice Springs and mistake the conception sites of their ancestors with a place they may claim as their own, believing that it confers primary rights to a place or country. Also the memory of apical ancestors was not preserved in Aboriginal societies. It is only with genealogical records like the ones produced by the Strehlows, Tindale and the Finke River Mission that Aboriginal people today are able to reproduce such 'deep' genealogies. As already mentioned this is not likely to have been the way Aranda people perceived their relatedness. The reality of desert life with its particular social circumstances and traditions determined who was emphasised in a person's kinship net. The cultural significance and the appropriate interpretation of the information on these family trees can only be understood through close reading of the ethnographic works of both Strehlows. This means they have to be set in their theoretical and historical context with consideration of contemporary indigenous community politics.

---

21   See Kenny (2004a,b) for more on this term.

Hesekiel's family tree is recorded within the Strehlow Research Centre's archives.

Born in March 1889 at Ellery Creek. Hesekiel belonged to the Knuarea skin group, and his personal totem was Jiramba (honey pot ant).

His parents were Ḷṭálaḷṭúmarínja and Rákụa, and his father's parents were Máŋina and Kámbarknáṇaka. Hesekiel had five brothers, David, Jakobus, Jakob, Markus and Alexander. He married Jūlajindāka, with whom he had seven children.

Épa f.

Iŋjúnaŋa m.
(Paḷṭara)
From Tnỗrula;
iŋjúnaŋa kŋ.

Máŋina m.
(Kŋuarea)
From Tnỗrula.

Ḷṭálaḷṭúmarínja m.
(Paḷṭara)

Kámbarknáṇaka f.
(Ṭjala)
From Ntjárkítnáma;
ṭjỗṭba kŋ.

Rákụa f.
(Kamara)
From Tnúluŋa;
tnúruŋáṭja kŋ.

Hesekiel m.
(Kŋuarea)
From Ellery Ck.;
jíramba kŋ.
B. 28.3.89.

=

Jūlajindāka f.
(Purula)
From Ṭjálakíti;
ṭjíḷpa kŋ.

David II m.
(Kŋuarea)
From Njárea;
rátapa kŋ.
B. 15.3.87;
d. 16.4.88

Gustav m.
(Paḷṭara)
B. 11.2.09.

Emma f.
(Paḷṭara)
B. 25.2.11.

Jeremias m.
(Paḷṭara)
B. 4.12.13.

Lucia f.
(Paḷṭara)
B. 23.1.16.

Ferdinand m.
(Paḷṭara)
B. 13.12.18;
d. 19.12.18.

Jakobus II m.
(Kŋuarea)
From Njárea;
rátapa kŋ.
B. 9.6.91;
d. 1.3.93.

Kordula f.
(Paḷṭara)
B. 13.12.19.

Jakob II m.
(Kŋuarea)
From Njárea;
rátapa kŋ.
B. 18.1.00;
d. 20.5.00.

Traugott m.
(Paḷṭara)
B. 8.10.22.

Markus m.
(Kŋuarea)
From Njárea;
rátapa kŋ.
B. 24.12.06.

Alexander m.
(Kŋuarea)
From Njárea;
rátapa kŋ.
B. 25.7.10.

20. Hesekiel Malbunka's family tree drawn by T.G.H. Strehlow. Exhibited in 2007 with the consent of the Malbunka family in the tourist facility of the Museum of Central Australia in Alice Springs.

Source: Strehlow Research Centre, Alice Springs.

The concept of Western Aranda families, resulting from a long influence of constant reinforcement of family trees produced by the Finke River Mission, T.G.H. Strehlow and the Central Land Council, may be seen as a paradigm for Sutton's (2003: 206–231) conceptualising his 'Families of Polity' as a modern kinship form among indigenous Australians that are not residential or local groups (Austin-Broos 2004: 61). Generally these 'families' are today characterised by a patronymic identity and cognatic descent many generations deep. A different treatment of this phenomenon takes a view of kinship application in the contemporary social context of day-to-day living in which elaborate and complex networking by individuals takes place (Austin-Broos 2003a, 2006, 2009). Carl Strehlow's treatment of kinship was still at a considerable distance from such a description and analysis of social organisation.

T.G.H. Strehlow's genealogies, by extension also his father's and other family trees of the Finke River Mission, and more recently family trees generated by the Central Land Council during the land rights era, have assumed new meanings in the context of land-ownership. Genealogies are increasingly the way to claim affiliation or connection to Aranda country rather than through esoteric knowledge of myth which is in decline (Oberscheidt 2005). Sometimes T.G.H. Strehlow's genealogical information is almost treated as secret-sacred material. There is a perception that once on a family tree one is 'in', even if the connection is marginal or affinal.[22] T.G.H. Strehlow's genealogies are often perceived as the last word on traditional membership of a landholding group by some indigenous people, and used by them as evidence for membership. However, they do not define how kinship confers particular rights and obligations in land or how kin networks function. In addition, placing weight on these genealogical records can obscure other processes including fission, fusion, the end of patrilines and political alliances of particular families.

Is there a responsible use of family trees?

In November 2007, Central Land Council anthropologists, Helen Wilmot and Rebecca Koser, presented at the conference of the Australian Anthropological Society a paper in which they addressed problems in the context of Aboriginal land claims, mining and royalty distribution processes created by genealogical materials obtained from archives. They raised the question: how are anthropologists to deal with problems, generated by archival materials, in particular by family trees, amongst Aboriginal people in central Australia. People are gaining positions of power and influence in Aboriginal decision making with these documents that under traditional laws and customs they

---

22   Affines can have contingent rights under certain conditions (see Sutton 2003: 12–13).

would not be able to gain, and are rejecting others. They discussed how some facets of identification are based on these documents that are perceived as 'quasi-traditional authority' and how this information is reified.

Land Council anthropologists are witnessing that written documents are used as 'proof' of ownership and connections to land. They have observed that parts of genealogies, such as a footnote, are internalised even by senior people. These snippets of genealogical information, which may or may not be wrong, are on occasions recited as if they were traditional knowledge and misconstrue traditional ownership. Morgan and Wilmot (2010: 9) give an example of such a situation. As an explanation for how certain families were related to each other, various senior members of a particular group had repeatedly told a Land Council anthropologist that 'All our mothers were sisters from Bambi Springs (location a pseudonym)'. Some time later it was discovered that this sentence had been plucked from a footnote of a Strehlow genealogy (the traditional owners had in the meantime lost their copy of this family tree), and after careful analysis of the genealogy it emerged that the connections claimed had been based on a misunderstanding of the document with significant implications for claims to land.

Ethically it is difficult for anthropologists and institutions, who hold this type of genealogical material, to address these issues (Morgan and Wilmot 2010: 3–4). Once such material enters the public domain it is not possible to control or guide what people do with this material, how they interpret it or base their identity on it. The use of written material as proof of identity is not common to all Arandic regions; degrees of urbanisation and westernisation in central Australia differ. There are Arandic people who barely speak English, and are embedded in their traditional laws and customs. These are often the people who suffer when the written artefact takes on a new life in the hands of relatives who are proficent English speakers and familiar with modern mainstream life and administration. Morgan and Wilmot remark that one of the issues of the rise of genealogical documentation as a new form of authority, is that it is used by Arandic people, who are print-literate and adept in processes of negotiation within the wider society, to successfully demand recognition as traditional owners or native title holders from recognised senior, knowledgeable people based on these genealogies. They write:

> In these scenarios, it is often the case that such a heavy reliance on genealogical documentation is the result of limited knowledge about kinship rules, how country is inherited or knowledge of the country purported to be owned and even, in some cases, where that country is located. It is not uncommon to receive requests from senior traditional owners to hold workshops about some of these issues in order to pass on cultural information. There is clearly recognition that knowledge and

traditional hierarchies are diminishing, which is related to socio-cultural change between generations, in a context of reinvented post-traditional forms of knowledge. (Morgan and Wilmot 2010: 9)

On the other hand Carl and T.G.H. Strehlow's family records are highly valued today among many Aboriginal people in central Australia. For some descendants, to possess excerpts of T.G.H. Strehlow's genealogies showing one's ancestors is one of the most precious and cherished possessions, giving some indigenous people a kind of sense of belonging, and the feeling of empowerment knowing 'who' they are and from 'where' they come.

VII. Territorial Organisation

Although Carl Strehlow was not documenting territorial organisation, and did not elaborate on Aranda and Loritja land tenure as such,[1] he made some explicit remarks about an individual's rights to and affinities with his or her conception site and about mother's conception site. He took these to be links to places and their dreamings. He also recorded, though less systematically, data on patrilineal descent, inheritance rights through fathers, and rights to ritual knowledge. These data give evidence of a number of pathways to connections to land or place and show the relevance of Carl Strehlow's work today in the context of land and native title claims. They provide some of the earliest evidence for ways of being connected to country other than through patrilineal principles among Aranda and Loritja people. The data allow us to canvas various dimensions of traditional laws and customs relating to land ownership as it may have existed at the time of Northern Territory sovereignty in 1825.[2]

In the course of the twentieth century a number of researchers passed through the area and made observations that clarify Carl Strehlow's findings. Some of these were based on views of informants who were born before the incursion of white people into Aranda and Loritja lands. These later records have expanded in a major way our knowledge of traditional ownership and the nature of contemporary landholding groups. Carl Strehlow's material indicates that even the Western Aranda, who are often viewed as the paradigm of patriliny in central Australia, had a system of land tenure that offered 'multiple pathways' to 'belonging to country' (Myers [1986] 1991: 138ff). This does not mean that these connections were not ranked, qualified or otherwise proposed mainly as cultural norms, as can be the case today. Before I consider Carl Strehlow's contributions, an outline of what a 'country' implies today in central Australia and an overview of the history and twentieth century issues and debates of Australian land tenure are important to understanding the significance of his ethnography.

---

1   The focus in this chapter is on Aranda land tenure, because the Loritja Carl was mainly writing about, the Kukatja-Loritja, had similar social institutions (Strehlow 1908, 1910: 1; 1913); and according to T.G.H. Strehlow, Western Aranda and Kukatja had virtually the same land tenure system (Strehlow 1970: 99).
2   British sovereignty over Australia was aquired in several stages. In 1788 it extended westwards from the east coast of the continent to longitude 135 degrees taking in what is now the eastern third of the Northern Territory. In 1825 sovereignty was extended to around the present day western border of the Territory. Western Australia was claimed in 1829. In a native title claim the claimants are required to prove that their system of land-ownership is consistent with the system that might have been in place at 'sovereignty' or at effective 'sovereignty' as far as Aboriginal life was concerned. Under the *Native Title Act 1993* (Cth) Aboriginal people also have to prove that their ancestors were the original inhabitants and traditional owners of the area claimed.

Pmara and Ngurra

Today, Western Aranda people refer to countries that they may claim, usually through their grandparents, and its associated esoteric knowledge, as pmara (pmere), called 'country' in Aboriginal English and 'estate' in the anthropological literature. Luritja call it 'ngurra' and it can mean place, camp or country depending on context (see also Myers [1986] 1991: 54–57). Carl Strehlow spelled pmara 'tmara'. He recorded tmara altjira, tmara runga or tmara rungatja as well as the term knanakala for 'totem place' in general and the terms mbatjita (*grosser Totem-Platz*, big totem place), tmarutja (*ewiger Platz*, eternal place) and takuta (*immerwährender Platz*, everlasting place) for important places associated with particular ancestral beings (Strehlow 1907: 5). In his son's work these places were called pmara kutata (everlasting place). Today, Western Aranda people use the term mekemeke for 'sacred site' (Kenny 2004a: 20), which also means 'dangerous place' due to its spiritual powers. T.G.H. Strehlow's unpublished material records makamaka (mekemeke) as meaning 'to be avoided' or 'sacred cave'[3] and defines 'pmara makamaka' as 'asylum, a place whither men in danger of death can flee for safety, e.g. the area around an arknganaua, where nothing could be killed and within whose precincts not even a hunter could pursue an animal that already had a spear stuck into it'.[4]

The country of a landholding group generally comprises a set of significant sites or areas that are associated with one or more dreamings. Each country is usually associated with a particular patricouple, i.e. subsection couple as discussed in the previous chapter. These local group countries were called 'njinaŋa (patricouple) section areas' by T.G.H. Strehlow. It is also identified with predominant dreaming tracks, sites, site names and particular families or groups. Aranda people usually think of their country in terms of sites and the dreamings connected to them rather than as a bounded area. Although, sometimes the notions of boundaries, 'blocks of land' (as may be used in the pastoral context) and even the word 'estate' (as used in anthropological reports for legal proceedings) appear in conversations with Aranda people. While people do speak of 'boundaries' this cannot be taken at face value as it really denotes areas which can be up to several kilometres wide. Where boundaries of neighbouring estates converge or become better defined is often at a site or sites along tracks of travelling dreamings, so that each estate group has interests in such a site or sites.

For these reasons, and due to the aridity of the environment, boundaries are not always clear. Pink observed during her work on Northern Aranda territory

---

3   T.G.H. Strehlow's Diary 38 (1968: 39).
4   T.G.H. Strehlow's unpublished dictionary M: 126.

that 'on the outer edges the boundaries of individual estates became somewhat indefinite' (Pink 1936: 283), while T.G.H. Strehlow recorded boundary points between countries called 'arkngata' or 'barrier':

> It marked the limit beyond which a myth might not be told, a song not sung, nor a series of ceremonies performed by members of a njinaŋa section area who shared these traditions with neighbours. (Strehlow 1965: 138)

He remarked that such sites could figure equally prominently in a number of myths held by different people or groups of people (Strehlow 1947). In the Palm Valley Land Claim Justice Gray heard evidence and found that definitive boundaries were rare (Gray 1999: 116). Earlier, Stanner noted that the 'known facts of inter-group relations simply do not sort with the idea of precise, rigid boundaries jealously upheld in all circumstances' (Stanner 1965: 11).

Knowledge about country, that is the knowledge of the cultural geography and associated mythology, is one of the defining principles for traditional Aboriginal land ownership. According to T.G.H. Strehlow (1965: 135), the extent of a Western Aranda local group's country was defined geographically and validated by episodes mentioned in the sacred myths. Pink made the observation among her Northern Aranda informants:

> The songs, according to my Aranda informants, definitely establish a man's title, to use legal phraseology, for the site a man inherits has a song, or songs, associated with it; to inherit the song is to inherit the estate. (Pink 1936: 286)

This knowledge relating to land was well-guarded and concealed – not freely transmitted – because rights to country hinged on it. Great effort was invested in the acquisition of knowledge which was not evenly distributed in central Australian Aboriginal societies, as Róheim observed ([1945] 1971: 2). Claims to country are still commonly based on knowledge of the associated dreaming stories and places, about which members of a landholding group simply know more than others. T.G.H. Strehlow in *Aranda Traditions* (1947) writes that his informants, even the best informed, would not know the entire body of myths, and Spencer and Gillen (1899: 10) observed that 'Old age does not by itself confer distinction, but only when combined with special ability'. Carl Strehlow (1915: 1–2) wrote in a similar vein that it was knowledge that made an 'inkata knara' (great chief), while 'inkata kurka' (little chief) was a title to father's country inherited simply through descent. People with knowledge are still respected in Western Aranda society, and are frequently referred to, because ritual knowledge is and was highly valued and the basis of prestige. Knowledgeable people have the right and duty to be involved in the management of mythology and land; and are entitled to some kind of payment for the knowledge they transmit to others.

Although Carl Strehlow's myth collection has been effectively used in the context of land claims over traditional Arandic lands and in native title determinations, nowhere does he explicitly indicate that these narratives are owned by particular individuals or groups of individuals. He seems not to have realised that ownership of myths played an important role in connecting people to their countries and conferring rights and responsibilities both to individuals and groups. This creates a distance between Carl Strehlow's view of myth and the political and legal contexts in which myth is often canvassed today, as land ownership has become a topic of enduring debate within Australian anthropology.

A brief account of research into traditional land ownership

The study of territoriality, called local organisation in early ethnography, did not feature prominently on the agenda of the emerging discipline of anthropology in the nineteenth century. The documentation of rights to country is incidental and linked to other aspects of Aboriginal life. Early writers did not canvas clear structures of land ownership. They paid little attention to indigenous land rights, decision-making processes, succession and many related subjects that are relevant for a systematic treatment of Aboriginal land tenure. Nevertheless they collected some limited data on local (territorial) organisation that indicates that Aboriginal Australians had rights in land (Peterson 1986: 13). In 1839 Reverend John Dunmore Lang, for example, suggested that property rights certainly existed among Aboriginal people in Australia (Grey 1841: 232–236; Hiatt 1996: 18). He wrote that:

> I have already observed that the aborigines of Australia are universally divided into distinct and independent tribes, each occupying as their hunting-grounds a certain portion of territory, of which the limits are generally well defined by prominent features in the natural scenery of the country, and well known to all the neighbouring tribes. This division appears to have taken place from time immemorial, as there is no part of the available portion of the country to which some tribe or other does not lay claim. (Lang 1861: 335)

> The territory of each tribe is subdivided, moreover, among the different families of which it consists, and the proprietor of any particular subdivision, has the exclusive right to direct when it shall be hunted over, or the grass burned, and the wild animals destroyed. (Lang 1861: 336)

In 1865 August Oldfield who had spent many months with the Nanda people in Western Australia remarked on the general nature of 'tribes' that their territorial boundaries were well defined and that Aboriginal people had not been able to retreat 'before the white invader, for to pass beyond their own limits would be to expose themselves to the hostilities of some other tribe' (Oldfield 1865: 221). In Aboriginal Australia land ownership often manifested itself in strict rules relating to trespass and elaborate invitation and welcome rituals that commonly regulated access to and control over country (Peterson 1986: 27). The use of the concept of 'tribe'[5] by early writers is often confusing as it can refer to anything from an extended family to a linguistic grouping; the implication that groups at the linguistic level had property rights and ownership in land was clearly wrong. However, the use of this concept indicated to some degree that early writers departed from some kind of assumption that tribes had rights to land (see Hiatt 1996: 18).

Some early writers observed that 'tribes' were divided into smaller landed units and found hints that patrilineal descent, totemic affiliation, birthplace and knowledge pertaining to place played a role in conferring rights to land. Smaller landholding groups belonging to distinct areas in south-east Australia, for example, were mentioned by early writers such as Breton (1833), Barlow (1873: 174), Howitt and Fison (1883), Howitt (1884, 1904), Mathews (1906, 1912, 1917), Parker (1905) and Mathew (1910: 129, 147).

In 1880 Lorimer Fison and A.W. Howitt published *Kamilaroi and Kurnai: Group Marriage and Relationship, and Marriage by Elopement* and in 1883 'From Mother-right to Father-right'. While their book focuses on the social organisation of these groups (kinship, moieties, section system), their article was of 'seminal importance' (Hiatt 1996: 20) in some ways, because it progressed the discussion about territoriality by distinguishing between the social and local (territorial) organisation. They showed that traditional societies had two separate but interconnected institutions (Howitt and Fison 1883: 33–34). One was a system determined by totems and exogamous intermarrying classes in which descent was traced in the matri line and, the other system in which country was inherited 'with descent through the father'. They wrote:

> The Australian tribe (or community) presents itself under two aspects, and it is very necessary to see clearly, and to keep in view, the distinction

---

5   It has been clear for some time that the 'concept of tribe' is inadequate to describe traditional landowning units in Aboriginal Australia. See, for instance, Strehlow (1947) and Berndt (1959).

between them. We may view the tribe as a whole made up of certain exogamous intermarrying classes, or we may study it as a whole made up of certain local divisions, each of which may contain classes aforesaid. The former may be called its social aspect, the latter we may speak of as its local and physical aspect. The two are co-existent and conterminous; they cover and inter-penetrate each other, and yet the classes of the one are distinct from the divisions of the other, excepting in rare cases to be mentioned by-and-by, and are subject to quite different organic laws. Let us for the sake of convenience call the former the social organisation, and the latter its local [territorial] organisation. (Howitt and Fison 1883: 3)

They maintained that a tribe was composed of a number of local groups or clans, each having 'a local position in some part of the tribal territory' and that 'perpetual succession through the males, who hunt over the same tracts of country over which their fathers hunted before them' took place (Howitt and Fison 1883: 34). In 1904 Howitt restated that 'the principal geographical and territorial division of a tribe', the 'clan', recruited its members by 'descent in the male line' (Howitt 1904: 89).

A.R. Brown, better known as A.R. Radcliffe-Brown, was the first professional anthropologist in Australia to make a serious attempt to systematise the entire study of social and local organisation of Aboriginal Australians. Soon after his Western Australian fieldwork in 1911 he reinforced the notion that the basic land-owning unit 'forms what we may call a "clan" with male descent, all the male members of the clan being "father's father," "son's son," "father," "son," or "brother," to each other' (Brown 1913: 160). He suggested that 'tribes' (linguistic groups) were divided into small landed units and that patrilineal descent in particular, as well as knowledge of country and totemic affiliation pertaining to place and land together played a role in conferring rights and interests to country in all traditional Aboriginal societies.

During his work in Western Australia he had found 'over a considerable area from the Western Kimberley district in the north to the Murchison River in the south' (Radcliffe-Brown 1929: 399) the existence of localised rites and ceremonies for the increase of natural species that were tied to local totemic centres and owned by particular clans.[6] These localities were associated with certain mythical beings who were believed to have existed at the beginning of time and who were 'responsible for the formation of the totem centres' which were in the territory of different clans. A clan's country he generally defined as 'a certain area of territory, the boundaries of which are known', and the persons belonging to the horde [sic clan] as 'possessing in common proprietary rights

---

6   To clarify Radcliffe-Brown's model in this paragraph 'clan' has been inserted where he often used 'horde'. The reason for this is set out in the following paragraphs.

over the land and its products'. He maintained that the clan 'is the primary land-owning or land-holding group' and membership of a clan 'is determined in the first place by descent' (Radcliffe-Brown 1930: 35). He found that each clan had a number of different totem centres, some more important than others (see Radcliffe-Brown 1930: 60–63). He wrote about the close connection of people and country in the following manner:

> It should be noted that the most important determining factor in relation to this wider structure is the strong social bond between the horde or local clan and its territory. The strong local solidarity, which is the most important thing in the social life of the Australians, is correlated with a very strong bond between the local group and its territory. There is an equally strong and permanent association between the territory and the animals and plants that are found on it. It is this intimate association of a group of persons with a certain stretch of country with its rocks and water-holes and other natural features, and with the natural species that are abundant in it, that provides the basis of that totemism of local totemic centres that is so widespread and so important in the Australian culture. (Radcliffe-Brown 1930: 63)

Radcliffe-Brown's early model of local organisation remained unchallenged until 1962 (Hiatt). In that year Hiatt pointed out that Radcliffe-Brown did not distinguish between a descent based land owning group, and the land using residential group, collapsing the distinction by using the term horde for both. This has led to his version of the land using group being referred to as the 'patrilineal band'. In fact he did recognise a distinction but did not see it as relevant. All males in the patrilineal band, like the clan, were of the land owning group, in his view, but because of exogamy only unmarried girls of the clan were part of the band, all adult women were in-marrying wives from diverse clans and the adult women of the clan off elsewhere living with their husbands. After a comprehensive literature review Hiatt (1962) argued that the patrilineal band in Radcliffe-Brown's sense was unrecorded, and had probably never existed (see also Peterson 1970: 9).

Stanner contested Hiatt's criticism of Radcliffe-Brown in his 1965 article 'Aboriginal Territorial Organisation; Estate, Range, Domain and Regime'. He suggested that any examination of Aboriginal land tenure patterns (territoriality) should take the distinction between 'estate' and 'range' into account. He described 'estate' as 'the traditionally recognized locus ("country", "home", "ground", "dreaming place"), of some kind of patrilineal descent-group forming the core or nucleus of a territorial group' and 'range' as 'the tract or orbit over which the group, including its nucleus and adherents, ordinarily hunted and foraged to maintain life'. The range normally included the estate, and together Stanner called them (1965: 2) a 'domain'. The domain was the ecological 'life-space' of a group. He proposed that issues concerning ecology and season could be seen to influence the composition of a residential group at any particular point in time so that males of several clans could be found living together.

He departed from a static model of a residential group strictly composed according to patrilineal principles by adding some flexibility, which allowed the incorporation of other kin to join the group to hunt and gather on a certain stretch of country which belonged at its core to a patrilineal group. He concluded that a local or residential group was of mixed clan composition for males as well as females and that 'visitations of cognates and affines' (Stanner 1965: 15) was common. However, he insisted that it was generally true to say that:

> (1) Some sort of exogamous patrilineal descent-group was ubiquitous. (2) It had intrinsic connection, not mere association, with territory. (3) There was a marked tendency towards, though not iron rule requiring, patrilocality and virilocality. (4) The group thus formed was basic to both territorial and social organisation, however concealed by other structural groups (e.g. phratries, moieties, sections, etc.) or by dynamic emphasis. (Stanner 1965: 16)

Stanner (1965: 3) conceded that patri-virilocal residence on account of ecology was at best a hypothetical assumption. Factors other than patri-focal criteria influenced residence and group composition. Male knowledge of a tract's resources could easily be exaggerated. Moreover, foraging by women was just as if not more crucial to a group's survival. Peterson (1970) affirmed that links through women were an important factor that determined the composition of residential groups in Aboriginal society. Both sociological and ecological considerations had an impact. It was quite common for a man's first marriage to require uxoripatri-local residence so that he could fulfil bride-service obligations towards his in-laws. In Aranda society, for example, Carl Strehlow (1913) recorded that young spouses had to supply food to their in-laws, and this would have had an impact on where and with whom the couple would live. Another reason why a newly married man might reside with his wife's father's group involved a senior man's desire to keep his (female) labour force together, observed by Peterson in Arnhem Land (1970: 14). Alternatively, in the Western Desert, a young woman may have wanted to remain close to her parents because she received meat from her mother and father (Hamilton 1987: 41). These individual choices of everyday life explain many aspects of group composition. Myers demonstrates that among the Pintupi individual choice determines how people see themselves as part of a group and that there are multiple pathways to claim connection to a place and country (Myers [1986] 1991: 129–130, 138–140).

In the eastern Western Desert, Hamilton (1987: 38–39) suggested that an important tool used for grinding seeds by women, and exclusively owned and inherited by women, influenced the local organisation. These implements, belonged to groups of uterine kinswomen and were left behind in countries affiliated to mothers as they were often large and heavy sometimes weighing as much as 22.5 kg. During major ceremonies, when the men were dependent on the labour of women who produced much of their foodstuff, the location of these grinding stones influenced where and who would have been present. She writes that 'this aspect of women's labour around a single scarce resource (the grindstone and mill) acted as a kind of perpetual opposition to the men's desires to promote patrilocal residence' (Hamilton 1987: 40).

Hamilton writes, that the 'Hiatt-Stanner debate led to a crucial clarification — that is, the necessity to maintain a clear distinction between economic and ritual relationship to land — so that instead of a horde there is both a ritual and an economic group' (Hamilton 1998: 91). Notwithstanding, the ritual group also has economic roles (Hamilton 1998: 94). In this context she cites T.G.H. Strehlow:

> Each Aranda local group was believed to perform an indispensable economic service not only for itself but for the population around its borders as well … the religious acts performed by the totemic clan members of all the inland tribes at their respective totemic centres were regarded as being indispensable for the continuation of all human, animal and plant life in Central Australia. (Strehlow 1970: 103)

Thus, it is important not to confuse the ritual group (clan) with the residential/land-using/economic group (band). They are different groups with highly variable degrees of overlap in their composition.

The passing of the Commonwealth's *Aboriginal Land Rights (Northern Territory) Act 1976* and *Native Title Act 1993*, has led to a great deal more research into relationships to land for the preparation of land claims that these Acts make possible. The result has been a diversification of models of land tenure, ranging from strictly patrilineal to the fully-fledged cognatic, some, but not all of this diversity due to more recent changes in people's lives.

The *Aboriginal Land Rights (Northern Territory) Act 1976* (Cth) shifted focus onto the 'local descent group' as defined in the Act. In the initial claims this was equated with the clan but later expanded to include matrifiliates as people that also had a 'common spiritual affiliation' to a country as required by the Act. Under the *Native Title Act 1993* (Cth) no definition of traditional owner was provided and so the definition of land owner was left to the empirical situation in each case, although descent from the original owners at sovereignty is required. This research provoked considerable academic debate around land tenure issues.

Ian Keen's paper 'Western Desert and the Rest' (Keen 1997: 66) provoked debate on the nature and the significance of descent groups. Keen's research among the Yolngu in the 1970s and 1980s, and strategies of belonging to country by individuals in the McLaren Creek Land Claim,[7] threw doubts on the existing assumptions regarding patrilineal dogma, in particular the clan system in Arnhem Land. In his article, 'The Western Desert vs the Rest: Rethinking the Contrast', he reinforced his view that in Arnhem Land groups were not as strictly patrilineally organised as portrayed in the literature, but that individual choice played an important role. Keen argued that rather than being clan-based, Yolngu society is more appropriately thought of in terms of a kindred (Keen 1997: 66–67; Morphy 1997: 130). He offered a re-analysis of the patrifilial identity of the Yolngu clan which he preferred to call 'group', and put forward that it would be more appropriate to use metaphorical expressions, such as 'strings' of connectedness, rather than the terms 'patrilineal descent group', 'clan' or 'corporation' (Keen 1997: 67), which he maintains do not capture the 'Yolngu constructs related to identity, country and ancestors' (Keen 2000: 32). Morphy (1997) responded by offering a processual model that maintains the clan-based model taking individual behaviour that determines variation in a system into account and thus, aims 'to transcend such divisions and to show how structural factors, such as an on-going system of clan organisation, can be integrated into a praxis-oriented framework in which the individual has a role in the transformation and the reproduction of the system over time' (Morphy 1997: 124).[8] This seemed to a degree acceptable to Keen (2000) provided social change is considered alongside ancestral law and politics; though he added that 'the concept of the "clan" is perhaps the last vestige of the Radcliffe-Brown synthesis to remain' and that 'it has long been unsafe to assume a fundamental uniformity in aboriginal social arrangements' (Keen 2000: 39).

Sansom (2006, 2007) also critiqued Keen and his 'West' is not all that much different to the 'Rest'. He was not necessarily opposing Keen's view that patriliny did not have such an exclusive position, but he thought that Keen ignored underlying social structures and norms. Sansom writes:

> Those (like me) who radically distinguish the contemporary desert West from the contemporary Rest, do so by pointing to normative difference. In The West there are nowadays 'multiple pathways' to land. Outside the Western Desert, specific rules of kinship traditionally prescribe that primary right-holders in land would be patrifilial inheritors of estates in land, and that holders of secondary (and mediated) rights constitute a limited set of persons who have particular and specified relationships

---

7   See quotation of claim book (exhibit CLC 3) in Aboriginal Land Commissioner's report (Olney 1991: 11–13).
8   Myers' emphasis on 'multiple pathways' and his re-rendering of kinship in terms of relatedness and identity have affinities with these more praxis-oriented approaches.

that link them to those who hold the primary rights. Keen sets aside modelling that emphasises explicitly rendered ideological rules (or 'normative norms') by shifting the emphasis from normative norms to statistical norms. He then looks past ideologies to instances of behaviour and to rates that describe trends to actions. (Sansom 2007: 79–80)

Keen's response was that he clearly accords 'patrifiliation rather more than mere rhetorical value', and while he had 'certainly questioned the usefulness of the concept of corporate "clan" to Aboriginal relations to country and sacra', he had not thrown into doubt 'the concept of social structure as a whole' (Keen 2007: 170).

In general, Western Aranda today emphasise patrifilial connections to land strongly, making it part of the 'Rest'. They are disposed towards a tighter land tenure model than Western Desert peoples, mainly because their country belongs to the better-watered areas in central Australia. In his essays written in the 1930s, later published in *Aranda Traditions*, and in particular in his article 'Culture, social structure and environment in Aboriginal Central Australia' (1965), T.G.H. Strehlow maintained that the landholding group was strictly patrilineal (Strehlow 1947: 139; 1965). In these works he appears to present an ideal group that is mainly determined by ritual and not by 'secular' links which would have determined the everyday composition of an Aranda residential group. He wrote that due to harsher environmental conditions Western Desert peoples had a local organisation that was of much looser and fluid nature, but that the Kukatja-Loritja were an exception, because their social and local system was very similar to the Aranda's, although linguistically they belong to the Western Desert people (Strehlow 1965: 143; 1970: 99).

Hamilton observed in the eastern Western Desert during 1970–71 an ideological preference for patrilineal and patrifocal structures amongst her informants, that were counterbalanced by women's labour organisation and female secret ritual life, as well as by the climatic and environmental conditions (Hamilton 1987, 1998). Munn wrote about the residential foci of Pitjantjatjara that 'the men of the group ideally based themselves after marriage in their father's home country (even though at any given time they might actually have been living or hunting elsewhere)' (Munn 1970: 146). In the anthropologists' report of the Yulara Native Title Claim another factor is mentioned that determines the connection of a woman to an area:

> There is some tendency for men to have a special relationship to their fathers' and fathers' fathers' places, and for women to have a similar connection to those of their mothers and mothers' mothers, though this is not a uniform rule. It appears in some kin sets but not in others. (Sutton and Vaarzon-Morel 2003: para. 7.55 cited in Sutton 2007: 178)

It is likely that T.G.H. Strehlow's informants, who were male, stressed this patrilineal preference. However, his own work (Strehlow 1971, 1999) shows how men have ritual rights and links to country based on a range of other claims. Connections to country through mothers are already mentioned in his first essays written in 1934, as well as individual rights through conception at a particular place. These people with matrifilial rights, he called kutuŋula (kwertengerle). Its role in central Australia is well understood now (see Pink 1936; Meggitt [1962] 1986; Morphy and Morphy 1984; Peterson 1986; Myers [1986] 1991; Morton 1997a,b; Vaarzon-Morel and Sackett 1997; Elliott 1999: 105–110; 2004: 74–76). It became clear during the land claim era that claims to membership of a landholding group through matrifiliation were and are of great importance and that these people hold distinct and significant rights and responsibilities in relation to land. In the Palm Valley Land Claim under the *Aboriginal Land Rights (Northern Territory) Act 1976* (Cth), Justice Gray recognised in addition to patriliny and matrifiliation, cognatic descent as a basis for membership of the Western Aranda landholding groups involved in the claim (Gray 1999: 17–18). These other connections provided the land tenure system with (strong) provisions for ways to claim places and dreamings other than through the patriline, which is evident in a large number of land and native title claims in the Northern Territory and elsewhere in Australia.

These various pathways to 'belonging to country' find early support in Carl Strehlow's data. They suggest that around 1900 the Western Aranda had beside patrilineal connections to country, connections to their own conception site and their mother's conception place, (i.e. where mother's mother conceived mother). This mother's place may or may not have been located on mother's father's country. He wrote:

> Every individual, then, is placed into a relationship with two totems. He belongs to one totem by virtue of his birth[9] and is related to another because he inherits it from his mother. He may actively participate in the cult of both totems. (Strehlow 1908: 58)[10]

In the following sections I will show how Carl Strehlow's material does not support the Radcliffe-Brownian view though one might expect this from data collected from Aranda during the late nineteenth and early twentieth century. It is not my contention that Carl Strehlow's true account is only now being discovered through land claim debates. Rather, the fact that Carl Strehlow emphasised conception and mother's conception place and not father's father's place suggests that systems may be dynamic over time, and subject to varieties of representation – what is said and to whom in the micro-politics of relationships and translation.

---

9   He means here the dreaming from an individual's conception site.

10   See also Strehlow (1910: 2).

Rights to country through conception

The literature on Arandic cultures shows consistently that conception was important in conferring rights in or 'belonging' to country in the first part of the twentieth century (Spencer and Gillen 1899: 121–127; Strehlow 1908: 52–61; T.G.H. Strehlow 1947: 86–96; [1964] 1978: 20–23; 1971: 158, 596). In Carl Strehlow's work the conception dreaming is called 'ratapa' which can mean totem in general or spirit child; and the conception site of a person is called 'tmara runga' or 'tmara rungatja'. This place is where a person entered 'his mother as a ratapa, and where his tjurunga is kept' as well as where she felt the first movement of the foetus in the womb (1908: 53, 56). The terms 'tmara runga' or 'tmara rungatja' mean 'my own place' (Strehlow 1908: 57–58). He also used the general term for 'totem place', 'knanakala', for conception site (Strehlow 1907: 5; 1920). He remarked on Aranda and Loritja conception beliefs:

> The totemic conceptions of the Loritja are very closely related to those of the Aranda. Every Loritja also belongs to two totems, a personal totem which he calls aratapi (= (A) ratapa), and a maternal totem which he calls altjiri (= (A) altjira). The manner by which children enter the womb of the mother is seen by the Loritja in exactly the same way as by the Aranda. Either an aratapi enters the woman or a totem ancestor emerges from the earth and throws a bullroarer at her, which changes into a child inside the woman. The Loritja say that the latter case is the more frequent. (Strehlow 1908: 60)

His son's earlier work (1947) and genealogy collection evokes the impression that T.G.H. Strehlow was mainly interested in conception sites of individuals to whom they were of great importance, as their significance as personal totems may have rested on a 'mythopoetic' and 'their experience of self in a world forged through hunting and foraging practice' (Austin-Broos 2004: 60). The conception site 'pmara kŋanintja' (Strehlow 1971: 596) was a well-defined place which was of particular significance to an individual, as his spirit or soul was believed to have come from there; one had the right to detailed knowledge about this place and conception bestowed on the owner a special connection to it (Strehlow 1947: 87; 1971: 158). In *Aranda Traditions* he placed great emphasis on them, writing that the conception site took 'by far the most important place in all the complex arguments which centre around the possession of the myths, chants, ceremonies and sacred objects owned by any large local totemic clan' (Strehlow 1947: 87), but at the same time he maintained that 'the doctrine of the conception site is deliberately counterbalanced by the strong emphasis laid upon the unifying ties represented by the allegiance claims of the pmara kutata and by membership obligations to the local njinaŋa section' (Strehlow 1947: 139–140).

The probability of being conceived on one's father's father's country was quite high (Pink 1936: 288; Austin-Broos 2004: 62; 2009: 114) when people resided on well-watered land, as did the Western Aranda. This seems to be broadly substantiated in T.G.H. Strehlow's genealogies (Austin-Broos 2009: 289, fn. 13).[11] If a person's conception site was on their father's father's country, they would quite likely have had a stronger connection to that site than to others. However, there were exceptions. A person conceived outside their father's father's country had a right to acquire detailed knowledge of their conception site, but required some personal efforts. In 'Agencies of Social Control in Central Australian Aboriginal Societies', T.G.H. Strehlow ([1950] 1997) described how Rauwirarka, a Western Aranda man, went to a substantial amount of trouble to acquire knowledge about his Anmatyerr conception site to the north of his primary estate on the Ellery Creek.

Under certain circumstances people with strong connections to and knowledge of their conception site and adjacent areas outside of their father's father's country could over time potentially establish themselves in a country as a new landholding group, if the original group had reached the end of their patriline. Although rare, it may even have resulted in a change in the patricouple associated with that country (Morton 1997a: 119), in situations where a person's conception site was located on a country associated with the opposite patrimoiety.[12]

Knowledge about one's conception site alone seems not to have been sufficient to entitle a person or group to make claims to hold rights and interests in the land concerned; other factors, such as long-term residence, neighbouring estate affiliation, intermarriage, and political negotiation skills also played a vital role in the process of succession and establishing a new landholding group where the original owners were extinct or the patriline severely depleted. Spencer and Gillen's work seems to support this proposition:

> Once born into a totem, no matter what his class may be, a man, when initiated, may witness and take part in all the sacred ceremonies connected with the totem, but, unless he belongs to the predominant moiety, he will never, or only in extremely rare cases, become the head man or Alatunja of any local group of the totem. His only chance of becoming Alatunja is by the death of every member of the group who belongs to the moiety to which the Alcheringa men belonged. (Spencer and Gillen 1899: 126)

Writing about Northern Aranda people, Pink maintained that the country of one's father's father was of primary significance in relation to land ownership,

---

11   Helen Wilmot, pers. comm., 2009.
12   More commonly the individual with the conception site is seen as either pmerekerteye or kwertengerle based on their subsection in relation to the known subsection identity of the land.

and the country on which one's conception occurred was 'only of personal and secondary importance' (Pink 1936: 285). Indeed today, people sometimes refer to it as one's 'own personal or little story', to which individuals have an emotional attachment. The conception site is sometimes conflated with birthplace, a tradition that may have been imported from neighbouring Western Desert areas, and has lost much of its significance as a basis for rights and responsibilities in relation to land. Justice Gray suggested a reason for the reduced significance of the conception site, when he observed that 'Otherwise the large number of people conceived and born at a place such as at Hermannsburg would have the potential to swamp the land tenure system' (Gray 1999: 18). Indeed, settlement seems to be the main component for conception's loss of relevance. The multiple demographic and land use factors involved in settlement seemed to undermine the imagination of a social world embedded in country, in which conception had a central part (Austin-Broos 2004: 60). Initially, movement over Aranda country was restricted by pastoral expansion into the region and the efforts of both the church and state to settle Aranda people at missions and in other permanent settlements. More recently, settled community life and employment have resulted in fewer opportunities for people to be permanently present on their country. Austin-Broos writes that Christianity's creationism as well as sedentary life and the attenuation of practical and ritual knowledge it brought contested the Western Aranda's notion of conception (Austin-Broos 2009: 128–129) and may have caused an ontological shift (Austin-Boos 2009: 5–7, 112; 2010: 15).

It is noteworthy that today many Western Aranda people speak in terms of a 'conception dreaming' rather than conception site. The place of conception is not necessarily associated with a particular site, but rather with one of the dreamings found in an area. A particular encounter with an animal or natural phenomenon ultimately confirms what kind of spirit or spirit child has entered a woman. An encounter with an animal that might determine the dreaming of conception can be connected to an incident experienced by the father of a child while out hunting, according to Aranda woman Mavis Malbunka (2004: 13). They speak affectionately of their 'dreaming mark' or 'birthmark dreaming' and use the word tnengkarre when they refer to it (Kenny 2003: 35). Munn (1970: 146) found in the mid 1960s among the Pitjantjatjara living at Areyonga that such birthmarks were believed to be 'marks left by the ancestors at their birthplace'.

Unless conception has occurred on one's father's father's country, which is very rare in the contemporary context, it appears that today relatively little significance is placed on site of conception by Western Aranda in regard to claims to land.

Belonging to country through matrifiliation

The first remark on matrifiliation to Aranda country was made by the Lutheran missionary Louis Schulze (1891: 238–239). He recorded the term 'tmara altjira' meaning 'the place where mother of the dead person was born'. Likewise Carl Strehlow mentioned as one of his first encounters with connection to country, mother's conception dreaming, called in Aranda 'altjira'. He described the relationship of an individual to mother's dreaming, 'altjira', also called 'garra altjira' or 'deba altjira', and to mother's conception site, called 'tmara altjira or more precisely, tmara altjirealtja, i.e. the place of the totem associated with me' (Strehlow 1908: 57; 1910: 2). Altjira is used in this context as meaning mother's conception dreaming. He lists these in his published family trees (Strehlow 1913: Attachments) as 'ara' (kangaroo), 'ilia' (emu), 'jerramba' (honeyant), etc. and mentioned how to ask properly about this particular place:

> The following question should be put to him in order to ascertain the totem place of his mother, tmara altjira (or altjirealtja) unkwanga ntana? i.e. Where is the place of the totem associated with you? (Strehlow 1908: 58)

He observed that sets of siblings with the same mother shared a dreaming and the associated site. He had found that an 'altjira (totem)' could be inherited from mothers.[13] There seems to be an emergent thought here that mother's dreaming and place were collectively held, as all children of one mother had the same altjira implying ownership rights to mother's place, and that at different times, different 'totem' affiliations were more or less important. Unfortunately these thoughts were not developed any further. Nevertheless, it shows, that the right questions, thoughts and concepts were emerging. A passage written on the 6 April 1907 to von Leonhardi indicates this clearly:

> As the tjurunga [sacred property or object] is the symbol of the personal totem, some blacks have told me, that the wonninga can be seen as the symbol of the maternal totem or altjira. However, I am not yet certain about this, and will make further inquires. While the tjurunga of individuals are different (each individual has his own totem ancestor), the wonninga as the symbol of altjira would tie the members of a family together, because they all have the same altjira, but all have different ratapa ancestors. It is hard to tell which of the two totems is older, the personal or the one inherited from one's mother.[14]

The altjira, Strehlow wrote, had a providing and protecting role 'like a mother feeds and protects her children during the early years of their lives' and appears

---

13 Von Leonhardi to Carl Strehlow, 2.6.1907.
14 Carl Strehlow to von Leonhardi, n.d. possibly 6.4.1907 (SH-SP-11-1).

in dreams to warn from danger but also to tell friends about a person's well-being (Strehlow 1908: 57). The particular tjurunga associated with a man's mother, he regarded 'as the body of his altjira (mother's totem ancestor), who would accompany him on his lonesome journeys' (Strehlow 1913: 25). He also recorded some interesting details surrounding the 'altjira' and 'tmara altjira':

> After the boy has carried his knocked out tooth about with him for several weeks, he tosses it into the direction of his tmara altjira. (Strehlow 1911: 9)

> After a person's death, his spirit goes first to his grave where he remains until the completion of the second burial ceremony. Then he goes to the tmara altjira to collect his tooth, which will show him the way to the Island of the Dead. From there he returns with the tooth and presses it into the arm or a leg of a former camp companion, causing him to become very ill. The magic doctor, however, is able to remove the tooth. (Strehlow 1911: 9, fn. 4)

Another aspect of its importance is expressed in death and burial customs and beliefs. At the death of a person, he is laid into his grave facing his tmara altjira ('maternal totem place') (Strehlow 1915: 16).[15]

Radcliffe-Brown, writing about the Arandic type of social organisation, had also noted 'that there is an important relation between an individual and the totem and totem-centre of his mother' (1930: 325). He did not elaborate on this observation while T.G.H. Strehlow wrote in the 1930s that people connected to land through their mothers had rights to 'mother's tjurunga' and were called kutuŋula, but did not define this role precisely. He wrote of 'mother's tjurunga':

> In Western and Southern Aranda territory claims are frequently put forward by the older men to a share in the possession of the tjurunga which were once regarded as the property of their own mothers. (Strehlow 1947: 137)

A kutuŋula, according to Olive Pink, was a father's sister's son or a mother's brother's son, who should be theoretically the same person, however, in reality, she remarked in a footnote, that 'they seldom are in these days of diminished numbers' (Pink 1936: 303). At any rate these relatives are of the opposite moiety and of the same subsection. A male ego, for example, from the Mbitjana (Mpetyane) subsection, has a Paltara (Peltharre) man as his kutuŋula, who can also be classified as his mother's father. If close relatives are not available to deal with issues arising in relation to land and for this role then classificatory

---

15   T.G.H. Strehlow wrote in 1964 that 'when a man died, he was buried (generally in a sitting position) in such a way that his face was turned towards the conception site of his mother: for that was his pmara altjira, his "eternal home"' (Strehlow [1964] 1978: 39).

kinsmen from the opposite moiety with appropriate subsections and knowledge or seniority will be recruited for this position. Myers observed among the Pintupi that this type of process was 'to fill the ranks of an estate group depleted of personnel' (Myers [1986] 1991: 149) and Bell (1983) called it 'sufficiency of minds' concept. Accordingly, the division into intermarrying moieties has the potential to create and establish alliances between particular members of two social groups, neighbouring opposite moiety estates, even if no actual marriages or genealogical links otherwise exist, which is rather rare.

Today it is quite common for people of neighbouring countries who belong to opposite patrimoieties to express their rights and interests in those countries by saying that they are 'kwertengerle [kutuŋula] for each other'. This kind of reciprocity is based on the fact that one can find in neighbouring estate groups of the opposite patrimoiety, potential spouses, mothers, mother's brother's sons, sister's sons, and mother's fathers, all of whom can assume the important role of kwertengerle. The strength of any reciprocal rights is dependent on various factors, including the perceived closeness of kinship and personal relationships, intermarriage, knowledge of shared dreaming stories and associated sacra. In the course of the 1960s and 1970s the concept of kutuŋula/kwertengerle became well understood, in particular through the land claim process under the *Aboriginal Land Rights (Northern Territory) Act 1976* (Cth). The first 'claim book' by Peterson and others (1978) for central Australian Aboriginal people under this legislation, outlines clearly the role and recruitment of the kurdungurlu amongst Warlpiri people, for example.

In Western Aranda society today kutuŋula/kwertengerle are usually said to be people who claim rights to land through their mother's fathers, tyemeye, which is the other main way to claim country beside one's father's father, arrenge. Also people who claim country through their father's mother, perle, and mother's mother, ipmenhe, are often called kwertengerle, however, they may require the recognition and support of primary patrifilial landholders to ascertain their rights (see Morton 1997b: 26). Although kwertengerle who acquire rights and responsibilities in this way have incontestable rights to country, they are usually not as strong as rights derived through father's father and mother's father.

In 1947 T.G.H. Strehlow made general remarks on the kutuŋula's role and in his later work he wrote that kutuŋula status was gained through 'matrilineal inheritance' and that 'they did have the right at all times to be present at performances of the totemic acts that belonged to their mothers' (Strehlow [1964] 1978: 25, 38). The kutuŋula remains loosely defined in his work; it is not clear what the exact matrifilial requirements were to become one. He did not define precisely how the kutuŋula is recruited in kin terms, but rather recorded that this role involved ritual preparation and was crucial in the preservation of knowledge, calling them 'servants' and 'ceremonial assistants' (Strehlow 1947:

123–125, 132, 148–150, 164, 170; 1971: 248, 752). It was not simply a kinship connection to country among the Aranda for him (see also Meggitt 1966: 30; Nash 1982: 149). In his earlier work, Morton (1992) found that kwertengerle was not strictly defined among Western Aranda people. Central Arrernte in Alice Springs told him (Morton 1997b) during native title claim research, and I also have been told by Western Aranda, that people who claim country through their father's mother and mother's mother are called kwertengerle.[16]

It should be noted here that the term kutuŋula/kwertengerle seems to be a relatively recent introduction into Arandic cultures while the underlying concept pre-existed in Aranda thought. Nash suggests, that kurdungurlu is a Warlpiri word that diffused southwards (Nash 1982: 149–151). A letter written in Aranda by Nathanael Rauwirarka to Carl Strehlow, suggests that Ilpara men from the north, believed to be Warlpiri people, had visited Hermannsburg in the first decade of the twentieth century.[17] This Warlpiri term, kurdungurlu, is composed of 'kurdu' and -ngurlu. Nash suggests that kurdu in this context is most likely to mean 'sister's child' (Nash 1982). The word does not seem to appear in Carl Strehlow's or in Spencer and Gillen's published work. It features only in Carl Strehlow's unpublished dictionary spelled kutungula in Aranda and pipawonnu in Loritja meaning 'subject, servant'.[18] In his bible translations and the small primer he wrote for Aranda children it is used for 'disciple' or 'evangelist' (Austin-Broos 2010: 21).

In the anthropological literature on Arandic people the term kutuŋula is first documented in the 1930s in Olive Pink's *Oceania* articles (1936) and T.G.H. Strehlow's unpublished essays (1934). The recent importation of this term may also account for its various concepts among people speaking different Arandic languages. Considering the concept under these diffusionist and linguistic aspects, it is no wonder that anthropologists have found a number of variations of the kutuŋula (kwertengerle) concept in Arandic areas. They explain to some degree why it has been difficult to find and describe the meaning of the term. Some Arandic people seemed to define the concept of kwertengerle more broadly than others. It was, and maybe still is, evolving, and meanings from other terms moved to such newly acquired words and concepts. It seems, for example, that some Western Aranda meanings of altjira, in the sense of mother's dreaming, was shifted to this newly adopted expression, while other parts of altjira's semantic field moved to tnankara (tnengkarre) as discussed in Chapter V.

---

16 Connections to country through one's mother's mother may be construed to pmerekwerteye, because ego and his mother's mother are in the same patrimoiety. However, mother's mother connections are usually understood as conferring kwertengerle status among Western Aranda people, in my experience.

17 Letter from Nathaneal (and Moses) to Carl Strehlow, 30.4.1911.

18 Carl Strehlow's handwritten unpublished Aranda-German-Loritja dictionary manuscript (c.1890s–1909) held at the Strehlow Research Centre in Alice Springs.

Carl Strehlow's record of altjira meaning 'mother's dreaming' provides one of the earliest comprehensive pieces of evidence that rights to country could be gained through mothers and determine a number of entitlements, including ritual rights. He writes concerning these ritual rights that actors for certain ceremonies should be of the appropriate 'ratapa' or 'altjira':

> During the mbatjalkatiuma the men selected as actors for the respective ceremonies must belong to the totem concerned, or at least it must be their maternal totem (altjira). For example, if a kangaroo cult ritual is to be held the actors may be chosen only from among those whose ratapa or altjira was a kangaroo-altjirangamitjina. In the case of the intitjiuma, however, men belonging to the totem concerned will be preferred, but men of other totems may also appear as actors. Hence, a lizard-man may play an active role in a kangaroo ceremony. (Strehlow 1910: 1–2)

Altjira, meaning mother's dreaming in this context, seems to indicate that Western Aranda land tenure was somewhat differently orientated during Carl Strehlow's time, although it still confers rights through mothers. These affiliations are now articulated through the concept of kwertengerle in Western Aranda society. The rights to be a kwertengerle come mainly through mother's father, and sometimes through father's mother and mother's mother. In other Arandic languages the term altjira still denotes today similar meanings to those Carl Strehlow elicited from his informants (see, for instance, Green 2012: 167). Altyerre in North-Eastern Arrernte (Henderson and Dobson 1994: 105) and altyerr in Alyawarr[19] (Green 1992: 29–30) and Anmatyerr[20] (Green 2010) which are often glossed as 'dreaming' in English, can also refer to the dreaming tracks, places and stories which are inherited through maternal ancestry, and can mean mother's place. Green writes:

> The compound from ALYERR-ANKETHENH (lit. 'having Dreaming') refers to 'those related to a place or Dreaming through their mothers'. (Green 1998: 57)

Father's father's country

There are no explicit remarks on land ownership through a patrilineally inherited 'totem' (dreaming) in Carl Strehlow's work. However, belonging to land through fathers appears in some ways 'at the beginning of time'. It is striking how the mythological account of primordial times on earth, that presents embryonic

---

19 Arandic language spoken in parts of north-eastern central Australia.
20 Arandic language spoken in parts of north-western central Australia.

people slumbering under the earth's surface, divides them into patrimoieties and patricouples, although at the time the subsection system was believed to have been a very recent introduction into Arandic cultures:

> The rella manerinja, who lived on the slopes of the mountain, were divided into four classes: Purula, Kamara, Ngala and Mbitjana. Because these people lived on dry land they were referred to as alarinja [land dwellers]. However, there were other undeveloped people who lived in the water, called kwatjarinja, water dwellers. These people had long hair and their food consisted of raw meat. They were also divided into four classes: Pananka, Paltara, Knuraia and Bangata. More of these undeveloped people lived at Rubuntja [Mt Hay] in the north-east and at Irbmankara on the Finke River, now known as Running Waters. (Strehlow 1907: 2)

It was only with Mangarkunjerkunja who had come from the north that the helpless rella manerinja's lot was improved. It was he who awoke them, explained to them how their subsection system worked and who should marry whom. In addition, he allocated patricouples to all areas in the Aranda landscape (Strehlow 1907: 6–7; 1915: 1).

The mythology of the Loritja provides similar data on this issue. Carl Strehlow wrote that 'the undeveloped people matu ngalulba of primordial times were already divided into 8 marriage classes [that is, a subsection system] and lived in the vicinity of Unkutu-kwatji' (Strehlow 1908: 4). Unlike the 'rella manerinja' of the Aranda who were divided into land dwellers and water dwellers, the 'matu ngalulba' of the Loritja lived beside each other; 'one group resided in the north and east and the other group lived in the south and west' (Strehlow 1913: 79).

In a chapter called 'The Constitutional and Legal Order' of the Aranda (Strehlow 1915: 1–15) he refers again to the fact that country is allocated to subsections and talks about what can perhaps be described as estates, or at least, as forerunners of what his son would call the 'njinaŋa (nyenhenge) section areas':

> According to the primordial legends, Mangarkunjerkunja had already partitioned the vast territory of the Aranda among the individual marriage-classes (Aranda Legends, page 6,7). *This division of territory, presented in detail in Part I, p.6f., is important to the extent that the individual marriage-classes still regard the tracts of land given to them at that time as their property and claim chieftainship over them.*[21] For example, in the first mentioned western territory of the Aranda the chief has to belong to either the Purula class or the Kamara class. In Alice Springs and the surrounding region he must be a Paltara or a Knuraia. In

---

21   Emphasis added.

the Ellery Creek territory he must be a Pananka or a Bangata; whilst in the territory south of Rubula only an Ngala or Mbitjana may claim the honour of a chief. (Strehlow 1915: 1)

He goes on to explain that the chief of an estate is called 'inkata' (chief or father of all), but on a general level he is only a 'primus inter pares', and that his position is hereditary.[22] He wrote:

> The Aranda and Loritja do not elect their chief. He is, as it were, born into that position. The chieftainship is always inherited by the next younger brother, and after the death of the youngest brother it passes to the oldest son of the oldest brother, should he still be alive. If that is not the case, then it passes to a younger son of the oldest brother, etc.

> The greater or lesser esteem for a chief depends on his personal achievements. Although every larger settlement has a resident chief who presides at meetings, only those from among them who have distinguished themselves by their courage and strength would be called inkata knara (= great/big chief) and held in higher esteem than the inkata kurka (= little chief), who holds this honour merely by virtue of his inheritance and does not exceed the other men of his camp in terms of personal achievements. (Strehlow 1915: 1–2)

The old men were called 'knaribata (kngerrepate)', 'pintulara' in Loritja and 'pinaru' in Diyari meaning 'the big man, the older man of high status)' in Carl Strehlow's time[23] and these men were highly esteemed according to their level of knowledge (see also Spencer and Gillen 1899: 10). This term appears in volume one (1907), but is only much later explained and translated in Carl's work (1913). T.G.H. Strehlow also uses the term 'knaribata' which 'always refers to an old man who knew all the sacred traditions of his clan or group, and is therefore fit to be a member of the council of elders of his group'.[24]

Carl Strehlow writes that the subsection 'is passed on from grand-father to grand-child or, to put it in other words, that the class continues along patrilineal and not matrilineal lines' (Strehlow 1913: 71). He concurs with the findings of Spencer and Gillen (1899: 115) that 'so far as the class [subsection] is concerned, descent is counted in the male line' from one's father's father. In this context, Spencer and Gillen make an interesting comment on the way in which a 'churinga' dropped by a spirit child is found, once it has entered the mother:

---

22 Inkata (A) = tina, atunari (L) = Kapara (D): Häuptling, Herr (allg. Vater) (Carl Strehlow's unpublished dictionary c.1900–1909).
23 Knaribata is composed of knara (big) and ata a contraction of atua (man). It was used for 'old man' (Carl Strehlow's unpublished dictionary c.1900–1909).
24 T.G.H. Strehlow's unpublished dictionary K (n.d.): 92a.

Sometimes it is found, sometimes it is not. In the former case, which is stated to occur often, we must suppose that some old man — it is most often the Arunga or paternal grandfather who finds it — has provided himself with one for the occasion, which is quite possible, as Churinga belonging to their own totem are not infrequently carried about by the old men, who obtain them from the sacred storehouse in which they are kept. (Spencer and Gillen 1899: 132)

It is noteworthy, that Carl Strehlow very rarely recorded any explicit remarks on subsection affiliations of myths in either prose or poetic texts. He only made a comment on the subsection affiliation of the frog ancestors. He wrote that they 'belonged to the Mbitjana class', and it was the only myth and song in his entire oral text collection (Strehlow 1910: 72–73; 1911: 37) in which his informants had made an explicit remark that it was about ancestors of a particular subsection:

> It will be noticed that the marriage-class of the altjirangamitjina concerned is mentioned in this legend only, while in the legends passed on by Spencer and Gillen they are almost always specified. However, the marriage-class was given to me only in this case. I suspect that Spencer and Gillen made it a practice to ask for the class to which the respective totem ancestor belonged. I have deliberately avoided this, the black can, by means of simple deduction, state the marriage-class of a particular totem ancestor (iningukua) because every individual is born into the same class as his specific iningukua. Therefore, if one knows a person whose ratapa has emerged from a rock, tree, or tjurunga of a particular altjirangamitjina, and if one takes into account the marriage-class of the mother, then it is easy to state the marriage-class to which the iningukua must have belonged. It should be obvious, however, that such a subsequent determination by the various black narrators is without value. (Strehlow 1907: 82)

It seems to have been taken for granted by his informants that he knew, as they did, that a myth was about a particular country and ancestors with particular subsection affiliations. In 1932 his son went to considerable trouble to find out to which subsections the protagonists of the myth 'atua arintja' of Ulamba belonged. He found out that the father, Toppatataka, was a Purula and his son, the atua arintja (monster man), a Kamara.[25] It may have been taken for granted and, thus, completely unnecessary to mention that a myth or an ancestor was of a particular subsection, as it was clear to everyone at that time that country had subsections.

---

25   T.G.H. Strehlow's Diary I (1932: 145).

In the 1930s, Olive Pink witnessed an emphasis on traditional estates associated with patricouples and owned through the patriline among Northern Aranda people and T.G.H. Strehlow among the Western Aranda. In his early work, although it was not the centre of his attention, T.G.H. Strehlow defined the landholding group as consisting of 'all men, women and children of a given totemic clan who stand to one another in the relation of fathers, sons, brothers, sisters, and daughters, relationship being determined both by actual and by class ties' (Strehlow 1947: 139).

A tight reading of this statement and of T.G.H. Strehlow's 1965 view on Aranda land tenure appears in the 'Summary Statement' of a Finke River Mission report. The authors of this statement appear to be perpetuating and emphasising a patrilineal and patriarchal model, although they add the role of the kutungula, defined as 'custodians or managers of the tjurunga, and so also the land' who are the 'male descendants from women belonging to the land-owning group'. They wrote that:

> The most important kin grouping in relation to land ownership is the patrilineal descent group, composed of people descended from a common male ancestor through the male line. Each patrilineal descent group belongs to a particular tract of land and its member are called the Pmarakutwia (people belonging to the land, the land owners) for that particular area of land. A clearly defined system of leadership, and a recognised leader, exist within each of these groups. The female descendants from the male line are part of the patrilineal land-owning group, but only the fully initiated males are taught the secret knowledge relating to the land and its tjurunga. (Albrecht et al. 1976: 1)[26]

T.G.H. Strehlow called the country of a patrilineal descent group the 'njinaŋa (nyenhenge) section area'. Rights and interests in such an area were and still are articulated in terms of knowledge of particular dreaming tracks or segments of dreaming tracks and sites, as well as in terms of kinship links. Aranda people affiliated with a landholding group and its country through their fathers and father's fathers are today called pmerekwerteye (Morton 1992, 1997a,b; Kenny 2003: 31). According to Morton, T.G.H. Strehlow's 'njinaŋa' group more or less corresponds with what is understood under the term pmerekwerteye (Morton 1997a: 117). In land rights and native title claims this was found to be one of the principal ways to become a member of a landholding group and thereby acquire rights and responsibilities in relation to land. The other principal way today is through mother's father discussed above. Pmerekwerteye means literally 'country-owner'. It is a compound: pmere-ke-rtweye. The -ke is a dative suffix, which is very common, and -rtweye is the same as artweye (Henderson and

---

26   This summary statement has been reproduced in Albrecht (2002: 80–82).

Dobson 1994: 286–287) in Eastern Arrernte and means 'owned or owner'. However, in Western Aranda it does not seem to be used as an independent word (as artweye can be, but is not usually); -rtweye is rare in other combinations, and so people do not think of it as a unit.[27] Gillen in 1899 mentioned 'Kartwia Quatcha' to Spencer 'meaning rain or water country and applied to the district occupied by a water totem group' (Wilkins 2001: 508). Wilkins continues:

> It is not clear whether kartwia is really intended as a separate word or not. The form artweye means 'custodian of, person having major responsibility for something' and it typically follows a noun in the dative case -ke. For instance traditional owners of country are Pmere-k-artweye (country-DATIVE-custodian). Thus k-artweye could be a mis-parsing of some more complex construction. Kwatye-k-artweye would be the term referring to custodians of rain and water Dreaming country. (Wilkins 2001: 508–509)

The term pmerekwerteye seems to have emerged in the context of land right claims in the Northern Territory. In written records pmerekwerteye seems to appear for the first time in 1976 in a land rights submission of the Finke River Mission (FRM), spelled 'pmarakutwia' (Albrecht et al. 1976). Garry Stoll[28] remembers hearing it in the late 1960s. This expression does not seem to appear in either of the Strehlows' or Pink's work. It appears as 'Atwia-atwia' in Spencer and Gillen's work where it is said to be the 'name applied to the men who operate at the ceremony of circumcision' (Spencer and Gillen 1899: 647). It appears that one of the two 'Atwia-atwia' of the ceremony they witnessed in Alice Springs was the novice's father (Spencer and Gillen 1899: 241–248). According to Wilkins, this Central (Mparntwe) Arrernte term artweye-artweye can be understood in the following way:

> The form artweye means the person/people who have the primary responsibility for looking after something; the custodians or 'owners' of something. This form shows up in the term for parents, the term for traditional owners of country and the term for the ancestors ('the custodians of us all'). In Arrernte the term artweye-ke-artweye means related to one another in kinship. (Wilkins 2001: 496)

The suffix -gatuia appears on T.G.H. Strehlow's genealogies collected from Anmatyerr people in July/August 1968 at Alcoota and Laramba.[29] Imora-gatuia, for example, translates as 'possum dreaming owner' or 'belonging to possum

---

27   Gavan Breen, email, 17.9.2007.
28   Garry Stoll worked for over three decades at Hermannsburg. Initially he worked as a mechanic and later became the executive officer of the Finke River Mission. He is a fluent speaker of Aranda and was involved in most aspects of public Western Aranda life, including the land rights movement.
29   T.G.H. Strehlow's Diary 38 and Anmatjerra FT series IX.

dreaming'. The same dreaming affiliation appears on a Western Aranda family tree as 'imora kŋ. (kŋanintja)'. However, the suffix -gatuia appears in the word pmaragatuia used in documents written for the Palm Valley Land Claim (Morton 1992 and Gray 1999).[30] In the Land Claim by Alyawarra and Kaititja (Toohey 1978: 5) and Utopia Land Claim by Anmatjira and Alyawarra to Utopia Pastoral Lease (Toohey 1980: 5) some patriclans had the tendency to add the suffix -rinya (meaning 'belonging to') to their estate name. This though is another suffix.

In sum, Carl and T.G.H. Strehlow use inkata and knaribata to reference what we today understand as primary Aranda land-owners. The term pmerekwerteye that carries connotations of ownership has replaced some of the meaning that was covered by the terms inkata and knaribata which implied ritual authority and power.[31] Austin-Broos (2004: 63) suggests that the impact of settlement life, pastoralism with its ideas and notions of 'ownership' and the state's jural order shifted the focus from custodianship of rites and sites to 'blocks' of land and 'bounded patrilineal estates'. A term such as pmerekwerteye with its affinity to notions of European ownership possibly was a convenient one in the land claim context and seems to have been reinforced by its use in legal procedures.

Change and continuity?

Clearly there is a tension between Carl and T.G.H. Strehlow's respective emphasis concerning connections to country in Western Aranda culture. While both documented conception as important, their data seem to diverge with regard to mother's and father's connections to place and dreaming. In fact Strehlow senior did not even mention explicitly a connection to a father's 'totem', only to a patch of country that was inherited through patrilineal descent and associated with patricouples. His data on ratapa (conception dreaming) and altjira (mother's conception dreaming) and associated places stands in contrast with the emphasis that his son and others have given to dreamings and places inherited through patrilineal principles. Carl's altjira as well as ratapa were connected to mother, both her own conception and that of her child. These personal details seem to give 'mother's side' some significant meaning in belonging to country. T.G.H. Strehlow did not explore these mother's connections in detail. His father's 'altjira' would appear in some way in connection with the kutuŋula's rights to mother's tjurunga ([1964] 1978: 38). In his work patrilineal connections conferred primary land-ownership rights which were transferable through the

---

30 '-gatuia' meaning 'own' or 'self' (Morton 1992).
31 The term pmererenye (A) meaning 'belonging to country' seems to give in the contemporary context some counterbalance to the notions of 'owner' in the word pmerekwerteye. (Ngurraritja (L) has been translated to me as pmererenye.) However, I have not discussed its translation and its underlying concepts sufficiently yet with Aranda and Loritja people to make a conclusive statement here.

patriline. Connections and rights to a conception site he seems to have mainly understood as an individuating characteristic within the context of a patrilineal descent group, his njinaŋa group, and were generally not transferable. This may have given the ritual group balance within their estate, as the people involved shared a ritual focus but also had their own personal identity (Austin-Broos 2009: 116).

One wonders if Carl Strehlow's informants provided him with these personal details because that is what he seemed to ask rather than for an account of a located socio-territorial order. Perhaps his style of questioning elicited personal details most readily, or perhaps the personal details were the most readily provided information. These seem to be egocentric principles, as described by Myers ([1986] 1991), that are operating at the turn of the twentieth century. Or, possibly, Carl Strehlow's informants took it as evident that every person was connected to a father's dreaming, as it was obvious that all country on Western Aranda territory had subsection affiliations, that is the bond between fathers and their offspring was embedded in land.

A tight and literal reading of T.G.H. Strehlow's work and the ideologies he presented at different times during his long career as an anthropologist, have led to the view that he promoted a rigid patrilineal model or gave too much prominence to conception sites. It seems he was trying to grasp a land tenure system which was undergoing shifts due to a number of events that had been occurring since the 1870s, and focused at different times on different aspects of the system. To understand the Western Aranda's land ownership system and the changes it was undergoing in the twentieth century, T.G.H. Strehlow's complete work spanning over four decades has to be considered. It shows that he had found evidence for multiple paths to be included even in a system such as the one of the Western Aranda (though the rights are not all equal) and that it was changing as he was researching it. In his publications he seems to have been oblivious of socio-cultural changes, as he opted to present the Aranda's 'classical' system as if it had been handed down unchanged 'since time began'.

The fact that T.G.H. Strehlow tried to capture an untouched, pre-contact world of the Western Aranda people – an ideal Aranda world – in which demographic and climatic accidents of a desert environment, like long droughts or the end of a patriline, were not taken into account, shows clearly that he was not formally trained in modern anthropology. Morton has argued that Strehlow junior attempted 'to over systematise a dynamic framework of land tenure in which contradictions have been as historically significant as harmony and integration' (Morton 1997a: 109). While the patrilineal model was likely to have been an ideal even in a desert environment that was relatively well watered, such as the areas of the Aranda, it would have been impractical, if not unrealistic. People had to move to survive – and to maintain their far flung social networks, as they still do. In an environment as unpredictable and harsh as that of central Australia, mechanisms to ensure the maintenance of knowledge and land ownership needed to be inherent in a land tenure system. Their system had to survive in a desert environment which only allowed a low demographic density; the population was made up of very small groups, with lineages that constantly expanded or diminished in numbers in unpredictable ways. T.G.H. Strehlow's model of Western Aranda land ownership does not always reflect what contemporary indigenous landholding groups regard as true.

It also has to be kept in mind that Strehlow junior worked with men and did very little research into the world of Aboriginal women. He made a remark late in his oeuvre about women and their ritual knowledge. In *Songs of Central Australia*, he writes briefly how little is known about the sacred life of Aboriginal women and how regrettable this is (1971: 647–653). He remarked that women 'were aware of *all*[32] the landscape features associated with the various totems located in their area of residence' (Strehlow 1971: 648) as they were the ones who ultimately determined the conception sites of their children, and that there 'is the undoubted existence of a body of unknown dimension of special women's lore, which used to be kept jealously secret from the men' (Strehlow 1971: 649). His work depicts largely a male Aranda worldview. His bias towards a patrilineal land tenure model may to a certain degree be the result of the lack of consultation with women.

Nevertheless, there seems to be little doubt that Western Aranda society had and still has a preference for the inheritance of knowledge through the patriline connecting people to father's father's country. Carl Strehlow's references on how country is associated with subsections, and chieftainship is inherited through the male line as well as his position on patrilineal descent, seem to point to a patrilineally biased model, despite his evidence that matrifiliation and conception were other pathways that were valid ways to claim rights to land and very possibly emphasised by individuals.

In sum, we find generally in contemporary Western Aranda culture that the group of landholders of a country consists of pmerekwerteye, who connect to their land through their father's father, and kwertengerle, whose rights and responsibilities are mainly derived through mother's father. They are the core members of a landholding group under traditional laws and customs. People who are connected to country and have rights and responsibilities in relation to it through their father's mother and mother's mother are also called kwertengerle and can acquire membership in a landholding group. Long-term residence, conception sites, responsibility of shared dreaming tracks, and knowledge and authority in relation to dreaming tracks and stories enhance the status of the

---

32 T.G.H. Strehlow's emphasis.

latter kwertengerle (Kenny 2010: 42–48) – in rare cases this includes exceptional individuals without descent links. Morton described a comparable situation among Central Arrernte people:

> While a person's connections to, and rights in, all four grandparental estates are held simultaneously, those connections tend to be more or less ranked in people's minds. One belongs first to the estate on one's father's father; second to the estate one's mother's father; third to the estate of one's father's mother; and fourth to the estate of one's mother's mother. However, there may be exceptions to this ranking system based on factors such as knowledge, seniority and long term residence. (Morton 1997b: 26–27)

This type of model based on traditional principles manifests itself in the context of land and native title claims and decision-making with regard to some infrastructure and mining developments on Aboriginal land rather than in everyday life. It is determined by dreaming associations and certain kinship links, because many principles of land ownership are based on descent and who has a right to acquire knowledge of the mythology associated with particular parts of the landscape. Indeed, kin or rather descent-based connections to land are becoming in the contemporary setting more prominent in claiming rights and the accepted way to be part of a landholding group, in particular when the distribution of resources from mining ventures or joint management of National Parks are involved. Sutton (2003: 252) has observed that there is a tendency in settled areas of Australia to move towards a cognatic model of inheritance to rights in land. Western Aranda people seem to oscillate between a patrilineal 'biased' and a cognatic model depending on the social, economic and political context.

Carl Strehlow's material, and its many imponderable dimensions, especially when it is placed beside that of his son, suggests something other than a mere developmental sequence or a static model. Aboriginal rights to land in central Australia have involved a significant range of personal as well as socio-centric links. These have been ranked in a variety of ways, and can be made more or less prominent, according to context. This is unsurprising in view of the Aranda's twentieth century history.

VIII. Positioning Carl Strehlow in Australian Anthropology and Intellectual History

Histories of Australian anthropology have had an overwhelmingly Anglophone focus rendering invisible the contribution of the German humanistic tradition. In this chapter I will make some suggestions as to how Carl Strehlow's work might be positioned in Australian anthropology and the implications of this for a re-assessment of the work of Spencer and Gillen and T.G.H. Strehlow as well as the history of the discipline more generally.

Old texts or ideas can become the object of current debate and reflection in a discipline (Langham 1981: xxii). Carl Strehlow's text, for instance, suggests new forms of reflection on contemporary Australian anthropology and especially on the way in which professionalism can promote research but also narrow the history of a discipline. There are other early ethnographic writers including W. Ridley, A.H. Howitt, R.H. Mathews, K. Langloh Parker and W.E. Roth from whom new insight might be gained concerning how anthropology was shaped specifically in Australia across the nineteenth and early twentieth centuries. Using translations both from French and German, Martin Thomas (2007, 2011) has made an impressive start on the work of R.H. Mathews. His tracing of the linguistic journey involved in the publication of Mathews' work, suggests that Australian anthropology then may have been more cosmopolitan than it is today. Chris Nobbs' 'The Bush Missionary's Defence' (Nobbs 2005: 26–53) on missionary Otto Siebert makes a start on showing underlying premises that lie outside an Anglophone tradition of a modern anthropology and its field method. Once again, there is more than one route to an empirical discipline. Silverman (2005) suggests national anthropologies should be aiming towards a cosmopolitan discipline and Austin-Broos (1999: 215) proposes that to engage with anthropology's maturing path in the course of the twentieth century, it is paramount in the Australian context to consider traditions outside of a British-Australian intellectual world, that takes the psychological and hermeneutic traditions of European anthropologies into account.

There are two forms of mainly Australian writing that frame Carl Strehlow's work. The first are comments, sketches and longer studies contemporaneous with *Die Aranda- und Loritja-Stämme in Zentral-Australien* and produced by others interested in or engaged with Aboriginal people. These writings provide a further important background to *Die Aranda- und Loritja-Stämme in Zentral-Australien*. To ultimately place his work in perspective, and the work of Spencer and Gillen, it is important to compare and contrast what they achieved with other writers of the time. The focus should not be just on the 'armchair' anthropologists of Europe and Great Britain but also on the diarists, chroniclers and policeman-scribblers who shaped popular attitudes to Aboriginal people. It may have been some of the work of this latter group that most influenced settler society in its view of indigenous Australians. It is in comparison with this work that Australia's transitional ethnographers need to be judged, for what they achieved in a nascent science rather than for ways in which they fell short of a modern anthropology. A history of how anthropology in Australia enlightened its readers, rather than reinforced colonial prejudice, is still to be written, although Hiatt's *Arguments about Aborigines* (1996) makes a start.

The second set of literature I will address are some relevant discussions in the history of Australian anthropology that bear on my study of *The Aranda's Pepa* and also differ from it. This book is unusual to the extent that it focuses only on one major text, in this case of a missionary-scholar. It is the unique circumstance of Carl Strehlow's work, largely forgotten in Germany and hardly known in Australia, that led me to this particular focus especially when I discovered the von Leonhardi correspondence at the Strehlow Research Centre in Alice Springs. It seemed a fitting redress for Carl Strehlow's opus. The contemporary writings that correspond most directly with this study are those by John Mulvaney and his co-authors and co-editors in their works on both Spencer and Gillen. Although these are not the only writings on a transitional figure in Australian anthropology, they are certainly the most important. Possibly, the other major work to consider beside these is Ian Langham's study of 'the "school" of Cambridge Ethnology' in which the roles of W.H.R. Rivers and A.R. Radcliffe-Brown are central (Langham 1981: xxiii). His approach was influenced by George Stocking's mode of writing about anthropology, which he usefully applied to early Australian anthropology.

Early contemporaneous work

In the 1860s and early 1870s J.M. Stuart (1865), W.C. Gosse (1873), P.E. Warburton (1875), E. Giles (1889), and other explorers, recorded the presence of Aboriginal people in central Australia by making some occasional remarks on brief encounters and indigenous terms. These accounts were followed by a number of books with contributions from a variety of people including surveyors, missionaries, policemen and telegraph masters. Examples of this genre which often came in the form of collations, are: R.B. Smyth's *The Aborigines of Victoria with notes relating to the habits of the natives of other parts of Australia and Tasmania* (1878), G. Taplin's *The Folklore, Manners, Customs and Languages of the South Australian Aborigines* (1879), J.D. Woods' *The Native Tribes of South Australia* (1879) and E.M. Curr's *The Australasian Race* (1886–

1887). These collections cover subjects such as the origin of the Australian race, their languages (usually wordlists and occasionally skeletal grammars) and their 'customs, manners and habits' in general. 'Ethnographic' writing by troopers, such as Gason (1874) and Willshire (1888), were also published.

Samuel Gason, a mounted constable of the South Australian police force was stationed at Lake Hope in the early 1870s, and took an interest in the Diyari people of the region collecting ethnographic data on their social and religious life. In 1874 he published *The Dieyerie Tribe of Australian Aborigines;* in the same year he led punitive expeditions near Barrow Creek on Kaytetye country (Nettelbeck and Foster 2007: 7). In 1888 William Willshire's *The Aborigines of Central Australia* appeared, which, according to Nettelbeck and Foster, 'is more tellingly a literary reconstruction of his experience and opinions as a Mounted Constable in the Interior' than an account of the 'manners, customs and languages' (Nettelbeck and Foster 2007: 53).

Also noteworthy are Thomas Worsnop's *The Prehistoric Arts, Manufactures, Works, Weapons, etc., of the Aborigines of Australia* (1897), a survey of Aboriginal art and material culture, and John Mathew's *Eaglehawk and Crow* (1899). Mathew attached special importance to his linguistic studies and was interested in diffusionist thought. His data seemed to indicate that the distribution of language proved that settlement of the continent was first in the north-east where the lines of language converged and not, as was put forward in an earlier hypothesis by Eyre and endorsed by Curr, that the first settlement was in the north-west, and that the distribution of population was effected by the original stream of people crossing to the south of Australia in three broad separate bands (Mathew 1899: ix–xi).

W.E. Roth, Oxford educated, published in 1897 *Ethnological Studies among the North-West-Central Queensland Aborigines*, a classic in Australian anthropology. Roth was a surgeon working in Boulia, Cloncurry and Normanton, where he made his own empirical investigations into the languages and traditions of the Aboriginal people of North-West-Central Queensland. He concluded that 'his tribes lacked any totemic beliefs, a finding which Spencer condemned as heresy' (Mulvaney and Calaby 1985: 209). Spencer set out to demonstrate its falsity and made derogatory remarks about Roth, as he did about R.H. Mathews (Mulvaney and Calaby 1985: 195; Thomas 2004, 2011).

Like other Australian ethnographic writers of the time, R.H. Mathews (1841–1918) was a self-taught anthropologist. Between 1893 and 1918, he published 171 anthropological reportages in English, French and German (Thomas 2007). Some of it was based on his own observations, but like most of his contemporaries, he also had to rely on the information supplied by others through correspondence. Among his prolific writings were a number of articles on Aranda people

(Mathews 1906, 1907a,b,c, 1908) although he never visited central Australia and seemed to base his accounts at least in part on his letter exchange with Carl Strehlow.

E. Eylmann (1860–1926), a German doctor and adventurer, also had contact with Strehlow. In 1908 he published *Die Eingeborenen der Kolonie Südaustralien*. During his travels in remote Australia, he had been a guest of Carl Strehlow at Hermannsburg Mission in 1898. His account contains some interesting ethnographic and historical data on Aboriginal Australia as well as an ungracious account of the Lutheran missions of the inland (Eylmann 1908: 464–482) who had been his hosts. Monteath (2013) writes that Eylmann stood in the camp of the anti-humanists who were also well represented amongst Germans, and that his views differed fundamentally from those of the German missionary anthropologists, above all Carl Strehlow.

In the 1860s with a stream of Protestant missionaries arriving in the Lake Eyre region the Diyari language and culture received a great deal of attention. One of the first missionaries at Killalpaninna Mission, Carl Schoknecht, wrote a Diyari grammar and wordlist within two years of his arrival (Schoknecht 1997: 16, 80). His successors continued to collect data on the Diyari language and culture until the mission was closed in 1917 (see Kneebone 2001; Stevens 1994). The Lutheran ethnographers of this region are fairly well-known today. Among these, missionaries Siebert and Reuther made outstanding contributions (Völker 2001; Hercus and McCaul 2004; Nobbs 2005). Reuther left a monumental work behind called *Die Diari*. It remains unpublished despite Tindale's efforts. In 1902 Siebert co-authored with M.E.B. Howitt 'Some Native Legends from Central Australia' in *Folklore* and in 1910 his article 'Sagen und Sitten der Dieri und Nachbarstämme in Zentral-Australien' was published in *Globus* with the help of von Leonhardi (Völker 2001). Siebert's unpublished correspondence with Howitt remains a valuable source for the cultures of the Cooper Creek area (see Hercus and McCaul 2004; Nobbs 2005). However, others also made records of the Diyari. A.W. Howitt who had corresponded with S. Gason between 1879 and 1888 published 'The Dieri and other kindred Tribes of Central Australia' in 1891, which according to Nobbs (2007: 3), is the first comprehensive ethnography about Aboriginal people in the Cooper Creek region.

However, among Aboriginal peoples in central Australia and in Australian anthropology generally, the Aranda are now one of the best-documented Aboriginal groups. The Aranda, as John Morton remarks, 'need no introduction' as they and their first significant ethnographers, Spencer and Gillen, were propelled around the 1900s to international celebrity (Morton 1985: 3) and are one of the 'best-known Aboriginal groups in world anthropology' (Morton 1992: 24; see also McKnight 1990). Their ethnographers and anthropologists are among the finest.

The documentation of Aranda culture began when the first Lutheran missionaries, A.H. Kempe, L. Schulze and W.F. Schwarz, arrived in 1877 at the site of Ntaria in central Australia where they set up the Lutheran mission. As soon as they had made first contacts with the indigenous population, they started to study the language of the local people and collected material on their customs. By 1880–1881 they had produced a school primer and a book with bible stories, psalms, hymns and prayers in the local language. In 1883 Kempe published his first ethnographic account of the 'Aldolinga', as the people he had met at Ntaria called themselves, 'Zur Sittenkunde der Centralaustralischen Schwarzen'. In 1886 and 1887, F.E.H. Krichauff published 'Customs, Religious Ceremonies, etc., of the "Aldolinga" or "Mbenderinga" Tribe of Aborigines of the Krichauff Ranges', which was based on data collected by Kempe and Schulze. By the time these missionaries left Hermannsburg Mission in the early 1890s they had also published 'A grammar and vocabulary of the language spoken by the Aborigines of the MacDonnell Ranges' (Kempe 1891) and 'The Aborigines of the Upper and Middle Finke River: their habits and customs' (Schulze 1891). Schulze had also corresponded with Howitt.[1]

After these early anthropological accounts on Aranda people and language by the German missionaries, they became the subject of scientific research during the Horn Scientific Expedition of 1894. E.C. Stirling, the expedition's anthropologist and the director of the South Australian Museum, collected ethnographic data principally on the 'Arunta' (Stirling 1896: 9) which was published as the fourth volume, *Anthropology,* in the expedition's report. This volume also contains a piece on Aboriginal beliefs by Frank Gillen. Baldwin Spencer, the expedition's zoologist and editor of the reports, made some remarks on the Aboriginal people he had encountered in central Australia, which includes Gillen's famous coining of 'alcheringa' as the 'dreamtime' (Spencer 1896: 111). Gillen's contribution was not his first anthropological or linguistic attempt. Previously, he had collected wordlists, and one of them had been published in Curr's third volume of *The Australasian Race* in 1886. He had also made field notes, some of which were published posthumously (Gillen 1968, 1995).

Based on the observation of ceremonial cycles performed in 1896 for a number of weeks at the Alice Springs telegraph station, and Gillen's previous and subsequent field research, Spencer and Gillen's first classic *The Native Tribes of Central Australia* appeared in 1899. It was followed by *The Northern Tribes of Central Australia* in 1904 which was the result of a long fieldtrip from Alice Springs north along the Telegraph Line in 1901. One year earlier Gillen read and published a Frazerian paper, called *Magic amongst the Natives of Central Australia* in Melbourne which Spencer had written (Morphy [1997] 2001: 28). Their work was 'in no small measure sponsored' (Morton 1985: 12) and mentored by James

---

1 Schulze's letters to A.W. Howitt, 1887–1889 (State Library of Victoria, Howitt Papers MF 459, Box 1051/Icc).

Frazer (Marett and Penniman 1932). These books address both physical and social aspects of Aboriginal people, but focus on totemic beliefs and ceremonial practices. After Gillen's death in 1912, Spencer continued publishing and his oeuvre amounted to several more books and reports on Aboriginal people of the Northern Territory, culminating just before his death in two volumes called *The Arunta* (1927), which included Gillen as co-author.

Another anthropological classic called *The Native Tribes of South-East Australia* by A.W. Howitt (1830–1908) was published in 1904. It was based on his field-data and the data of dozens of others with whom he corresponded. In 1873 he had joined 'Dr Lorimer Fison in investigating the classificatory system of relationships, which obtains among these savages' (Howitt 1904: vii). Their results had been published in *Kamilaroi and Kurnai: Group Marriage and Relationship, and Marriage by Elopement* in 1880 and 'From Mother-right to Father-right' in 1883 and were indebted to Morgan's approach to kinship studies. These publications which were concerned with origins of group-marriage maintained they had found evidence for the practice, which, according to Hiatt, belongs to 'one of the most notable fantasies in the history of anthropology' (Hiatt 1996: 56). Howitt understood wife-sharing between two brothers as group marriage, evident in a practice called pirrauru, by which an older brother granted access to his wife to a younger brother. In 1899 Spencer and Gillen reported a similar institution among the Urabunna giving Howitt's finding powerful backing. However, Malinowski would seal the fate of group marriage in 1913 with his *The Family among the Australian Aborigines* that showed that Howitt and Spencer's theoretical loyalties had led them to distort the facts of Aboriginal family life (Hiatt 1996: 45, 51).

Earlier in 1906 N.W. Thomas had taken issue with the existence of group marriage in *Kinship Organisations and Group Marriage in Australia*, a summary of the existing Australian material on kinship study (Thomas 1906a: 123; Hiatt 1996: 46–47). Generally N.W. Thomas belonged to those who did not accept many of the assumptions generated by evolutionistic thinking. He commented on Australian anthropology in German and English journals. In 1905, for example, he wrote 'Über Kulturkreise in Australien' in the *Zeitschrift für Ethnologie* and in 1906 'Dr. Howitt's Defence of Group-Marriage' in *Folklore*. In the same year he also published *Natives of Australia,* a summary of the existing literature on the Aborigines of Australia, and an article called 'The Religious Ideas of the Arunta'. These works were literature based and relied on information obtained from people in the field. For example, Thomas corresponded briefly with Carl Strehlow asking him to fill in some gaps left by Spencer and Gillen's publications.[2]

---

2   See for example N.W. Thomas to Carl Strehlow, 22.10.1904 (SRC 1904/39) and 27.4.1905 (SRC 1905/58).

Andrew Lang, another armchair anthropologist, also rejected the idea of group marriage that led him to an interest in K. Langloh Parker's work. In the foreword of her book *The Euahlayi Tribe: A Study of Aboriginal Life in Australia* (1905), he remarked that she had *not* found the custom 'by which married men and women, and unmarried men, of the classes which may intermarry, are solemnly allotted to each other as more or less permanent paramours' (Lang 1905: xi). He also took the opportunity to hint that Parker's collections of certain beliefs might be styled as 'religious'.

Some press notices of K. Langloh Parker's earlier compilations of folklore, *Australian Legendary Tales* and *More Australian Legendary Tales*, remark that 'the wild man of that land deserve to occupy a somewhat higher position in the scale of intelligence than that which is generally attributed to them' and that 'The poetic and imaginative quality of these tales will surprise readers who are chiefly impressed by the savagery and the degraded condition of the Australian blacks' (advertising space in Mathew's *Eaglehawk and Crow* 1899).

A number of English intellectuals were sceptical about the wide-sweeping generalisations made by the evolutionists, who were often lawyers or natural scientists. The literature generated by people with clerical or humanistic backgrounds tended to avoid the sweeping generalisations of natural scientists and focused more on specific cultures and groups. But as natural science was the dominant paradigm and a new era seemed to be dawning, it dominated mainstream thinking – not least because it delivered some readily understandable generalisations such as progressive moves from 'magic, religion to science' that were attractive to the Victorian mind (see Stocking 1987, 1995).

Historical writing on transitional Australian anthropology (c.1890–1920)

Without doubt the most impressive corpus of commentary to consider in relation to Carl Strehlow's work is the body of work produced by John Mulvaney and his associates that celebrates the life of Baldwin Spencer and, to a lesser degree, that of Frank Gillen. These works include Mulvaney and Calaby's biography of Baldwin Spencer, not only as anthropologist but also as biologist, public man of letters and administrator (Mulvaney and Calaby 1985). This corpus includes the collection of Baldwin Spencer's photographs selected and annotated by Geoffrey Walker and edited by Ron Vanderwal to which Mulvaney wrote an introduction (Walker and Vanderwal 1982). Interestingly, a second edition of Spencer's photographs, this time edited by Philip Batty, Lindy Allen and John Morton was produced in 2005. It reflects the impact of historical perspectives in anthropology and a consequent effort in the selection to underline both the specificity of Aboriginal people, especially in their ritual life, and the colonial context in which Spencer took his photographs. For example, the second edition includes photographs of body decoration and ritual acts not included in the earlier selection, and photographs of living conditions, on the fringe of Darwin, for instance, that help contextualise Spencer's other images.

In his introduction to the first collection of Baldwin Spencer's photographs, Mulvaney canvases the view of Spencer that he, and Howard Morphy in particular, would develop in their later work. The latter involved editing the correspondence of Gillen to Spencer and also other outback correspondence with Spencer especially from Constable Ernest Cowle who resided for some time south of Hermannsburg at Illamurta (see Mulvaney, Morphy and Petch [1997] 2001; Mulvaney, Petch and Morphy 2000). While neither Mulvaney nor Morphy deny Spencer's strong evolutionary views, they tend to give them less weight by emphasising their data collection through fieldwork that was the product of the Gillen-Spencer partnership. Mulvaney sums up Spencer's evolutionary position quite precisely:

> Spencer believed that biological evolution went along with mental development and material progress. He conceived of Aborigines as surviving fossil remnants from the remote past, whose social and belief systems reflected this pristine condition. (Mulvaney 1982: x)

At the same time, Mulvaney observes that Spencer was a 'generous' man who attended to the 'individuality' of his indigenous photographic subjects. He underlines that Spencer and Gillen's research, due to its density, can be revisited and has been by other anthropologists. Morphy goes further to propose that the partnership of Spencer and Gillen involved an example of the newly emerging 'fieldworker theorist' with one particular twist: '[R]ather than being combined in a single person [the fusion results from] their separate identities in joint research and co-authorship' (Morphy [1997] 2001: 43). Morphy seems to suggest that by over-emphasising Spencer's evolutionary concerns, the partnership has been done an injustice in histories of social anthropology (Morphy [1997] 2001: 30, 46). As a consequence, Radcliffe-Brown and Malinowski have been given more prominence than Spencer and Gillen as trail-blazers of modern fieldwork and the ethnographic method. Morphy seems to propose that 'theory' in this work ultimately has been less important than the actual data, and he also seems to give Baldwin Spencer equal credit with Frank Gillen for the production of that data in *The Native Tribes of Central Australia*.

This argument is difficult to sustain when it is juxtaposed with Philip Jones's preliminary research on the relative ethnographic contributions of Gillen and Spencer to *The Native Tribes of Central Australia*. His examination of correspondence and text reveals that, notwithstanding Gillen's acknowledgements of Spencer, the latter more often acted as editor than as original contributor to the work. In addition, many of the original photographs in their first publication were Gillen's rather than Spencer's (see Jones 2005). If Spencer was mainly the theorist in this fieldwork-theorist fusion, then his contribution to this partnership needs to be carefully re-assessed for, as Mulvaney indicates, his theory was a radical evolutionary type that would soon be superseded by others.

Notable in these discussions is the absence of any sustained attempt to assess the impact of Spencer's evolutionism on the ethnography and interpretations that the pair produced, whether it be their views on conception (but see Wolfe 1999), the controversy about *altjira* and the presence or absence of a high god, or their views on the inheritance of totems. Morphy ([1997] 2001, 2012) focuses mainly on the production of fieldwork data *per se* and Mulvaney in his biography of Spencer, authored with Calaby, addresses a host of activities well beyond anthropology (Mulvaney and Calaby 1985), which included some foundational ideas and projects for future assimilation policies (Ganter 2005: 124–129). However, Mulvaney and Calaby do suggest that the feuding relation between 'Spencer and the Lutheran authorities' was regrettable and detrimental to the advancement of anthropological research in Australia and that Gillen's view of Strehlow contributed to Spencer's attitudes towards the Lutherans (Mulvaney and Calaby 1985: 391). Mulvaney and Calaby remark:

> The fact that Strehlow was to publish significant studies of Aranda religion, the only other major anthropology of this area, was to compound the rancour which developed between Spencer and the Lutheran authorities, for they conflict with his own interpretations. (Mulvaney and Calaby 1985: 124)

Furthermore, the biographers also suggest that whatever his critiques of the Christian Strehlow, Spencer's own research methods were by no means beyond reproach. They note that in Spencer's *The Arunta* (1927), he virtually claims a 'monopoly of knowledge':

> He [Spencer] disposed of Strehlow's conflicting evidence as unreliable, because his informants were not "unspoilt" by culture contact, whereas he assumed that Gillen's elders were authentic "primitives". He felt confident that no future anthropologist "will ever be able" to add anything substantial to the Arunta testament according to Spencer and Gillen. Their record provided "as much insight as we are now ever likely to gain into the manner of life of men and women who have long since disappeared in other parts of the world". However, because their traditional informants were now dead, he had the comforting sense that their veracity was unassailable. This was, however, a sad reflection on his

conception of scientific research method in anthropology. He disparaged
Strehlow's informants, but his own were safely beyond questioning
in this world. In this sense, Spencer was the classic example of the
proprietorial anthropologist, who claimed a people as "his."' (Mulvaney
and Calaby 1985: 379)

Morphy proposes that it does 'not matter what Spencer and Gillen labelled
Arrernte rituals and ceremonies – whether they classified them as religious or
magical practices' (Morphy [1997] 2001: 37). This underestimates a powerful
underlying framework in both academic and popular life that, in Australia,
has treated indigenous practices and belief as survivals of an earlier time, and
thereby with contempt.

Austin-Broos has argued that although 'Gillen's knowledge of the marriage
system and churinga led him beyond the issues of primitive promiscuity and
totemic cannibalism as they had been posed by Baldwin Spencer', Gillen failed
nonetheless to formulate either anthropological or historical questions to
replace 'these spurious evolutionary ones' (Austin-Broos 1999: 210–211). Thus,
she argues, it is 'inappropriate to compare, as Morphy does, Gillen's historical
interests with the interests of anthropologists today in their discussions of myth
and historical transformations' (Austin-Broos 1999: 211). Rumsey also questions
Morphy's claims for Spencer and Gillen. Morphy argues that some of their
'key concepts', 'the network of ancestral tracks that intersect the landscape',
actually specified an Aboriginal ontology (see Morphy [1997] 2001: 37). In reply,
Rumsey showed that 'the centrality of place in the people-totem-place nexus'
was a theme that Spencer and Gillen did not even closely apprehend (Rumsey
2001: 42). These views suggest that the advances of theory in conjunction with
ethnography that Morphy imputes to Spencer and Gillen would only emerge
some decades later as a professional anthropology developed. Once again,
this is not to diminish the achievements of Spencer and Gillen as early field
anthropologists of central Australia, but rather to locate them appropriately in
terms of subsequent as well as previous work.

Beyond the status of their field research, it is Spencer and Gillen's influence
on public and political life that makes them a difficult case. It seems clear
that they had a major impact on public opinion that shaped negative views of
Aboriginal Australians (Mulvaney [1997] 2001: 9; Ganter 2005). In the context
of this opinion, functionalism for all its limitations was critical and almost
revolutionary. In arguing that all the elements of a people's practice and belief
are 'functional' in the present, it eschewed the evolutionary assumption of
lower level survivals from the past in a superior present. As Morphy remarks,
Spencer and Gillen were 'by no means embryonic functionalists' (Morphy [1997]
2001: 50). They belonged to a Victorian past that subscribed to evolutionism;
one that W.H.R. Rivers, Radcliffe-Brown and Malinowski had to reject as they

developed the discipline. Therefore it is fair to conclude that their work, like Strehlow's as well, requires very careful and dispassionate treatment concerning both its strengths and its limitations. Few would argue with the view that both Christianity *and* social Darwinism can impair ethnography (Austin-Broos 1999: 214). Carl Strehlow and Baldwin Spencer each instituted a different way of looking at Aboriginal futures. Overall for the Lutherans, the idea was adaptation to the new circumstances if not assimilation; and for Spencer and the like, reserves, where Aboriginal people could remain much as they always had been and 'humanely' die out. Both ideas were highly problematic. Nonetheless, the idea that Aboriginal people could not or should not have engaged with the new world that was clearly overtaking them was fundamentally flawed.

As Mulvaney and Calaby indicate, and as Hiatt (1996) confirmed, these types of anthropological debate have continued throughout the twentieth century. Teasing out the real value of works that have been tainted by their own times cannot be done by 'exonerating accounts', critiques of other researchers who might have incorrectly read something into it, textual analysis, or a personal, purposive or interpretive reading of early ethnographic texts (see for instance Morphy 2012: 545–560). Indeed, it does not do these texts justice. Forms of work are needed that integrate personal and institutional agendas with the particular intellectual issues and debates that engaged practitioners and shaped anthropology. Intellectual biographies that address the anthropology produced by these early writers furthers our understanding of ongoing issues in modern anthropology and helps to identify the shadows of early paradigms in contemporary thought. Austin-Broos (1999: 215) writes, for example, that a 'thorough assessment of Baldwin Spencer would require at least a careful comparison of his work with that of W.H.R. Rivers and Franz Boas, in addition to a comparative assessment of Frank Gillen's regional ethnographic achievements'. In this light R.H. Mathews' work on Bora type initiation ceremonies should also be carefully examined (Mathews 1894, 1895, 1896, 1897). It appears likely that Mathews' extensive work on these matters influenced Spencer. For example, Spencer had 'communicated' in 1896, Mathews' paper on 'The Bora of the Kamilaroi' (Mathews 1897: 137–173), to the Royal Society of Victoria just before he left for his fieldwork on central Australian ceremonies in 1896.

In his account of the early '"school" of Cambridge Ethnology', Langham (1981) analyses a range of work conducted mainly in Oceania and the Pacific that forged the method of early professional social anthropology as a fieldwork discipline. Central to his account are W.H.R. Rivers and his genealogical method, developed in the course of the 1898 Torres Strait Expedition with Haddon, Seligman and others, and the innovations of Radcliffe-Brown following his West Australian fieldwork in 1910–1912 and his earlier writings on Australian social organisation.[3] Langham stipulates clearly the bases on which he distinguishes the discipline of social anthropology: First, it had some key terms, 'society', 'function' and 'structure', meaning in the latter case, for instance, 'the combination of behavioural options employed by the society' and reflected in further terminological distinctions such as 'patrilineal' and 'matrilocal' (Langham 1981: xii–xiv). Second, this anthropology provided 'exhaustive treatment of restricted social groups' produced through 'intensive and prolonged fieldwork' (Langham 1981: xv). A third feature was that the discipline had 'close links with British imperialism', being largely dependent on government grants for the intensive fieldwork pursued. He comments:

> An anthropology with the avowed aim of uncovering the factors which kept societies in smoothly-functioning harmony, and a national colonial policy which imposed its will upon distant peoples by plugging into the indigenous political organization, could not have been innocent playmates. (Langham 1981: xv)

Finally, he notes the centrality of kinship studies as the major component of comparative work in forms of social organisation in British social anthropology. Namely, a style of study that focused directly on investigated forms of social relatedness, like Meggitt's *Desert People* (1962), rather than notions projected from Europe.

With Radcliffe-Brown's appointment in Sydney, Langham notes the beginnings in Australia of social anthropology as a professional discipline (see also Gray 2007). Once again, he is careful to stipulate the criteria: (i) that there exist the opportunity for rigorous training by practitioners; (ii) that an income is earned from 'contributions to the subject'; (iii) that scientific findings are propagated systematically;[4] (iv) that institutionalisation occurs, preferably at universities; and (v) that the scientific output becomes sufficiently technical to command a specialist 'group of fellow practitioners' (Langham 1981: 245).

These specifications of a particular anthropology that is also a professional discipline, frame Langham's discussion of the various debates around kinship analysis that progressively marked out the parameters of social anthropology. His study helps to locate the phenomenon of 'transitional' anthropology exemplified by Carl Strehlow as well as Spencer and Gillen. In his terms, neither Spencer and Gillen nor Carl Strehlow were engaged in a modern and professional anthropology. And he makes a further pertinent observation on why he would consider this to be the case. At the end of the nineteenth century, the agenda for research was very much set by comparative religionists so that Frazer (Spencer's

---

3 A.R. Radcliffe-Brown was professor of the Department of Anthropology at Sydney University between 1926 and 1929 before he travelled to Chicago and thence back to England where he became Professor at Oxford.
4 The journal *Oceania* was first published in 1930.

patron), outside of anthropology, and Tylor within it, were both focused on issues of religion and evolution rather than matters of comparative social organisation (Langham 1981: xviii, xx, 49). These were also issues that absorbed Carl Strehlow and Baldwin Spencer. While they collected data on class systems and Strehlow additionally genealogical data, these did not yet present analyses in comparative social organisation as such. Spencer and Gillen in particular took their lead from Lewis Henry Morgan (1871) and his interest in classificatory terminologies. It would not be until the impact of Rivers, and his genealogical method, that this interest would be refined in Australia and elsewhere.

Langham designated Radcliffe-Brown as the anthropologist writing on indigenous Australia who took the next step. Here he mirrors the mainstream of Australian anthropology that excluded T.G.H. Strehlow's work for a lengthy period, not least because he pursued his father's central interest in language and myth and augmented these with his seminal work on indigenous Australian ontology. Issues of social organisation were secondary to Strehlow jnr and would remain so, due to the intellectual tradition in which he had been raised. Géza Róheim also pursued a tradition somewhat foreign to British social anthropology though Hiatt, with his interest in psychoanalysis, engaged with this work, and the Berndts who contributed to Róheim's Festschrift *Psychoanalysis of Culture*. However, where central Australian ethnography is concerned, it took the work of Nancy Munn (1970) and her interest in the relationship between the individual and the collectivity as mediated by the object world to begin the contemporary re-integration of this tradition into Australian anthropology. Recent interests in a contemporary phenomenology, or social phenomenology, have redeemed T.G.H. Strehlow's work for an interested audience (see, for instance, Myers [1986] 1991; Morton 1987; Redmond 2001; Musharbash 2008; Austin-Broos 2009).

These issues bear on Langham's proposal that his study of the British tradition is intended to echo the work of George Stocking who, although his essays range widely through many terrains of mainly 'Victorian' and early modern anthropology, tends to take his standpoint from contemporary cultural anthropology as it is practised in the United States. This means that Baldwin Spencer, whom Stocking takes to be 'the ethnographer' in the pair of Spencer and Gillen, figures fleetingly in some of his essays, while Carl Strehlow does not figure at all, and his son T.G.H. Strehlow only in a footnote (see Stocking 1987, 1995: 97). Langham suggests that history writing in anthropology should take contemporary issues into account and use older texts to interrogate present assumptions. He remarks that Stocking uses his histories often 'with the express purpose of demolishing myths about the history of anthropology' and to craft 'argument[s]' that 'modern practitioners of the trade will find challenging'

(Langham 1981: xxii). In this respect, Langham's and Stocking's work differs from that of Mulvaney and Calaby (1985) who produced a conventional biography of Spencer, independent of specific anthropological reference points.

This discussion of the contrast between the British and German-American traditions has relied on the initial contrast between Spencer's Darwinism and Strehlow's humanism. To be fair it could be said that the continuity in the English tradition was its general materialism and instrumentalism, rather than Darwinism *per se*, which is partly what made it turn to or stay with kinship, politics and, to a lesser degree, economics. Religion, more in the sense of 'meaning', remained somewhat an add-on until perhaps the 1960s, although T.G.H. Strehlow was trying to straddle this divide in his early essays in the 1930s published as *Aranda Traditions* (1947). These matters have progressed much in contemporary work and in the Arandic context has led to a more mature state in Austin-Broos' *Arrernte Present Arrernte Past* (2009) in which she forcefully argues for the need to deal with 'economy' and 'culture' in the same breath.

Repositioning T.G.H. Strehlow

Carl Strehlow's opus has implications for the assessment of his youngest son's work. Without doubt the father's masterpiece furnished the foundation for the work of T.G.H. Strehlow. The myth and song collection in *Die Aranda- und Loritja-Stämme in Zentral-Australien* (1907–1920) provided a basic model for *Songs of Central Australia* (1971) – T.G.H. Strehlow's much celebrated work. Carl's genealogies gave his son the opportunity to construct family trees reaching sometimes back from the 1960s to the early decades of the nineteenth century. In both these domains of ethnographic work the achievements of the son far surpassed those of the father in volume and in acknowledgements. However, Carl Strehlow's unresourced and lonely work, with only von Leonhardi's support, was equally remarkable in its time. Although T.G.H. Strehlow was marginalised from academic anthropology, he had the support of the University of Adelaide and the Australian National Research Council for many of his ventures. Moreover, Carl Strehlow's massive handwritten dictionary that was intended to give 'anyone' the chance to know the significance of Aranda and Loritja myths,[5] sat for a lifetime unpublished on T.G.H. Strehlow's desk as his personal reference work. Finally, the father smoothed the path for the son in personal as well as scholarly ways. Carl Strehlow's standing among central Australian people conferred a privileged position on his youngest son that facilitated his collection of confidential and classified information. It is beyond the scope of these remarks to explore the reasons why T.G.H. Strehlow allowed his father's

---

5   Carl Strehlow to N.W. Thomas, mid to end of 1906 (SH-SP-6-1).

work to lie untranslated in obscurity throughout his own Australian research career. Why parts of Carl's work were not deposited at the Strehlow Research Centre and some material only discovered in the 1990s at the house of T.G.H. Strehlow's widow, Kathleen, are things that we may never know.

T.G.H. Strehlow gained crucial insights from his father's work, but also details such as his statistics on natural species in central Australia. He recorded these in his first diary (1932: 2), and this record subsequently found its way into the second seminal essay of *Aranda Traditions* (1947: 66–67) – based on his father's dictionary work.[6] *Aranda Traditions* (T.G.H. Strehlow 1947) is dedicated to the detailed explanation of the particularities of different Arandic groups and specification, which is reminiscent of early particularism and clearly references the German view that language, including the oral literature of a people, is the manifestation of the *Geist* of a people. All the essays in this publication draw on data or comments from Carl Strehlow's work and possibly from von Leonhardi's letters that were in his possession.

One of von Leonhardi's main concerns was with unwarranted generalisations, a view echoed by T.G.H. Strehlow when he rebutted Baldwin Spencer's attack on his father's work (Strehlow 1947: 68–69, 83). Spencer had alleged that it was nonsense to propose that tjurunga were ever mentioned in the presence of women or that, wrapped with strings to prevent women from seeing them, these tjurunga were laid in wooden baby-carrying trays to hasten children's growth (Strehlow 1908: 80; Spencer 1927: 586). When Strehlow junior defended his father he did so using not simply his own observation but also the carefully worded observations of both von Leonhardi (1904)[7] and Carl Strehlow (Strehlow 1910: 7–8).[8] T.G.H. Strehlow wrote:

> … European writers have fallen into serious mistakes owing to their fatal habit of dumping together irreconcilable beliefs collected from different Aranda groups and then attempting to work out a coherent system of religious thought and ceremonial customs for the 'tribe' regarded as a coherent whole. (Strehlow 1947: 69)

In making these remarks, my intention is not to disqualify T.G.H. Strehlow as a scholar – he was an excellent one – but rather to place the achievements of father and son in a more appropriate relation. He admitted that his own research was not completely created *ex nihilo*. Most great thinkers, he observed, have 'certainly been greatly indebted to their own cultures' (Strehlow [1967] 2005: 86). Despite a certain amount of unreferenced reliance on *Die Aranda- und Loritja-Stämme in Zentral-Australien* and his father's language studies, he took his father's work a

---

6 Quoted in Chapter V.
7 Von Leonhardi to Carl Strehlow, 28.8.1904. Quoted in Chapter IV.
8 Quoted in Chapter IV.

step further by conceptualising the specificity of an Aboriginal ontology and in so doing arguably made Aboriginal culture an object of wonder for many non-indigenous Australians. The father's work and intellectual background allowed the son to write about indigenous relations to land in a way that had not been done prior to the publication of *Aranda Traditions* (1947). T.G.H. Strehlow ends his first essay on Aranda traditions with a Herderian remark that may reflect his father's and his own German enculturement. He wrote what no Anglophone anthropologist would have penned[9] namely that 'the soul of a race is enshrined in its legends' (Strehlow 1947: 46).

It is therefore unfortunate that only late in his career did T.G.H. Strehlow start to look towards North America for ideas on how to integrate his thoughts on culture and language in a more explicit anthropological method. In 1967 he gave a talk entitled 'Man and Language' (Strehlow [1967] 2005: 76–88) at the University of Adelaide. In comments that were conversational in style, he presents in an idiosyncratic and almost anachronistic way, his views on the importance of language study to understanding culture, such that anthropology should be seen to entail appropriate training in linguistics. The divergence of British social anthropology from the language and culture studies of German particularism had made it necessary for T.G.H. Strehlow to state in an awkward fashion matters his father had seemed to take for granted. Far from criticising Strehlow junior, this event reflects the limited representation in Australia at the mid-century point of the style of anthropology that Franz Boas founded and promoted in the United States. At that time in Adelaide, T.G.H. Strehlow's talk was a plea for collaboration between the disciplines, an argument that the study of people must be accompanied by the study of language and vice versa (Kenny and Mitchell 2005: 5). In these remarks the son seemed to respond, albeit unconsciously, to his father's German intellectual and anthropological roots, as revealed in *Die Aranda- und Loritja-Stämme in Zentral-Australien*.

---

9   John Morton, pers. comm., 13.11.2012.

Conclusion

Perhaps it is fair to say that Carl Strehlow's masterpiece and its context, demonstrate that every 'hero' of past scholarship is but one notable route among others to better understand contemporary thought. This book has been devoted to elucidating his work, both its strengths and its limitations, and the tradition of German humanistic anthropology in Australia. In Part One of this book, I have addressed the wider intellectual context in Germany and in Lutheran Australia that might have shaped his ideas, directly or indirectly. In Part Two, I have discussed his legacy for today's anthropology, and also the ways in which his intellectual method fell short of a modern anthropology. Carl Strehlow's opus represents a transitional phase in modern anthropology.

Noting the transitional status of Carl Strehlow's text in its relation to modern anthropology, it is also worth noting what Carl Strehlow offered, and what modern ethnography has lost. A decade or a lifetime 'in the field' has become almost unknown in anthropological practice. An acute and effective fieldworker, a committed empiricist, he nonetheless brought with him implicit models from Europe that did not fit indigenous Australian cultures. Still, his European preconceptions and assumptions allowed him to begin systematic data collection in a way that was rare for the period and remains of immense value. This data as discussed in Chapters V to VII furnished many starting points for central developments in the modern field of twentieth century anthropology. In this sense he was collecting material for a new century of anthropology; the ingredients that would be essential for a modern comparative and specifying study of societies and their cultures are present in his work. While *Die Aranda-und Loritja-Stämme in Zentral-Australien* supplies source material for the study of religion and society, it serves another purpose which he could not have anticipated at the turn of the century: land rights, native title and mining and royalty agreements. These matters make *Die Aranda- und Loritja-Stämme in Zentral-Australien* a work of international significance in anthropology's history. It is a classic that stands beside other transitional Australian works of his time such as Howitt, Spencer and Gillen, Langloh Parker or Mathews, and even the early works of Franz Boas.

Carl Strehlow's importance into the present is particularly evident in the context of land and native title claims in which his materials have provided unmistakable evidence that connects claimants to named ancestors who occupied and exploited the area claimed before 'Sovereignty' occurred in 1825 in the Northern Territory. T.G.H. Strehlow integrated his father's data collection into his work and together they produced a truly unique record of marriage, relatedness, place and ritual significance. In the land rights movement and native title context the ethnographic detail of this record has not only shown the physical connection of named Aboriginal individuals to their traditional lands but has also demonstrated cultural continuity. No other indigenous Australian group can draw on such a rich cultural heritage record and deep and detailed genealogical documentation. Maybe ironically, this record has so impinged on Western Aranda consciousness that it has become an artefact in their modern culture, invested with their own use-values.

I have also sought to draw out some of the anthropological implications of Carl Strehlow's views in relation to the social Darwinistic work of his contemporaries, the role of language, the high god and 'altjira' issues, European frameworks that impinged on and limited Carl Strehlow's anthropology, and his humanistic position that accepted cultural diversity and the gamut of human possibilities among the Aranda and Loritja. The main difference between Strehlow's work and that of most other Australian researchers of his time is that he did not use ranked categories to position Aranda and Loritja beliefs at the baseline of mental development.

For an intelligent young missionary as Carl Strehlow was, educated in a Lutheran humanistic tradition, Baron von Leonhardi's request to train his gaze on language and myth, and those for further clarifications that followed, made sense. This was the simple foundation on which their collaboration was built. This simple fact reflects that Strehlow's orientation to the world and the people he encountered in it was shaped by a particular cultural milieu, intellectual life, theology and missionary practice. It is important to note that beyond von Leonhardi's engagements with Andrew Lang, and Lang's engagement with James Frazer, not to mention Baldwin Spencer's jousts with the shadow of Strehlow, von Leonhardi and Strehlow opened up a correspondence in which the recording of myth and language was foundational for learning about central Australian life. This was their route to an empirical science that differed in radical ways from the route through developmental stages as reflected in biology. Though engaged with ritual practice, Gillen and Spencer used their data on that practice to distance and subordinate Aboriginal intellectual life to that of Europeans. This was reflected especially in their views on Aranda nescience concerning human birth (see Hiatt 1996; Wolfe 1999: 9–42). Possibly the true nature of Strehlow's work was most evocatively rendered by Marcel Mauss when he remarked that the volumes represented a form of an Aranda Rig Veda (Mauss 1913: 103). This ancient collection of Hindu hymnal chants is also one of the earlier records of Indo-European language and thereby a philological treasure. Perhaps the same might be said of Carl Strehlow's work on myths collected in Aranda and Loritja language as well of his son's later work.

The singularity of Carl Strehlow's work is underlined not merely by the contrast it presents to Spencer's and Gillen's texts but also by the contrast that the work on Aboriginal myth of the Strehlows, father and son, presents to the rest of Australian anthropology. Save for the work of Róheim, also at Hermannsburg shortly after Carl Strehlow's time, there is nothing in the Australian literature quite like their early attempts to specify an indigenous ontology. Yet the manner in which Carl proceeded, supported by von Leonhardi, seems to have been nothing more than a shared and self-evident method. Carl Strehlow's route may have seemed the natural course for a German missionary-scholar. In the first instance, he lived intimately over a long period with a group of hunting and gathering people who were gradually becoming sedentary. He learned their languages as required by good missionary practice. But as he learnt, and began recording myth from his key Aranda collaborators Loatjira, Pmala, Tjalkabota and Talku, it became evident to him that their cultures were being revealed through their oral forms. So absorbing was this task, and illuminating, that less than a year before he died Strehlow confidently repudiated any suggestion that the Aranda's modest technology might reflect a limited intellectual life. 'Never' Strehlow said.[1]

This confidence was born of both extensive exposure 'in the field', and also of an environing intellectual milieu. This milieu was both secular and theological. It suggested the possibility of multiple cultures, once thought of as God's plenitude but, in Carl Strehlow's time, increasingly identified with a multiplicity of languages that each carried a people's *own spirit and intellect* but also the capacity to translate Euro-Christian truth. Through the particular inheritance embodied in the rise of nineteenth century German anthropology based on thought initiated by Herder and developed in the work of the von Humboldts and then Bastian and Virchow, an appreciation of the psychic unity of humankind was fostered along with an active engagement with language work. This line of thinkers preceded Graebner and Boas who began to shape a recognisably modern tradition within anthropology. Carl Strehlow's work falls in this German tradition of anthropological specification, which bears a strong resemblance to Franz Boas' approach. Although Boas entered the academy, while Strehlow remained a missionary-scholar in the field, Strehlow's opus sits comfortably as an early field project in the Boasian tradition of anthropology.

The Lutheran missionary training in Germany and missionary practice in colonial Australia demonstrates the types of tool and worldview that Strehlow brought to life in central Australia. To begin with, the German Lutheran tradition sustained at Neuendettelsau placed importance both on classical language study – Greek, Latin and Hebrew – and on the study of vernacular, the medium for worship in Lutheran churches. This emphasis on vernacular led at least some pastors to take an interest in the *Weltanschauung* (worldview) of the people they worked with. Strehlow was one of them. In addition, both Johannes Deinzer at

---

1   Carl Strehlow, *The Register,* 7.12.1921.

Neuendettelsau and Wilhelm Löhe, whose teachings Deinzer supported, placed an emphasis on the 'outer mission' to unbelievers as well as the 'inner mission' to those settlers in colonised areas already admitted to the Lutheran faith. This Lutheran emphasis on the vernacular and the fluid relation between an outside mission that might become an inside mission over time almost certainly informed Strehlow's practice in central Australia. It involved a Christian frame in which the Aranda and Loritja people who lived at the mission became his Lutheran community. The mutual engagement between Aboriginal people and the pastor is to some degree reflected in Basedow's comment:

> As a disciplinarian he has established himself at the head of the tribal group he manages, and even in quarrels and feuds of the bitterest nature his word is and must be final. Moreover the religion taught is sincere and not overdone. (Basedow 1920–22: 22)

This comment suggests that, possibly, the Western Aranda word inkata, or ritual leader, was more readily applied to Strehlow than it might have been to other missionaries. Facilitated both by his language studies and his particular missionary persona, Strehlow's engagement through research may have encouraged the Aranda to provide him with a status that referenced their world and very possibly tried to make him part of their world. It certainly appears that towards the end of his life, the Aranda had made him part of their world; whether he knew or felt this, is not known. Letters written in Aranda to him during his last days at Hermannsburg and later to Frieda Strehlow in South Australia show the emotional attachment his Aranda congregation had to him.[2]

The different types of intellectual context in which Carl Strehlow proceeded into the field also informed his collaboration with von Leonhardi. The foci that von Leonhardi suggested were just the ones that Strehlow with his Lutheran background would likely have chosen for himself. In addition, it is pertinent to underline again that, as an armchair anthropologist, von Leonhardi subscribed to the full range of professional journals, especially in German and English, that otherwise would have been unavailable to Strehlow. This bore on Carl Strehlow's work in two particular ways. First, it meant that von Leonhardi's comments kept current issues such as the 'high god' issue present. Through reference to Andrew Lang and others, von Leonhardi encouraged Strehlow to explore these matters as thoroughly as he could. Strehlow's view shifted over time as did his understanding of altjira. Whether or not a later ethnography would endorse all Strehlow's positions, the dimensions of meaning concerning these issues

---

2   Between 13 September and 9 October 1922 when Carl was still at the Hermannsburg Mission, Jakobus, Rufus, Nathanael and others wrote letters to their 'Inkata' and after his death letters written in 1923 from Mariana, Jacobus, Nathanael and Maria give touching testimony to the relationship between the missionaries and the Aranda people. Other letters written between 31.8.1903 and 28.8.1911 by Aranda people have survived and are held at the Strehlow Research Centre in Alice Springs.

that the correspondence with von Leonhardi brought to the fore reveals the subtlety of Aranda culture and belief in ways that are foreign to other works of early ethnographic work in Australia. Notwithstanding Strehlow's position as a missionary, the fact that he could consult with his informants in their language gave them some agency and allowed the building of an ethnographic record that still fascinates today. The correspondence between Strehlow and von Leonhardi had a second major impact. It reinforced Strehlow's own propensity to focus on the empirical record and turn away from premature theory. Time and again, von Leonhardi enjoined Strehlow to check his facts and to record the precise meaning of particular terms and the nature of particular practices. This focus on empirical particulars may have encouraged Strehlow towards a limited, yet refined diffusionism that his studies of the Aranda and Loritja involved. His recording of the ways in which forms of myth overlap and interpenetrate foreshadows the work of T.G.H. Strehlow and other subsequent field research.

The foregoing comments summarise some important issues I have discussed and underline the different factors that led Carl Strehlow towards the prolonged empirical study of individual cultures, one in particular among other cultures. Carl Strehlow was almost certainly Eurocentric in his view of central Australian indigenous people. He was not, however, an evolutionist who would present central Australians as simply culturally homogeneous. This gives his work a modern feel despite its transitional nature. Carl Strehlow was not yet a part of modern professional anthropology, notwithstanding the fact that he produced immensely valuable data in central areas of research. I have shown (i) that although his recording of myth lacked a truly comparative frame beyond the immediate region and a sense of symbolism, his ethnographic record began in earnest the specification of central Australian Aboriginal ontology of person-land relations (Róheim and Morton, not to mention Strehlow junior, have followed this route); (ii) that although Carl Strehlow collected genealogies as family trees rather than as data used to specify a social structure, his material make major contributions to our understanding of social classification among Aboriginal people and most importantly, has given the Western Aranda and Loritja a detailed record of their ancestry which they have successfully used in claims to their traditional lands; and finally (iii) that although Strehlow did not quite connect the issues of social classification, knowledge and land in an understanding of 'countries', territorial (local) organisation or land tenure, he recorded thought-provoking data on the different ways in which individual people could be connected with place. Most important, these data suggest that in his time and subsequently, what today we call 'land tenure' was involved in change that would be intensified with the impact of settlement. His data make a major contribution to loosening the 'straitjacket' of interpretation imposed by A.R. Radcliffe-Brown and resonate with current views on traditional Aboriginal land ownership.

Carl Strehlow's opus is a unique Australian work that allows us both to look back to a classical tradition not well represented or studied within Australia, and forwards to a modern anthropology that carried his interests, and others, in multiplicity into the academy and well beyond. Boas' critique of evolutionism rested on this German historical particularism, an appreciation of the historically conditioned plurality of human cultures, and thus his 'notion of culture also called for a stance of cultural relativism, the idea that it is necessary to understand cultures in their own terms and their own historical contexts before attempting generalisations' (Silverman 2005: 262). Both wrote within a tradition that acknowledged that all societies are equal, despite their different moral values, and have individual features that cannot be rendered in terms of generalised stages of development. Carl Strehlow's work reflected the aims of this early German anthropological tradition, which was to document the plurality of peoples and their cultures in their own right.

Appendix A

IAD Pronunciation Guide to Arrernte orthography[1]

a   Basically long 'ah' when stressed; 'uh' when not stressed at the beginning of a word. *ay* like 'ay' in 'hay' in a few special words and endings, and sometimes before rt, rn, or rl; like 'ie' as in 'lie' when stressed in normal words. *aw* like 'ow' in 'how' when stressed.

e   Basically like 'uh' or 'er' as in 'catcher', Like 'i' in 'bit' before ty, ny or ly. At end of words it is either like 'uh' or 'er' as in 'catcher or not pronounced at all. *ey* like 'ee' when stressed. *we* like 'oo' in 'wood' after another consonant; like 'woo' otherwise, except at ends of words. *wey* like 'wee'. *ew* like 'ow' in 'snow' when stressed.

h   A bit like 'w' as in 'wonder', but without rounded lips. Not used by some younger speakers.

i   Like 'i' in 'bit' or 'e' in 'bet'; like 'ee' before rn, rt, rl, ty, ny or ly.

k   Like 'k' or 'g'.

l   Like 'l'.

lh   Like 'l' but tongue touches back of upper teeth.

lth   = lh+th

lty   = l+ty or =ly+ty

ly   Like 'lli' in 'million.

m   'm'

n   'n'

ng   Like 'ng' in singer, not as in finger.

nh   Like 'n' but tongue touches back of upper teeth.

nth   = nh+th

nty   = n+ty or = ny+ty.

ny   Like 'ny' in 'canyon'.

p   Like 'p' or 'b'.

r   Normal Australian English 'r'.

rl   Like 'l' but tongue tip curled back up higher.

rn   Like 'n' but tongue tip curled back up higher.

rr   Hard or rolled 'r'.

---

1   Reproduced from Henderson and Dobson (1994).

rt   Like 't' or 'd' but tongue tip curled back up higher.

rtn   = rt+rn

t   Like 't' or 'd'.

th   Like 't' or 'd' but tongue touches back of upper teeth.

thn = th + nh

tnh = th + nh

tny = ty + n

ty   Like 'ch' or 'j'.

u   Like 'or' when stressed; like 'oo' in 'wood' when unstressed.

w   Like 'w'; also see ew and aw above.

y   Like 'y' in 'you', not as in 'city'; also see ey and ay above.

Pronunciation Guide to Western Arrarnta orthography[2]

a   This central vowel has several sounds. 1. The high sound, like 'u' in 'curt'. 2. The sound like 'er' I the English word, 'father'. 3. The sound like 'u' in the English word 'umbrella'. Nearly every Western Arrarnta word ends with *a*.

e   Like 'e' in 'every'.

h   A bit like 'w' as in 'wonder', but without rounded lips. Not used by some younger speakers.

i   Like 'i' in 'ink' or 'bit', like 'ee' in 'sheep' or like a soft 'e' in 'every'.

k   Like 'k' or 'g' in English. Most Aboriginal Australian languages do not distinguish between 'g' and 'k'.

l   Aveolar sound like 'l' in English.

lh   Dental sound like 'l' but tongue touches back of upper teeth.

ly   Palatal sound like 'lli' in 'million'.

m   'm'

n   'n'

ng Velar sound made at the back of the mouth like 'ng' in singer, not as in finger.

nh   Dental sound like 'n', but tongue touches back of upper teeth.

ny   Palatal sound like 'ny' in 'canyon'.

---

2 Adapted from Roennfeldt, D. with members of the communities of Ntaria, Ipolera, Gilbert Springs, Kulpitarra, Undarana, Red Sand Hill, Old Station and other outstations (2005).

p	Like 'p' or 'b'. Most Aboriginal Australian languages do not distinguish between 'b' or 'p'
r	Normal Australian English 'r'.
rl	Retroflex sound like 'l' but tongue tip curled back up higher.
rn	Retroflex sound like 'n' but tongue tip curled back up higher.
rr	Hard or rolled 'r'.
rt	Retroflex sound like 't' or 'd' but tongue tip curled back up higher.
rtn	Retroflex sound like rt+rn together.
t	Like 't' or 'd'. Most Aboriginal Australian languages do not distinguish between 'd' and 't'.
th	Dental sound like 't' or 'd' but tongue touches back of upper teeth.
tj	Like 'ch' or 'j' as in 'jaw'.
tnh	= th + nh
tny	= tj + ny
u	Like 'oo' in 'foot' or 'ou' in 'court', or as in 'two'.
w	Bilabial sound like 'w'.
y	Palatal sound like 'y' in 'you', not as in 'city'.

Short Pronunciation Guide to Luritja[3]

Point of Articulation	Stops	Nasals	Laterals
Bilabial	p	m	
Apico-Alveolar	t	n	l
Apico-Domal	rt	rn	rl
Lamino-Alveolar	tj	ny	ly
Velar	k	ng	

	Vibrants	Semiconsonants
Apico-Alveolar	rr	w
Bilabial		y
Apico-Domal		r

---

3 Reproduced from Heffernan and Heffernan (1999).

Vowels

	Short	Long
High front unrounded	i	ii
High back rounded	u	uu
Low central unrounded	a	aa

Appendix B

The glossaries list frequently occurring terms. I have included in the Western Arrernte/Arrarnta/Aranda glossary three different orthographic representations of each word, unless a reliable spelling was not available. The main difference between the Arrernte/Arrarnta modern orthographies is the representation of the vowels. The final 'e' is a marker of the IAD orthography and the final 'a' for the newer Ntaria orthography. The first entry in *italics* shows a word in the common IAD spelling system and the second one uses the most recent developments at Ntaria and the third entry lists Carl Strehlow's rendering of a word with its English translation.

Glossary of some Western Arrernte[1] / Arrarnta[2] / Aranda[3] terms

akeye / akia / agia. Bush currant, *Canthium latifolium*.

alkngarte / alkngaarta / alknata. Native pine tree, *Callitris glaucophylla*.

alknginere / alkngenara / alknenera. Cicada.

alturle / alturla / aldola. West.

altyemaltyirreme / [not available] / *altjamaltjerama*. Ancestors would altjamaltjerama into the landscape at particular places, which are named in Strehlow's work; it means 'become a hidden body, i.e. to assume a different form' (Strehlow 1907: 5).

altyerre / altjirra / altjira. Polysemic expression used for 'high god', dream, 'unmade', mother's dreaming, dreaming ancestor, mother's conception dreaming, mother's spirit double and 'totem'. 1. Dreaming, dream 2. Christian God.

altyerrengametyene / [not available] / *altjirangamitjina*. In Carl Strehlow's work generally used for 'totem ancestor', i.e. 'ancestral being'. This word is a compound of altjira (altyerre) and -ngamitjina (ngametyene and ngampetyene in modern Western Arrernte). According to Carl Strehlow altjirangamitjina means 'the eternal unmade ones'; altjira: unmade, ngamitjina: the eternal.

---

1 Compiled by Anna Kenny, checked by Gavan Breen and John Henderson.

2 Adapted from Roennfeldt, D. with members of the communities of Ntaria, Ipolera, Gilbert Springs, Kulpitarra, Undarana, Red Sand Hill, Old Station and other outstations (2005).

3 Carl Strehlow's published work and unpublished Aranda-German-(Kukatja)-Loritja-Dieri dictionary (c.1900-1909).

anpernentye / anparnintja / eknakilinja. Skin name, term of address or greeting.

anpernirrentye / [not available] */* [not available]. Subsection system, term of address or greeting, 'family' in everyday use. Anpernentye and anpernirrentye are derived from the verb anperneme 'call someone by a kinship term or describe them as being a particular relation'. Replacing the 'me' with 'ntye' turns it into a noun anpernentye that means something like 'what you call someone'. Adding the irr makes it reciprocal, 'what you call one another'. Anpernentye and anpernirrentye have the same gloss, but these words also have other similar meanings that differ. See also Dobson and Henderson (2013).

apme / apma / apma. Snake (generic, probably includes also other legless reptiles: burrowing skink and legless lizard).

arrenge / arranga / aránga. Father's father, brother's son's child.

arrethe / arratha / arata. Native fuchsia, *Eremophila freelingii.*

arretnurlke / arratnurlka / aratnolka. Mintbush, *Prostanthera striatiflora.*

arrkwetye / arrkutja / aragutja. Woman.

artwe / artwa / atua. Man.

helherenye / aalarinya / alarinja. 'Belonging to the earth'.

herre / arra / ara. Red kangaroo. Herre is not used by most people, only by a few of the oldest. Most people use kerarre, which is a compound of kere 'animal' and arre (coming from herre) 'kangaroo', or just arre. (Arre would often be preceded by kere anyway, but there is a clear difference in pronunciation between kere arre and kerarre.)

ilakekeye / [not available] */ nákarakia (or lakakia).* 'Us', meaning the people belonging to one's own patrimoiety.

Irlpere / Irlpara / Ilpara. Name of people who are said to be Warlpiri neighbours of Anmatyerr people; the Anmatyerr word is probably Arlper.

imurre / imurra / imora, antana. Possum, *Trichosurus vulpecula.*

inarlenge / enarlanga / inalanga. Echidna, *Tachyglossus aeuleatus.*

ingkarte / ingkaarta / inkata. 1. Chief, man (father in general). According to Strehlow (1915: 1) the chief of a traditional country (called in the anthropological literature 'estate') is called inkata or 'father of all', but on a general level he is only a 'primus inter pares', and his position is only hereditary, i.e. not necessarily achieved through knowledge or wisdom. T.G.H. Strehlow's gloss for 'ingkarte' is 'ceremonial chief'. – 2. Pastor. The word Ingkarte has changed its meaning significantly over the past century. It seems likely that the shift started to occur during Carl Strehlow's period, because he seems to have been their first white *ingkarte*. Today it is used for pastor. Austin-Broos (2004: 61) defines an *ingkarte* as 'a man who realised a balance between knowledge at his own place and at other sites'. – The original meaning of ingkarte has been replaced by the concepts of pmerekwerteye and kwertengerle in contemporary Arandic societies.

ingkwere / [not available] / *inkura*. Initiation ceremonies. Engwura in Spencer and Gillen's work. According to Strehlow (1913) inkura is only one part of the initiation ceremony not the entire process.

intaminte / [not available] / *ntamintana*. Species of fish found in Western Aranda waters. This is the same fish called *intamintane*. Alternative forms: intamintenhe and intamintame.

intetyiweme / [not available] / *intitjiuma*. 'To initiate into something, to show how something is done' (Strehlow 1910). Initiation ceremony.

irleye / *ilia* / *ilia*. Emu.

irrentye / *errintja* / *arintja*. Evil being, wicked spirit or devil.

irretye / *erritja* / *eritja*. Wedge-tailed eagle.

irrpenge / *irrpanga* / *irbanga*. Fish (generic).

karte / *kaarta* / *kata*. Father, father's brothers and SSS.

kawawe / [not available] / *kauaua*. Tall ceremonial pole with a bunch of feathers at the top. See also tnatantja meaning 'tall pole' in Strehlow (1910).

knganentye / [not available] / *knanakala*. Dreaming (totem), father's dreaming, conception dreaming. According to Breen, it means today mainly 'father's dreaming'. In T.G.H. Strehlow's unpublished dictionary knganintja [knganentye] means 'totem'. In the Eastern and Central Arrernte dictionary aknganentye's first meaning is given as 'the dreamings which are passed down through the father's side' (Henderson and Dobson 1994: 69). In Carl Strehlow's work the word knanakala means 'totem place', 'generated itself', 'coming out of itself', 'conception place' (Strehlow 1907: 5). According to Breen, 'knganintja' and 'knanakala' are related. They are both derived from the verb knganeme (in Eastern and Central Arrernte spelled aknganeme and defined as 1. originate in the Dreaming and exist forever, 2. be conceived in a place). The past tense form is knganeke. With the -ale ending it means 'the one who …' or 'the place where …'. So it could mean 'the one who was conceived' or 'the place where x was conceived'. With the ending -ntye it is converted into a noun referring to the dreamings or the place. – It is interesting to note here that the notion of 'father's dreaming' does not appear in any of the earlier records. If it had referred during T.G.H. Strehlow's time in any way to 'father's dreaming', I would have expected to have found it in his work.

kngerrtye / kngarritja / knaritja. Big. The extensions to father, chief etc. are like calling the person 'the great one'. In Carl Strehlow's work knaritja is used for father, chief, old man and totemic ancestor. In T.G.H. Strehlow's work kngaritja means 1. very large, huge. 2. totemic ancestor, may be translated as 'sire'.

kngerrepate / kngarripata / knaribata. Elder or ceremonial assistant, member of council of senior men. In Carl Strehlow's work knaribata (*zusammengesetzt aus knara (gross) und ata-atua (Mann): der grosse Mann, der ältere Mann, in angesehner Stellung, der älteste.* (Knaribata is composed of knara (big) and ata a contraction of atua (man). It was used for 'old man'.)

kngwelye / kngulya / knulja. Dog.

kwatye / kwatja / kwatja. Water, rain.

kwatyerenye / kwatjarinya / kwatjarinja. 'Belonging to water' or 'coming from the water'.

Kwerralye / Kwerralya / Kuralja. Pleiades.

kwertengerle / kurtungurla / kutungula. Landholder or belonging through descent other than father's father to land. This appears to be a Warlpiri term written in the Warlpiri language: kurdungurlu. In Carl Strehlow's unpublished dictionary recorded as 'subject, servant'.

larletye / lalitja / lalitja. Conkerberry, *Carissa lanceolata.*

latyeye / latjia / latjia. Yam, *Vigna lanceolata.*

lthane / lthaarna / ltana. Ghost. Ulthana, a spirit being (Gillen 1896: 183).

ltyarnme / [not available] / iltjenma. Freshwater crayfish found in Western Aranda waters.

lwengulpere / lhungurlpara / longulpura. Spangled grunter, *Leiopotherapon unicolor* (species of fish found in Aranda waters).

malyenweke / [not available] / maljanuka. 'Them', meaning the people in the opposite patrimoiety.

Mpeltyarte, twakeye / mpaltjarta / mbultjita. Bush-orange, *Capparis mitchellii.*

ngkwerlpe / ngkurlpa / inkulba. Wild tobacco (generic).

ngampekale / ngampakala / ngambakala. Eternal, everlasting, from always, from eternity. Carl Strehlow writes that 'The Aranda language has four words to describe eternal = ngambakala, ngambintja, ngamitjina, and ngarra' (Strehlow 1907: 1). – Ungambikula (out of nothing, self existing) or Numbakulla in Spencer and Gillen's work.

ngangkere / ngangkara / ngankara. Healer, native doctor.

nthepe / nthapa / ntape(rama). Dance of women at time of boys' initiation.

nturrerte / nturrurta / nturuta. Spinifex pigeon.

nyurrpe / nyurrpa / [not available]. Not eligible to marry someone, wrong skin for marriage (opposite generational moiety).

pangkelangke / pangkalangka / bankalanga. Dangerous hairy (male) spirit which may kill and devour humans. Sometimes also used for an evil female spirit, called arrkwetye irrentye (evil woman).

pepe, pipe / pepa / pepa. New word deriving from the English word 'paper'. Carl Strehlow (1915: 70) recorded a handsign for pepa meaning 'book, letter'.

pmere / pmara / tmara. Camp, land, place or country.

pmerekwerteye / pmarakurtwia / [not available]. Landowner through father's father. *Pmerekwerteye* means literally 'country-owner'. It is derived, via a minor sound change, from a compound: pmere-ke-rtweye. The -ke is a dative suffix, which is very common, and -rtweye is the same as artweye in Central and Eastern Arrernte (Henderson and Dobson 1994: 286–287) and means 'owned or owner'. In Western Arrernte it does not seem to be used as an independent word (as artweye can be, but isn't usually); -rtweye is rare in other combinations, and so people do not think of it as a unit (Gavan Breen email, 17.9.2007).

pmererenye / pmararinya / [not available]. Belonging to land/place. Very occasionally used to mean 'traditional owner' by people of Kukatja-Luritja descent today. Luritja and other Western Desert peoples use nguraritja.

pmere kwetethe / pmara kutatha / [not available]. Sacred site in T.G.H. Strehlow's work and today Western Aranda people use this expression to denote 'spirits of the land'.

rathepe / [not available] */ ratapa.* In Carl Strehlow's work ratapa means child spirit, offspring, baby, child, conception dreaming, 'totem'. In T.G.H. Strehlow's work it means mythical children or Twins of Ntaria (Strehlow 1947: 118; 1971).

renge / ranga / aranga. Euro, *Macropus robustus* (Gould).

-renye / -rinya / -rinja. Suffix meaning 'belonging to or in', 'coming from', 'out of' or 'originating from'.

rrweperrwepe / rrupa-rrupa / rubaruba. Whirlwind.

rwekerte / [not available] */ rukuta*. 'Young man who has been circumcised and has to keep himself hidden' (Strehlow 1907: 41).

taye / taiya / taia. Moon.

tnengkarre / tnangkarra / tnankara. Dreaming, dreaming ancestor, mythological past, birthmark, dreaming mark.

tnwerrengatye / tnurrangatja / tnurungatja. Species of caterpillar living on the emu bush. Came from Mt Zeil in the dreaming.

tnwerrenge / tnurranga / tnurunga. Emu bush, *Eremophila longifolia*.

Twanyirreke / [not available] */ Tuanjiraka*. One of the ancestral beings; but also meaning 'large bullroarer'. Twanyirika in Spencer and Gillen (1899: 264, 654) referring to a spirit being.

tyape / tjaapa / tjappa. Witchetty grub, edible grub (generic).

tyelpe / tjilpa / tjilpa. Western quoll, native cat, *Dasyurus geoffroii*.

tyemeye / tjimia / tjimia. Mother's father.

Tyurretye / Tjurritja / Tjoritja. The Western MacDonnell Ranges.

tywerrenge / tjurrunga / tjurunga. This term has a number of very complex meanings depending on its context. Tjurunga can mean songs, stories, dances, paraphernalia, sacred object, etc associated with the ancestral beings. The term tjurunga is a very complex term and depending on context means different things. (See also Carl Strehlow's unpublished dictionary in which 'heilig (sacred)' is part of its meaning, and T.G.H. Strehlow 1947: 84–86; 1971: 770–771). Tywerrenge usually means today 'sacred object' and is not often spoken about (Breen 2000: 60). Choringa in Spencer and Gillen's work.

tywerrengirreke / [not available] */ tjurungeraka*. 'Change into wood or stone' at the end of creative activities (Strehlow 1908: 77).

ure / ura / ura. Fire.

wanenge / [not available] */ wonninga*. Object used during ceremonies. Item made of hairstrings stretched over a wooden cross.

yerrampe / yirrampa / jerramba. Honey ant, *Camponotus inflatus*.

Glossary of some Western Arandic kin terms[4]

F: father, B: brother, M: mother, Z: sister, S: son, D: daughter, H: husband, W: wife, e: elder, y: younger, (m): male view, (f): female view.

arrenge / arranga / aránga, aranga. FF (paternal grandfather), FFB, FFZ, WFM, SS (m), SD (m), BSS, BSD, WZSS, WZSD, HFM, HZSS, HZSD.

perle / parla / palla. FM (paternal grandmother), FMZ, FMB, WFF, SS (f), SD (f), ZSS, ZSD, WBSS, WBSD, HBSS, HBSD and HFF.

tyemeye / tjimia / tjimia. MF (maternal grandfather), MFB, MFZ, WMM, HMM, DS (m), DD (m), BDS, BDD, WZDS, WZDD, HZDS and HZDD.

ipmenhe / ipmanha / ebmanna. MM (maternal grandmother), MMZ, MMB, WMF, DS (f), DD (f), ZDS, ZDD, WBDS, WBDD, FZSW, MBSW, HBDS, HBDD, FZDH and MBDH.

karte / kaarta / kata. F, FB, and SSS.

wenhe / wunha / wonna. Aunt, FZ, and MBW.

meye / mia / maia. M, MZ, SW (m), and FBW.

kamerne / kaamurna / kamuna. MB, FZH, DH (m), BDH (m), WZDH (m).

mare / mara / marra. Mother-in-law, WM, WMZ, DH (f), DHB (f), WBSW, WBDH, ZDH, ZSW.

kelye / kalya / kalja. eB, FeBS, MeZS, WeZH, HeZH.

kwaye / kwaiya / kwaia. eZ, FeBD, MeZD, WeBW, HeBW.

newe / nua / noa. Spouse, W, WZ, BW, FBSW, MZSW, H, HB, ZH, FBZH, and MZZH.

mparne / mparna / mbana. WB (man's brother-in-law), ZH (m), FBDH (m), MZDH (m).

tyeye / tjia / tjia. Younger sibling, yB, yZ.

ampe / ampa / amba. Child of woman, S (f), D (f), ZS, ZD, WBS, WBD, HBS, HBD, and HF.

lere / lira / alirra. Child of man, S (m), D (m), BS, BD, HZS, HZD, FFF.

ankele / ankala / ankalla. MBS (m) and FZS (m).

---

4   Based on Carl Strehlow (1913: 66–70); updated by Gavan Breen.

ltyele / ltjala / altjala or iltjala. MBD (f) and FZD (f).

Glossary of some Loritja terms[5]

ara. Skin-name.

aratjarra. Subsection system.

anumara. Caterpillar.

atanari. Ceremonial chief/leader (T.G.H. Strehlow 1970: 110).

inyurrpa. Not eligible to marry someone, wrong skin for marriage.

kami. Grandmother.

kuninka. Western quoll, native cat, *Dasyurus geoffroii*.

kungka. Woman.

kuniya. Carpet snake or children's python.

kuntanka (= tjurunga). According to Carl Strehlow kuntanka describes to a lesser degree a sacred object, but rather particular features of a landscape that represent dreaming beings or parts of them. See above 'tjurunga'.

kutintjingañi. 'To bring about, make fertile, improve the conditions of' (Strehlow 1910). Ceremony held at specific places for the increase and growth of particular species. In the Pintupi/Luritja dictionary kutinytjinganu is said to mean 'caused to roll'. In the Pitjantjatjara/Yankunytjatjara dictionary kutintjingani is glossed as 'turn over' (transitive). The Aranda word for 'turn over' is ikngarrpiweme or kngartiweme. The Aranda word mbatjalkatiuma in Strehlow's work is not known and no contemporary spelling can be found as the etymology is not certain.

merinangurrara. Belonging to Merina country.

ngananangarri. 'We all, we group, us mob' (Hansen and Hansen 1991: 78). *ngananukarpitina* ('all of us') recorded by Carl Strehlow (1913). Also *ngananankarpa* or *ngananiltja* (all of us).

ngurra. Camp, place, area, country.

-ngurrara. From, belonging to the place/country.

---

5   Based on Carl Strehlow's Kukatja-Loritja terms. Checked by Rhonda Inkamala.

ngurraritja. Owner of land. Spirits of the land.

papa. Dog.

pipawonnu. Subject, servant.

puntulara. Elder or ceremonial assistant, member of council of senior men. Dieri: pinaru.

tina or tjilpi. Elder or ceremonial assitant.

Talku. Bandicoot. Personal name of Carl Strehlow's main Loritja informant.

tananukarpitina. 'All of them' or tananilpa or tananitja or tananarata and sometimes the Aranda term ilakija.

tintinpungañi. Meaning 'to initiate into something, to show how something is done' (Strehlow 1910). Initiation ceremony.

tjamu. Grandfather.

tjukurrpa. Dreaming, Dreaming ancestor, mythological past.

tjuta. Many.

tukutita. 'The totem gods'; tuku: unmade and tita: the eternal, according to Carl Strehlow. According to Hansen and Hansen (1977: 149) tjukutitja means 'that which belongs to the dreaming'.

wanampi. Type of snake, rainbow snake, water serpent.

wapiti. Yam, bush potato.

wolkngati. Native pine tree, *Callitris glaucophylla*.

Glossary of some Luritja Kin Terms[6]

F: father, B: brother, M: mother, Z: sister, S: son, D: daughter, H: husband, W: wife, e: elder, y: younger, (m): male view, (f): female view.

tjamu. FF (paternal grandfather), FFB, FFZ, MF (maternal grandfather), MFB, WFM, SS (m), SD (m), BSS, BSD, WZSS, WZSD, HFM, HZSS, HZSD.

---

6   Based on Carl Strehlow (1913).

kami. FM (paternal grandmother), MFB, MFZ, WMM, HMM, DS (m), DD (m), BDS, BDD, WZDS, WZDD, HZDS and HZDD. MM (maternal grandmother), MMZ, MMB, WMF, DS (f), DD (f), ZDS, ZDD, WBDS, WBDD, FZSW, MBSW, HBDS, HBDD, FZDH and MBDH.

papa. F, FB, and SSS.

kuntili. Aunt, FZ, and MBW.

mama. M, MZ, SW (m), and FBW.

kamuru. MB, FZH, DH (m), BDH (m), WZDH (m).

waputju. Father-in-law, WF (man's father-in-law), WFB, WFZ; and HF, HFB, HFZ.

nunari or yumari. Mother-in-law, WM, WMZ, DH (f), DHB (f), WBSW, WBDH, ZDH, ZSW. (Also son-in-law?)

umari. HF (woman's father-in-law), SW (m), BSW (m), and WZSW.

kuta. Brother.

kangkurra. Sister, eZ, FeBD, MeZD, WeBW, HeBW.

malany(pa). Little sister or brother.

kuri. Spouse, W, WZ, BW, FBSW, MZSW, H, HB, ZH, FBZH, and MZZH.

marutju. WB (man's brother-in-law), ZH (m), FBDH (m), MZDH (m).

tjuari. HZ (woman's sister-in-law), BW (f), FBSW (f), MZSW (f).

malanypa. Younger sibling, yB, yZ.

pipiri/tjitji. Child of woman, S (f), D (f), ZS, ZD, WBS, WBD, HBS, HBD, and HF.

pipiri. Child of man, S (m), D (m), BS, BD, HZS, HZD, FFF.

ukari. MBS (m) and FZS (m); MBD (f) and FZD (f).

untalpi. MSD.

katja. MSS.

Appendix C

Some important dates in Strehlow's life and work

23.12.1871	Carl Friedrich Theodore Strehlow was born in Fredersdorf.
31.3.1888	Entry to the Neuendettelsauer Seminary.
31.8.1891	Graduates from the Seminary.
30.5.1892	Arrives in Australia to take his first posting at Bethesda near Lake Eyre on Diyari country up.
1894	Finishes translation of New Testament into Diyari with missionary J.G. Reuther. It was called *Testamenta marra*.
12.10.1894	Arrives at his second posting, the Hermannsburg Mission in Central Australia.
1895	Frieda Keysser arrives in Adelaide.
25.9.1895	Frieda marries Carl at Light Pass.
5.11.1895	Frieda and Carl reach Hermannsburg.
24.3.1897	Birth of first son Friedrich.
1897	Publication of J.G. Reuther and C. Strehlow's *Testamenta marra*.
8.2.1899	Birth of their only daughter Martha.
12.10.1900	Birth of Rudolf.
15.5.1901	Carl Strehlow's letter printed in *Kirchlichen Mitteilungen*.
10.9.1901	Moritz von Leonhardi writes first letter to Carl Strehlow.
20.12.1901	Carl Strehlow first letter to von Leonhardi.
16.6.1902	Birth of Karl.
1903/1904	Family Strehlow leaves Hermannsburg for a one year holiday in South Australia.
1904	Publication of *Galtjindintjamea-Pepa Aranda Wolambarinjaka,* an Aranda Service Book including 100 German hymns translated into Aranda.
15.5.1905	Birth of Hermann.
1907	Publication of first volume of *Die Aranda- und Loritja-Stämme in Zentral-Australien* in Germany.
6.6.1908	Birth of T.G.H. Strehlow.
1908	Publication of second volume of *Die Aranda- und Loritja-Stämme in Zentral-Australien* in Germany.

24.11.1909	Carl finishes his ethnographic research.
11.12.1909	Leonhardi's last letter.
June 1910	Family Strehlow departs Hermannsburg for Germany. Strehlow and von Leonhardi are planning to meet in October 1910 to discuss their scholarly future.
October 1910	Baron von Leonhardi's sudden death in late October.
1910	Publication of third volume of *Die Aranda- und Loritja-Stämme in Zentral-Australien* in Germany.
1911	Publication of fourth volume of *Die Aranda- und Loritja-Stämme in Zentral-Australien* in Germany.
5.4.1912	Carl Strehlow returns to Hermannsburg with his wife and youngest son. The other five children remain in Germany to be educated; he does not see them again.
1913	Begin of translation of New Testament into Aranda.
1913	Publication of fifth volume of *Die Aranda- und Loritja-Stämme in Zentral-Australien* in Germany.
1915	Publication of sixth volume of *Die Aranda- und Loritja-Stämme in Zentral-Australien* in Germany.
1919	Finishes first Aranda translation of the bible.
1920	Publication of seventh volume of *Die Aranda- und Loritja-Stämme in Zentral-Australien* in Germany.
20.10.1922	Carl Strehlow's tragic death at Horseshoe Bend.
1925	Part of the Aranda bible manuscript published posthumously as *Ewangelia Lukaka* without mentioning the translator.
1928	Part of the Aranda bible manuscript published posthumously as *Ewangelia Taramatara* without mentioning the translator.
1928	Publication of *Pepa Araquilinja*. Aranda school primer written by Carl Strehlow.
1943	Duplicates of Carl Strehlow's manuscripts of *Die Aranda- und Loritja-Stämme in Zentral-Australien* and his scientific letters destroyed during the bombing of Frankfurt.

Primary sources at the Strehlow Research Centre

Strehlow, C. (c. 1905–1908) Sagen. Unpublished Manuscript.

Strehlow, C. (c. 190?–1909) Cultus. Unpublished Manuscript.

Strehlow, C. (c. 190?–1909) Leben. Unpublished Manuscript.

Strehlow, C. (c. 1900–1909) Unpublished Dictionary Aranda, Loritja, Dieri.

Strehlow, T.G.H. Diary I, 1932.

Anmatjerra FT Series IX.

Strehlow, T.G.H. Diary 38, 1968.

Strehlow, T.G.H. Childhood Diary III, 1922.

Carl Strehlow to von Leonhardi, probably 8.4.1906 (SH-SP-1-1).

Carl Strehlow to von Leonhardi, 2.6.1906 (SH-SP-2-1).

Carl Strehlow to von Leonhardi, 19.9.1906 (SH-SP-3-1).

Carl Strehlow to Dr. W. Foy, late 1908 (SH-SP-4-1).

Carl Strehlow to von Leonhardi, 13.2.1907 or earlier (SH-SP-5-1).

Carl Strehlow to N.W. Thomas, mid to end of 1906 (SH-SP-6-1).

Carl Strehlow to von Leonhardi, probably 13.12.1906 (SH-SP-7-1).

Carl Strehlow to von Leonhardi, probably on 3.12.1906 (SH-SP-8-1).

Carl Strehlow to von Leonhardi, n.d. probably 1907 (SH-SP-9-1).

Carl Strehlow to von Leonhardi, n.d. probably 1907 (SH-SP-10-1).

Carl Strehlow to von Leonhardi, possibly 6. 4.1907 (SH-SP-11-1).

Carl Strehlow to von Leonhardi, n.d. probably 1907 (SH-SP-12-1).

Carl Strehlow to von Leonhardi, n.d. (SH-SP-13-1).

Carl Strehlow to von Leonhardi, 23.10.1907 (SH-SP-14-1).

Carl Strehlow to von Leonhardi, probably 10.12.1907 (SH-SP-15-1).

Carl Strehlow to von Leonhardi, 14.1.1908 (SH-SP-16-1).

Carl Strehlow to von Leonhardi, 30.7.1907 (SH-SP-17-1).

Carl Strehlow v von Leonhardi, n.d. (SH-SP-18-1).

Von Leonhardi to Carl Strehlow, 10.9.1901 (Gross Karben).

Von Leonhardi to Carl Strehlow, 28.8.1904 (Gross Karben).

Von Leonhardi to Carl Strehlow, 9.9.1905 (Gross Karben).

Von Leonhardi to Carl Strehlow, 17.3.1906 (Gross Karben).

Von Leonhardi to Carl Strehlow, 2.6.1906 (Gross Karben).

Von Leonhardi to Carl Strehlow, 7.8.1906 (Gross Karben).

Von Leonhardi to Carl Strehlow, 26.11.1906 (Gross Karben).

Von Leonhardi to Carl Strehlow, 10.3.1907 (from Darmstadt).

Von Leonhardi to Carl Strehlow, 10.4.1907 (Gross Karben).

Von Leonhardi to Carl Strehlow, 23.4.1907 (Gross Karben).

Von Leonhardi to Carl Strehlow, 29.5.1907 (Gross Karben).

Von Leonhardi to Carl Strehlow, 2.6.1907 (Gross Karben).

Von Leonhardi to Carl Strehlow, 10.7.1907 (Gross Karben).

Von Leonhardi to Carl Strehlow, 5.9.1907 (Gross Karben).

Von Leonhardi to Carl Strehlow, 30.9.1907 (Gross Karben).

Von Leonhardi to Carl Strehlow, 8.12.1907 (Gross Karben).

Von Leonhardi to Carl Strehlow, 11.12.1907 (Gross Karben).

Von Leonhardi to Carl Strehlow, 15.12.1907 (Gross Karben).

Von Leonhardi to Carl Strehlow, 10.1.1908 (Gross Karben).

Von Leonhardi to Carl Strehlow, 8.3.1908 (Gross Karben).

Von Leonhardi to Carl Strehlow, 9.4.1908 (Gross Karben).

Von Leonhardi to Carl Strehlow, 1.6.1908 (Gross Karben).

Von Leonhardi to Carl Strehlow, 7.6. 1908 (Gross Karben).[1]

---

1   Von Leonhardi wrote this letter on the letter Karl von den Steinen had written him on the 3.6.1908 in regard to C. Strehlow's article in the *Zeitschrift für Ethnologie*.

Von Leonhardi to Carl Strehlow, 29.7.1908 (Gross Karben).

Von Leonhardi to Carl Strehlow, 29.8.1908 (Gross Karben).

Von Leonhardi to Carl Strehlow, 24.9.1908 (Gross Karben).

Von Leonhardi to Carl Strehlow, 23.10.1908 (Gross Karben).

Von Leonhardi to Carl Strehlow, 23.12.1908 (Gross Karben).

Von Leonhardi to Carl Strehlow, 28.1.1909 (Gross Karben).

Von Leonhardi to Carl Strehlow, 12.2.1909 (from Darmstadt).

Von Leonhardi to Carl Strehlow, 26.2.1909 (from Darmstadt).

Von Leonhardi to Carl Strehlow, 2.3.1909 (from Darmstadt).

Von Leonhardi to Carl Strehlow, Easter Monday 1909 (Gross Karben).

Von Leonhardi to Carl Strehlow, 3.4.1909 (Gross Karben).

Von Leonhardi to Carl Strehlow, 1.5.1909 (Gross Karben).

Von Leonhardi to Carl Strehlow, 19.7. 1909 (Gross Karben).

Von Leonhardi to Carl Strehlow, 18.8.1909 (Gross Karben).

Von Leonhardi to Carl Strehlow, 31.8.1909 (Gross Karben).

Von Leonhardi to Carl Strehlow, 23.9.1909 (Gross Karben).

Von Leonhardi to Carl Strehlow, 31.10.1909 (Gross Karben).

Von Leonhardi to Carl Strehlow, 14.11.1909 (Gross Karben).

Von Leonhardi to Carl Strehlow, 16.11.1909 (Gross Karben).

Von Leonhardi to Carl Strehlow, 11.12.1909 (Gross Karben).

Carl Seidel to Carl Strehlow, 12.9.1908 (SH 1908-2-1).

Karl von den Steinen to Carl Strehlow, 3.6.1908.

Prof. Fincke to Moritz von Leonhardi, n.d.

F.C.H. Sarg to Carl Strehlow, 20.9.1912.

F.C.H. Sarg to Carl Strehlow, 18.11.1912.

B. Hagen to Carl Strehlow, 10.9.1913.

J.M. Bogner to Carl Strehlow, Bethesda, 8.5.1900 (1900-21-2).

Christian Keysser to Carl Strehlow, 4.9.1905 (SRC 1905/26(a)).

Von Leonhardi to R.H. Mathews, 9.6.1908 (from Gross Karben).

Von Leonhardi to R.H. Mathews, 27.9.1908 (from Gross Karben).

Von Leonhardi to R.H. Mathews, 23.7.1909 (from Gross Karben).

Von Leonhardi to R.H. Mathews, 22.6.1910 (from Gross Karben).

Strehlow, C. 1901 Ein Bericht ueber die Mission in Neu-Hermannsburg, Australien, in einem Brief von H. Missionar Stehlow vom 8. Januar 1901. In *Kirchlichen Mitteilungen* vom 15 May 1901.

Strehlow, C. 1904. *Galtjindintjamea-Pepa Aranda Wolambarinjaka* [Aranda Service Book including 100 German hymns translated into Aranda]. Tanunda: G. Auricht.

Strehlow, C. 1907a. Einige Sagen des Arandastammes in Zentral-Australien. In Sonder-Abdruck aus dem *Globus* Bd. XCII(8) ausgegeben am 29. August 1907: 123–126.

Strehlow, C 1907b. *Die Aranda- und Loritja-Stämme in Zentral-Australien I. Mythen, Sagen und Märchen des Aranda-Stammes in Zentral-Australien.* Frankfurt am Main: Joseph Baer & Co.

Strehlow, C. 1908. *Die Aranda- und Loritja-Stämme in Zentral-Australien II. Mythen, Sagen und Märchen des Loritja-Stammes; die Totemistischen Vorstellungen und die Tjurunga der Aranda und Loritja.* Frankfurt am Main: Joseph Baer & Co.

Strehlow, C. 1908a. Unsere Australische Mission, in einem Brief von H. Missionar Stehlow vom 30. Juni 1908. *Kirchlichen Mitteilungen* vom 22. Juli 1908.

Strehlow, C. 1908b. Einige Bemerkungen über die von Dr. Planert auf Grund der Forschungen des Missionars Wettengel veroeffentlichte Aranda-Grammatik. *Zeitschrift für Ethnologie* 5: 698–703.

Strehlow, C. 1910. *Die Aranda- und Loritja-Stämme in Zentral-Australien III (i). Mythen, Sagen und Märchen des Aranda-Stammes; die Totemistischen Kulte der Aranda-und Loritja- Stämme.* Frankfurt am Main: Joseph Baer & Co.

Strehlow, C. 1911. *Die Aranda- und Loritja-Stämme in Zentral-Australien III (ii). Mythen, Sagen und Märchen des Aranda-Stammes; die Totemistischen Kulte der Aranda-und Loritja- Stämme.* Frankfurt am Main: Joseph Baer & Co.

Strehlow, C. 1913. *Die Aranda- und Loritja-Stämme in Zentral-Australien IV (i). Das Soziale Leben der Aranda- und Loritja-Stämme*. Frankfurt am Main: Joseph Baer & Co.

Strehlow, C. 1915. *Die Aranda- und Loritja-Stämme in Zentral-Australien IV (ii). Das Soziale Leben der Aranda- und Loritja-Stämme*. Frankfurt am Main: Joseph Baer & Co.

Strehlow, C. 1920. *Die Aranda- und Loritja-Stämme in Zentral-Australien V. Die Materielle Kultur der Aranda- und Loritja*. Frankfurt am Main: Joseph Baer & Co.

Strehlow, C. 1925. *Ewangelia Lukaka*. Gospel of St Luke in Aranda. London: British and Foreign Bible Society.

Strehlow, C. 1928. *Ewangelia Taramatara*, The Four Gospels in Aranda. London: British and Foreign Bible Society.

Strehlow, C. 1928. *Pepa Aragulinja: Aranda Katjirberaka*. Aranda school primer. Tanunda: Auricht's Printing Office.

Von Leonhardi, M. 1907. Über einige religioese und totemische Vorstellungen der Aranda und Loritja in Zentralaustralien. *Globus* 91(18): 285–290.

Von Leonhardi, M. 1908. Über einige Hundefiguren des Dieristammes in Zentralaustralien. *Globus* 94: 378–380.

Von Leonhardi, M. 1909. Der Mura und die Muramura der Dieri. *Anthropos* 4: 1065–1068.

Von Leonhardi, M. 1910. Geschlechtstotemismus. *Globus* 97: 339.

Bibliography

Achelis, T. 1889. *Die Entwicklung der modernen Ethnologie*. Berlin: Ernst Siegfried Mittler und Sohn.

Achelis, T. 1896. *Moderne Völkerkunde*. Stuttgart: Verlag von Ferdinand Enke.

Adams, W.Y. 1998. *The Philosophical Roots of Anthropology*. Stanford: Centre for the Study of Language and Information Publications.

Albrecht, K. 1903. *Lehrbuch der Galelsbergerschen Stenographie*. Dresden: Verlag von Erwin Haendcke.

Albrecht, P.G.E., Pfitzner, J.C., Stoll, G., Ziersch, R.P. and Fargher, R.K. 1976. *Summary Statement: Objections of Traditional Aboriginal Land Owners to the Proposed Aboriginal Land Rights Legislation*. Finke River Mission. Typescript.

Albrecht, P.G.E. 2002. *From Mission to Church, 1877–2002*. Adelaide: Finke River Mission.

Albrecht, P.G.E. 2006. The journey broken at Horseshoe Bend: an examination of the events surrounding Carl Strehlow's death from the documents. Bowden: Friends of the Lutheran Archives.

Altmann, M. 1980. *The Silver Miner's Son: The History of Louis Gustav Schulze Missionary*. Hahndorf: Fox Publishing.

Amery, R. 2004. Beyond their expectation: Teichelmann and Schürmann's efforts to preserve the Kaurna Language continues to bear fruit. In W. Veit (ed.), *Strehlow Research Centre Occasional Paper* 3: 9–28.

Anderson, C. (ed.) 1995. *Politics of the Secret*, Oceania Monograph 45. Sydney: University of Sydney.

Ankermann, B. 1905. Kulturkreise und Kulturschichten in Afrika. *Zeitschrift für Ethnologie* 37: 54–84.

Ankermann, B. 1926. Die Entwicklung der Ethnologie seit Adolf Bastian. *Zeitschrift für Ethnologie* 58: 221–230.

Applegate, C. 1990. *A Nation of Provincials: The German Idea of Heimat*. Berkeley: University of California Press.

Austin-Broos, D.J. (ed.) 1987. *Creating Culture*. Sydney: Allen & Unwin.

Austin-Broos, D. 1994. Narratives of the encounter at Ntaria. In J. Beckett (ed.), *Aboriginal Histories, Aboriginal Myths. Oceania* 65(2): 131–150.

Austin-Broos, D.J. 1996a. 'Right Way 'Til I die': Christianity and kin on country at Hermannsburg. In L. Olson (ed.), *Religious Change, Conversion and Culture.* pp. 226–253. Sydney: Sydney Association for Studies in Society and Culture.

Austin-Broos, D. 1996b. Two laws, ontologies, histories: ways of being Aranda today. *The Australian Journal of Anthropology* 7(3): 1–20.

Austin-Broos, D.J. 1999. Review article, Bringing Spencer and Gillen home. *Oceania* 69(3): 209–216.

Austin-Broos, D. 2001. Whose ethics? Which cultural contract? Imagining Arrernte traditions today. *Oceania* 71(3): 189–201.

Austin-Broos, D. 2003a. Places, practices, and things. The articulation of Arrernte kinship with welfare and work. *American Ethnologist* 30(1): 118–135.

Austin-Broos, D. 2003b. The meaning of *Pepe*: God's law and the Western Arrernte. *The Journal of Religious History* 27(3): 311–328.

Austin-Broos, D. 2004. Western Arrernte endogenous change and the impact of settlement. In M. Cawthorn (ed.), *Proceedings of the Strehlow Conference 2002.* pp. 60–65. Alice Springs: Northern Territory Government.

Austin-Broos, D. 2006. 'Working for' and 'working' among Western Arrernte in central Australia. *Oceania* 76: 1–15.

Austin-Broos, D.J. 2009. *Arrernte Present Arrernte Past.* Chicago: Chicago University Press.

Austin-Broos, D. 2010. Translating Christianity. *The Australian Journal of Anthropology* 21(1): 14–32.

Bagshaw, G. 2003. *The Karajarri Claim.* Oceania Monograph 53. Sydney: University of Sydney.

Barker, G. 1976. The ritual estate and Aboriginal policy. *Mankind* 10: 225–239.

Barlow, H. 1873. Vocabulary of Aboriginal dialects of Queensland. *Journal of the Anthropological Institute of Great Britain and Ireland* 2(2): 166–175.

Barnard, A. 2000. *History and Theory in Anthropology.* London: Cambridge University Press.

Barnard, F.M. 1969. *J.G. Herder on Social and Political Culture*, translated and introduced by F.M. Barnard. London: Cambridge University Press.

Barnard, F.M. 2003. *Herder on Nationality, Humanity, and History*. Montreal: McGill-Queen's University Press.

Basedow, H. 1920–1922. Hermannsburg Mission Station. Medical Inspection of Natives of Southern Portion of N.T. Department of External Affairs, Correspondence files, N.T. Series. Typescript.

Basedow, H. 1925. *The Australian Aboriginals*. Adelaide: Preece and Sons.

Batty, P., Allen, L. and Morton, J. 2005. *The Photographs of Baldwin Spencer*. Melbourne: The Miegunyah Press.

Berlin, I. 1976. *Vico and Herder*. London: Hogarth Press.

Berlin, I. 1980. *Against the Current*. Middlesex: Penguin.

Berndt, R. 1959. The concept of 'the tribe' in the Western Desert of Australia. *Oceania* 30(2): 81–107.

Berndt, R. 1970. Traditional morality as expressed through the medium of an Australian Aboriginal religion. In R.M. Berndt (ed.), *Australian Aboriginal Anthropology*. pp. 216–247. Perth: University of Western Australia Press.

Berndt, R. and C. 1958. Aborigines: myths and legends. In *The Australian Encyclopaedia*. Vol 1 (2nd ed.). pp. 53–55. Sydney: Grolier Society.

Berndt, R. and C. 1970. *Man, Land & Myth in North Australia*. Sydney: Ure Smith.

Berndt, R. and C. 1989. *The Speaking Land*. Melbourne: Penguin Books.

Berndt, R. and C. 1993. *A World That Was: The Yaraldi of the Murray River and the Lakes, South Australia*. Melbourne: Melbourne University Press at the Miegunyah Press.

Boas, F. 1901. The mind of primitive man. *Journal of American Folklore* 14: 1–11.

Boas, F. 1904. Some traits of primitive culture. *Journal of American Folklore* 17: 243–254.

Boas, F. 1910a. Ethnological problems in Canada. *Journal of the Royal Anthropological Institute* 40: 529–539.

Boas, F. 1910b. Notes and queries to 'The Origin of Totemism'. *Journal of American Folklore* 23: 392–393.

Boas, F. 1911. *The Handbook of American Indian Languages, Part 1*. Washington: Government Printing Office.

Boas, F. [1911] 1963. *The Mind of Primitive Man*. New York: The Macmillan Company.

Boas, F. [1927] 1955. *Primitive Art*. New York: Dover Publications, Inc.

Boas, F. 1940. *Race, Language and Culture*. New York: Macmillan.

Bohansen, P. and Glazer, M. 1988. *High Points in Anthropology*. New York: McGraw-Hill Inc.

Bowman, B. 1989–1991. *A History of Central Australia, 1930–1980* (3 Vols). Alice Springs: Bryan Bowman.

Brandauer, A. and Veber, M. 2009. Missionary love and duty: Frieda Keysser's and Carl Strehlow's letters of courtship (1894–1895). In A. Brandauer and M. Veber (eds), *Migration and Cultural Contact: Germany and Australia*. pp. 113–130. Sydney: University of Sydney Press.

Brandt, R. 1994. Kants pragmatische Anthropologie: Die Vorlesung. *Allgemeine Zeitschrift für Philosophie* 19: 41–49.

Breen, G. 2000. *Introductory Dictionary of Western Arrernte*. Alice Springs: IAD Press.

Breen, G. 2005. A short history of spelling systems in Arrernte. In A. Kenny and S. Mitchell (eds), *Collaboration and Language, Strehlow Research Centre Occasional Paper* 4: 93–102.

Breton, R.N. 1833. *Excursions in New South Wales, Western Australia, and Van Dieman's Land, during the years 1830, 1831, 1832, and 1833*. London: Richard Bentley, New Burlington Street.

Broce, G. 1986. Herder and ethnography. *Journal of the History of the Behavioural Sciences* 22: 150–170.

Brown, A. 1913. Three Tribes of Western Australia. *Journal of the Anthropological Institute of Great Britain and Ireland* 43: 143-194.

Bunzl, M. 1996. Franz Boas and the Humboldtian tradition: From *Volksgeist* and *Nationalcharakter* to an anthropological concept of culture. In G.W. Stocking (ed.), *Volksgeist as Method and Ethic: Essays on Boasian Ethnography and the German Anthropological Tradition. History of Anthropology*. pp. 17–78. Madison: The University of Wisconsin Press.

Burns, R.M. 2002. Classical historicism. In R.M. Burns and H. Rayment-Pickard (eds.), *Philosophies of History: From Enlightenment to Postmodernity*. pp. 56–97. Oxford: Blackwell.

Cawthorn, M. and Malbunka, H. 2005. Hesekiel Malbunka. In A. Kenny and S. Mitchell (eds), *Collaboration and Language*, *Strehlow Research Centre Occasional Paper* 4: 71–75.

Cawthorn, M. 2006. Alienated Possessions: Repatriating *Tywerrenge*. Honours Thesis, The Australian National University.

Centre for Indigenous Development Education and Research 1996. *Keeping Company, an Inter-Cultural Conversation*. Wollongong: Centre for Indigenous Development Education and Research, University of Wollongong.

Chewings, C. 1936. *Back in the Stone Age*. Sydney: Angus & Robertson.

Clifford, J. 1982. *Person and Myth: Maurice Leenhardt in the Melanesian World*. Berkeley: University of California Press.

Cole, D. 1999. *Franz Boas. The Early Years, 1853–1906*. Seattle and London: University of Washington Press.

Conte, E. 1987. Wilhelm Schmidt: Des letzten Kaisers Beichtvater und das neudeutsche Heidentum. In H. Gerndt (ed), *Volkskunde und Nazionalismus.Münchner Beiträge zur Volkskunde* 7: 261–278.

Curr, E.M. 1886–1987. *The Australasian Race* (4 Vols). Melbourne, London: J. Ferres.

Darcy, A. 1987. Franz Boas and the concept of culture: a genealogy. In D.J. Austin-Broos (ed.), *Creating Culture*. pp. 3–18. Sydney: Allen & Unwin.

Darnell, R. 1990. *Edward Sapir: Linguist, Anthropologist, Humanist*. Berkeley, Los Angeles, London: University of California Press.

Darnell, R. 1998. *And Along Came Boas: Continuity and Revolution in Americanist Anthropology*. Amsterdam/Philadelphia: John Benjamins Publishing Company.

Darnell, R. 2001. *Invisible Genealogies: A History of Americanist Anthropology*. Lincoln: University of Nebraska Press.

Dixon, R.M.W. 2002. *Australian Languages*. Cambridge: Cambridge University Press.

Dobson, V.P. and Henderson, J. 2013. *Anpernirrentye. Kin and skin. Talking about family in Arrernte*. Alice Springs: IAD Press.

Donovan, P. 1988. *Alice Springs. Its History and the People who Made It*. Alice Springs: Alice Springs Town Council.

Dousset, L. 1999. On reading Theodor Strehlow's 'Aranda Regular and Irregular Marriages'. *Strehlow Research Centre Occasional Paper 2*: 45–60.

Dousset, L. 2005. *Assimilating Identities: Social Networks and the Diffusion of Sections*. Oceania Monograph 57. Sydney: University of Sydney.

Dousset, L. and Glaskin, K. 2007. Western Desert and native title: how models become myths. *Anthropological Forum* 17(2): 127–148.

Dumont, L. 1994. *German Ideology: From France to Germany and Back*. Chicago: The University of Chicago Press.

Duranti, A. 1997. *Linguistic Anthropology*. Cambridge: Cambridge University Press.

Durkheim, E. 1915. *The Elementary Forms of Religious Life*. London: Allen & Unwin.

Elkin, A.P. 1932. Social organization in the Kimberley Division, north-western Australia. *Oceania* 2(3): 296–333.

Elkin, A.P. 1975. R.H. Mathews: his contribution to Aboriginal studies (Part II). *Oceania* 46(2): 126–152.

Elliott, C., Green, J. and Vaarzon-Morel, P. 1995. *Alcoota/Waite River Land Claim Book*. Alice Springs: Central Land Council.

Elliott, C. 1999 (Nov.). *Alyawarr, Kaytetye, Warumungu, Wakaya, Native Title Application Anthropological Report*. Exhibit A 1. Alice Springs: Central Land Council.

Elliott, C. 2004. *Pine Hill Native Title Application Consent Determination Report*. Alice Springs: Central Land Council.

Evans, D.E. 2003. Anthropology at war: racial studies of POWs during World War I. In H.G. Penny and M. Bunzl (eds), *Worldly Provincialism: German Anthropology in the Age of the Empire*. pp. 198–229. Ann Arbor: University of Michigan Press.

Eylmann, E. 1908. *Die Eingeborenen der Kolonie Südaustralien*. Berlin: Dietrich Reimer (Ernst Vohsen).

Farnbacher T. und Weber, C. 2004. *Ein Zentrum für Weltmission – Neuendettelsau*. Neuendettelsau: Missionswerk Neuendettelsau.

Feest, C.F. and Kohl, K.H. (eds) 2001. *Hauptwerke der Ethnology*. Stuttgart: Kröner.

Fink, K.J. 1993. Storm and Stress anthropology. *History of the Human Sciences* 6: 51–71.

Fischer, H. 1996. *Lehrbuch der Genealogischen Methode*. Berlin: Dietrich Reimer Verlag.

Fison, L. and Howitt, A.W. 1880. *Kamilaroi and Kurnai: Group Marriage and Relationship, and Marriage by Elopement*. Melbourne: George Robertson.

Foertsch, H. 2001. Missonarsmaterialien und die Entdeckung amerikanischer Sprachen in Europa: vom Sprachensammler Lorenzo Hervas y Panduro zum Linguisten Wilhelm von Humboldt. In R. Wendt (Hrsg.), *Sammeln, Vernetzen, Auswerten. Missionare und ihr Beitrag zum Wandel europäischer Weltsicht*. pp. 75–130. Tübingen: Gunter Narr Verlag.

Foy, W. 1909. Das städtische Rautenstrauch-Joest-Museum der Stadt Cöln. *Ethnologia* 1: 1–70.

Foy, W. 1911. Ethnology und Kulturgeschichte. *Petermanns Geographische Mitteilungen* 1(3): 230–33.

Fox, R. 1967a. *Kinship and Marriage*. Penguin Books.

Fox, R. 1967b. 'Totem and Taboo' reconsidered. In E. Leach (ed.), *The Structural Study of Myth and Totemism*. ASA Monographs 5. pp. 161–178. London: Tavistock Publications.

Frank, L. 1982. Herder's essay on the origin of language: forerunner of contemporary views in history, aesthetics, literary theories and philosophy. *Forum Linguisticum* 7: 15–26.

Franks, C. 1996. *Keeping Company*. Wollongong: Centre for Indigenous Development Education and Research, University of Wollongong.

Frazer, J.G. 1887. *Totemism*. Edinburgh: Adam & Charles Black.

Frazer, J.G. 1910. *Totemism and Exogamy*. London: Macmillan and Co.

Frazer, J.G. 1913. *The Belief in Immortality and the Worship of the Dead: The Belief Among the Aborigines of Australia, The Torres Straits Islands, New Guinea and Melanesia* (Vol. 1). London: Macmillan and Co.

Frazer, J.G. [1922] 1963. *The Golden Bough: A Study in Magic and Religion*. Abridged Edition. London: Macmillan & Co. Ltd.

Frobenius, L. 1897. Der westafrikanische Kulturkreis. *Petermanns Geographische Mitteilungen* 43: 225–236, 262–267.

Frobenius, L. 1898. Der Ursprung der afrikanischen Kulturen. *Zeitschrift für Erdkunde zu Berlin* 33: 111–125.

Gaier, U. 1996. Von nationaler Klassik zur Humanität: Konzepte der Vollendung bei Herder. In R. Otto (ed.), *Nationen und Kulturen*. pp. 49–64. Würzburg: Königshausen & Neumann.

Ganter, R. 2005. *Mixed Relations: Asian-Aboriginal Contact in North Australia*. Crawley: University of Western Australia.

Gason, S. 1874. *The Dieyerie Tribe of Australian Aborigines*. Edited by George Isaacs. Adelaide: Government Printer.

Geertz, C. 1973. *The Interpretation of Culture*. New York: Basic Books.

Gennep, A.v. [1906] 1975. 'Myth and Rite' and 'The Content of the Legends', translated by Enid Watkin Jones, with an introduction by L.R. Hiatt. In L.R. Hiatt (ed.), *Australian Aboriginal Mythology: Essays in Honour of WEH Stanner*. pp. 183–206. Canberra: Australian Institute of Aboriginal Studies.

Gennep, A.v. 1908. Die Aranda und Loritja Stämme in Zentral-Australien (I), Questions Australiennes (II). *Man* 8: 17–18, 37–41.

Gent, J.v. 2001. Carl T.F. Strehlow. In C.F. Feest and K.H. Kohl (eds), *Hauptwerke der Ethnologie*. pp. 459–469. Stuttgart: Alfred Kröner Verlag.

Giles, E. [1889] 1995. *Australia Twice Traversed* (2 vols). London: Sampson, Lowe, Marston, Searle & Rivington.

Gillen, F.J. 1901. *Magic amongst the Natives of Central Australia*. Melbourne: McCarron, Bird and Co.

Gillen, F. J. and Gillen, R.S. 1995. F.J. *Gillen's First Diary 1875: Adelaide to Alice Springs, March to June*. Edited by Robert S. Gillen. Kent Town: Wakefield Press.

Gillen, R.S. 1968. *Gillen's Diary: The Camp Jottings of F.J. Gillen on the Spencer and Gillen Expedition across Australia 1901-1902*. Adelaide: Libraries Board of South Australia.

Gingrich, A. 2005. The German speaking countries. Ruptures, schools, and nontraditions: reassessing the history of sociocultural anthropology in Germany. In F. Barth, R. Gingrich, A. Parkin, S. Silverman, *One Discipline, Four Ways: British, German, French and American Anthropology*. pp. 76–153. Chicago: Chicago University Press.

Goethe, J. 1998. *Dichtung und Wahrheit*. Stuttgart: Reclam.

Graebner, F. 1905. Kulturkreise und Kulturschichten in Ozeanien. *Zeitschrift für Ethnologie* 37: 28–53.

Graebner, F. 1906. Wanderung und Entwicklung sozialer Systeme in Australien. *Globus* XC(12): 181–186, 207–210, 220–224, 237–241.

Graebner, F. 1911. *Methode der Ethnology*. Heidelberg: Winter.

Gray, G. 2007. *A Cautious Silence: The Politics of Australian Anthropology*. Canberra: Aboriginal Studies Press.

Gray, P.R.A. 1999. *Palm Valley Land Claim No. 48: Report and Recommendations of the Aboriginal Land Commissioner, Justice Gray*. Canberra: Aboriginal and Torres Strait Islander Commission.

Green, J. 1988. *Pmere: Country in Mind*. Alice Springs: Tangentyere Council.

Green, J. 1992. *Alyawarr to English Dictionary*. Alice Springs: Institute for Aboriginal Development.

Green, J. 1998. Kin and Country. Aspects of the Use of Kin Terms in Arandic Languages. MA thesis, University of Melbourne.

Green, J. 2010. *Central and Eastern Anmatyerr to English dictionary*. Alice Springs: Institute for Aboriginal Development Press.

Green, J. 2012. The Altyerre story – 'Suffering badly by translation'. *TAJA* 23(2): 158–178.

Grey, G. 1841. *Journals of Two Expeditions of Discovery in North-West and Western Australia, during the years 1837, 38, and 39* (2 vols). London: T. and W. Boone.

Haberland, M. 1911. Zur Kritik der Lehre von den Kulturschichten und Kulturkreisen. *Petermanns Geographische Mitteilungen* 1(3): 113–118.

Hahn, H.P. 2001. Fritz Graebner. In C.F. Feest und K.H. Kohl (eds), *Hauptwerke der Ethnologie*. pp.137–142. Stuttgart: Alfred Kröner Verlag.

Hamilton, A. 1987. Dual social system: technology, labour and women's secret rites in the eastern Western Desert of Australia. In W. Edwards (ed.), *Traditional AboriginalSociety* (1st ed.). pp. 34–52. Melbourne: Macmillan Education Australia Pty Ltd.

Hamilton, A. 1998. Descended from father, belonging to country: rights to land in the Australian Western Desert. In W. Edwards (ed.), *Traditional Aboriginal Society* (2nd ed.). pp. 90–108. Melbourne: Macmillan Education Australia Pty Ltd.

Hansen, K.C. and Hansen, L.E. 1992. *Pintupi/Luritja Dictionary*. Alice Springs: Institute for Aboriginal Development.

Hardy, J., Megaw, J.V.S. and Megaw, M.R. (eds) 1992. *The Heritage of Namatjira*. Melbourne: William Heinemann.

Harms, H.F. 2003. *Träume and Tränen*. Hermannsburg: Verlag Ludwig-Harms-Haus.

Harms, V. 1990. The aims of the Museum for Ethnology: debate in the German speaking countries. *Current Anthropology* 31(4): 457–463.

Hartwig, M. 1965. The Progress of White Settlement in the Alice Springs District and its Effects upon the Aboriginal Inhabitants, 1860–1894. PhD thesis, University of Adelaide.

Harvey, D. 2001. Cosmopolitanism and the banality of geographic evils. In J. Comaroff and J. Comaroff (eds), *Millennial Capitalism and the Culture of Neoliberalism*. pp. 271–309. Durham and London: Duke University Press.

Hassel, M.v. 1981. Johann Gottfried Herder, a lost ancestor. *Dialectical Anthropology* 5: 331–339.

Hebart, T. 1938. *The United Lutheran Church in Australia: Its History, Activities, and Characteristics*. Adelaide: Lutheran Book Depot.

Heffernan, J. and Heffernan, K. 2005. *A Learner's Guide to Pintupi-Luritja*. Alice Springs: IAD Press.

Heidegger, M. 2002. The worldhood of the world. In D. Moran and T. Mooney (eds), *The Phenomenological Reader*. pp. 288–307. London and New York: Routledge.

Heinrichs, H.J. 1998. *Die fremde Welt, das bin ich: Leo Frobenius, Ethnologie, Forschungsreisender, Abendteurer*. Wuppertal: P. Hammer.

Henderson, J. and Dobson, V. 1994. *Eastern and Central Arrernte to English Dictionary*, Alice Springs: IAD Press.

Henson, B. 1992. *A Straight-Out Man: F.W. Albrecht and Central Australian Aborigines*. Melbourne: Melbourne University Press.

Hercus, L. and McCaul, K. 2004. Otto Siebert: The Missionary-Ethnographer. In W. Veit (ed.), *Strehlow Research Centre Occasional Paper* 3: 36–50.

Herder, J.G. [1772] 1966. *Abhandlung über den Ursprung der Sprache*. Stuttgart: Reclam.

Herder, J.G. 1966. Essay on the origin of language. In *Milestones of Thought. On the Origin of Language*. pp. 87–166. New York: Frederick Ungar Publishing Co.

Herder, J.G. 1969a. Yet another philosophy of history. In *J.G. Herder on Social and Political Culture*, translated and introduced by F.M. Barnard. pp. 179–224. London: Cambridge University Press.

Herder, J.G. 1969b. Ideas for a philosophy of the history of mankind. In *J.G. Herder on Social and Political Culture*, translated and introduced by F.M. Barnard. pp. 253–326. London: Cambridge University Press.

Herder, J.G. [1774] 1990. *Auch eine Philosophie der Geschichte zur Bildung der Menschheit*. Stuttgart: Reclam.

Herder, J.G. 1992. Shakespeare. In T. Chamberlain (ed.), *Eighteenth-Century German Criticism*. pp. 143–163. New York: Continuum.

Hiatt, L.R. 1962. Local organization among the Australian Aborigines. *Oceania* 32: 267–286.

Hiatt, L.R. 1966. The lost horde. *Oceania* 37: 81–92.

Hiatt, L.R. 1969. Totemism tomorrow: the future of an illusion. *Mankind* 7: 85–87.

Hiatt, L.R. 1975. *Australian Aboriginal Mythology. Essays in Honour of WEH Stanner*. Canberra: Australian Institute of Aboriginal Studies.

Hiatt, L.R. 1984. *Aboriginal Landowners: Contemporary Issues in the Determination of Traditional Aboriginal Land Ownership*. Oceania Monograph 27. Sydney: University of Sydney.

Hiatt, L.R. 1996. *Arguments about Aborigines: Australia and the Evolution of Social Anthropology*. Cambridge: Cambridge University Press.

Hill, B. 2002. *Broken Song: T.G.H. Strehlow and Aboriginal Possession*. NSW: Knopf, Random House Australia Pty Ltd.

Hoenigswald, H.M. 1963. On the history of the comparative method. *Anthropological Linguistics* 5(1): 1–11.

Hoenigswald, H.M. 1974. Fallacies in the history of linguistics: notes on the appraisal of the nineteenth century. In D. Hymes (ed.), *Studies in the History of Linguistics*. pp. 347–359. Bloomington/London: Indiana University Press.

Holcombe, S. 1998. *Amunturrngu*: An Emergent Community in Central Australia. PhD thesis, University of Newcastle.

Holcombe, S. 2004. The politico-historical construction of the Pintupi-Luritja and the concept of tribe. *Oceania* 74: 257–275.

Howitt, A.W. and Fison, L. 1883. From mother-right to father-right. *Journal of the Anthropological Institute of Great Britain and Ireland* 12: 30–46.

Howitt, A.W. 1884. On some Australian ceremonies of initiation. *Journal of the Anthropological Institute of Great Britain and Ireland* 13: 432–459.

Howitt, A.W. 1891. The Dieri and other kindred Tribes of Central Australia. *Journal of the Royal Anthropological Institute* 20: 30–104.

Howitt, A.W. 1904. *The Native Tribes of South-East Australia*. London: Macmillan and Co Limited.

Humboldt, W.v. 1994. *Über die Sprache*. Tübingen und Basel: A. Francke Verlag.

Humboldt, W.v. 1999. *On Language. On the Diversity of Human Language Construction and its Influence on the Mental Development of the Human Species*. Cambridge: Cambridge University Press.

Hymes, D. 1974. *Studies in the History of Linguistics*. Bloomington/London: Indiana University Press.

Inkamala, J. 1988. *Yeye Apme Kwerlaye-Iperre*. Alice Springs: Yeperenye School.

Jacknis, I. 1985. Franz Boas and exhibits: on the limitations of the museum method of anthropology. In G.W. Stocking (ed.), *Objects and Others. Essays on Museums and Material Culture*. No. 3. Madison: The University of Wisconsin Press.

Jacknis, I. 1996. The ethnographic Object and the Object of Ethnography in the Early Career of Franz Boas. In G.W. Stocking (ed.), *Volksgeist as Method and Ethic: Essays on Boasian Ethnography and the German Anthropological Tradition. History of Anthropology*. pp. 185–214. Madison: The University of Wisconsin Press.

Jacknis, I. 2002. The First Boasian: Alfred Kroeber and Franz Boas, 1896–1905. *American Anthropologist* 104(2): 520–532.

Jenner, H. 2004. *Von Neuendettelsau in alle Welt*. Neuendettelsau: Diakonie Neuendettelsau.

Jensen, A.E. 1963. *Myth and Cult among Primitive Peoples*. Chicago: The University of Chicago Press.

Jones, P.G. 1996. 'A Box of Native Things': Ethnographic Collectors and the South Australian Museum, 1830s–1930s. PhD thesis, University of Adelaide.

Jones, P. 2005. 'Indispensable to each other': Spencer and Gillen or Gillen and Spencer. In A. Kenny and S. Mitchell (eds), *Collaboration and Language*, *Strehlow Research Centre Occasional Paper* 4: 6–25.

Kaiser, S. 2004. The Stern Case. In M. Cawthorn (ed.), *Proceedings of the Strehlow Conference 2002*. pp. 66–76. Alice Springs: Northern Territory Government.

Kearney, W.J. 1985. *Warlpiri Kukatja and Ngarti Land Claim*. Canberra: Australian Government Publishing Service.

Keen, I. 1994. *Knowledge and Secrecy in an Aboriginal Religion*. Oxford: Clarendon Press.

Keen, I. 1997. The Western Desert vs the Rest: rethinking the contrast. In F. Merlan, J. Morton and A. Rumsey (eds), *Scholar and Sceptic: Australian Aboriginal Studies in Honour of L.R. Hiatt*. pp. 65–93. Canberra: Aboriginal Studies Press.

Keen, I. 2000. The debate over Yolngu clans. *Anthropological Forum* 10(1): 31–42.

Keen, I. 2004. *Aboriginal Economy and Society: Australia at the Threshold of Colonisation*. Oxford: Oxford University Press.

Keen, I. 2007. Sansom's misreading of 'the Western Desert vs. the Rest'. *Anthropological Forum* 17(2): 168–170.

Kempe, H. 1883. Zur Sittenkunde der Centralaustralischen Schwarzen. *Mitteilungen des Vereins für Erdkunde zu Halle* (Journal of the Halle Geographical Society): 52–56.

Kempe, H. 1891. A grammar and vocabulary of the language spoken by the Aborigines of the MacDonnell Ranges. *Transactions and Proceedings ofRoyal Society of South Australia* 14: [1]–54.

Kenny, A. 2003. *Anthropologist's Report for Western MacDonnell National Park*. Alice Springs: Central Land Council.

Kenny, A. 2004a. Pmara Kutata – Pmerekwetethe. In M. Cawthorn (ed.), *Proceedings of the Strehlow Conference 2002*. pp. 20–25. Alice Springs: Northern Territory Government.

Kenny, A. 2004b. Western Arrernte pmere kwetethe spirits. *Oceania* 74(4): 276–289.

Kenny, A. 2005. A sketch portrait: Carl Strehlow's editor Baron Moritz von Leonhardi. In A. Kenny and S. Mitchell (eds), *Collaboration and Language,Strehlow Research Centre Occasional Paper* 4: 54–70.

Kenny, A. and Mitchell, S. (eds) 2005. *Collaboration and Language, Strehlow Research Centre Occasional Paper* 4.

Kenny, A. 2009a. Carl Strehlow's mission. In A. Brandauer and M. Veber (eds), *Migration and Cultural Contact: Germany and Australia*. pp. 91–112. Sydney: University of Sydney Press.

Kenny, A. 2009b. Inland Australia's first Muslims. In J. Jupp (ed.), *Cambridge Encyclopaedia of Australian Religion*. pp. 436–439. Melbourne: Cambridge University Press.

Kenny, A. 2010. *Anthropology Report. Glen Helen Native Title Consent Determination, NT*. Alice Springs: Central Land Council.

Kessing, R.M. 1975. *Kin Groups and Social Structure*. New York: Holt, Rinehart and Winston, Inc.

Kluckhohn, C. 1936. Some reflections on the method and theory of the Kulturkreislehre. *American Anthropologist* 38: 157–196.

Kneebone, H. 2001. "Was hat die gegenwärtige Mission für die Sprachwissenschaft geleistet?" Missionare und die vergleichende Philologie im 19. Jahrhundert. In R. Wendt (Hrsg.), *Sammeln, Vernetzen, Auswerten. Missionare und ihr Beitrag zum Wandel europäischer Weltsicht*. pp. 145–172. Tübingen: Gunter Narr Verlag.

Knoll, S.B. 1982. Herder's concept of Humanität. In W. Koepke (ed.) in cooperation with S.B. Knoll, *Johann Gottfried Herder, Innovator through the Ages*. pp. 9–19. Bonn: Bouvier Verlag Herbert Grundmann.

Kohl, K.H. 1999. Der sakrale Königmord. Zur Geschichte der Kulturmorpholgie. *Paideuma* 45: 62–82.

Kohl, K.H. 2001. Ernst Vatter. In C.F. Feest and K.H. Kohl (eds), *Hauptwerke der Ethnologie*. pp. 498–502. Stuttgart: Alfred Kröner Verlag.

Kohl, K.H. 2002. *Die Macht der Dinge*. München: Verlag C.H. Beck.

Kolig, E. 1992. Religious power and the All-Father in the sky: monotheism in Australian Aboriginal culture reconsidered. *Anthropos* 87: 9–31.

Koepping, K.-P. 1983. *Adolf Bastian and the Psychic Unity of Mankind: The Foundation of Anthropology in Nineteenth Century Germany*. London: Queensland Press.

Koepping, K.-P. 1995. Enlightenment and Romanticism in the work of Adolf Bastian. The historical roots of anthropology in the nineteenth century. In H.F. Vermeulen and A.A. Roldan (eds), *Fieldwork and Footnotes. Studies in the History of European Anthropology*. pp. 75–91. London and New York: Routledge.

Koller, W. 1924. *Die Missionsanstalt in Neuendettelsau. Ihre Geschichte und das Leben in ihr*. Neuendettelsau: Verlag des Missionshauses, Nummer 7.

Kral, I. 2000. The Socio-Historical Development of Literacy in Arrernte. MA Thesis, University of Melbourne.

Kramer, F. 1977. *Verkehrte Welten: Zur imaginären Ethnographie des 19. Jahrhunderts*. Frankfurt am Main: Syndikat.

Kräuser, A. 1990. Anthropologie und Ästhetik im 18. Jahrhundert. *Das achtzehnte Jahrhundert* 14(2): 196–206.

Kreinath, J. 2012. Discursive formation, ethnographic encounter, photographic evidence: the centenary of Durkheim's basic forms of religious life and the anthropological study of Australian Aboriginal religion in his time. *Visual Anthropology* 25(5): 367–420.

Krichauff, F.E.H. 1886. Customs, religious ceremonies, etc., of the "Aldolinga" or "Mbenderinga" Tribe of Aborigines of the Krichauff Ranges, South Australia. *Proceedings of the Royal Society of Australia*, S.A. (1886–1887): 32–37, 77–80.

Kroeber, A. 1935. History and science in anthropology. *American Anthropologist* 37(4): 539–569.

Kroeber, A. 1956. The place of Boas in anthropology. *American Anthropologist* 58: 151–159.

Kuklick, H. 1991. *The Savage within: The Social History of British Anthropology, 1885–1945*. Cambridge: Cambridge University Press.

Kuklick, H. 2006. Humanity in the chrysalis stage. *British Journal for the History of Science* 39: 535–568.

Kuklick, H. (ed.). 2008. *A New History of Anthropology*. Malden: Blackwell Publishing.

Kuper, A. 1988. *The Invention of Primitive Society*. New York: Routledge.

Kuper, A. 1999. *Culture: The Anthropologists' Approach*. Cambridge: Harvard University Press.

Lally, J. 2002. The Australian Aboriginal Collection in the Museum für Völkerkunde, Berlin and the Making of Cultural Identity. PhD Thesis, University of Melbourne.

Lang, A. 1901. *Magic and Religion*. London: Longmans, Green and Co.

Lang, A. 1905. *The Secret of the Totem*. London: Longmans, Green and Co.

Lang, A. 1909a. Die Aranda- und Loritja-Staemme in Zentral-Australien by C. Strehlow, 1907 u. 1908, Teil I & II. *Man* 14: 26–28.

Lang, A. 1909b. The Alcheringa and the All Father. *Revue des Etudes Ethnographiques et Sociologiques* 2: 141–154.

Lang, J. D. 1861. *Queensland, Australia; A highly eligible field for emigration, and the future cotton–field of Great Britain: with a disquisition on the origin, manners, and customs of the Aborigines*. London: Edward Stanford.

Langham, I. 1981. *The Building of British Social Anthropology*. London: D. Reidel Publishing Company.

Langness, L.L. 1975. *The Study of Culture*. San Francisco: Chandler & Sharp Publishers, Inc.

Lawrence, P. 1987. Tylor and Frazer: the intellectualist tradition. In D. Austin-Broos (ed.), *Creating Culture*. pp. 18–34. Sydney: Allen & Unwin.

Layton, R. 1997. *An Introduction to Theory in Anthropology*. Cambridge: Cambridge University Press.

Leach, E. 1970. *Lévi-Strauss*. London: Fontana/Collins.

Lepenies, W. 1980. Germany: the search for a new ancestor. In S. Diamond (ed.), *Anthropology: Ancestors and Heirs*. pp. 395–430. The Hague: Mouton.

Leser, P. 1963. Zur Geschichte des Wortes Kulturkreis. *Anthropos* 58: 1–36.

Leser, P. 1977. Fritz Graebner – Eine Würdigung. Zum 100. Geburtstag am 4 März 1977. *Anthropos* 72: 1–55.

Leske, E. (ed.) 1977. *Hermannsburg: A Vision and a Mission*, Adelaide: Lutheran Publishing House.

Leske, E. 1996. *For Faith and Freedom*. Adelaide: Openbook Publishers.

Lessa, W. and Vogt, E. 1965. *Reader in Comparative Religion: An Anthropological Approach*. New York: Harper & Row Publishers.

Lévi-Strauss, C. 1963. *Structural Anthropology*. Translated by Claire Jacobsen and Brooke Grundfest Schoepf. New York and London: Basic Books.

Lévi-Strauss, C. 1966. *The Savage Mind*. Chicago: University of Chicago Press.

Liebel-Weckowicz, H. 1984. Herder's place in the development of ideas on human genesis and evolution. *Eighteenth-Century Life* 9: 62–82.

Liebermeister, B. 1998. Leben und Werk Carl Strehlows, des Erforschers der Aranda-und Loritja Stämme in Zentralaustralien. MA thesis, University of München.

Liss, J.E. 1996. German culture and German science in the Bildung of Franz Boas. In G.W. Stocking (ed.), *Volksgeist as Method and Ethic: Essays on Boasian Ethnography and the German Anthropological Tradition. History of Anthropology*. pp. 155–184. Madison: The University of Wisconsin Press.

Losonsky, M. 1999. Introduction. In W. Von Humboldt, *On Language. On the Diversity of Human Language Construction and its Influence on the Mental Development of the Human Species*. pp. vii–xxxix. Cambridge: Cambridge University Press.

Lowie, R. 1937. *The History of Ethnological Theory*. New York: Holt, Rinehart and Winston.

Lueker, E.L. (ed.) 1954. *Lutheran Cyclopaedia*. Saint Louis, Missouri: Concordia Publishing House.

Maddock, K. 1982. *The Australian Aborigines: A Portrait of their Society* (2nd ed.). Ringwood: Penguin Books.

Maher, T.P. 1966. More on the history of the comparative method. *Anthropological Linguistics* 8(3): 1–12.

Malbunka, M. 2004. Accessing family information at the Strehlow Research Centre. In M. Cawthorn (ed.), *Proceedings of the Strehlow Conference 2002*. pp. 13–15. Alice Springs: Northern Territory Government.

Malinowski, B. 1913. *The Family among the Australian Aborigines*. London: University of London Press.

Malinowski, B. 1979. *The Ethnography of Malinowski: The Trobriand Islands, 1915–1918*. Edited by Michael Young. London: Routledge and Kegan Paul.

Maranda, P. (ed.) 1972. Introduction. In *Mythology: Selected Readings*. pp. 7–20. Harmondsworth: Penguin Education.

Marchand, J.W. 1982. Herder: precursor of Humboldt, Whorf, and modern language philosophy. In W. Koepke (ed) in cooperation with S. B. Knoll, *Johann Gottfried Herder, Innovator through the Ages.* pp. 20–34. Bonn: Bouvier Verlag Herbert Grundmann.

Marchand, S. 2003. Priests among the Pygmies: Wilhelm Schmidt and the Counter-Reformation in Austrian Ethnology. In H.G. Penny and M. Bunzl (eds), *Worldly Provincialism: German Anthropology in the Age of the Empire.* pp. 283–316. Ann Arbor: University of Michigan Press.

Marett, R.R. and Penniman, T.K. 1932. *Spencer's Scientific Correspondence with Sir J.G. Frazer and Others.* Oxford: Clarendon Press.

Marquard, O. 1982. Zur Geschichte des philosophischen Begriffs 'Anthropologie' seit dem Ende des 18 Jahrhunderts. In *Schwierigkeiten mit der Geschichtsphilosophie: Aufsätze.* pp. 122–144. Frankfurt: Suhrkamp.

Marzan, de P.J. 1907. Le totemisme aux Iles Fiji. *Anthropos* 2: 400–405.

Massin, B. 1996. From Virchow to Fischer: physical anthropology and 'modern race theories' in Wilhelmine Germany. In G.W. Stocking (ed.), *Volksgeist as Method and Ethic: Essays on Boasian Ethnography and the German Anthropological Tradition. History of Anthropology.* pp. 79–154. Madison: The University of Wisconsin Press.

Mathew, J. 1899. *Eaglehawk and Crow.* Melbourne: Melville, Mullen and Slade.

Mathew, J. 1910. *Two Representative Tribes of Queensland: With an Inquiry Concerning the Origin of the Australian Race.* London: T. Fisher Unwin.

Mathews, R.H. 1894. Aboriginal Bora held at Gundabloui in 1894. *Journal and Proceedings of the Royal Society of New South Wales* 28: 98–129.

Mathews, R.H. 1895. The Bora, or initiation ceremonies of the Kamilaroi tribe. *Journal of the Anthropological Institute of Great Britain and Ireland* 24: 411–427.

Mathews, R.H. 1896. The Bora, or initiation ceremonies of the Kamilaroi tribe (Part II). *Journal of the Royal Anthropological Institute of Great Britain and Ireland* 25: 318–339.

Mathews, R.H. 1897. The Bora of the Kamilaroi tribes. *Proceedings of the Royal Society of Victoria* 9: 137–173.

Mathews, R.H. 1898. Initiation ceremonies of Australian tribes. *Proceedings of the American Philosophical Association* 37(157): 54–73.

Mathews R.H. 1899. Divisions of some Aboriginal Tribes, Queensland. *Journal and Proceedings of the Royal Society of New South Wales* 33: 103–111.

Mathews, R.H. 1906. Australian tribes – their formation and government. *Zeitschrift für Ethnologie* 38: 939–946.

Mathews, R.H. 1907a. Notes on some Aboriginal tribes. *Journal and Proceedings of the Royal Society of New South Wales* 41: 67–87.

Mathews, R.H. 1907b. Notes on the Arranda Tribe. *Journal and Proceedings of the Royal Society of New South Wales* 41: 146–164.

Mathews, R.H. 1907c. The Arran'da language, Central Australia. *The Proceedings of the American Philosophical Society* 46: 322–339.

Mathews, R.H. 1908. Marriage and descent in the Arranda Tribe, Central Australia. *American Anthropologist* 10: 88–102.

Mauss, M. 1913. Les Aranda et Loritja d'Australie centrale. II. *L'Année sociologique*: 101–104.

McConvell, P. 1985. The origin of subsections in northern Australia. *Oceania* 56(1): 1–33.

McKnight, D. 1990. The Australian Aborigines in anthropology. In Richard Fardon, (ed.), *Localising Strategies, Regional Traditions of Ethnographic Writing*. pp. 42–70. Edinburgh and Washington: Scottish Academic Press and Smithsonian Initiation Press.

Meggitt, M.J. [1962] 1986. *Desert People*. Sydney: Angus and Robertson.

Meggitt, M. 1966. *Gadjari among the Walbiri Aborigines of Central Australia*. Oceania Monograph 14. Sydney: University of Sydney.

Merlan, F., Morton, J. and Rumsey, A. 1997. *Scholar and Sceptic: Australian Aboriginal Studies in Honour of LR Hiatt*. Canberra: Aboriginal Studies Press.

Middendorf, H.J. 2006. Der Barbarische Geschmack. PhD Thesis, University of Heidelberg.

Monteath, P. 2013. Globalising German anthropology. Erhard Eylmann in Australia. *Itinerario* 37(1): 29–42.

Moore, D.C. 2003. TGH Strehlow and the Linguistic Landscape of Australia 1930–1960. Honours Thesis, University of New England.

Morgan, L.H. 1871. *Systems of Consanguinity and Affinity of the Human Family*. Washington, D.C.: Smithsonian Institute.

Morgan, R. and Wilmot, H. 2010. *Written Proof: The Appropriation of Genealogical Records in Contemporary Arrernte Society*. AIATSIS Native Title Research Unit Issue Paper Vol. 4, No. 5. Canberra: AIATSIS.

Morphy, F. and Morphy, H. 1984. Owners, managers and ideology: a comparative analysis. In L. Hiatt (ed.), *Aboriginal Landowners: Contemporary Issues in the Determination of Traditional Aboriginal Land Ownership*. pp. 46–66. Sydney: University of Sydney.

Morphy, H. 1996. More than mere facts: repositioning Spencer and Gillen in the history of anthropology. In S.R. Morton and D.J. Mulvaney (eds), *Exploring Central Australia Society, the Environment and the 1894 Horn Expedition*. pp. 135-149. Chipping Norton, NSW: Surrey Beatty & Sons.

Morphy, H. 1997. Death, exchange and the reproduction of Yolngu society. In F. Merlan, J. Morton and A. Rumsey (eds), *Scholar and Sceptic: Australian Aboriginal Studies in Honour of L.R. Hiatt*. pp. 123–150. Canberra: Aboriginal Studies Press.

Morphy, H. [1997] 2001. Gillen – man of science. In J. Mulvaney, H. Morphy and A. Petch (eds), *'My Dear Spencer', the Letters of F.J. Gillen to Baldwin Spencer*. pp. 23–50. Melbourne: Hyland House.

Morphy, H. 2012. Reading Spencer and Gillen. *Sophia* 51: 545–560.

Morris, B. 1987. *Anthropological Studies of Religion: An Introductory Text*. London: Cambridge Press.

Morton, J. 1985. Sustaining Desire: a structuralist interpretation of myth and male cult in Central Australia. PhD Thesis, The Australian National University.

Morton, J. 1987. Singing subjects and sacred objects: more on Munn's 'Transformation of Subjects into Objects' in Central Australian myth. *Oceania* 58(2): 100–117.

Morton, J. 1988. Introduction: Géza Róheim's contribution to Australian ethnography. In J. Morton and W. Muensterberger (eds), *Children of the Desert II. Myths and Dreams of the Aborigines of Central Australia*, pp. vii–xxx. Sydney: Oceania Ethnographies.

Morton, J. 1992. Country, people, art: the Western Aranda 1870–1990. In J. Hardy, J.V.S. Megaw and M.R. Megaw (eds), *The Heritage of Namatjira*. pp. 23–62. Melbourne: William Heinemann.

Morton, J. 1995. Secrets of the Aranda: T.G.H. Strehlow and the course of revelation. In C. Anderson (ed.), *Politics of the Secret*. Oceania Monograph 45. pp. 51–66. Sydney: University of Sydney.

Morton, J. 1997a. Arrernte (Aranda) land tenure: an evaluation of the Strehlow Model. *Strehlow Research Centre Occasional Paper* 1: 107–127.

Morton, J. 1997b. *Alice Springs Arrernte Native Title Determination Application Anthropologist's Report*. Exhibit 3. Alice Springs: Central Land Council.

Mühlberg, D. 1984. Herders Theorie der Kulturgeschichte in ihrer Bedeutung für die Begründung der Kulturwissenschaft. *Jahrbuch für Volkskunde und Kuturgeschichte* 27: 9–26.

Mühlmann, W.E. 1968. *Geschichte der Anthropologie*. Frankfurt am Main: Enke.

Müller, K.E. 1993. Grundzüge des ethnologischen Historismus. In W. Schmied-Kowarlik and J. Stagl (eds), *Grundfragen der Ethnologie*. pp. 197-232. Berlin: Dietrich Reimer Verlag.

Mulvaney, D.J. and Calaby, J.H. 1985. *'So Much that is New', Baldwin Spencer, 1860–1929*. Melbourne: Melbourne University Press.

Mulvaney, J., Morphy, H. and Petch, A. (eds) [1997] 2001. *'My Dear Spencer', the Letters of F.J. Gillen to Baldwin Spencer*. Melbourne: Hyland House.

Mulvaney, J. [1997] 2001. F.J. Gillen's life and times. In J. Mulvaney, H. Morphy. and A. Petch (eds), *'My Dear Spencer', the Letters of F.J. Gillen to Baldwin Spencer*. pp. 1-22. Melbourne: Hyland House.

Mulvaney, J., Morphy, H. and Petch, A. 2000. *From the Frontier: Outback Letters to Baldwin Spencer*. Sydney: Allen & Unwin.

Musharbash, Y. 2008. *Yuendumu Everyday: Contemporary Life in Remote Aboriginal Australia*. Canberra: Aboriginal Studies Press.

Munn, N. 1970. The transformation of subjects into objects in Walbiri and Pitjantjatjara myth. In R.M. Berndt (ed.), *Australian Aboriginal Anthropology*. pp. 141–163. Perth: University of Western Australia Press.

Myers, F. 1976. To Have and to Hold: A Study of Persistency and Change in Pintupi Social Life. PhD thesis, Bryn Mawr College, Pennsylvania.

Myers, F. [1986] 1991. *Pintupi Country, Pintupi Self*. Los Angeles: University of California Press.

Nash, D. 1982. An etymological note on Warlpiri kurdungurlu. In J. Heath, F. Merlan and A. Rumsey (eds), *Languages of Kinship in Aboriginal Australia*. Oceania Linguistic Monographs No. 24. pp. 141–159. Sydney: University of Sydney.

Nettelbeck, A. and Foster, R. 2007. *In the Name of the Law: William Willshire and the Policing of the Australian Frontier*. Adelaide: Wakefield Press.

Nisbet, H.B. 1992. Herders anthropologischen Anschauungen in den 'Ideen zur Philosophie der Geschichte der Menschheit'. In J. Barhoff and E. Sagarra (eds), *Anthropologie und Literatur um 1800*. pp. 1–23. Munich: Iudicium Verlag.

Nobbs, C. 2005. The bush missionary's defence: a key document in the history of Australian mission ethnography. In A. Kenny and S. Mitchell (eds), *Collaboration and Language, Strehlow Research Centre Occasional Paper* 4: 26–53.

Nobbs, C. 2006. Collectors on the Cooper Creek: 1860–1910. Typescript.

Oberscheidt, H. 2005. Translating Carl Strehlow's ethnological work. In A. Kenny and S. Mitchell (eds), *Collaboration and Language, Strehlow Research Centre Occasional Paper* 4: 89–92.

Ogden, C.K. and Richards, I.A. 1946. *The Meaning of Meaning: A Study of the Influence of Language upon Thought and of the Science of Symbolism*. New York: Harcourt, Brace & World.

Oldfield, A. 1865. On the Aborigines of Australia. *Transactions of the Ethnological Society of London* 3: 215-297.

Olney, H.W. 1991. *McLaren Creek Land Claim No. 32: Report by the Aboriginal Land Commissioner, Justice Olney*. Canberra: Australian Government Publishing Service.

Parker, K.L. 1905. *The Euahlayi Tribe: A Study of Aboriginal Life in Australia*. London: Archibald Constable and Company.

Penny, H.G. 1998. Municipal display: civic self-promotion and the development of German ethnological museums, 1870–1914. *Social Anthropology* 6(2): 157–168.

Penny, H.G. 1999. Fashioning local identities in and age of nation-building: museums, cosmopolitan traditions, and intra German competition. *German History* 17(4): 488–504.

Penny, H.G. 2002. *Objects of Culture. Ethnology and Ethnographic Museums in Imperial Germany*. Chapel Hill and London: University of North Carolina Press.

Penny, H.G. 2003. Bastian's museum: on the limits of empiricism and the transformation of German ethnology. In H.G. Penny and M. Bunzl (eds), *Worldly Provincialism: German Anthropology in the Age of the Empire*. pp. 86–126. Ann Arbor: University of Michigan Press.

Penny, H.G. and Bunzl, M. 2003. Introduction: rethinking German anthropology, colonialism, and race. In H.G. Penny and M. Bunzl (eds), *Worldly Provincialism: German Anthropology in the Age of the Empire*. pp. 1–30. Ann Arbor: University of Michigan Press.

Petermann, W. 2004. *Die Geschichte der Ethnologie*. Wupperthal: Peter Hammer Verlag.

Peterson, N. 1969. Secular and ritual links: two basic and opposed principles of Australian social organization as illustrated by Walbiri ethnography. *Mankind* 7(1): 27–35.

Peterson N. 1970. The importance of women in determining the composition of resident groups in Aboriginal Australia. In F. Gale (ed.), *Woman's Role in Aboriginal Society*. pp. 9–16. Canberra: Australian Institute of Aboriginal and Torres Strait Islander Studies.

Peterson, N. 1972. Totemism yesterday. *Man (N.S.)* 7: 12–25.

Peterson, N (ed.) 1976. *Tribes and Boundaries*. Canberra: Australian Institute of Aboriginal Studies.

Peterson, N., McConvell, P., Wild, S. and Hagen, R. 1978. *A Claim to Areas of Traditional Land by the Warlpiri and Kartangarurru-Kurintji*. Alice Springs: Central Land Council.

Peterson, N. 1983. Rights, residence and process in Australian territorial organisation. In N. Peterson and M. Langton (eds), *Aborigines, Land and Land Rights*. pp. 134–145. Canberra: Australian Institute of Aboriginal Studies.

Peterson, N. 1986. *Australian Territorial Organisation: A Band Perspective*. In collaboration with Jeremy Long. Oceania Monograph 30. Sydney: University of Sydney.

Peterson, N. 2000. An expanding Aboriginal domain: mobility and the initiation journey. *Oceania* 70(3): 205–218.

Peterson, N. 2006. 'I can't follow you on this horde-clan business at all': Donald Thomson, Radcliffe-Brown and a final note on the horde. *Oceania* 76: 16–26.

Petri, H. 1953. Leo Frobenius und die historische Ethnology. *Saeculum* 4: 45–60.

Pilhofer, G. 1967. *Geschichte des Neuendettelsauer Missionshauses.* Neuendettelsau: Freimund-Verlag Neuendettelsau.

Pink, O. 1933. Spirit ancestor in a Northern Aranda horde country. *Oceania* 4(2): 176–186.

Pink, O. 1936. The landowners in the northern division of the Aranda Tribe, Central Australia. *Oceania* 6(3): 275–305.

Planert, W. 1907. Aranda Grammatik. *Zeitschrift für Ethnologie* 39: 551–566.

Planert, W. 1908. Dieri Grammatik. *Zeitschrift für Ethnologie* 40: 686–697.

Povinelli, E.A. 2002. *The Cunning of Recognition: Indigenous Alterities and the Making of Australian Multiculturalism.* Durham: Duke University Press.

Preton, R.J. 1966. Edward Sapir's anthropology: style, structure and method. *American Anthropologist* 68: 1105–1127.

Preuss, K.T. 1908. Die Aranda und Loritja Stämme in Zentral-Australien. *Deutsche Literaturzeitung* 28.

Preuss, K.T. 1933. *Der Religiöse Gehalt der Mythen.* Tübingen: Verlag von J.C.B. Mohr (Paul Siebeck).

Radcliffe-Brown, A.R. 1929. Notes on Totemism in Eastern Australia. *The Journal of the Royal Anthropological Institute of Great Britain and Ireland.* 59: 399-415.

Radcliffe-Brown, A.R. 1930–31. The social organization of Australian tribes. *Oceania* 1: 34–63, 206–246, 322–341, 426–456.

Radcliffe-Brown, A.R. 1954. Australian local organisation. *American Anthropologist* 56(1): 105–106.

Redmond, A. 2001. Places that move. In A. Rumsey and J. Weiner (eds), *Emplaced Myth: Space, Narrative, and Knowledge in Aboriginal Australia and Papua New Guinea.* pp. 120–138. Honolulu: University of Hawai'i Press.

Redmond, A. 2005. Strange relatives: mutualities and dependencies between Aborigines and pastoralists in the Northern Kimberley. *Oceania* 75(3): 234–246

Reill, P.H. 1994. Science and the construction of the cultural sciences in late enlightenment Germany: The Case of Wilhelm von Humboldt. *History and Theory* 33(3): 345–366.

Ridley, W. 1861. Journal of a Missionary Tour Among the Aborigines of the Western Interior of Queensland, in the year 1855. In J.D. Lang, *Queensland, Australia*. Appendix I. London: Stanford.

Ridley, W. 1875. *Kamilaroi and other Australian Languages*. Sydney: Thomas Richards, Government Printer.

Ridley, W. 1878. Traditions of the Australian Aborigines on the Namoi, Barwan [sic], and other tributaries of the Darling. In R. Brough Smyth, *The Aborigines of Victoria*. Volume 2, Appendix B. Melbourne: Government Printer.

Rivers, W.H.R. 1910. The genealogical method of anthropological inquiry. *The Sociological Review* 3: 1–12.

Rivers, W.H.R. [1912] 1968. The sociological significance of myth. In R.A. George (ed.), *Studies on Mythology*. pp. 27–45. Homewood: The Dorsey Press.

Roennfeldt, D. with members of the communities of Ntaria, Ipolera, Gilbert Springs, Kulpitarra, Undarana, Red Sand Hill, Old Station and other outstations. 2005. *Western Arrarnta Picture Dictionary*. Alice Springs: IAD Press.

Rödiger, I. 2001. Gustav Friedrich Klemm. In C.F. Feest and K.H. Kohl (eds), *Hauptwerke der Ethnologie*. pp. 188–192. Stuttgart: Alfred Kröner Verlag.

Róheim, G. 1925. *Australian Totemism*. London: Allen & Unwin.

Róheim, G. 1932. The psycho-analysis of primitive cultural types. *International Journal of Psycho-Analysis* 13: 1–224

Róheim, G. [1945] 1971. *The Eternal Ones of the Dream: A Psychoanalytic Interpretation of Australian Myth and Ritual*. New York: International Universities Press.

Róheim, G. 1974. *Children of the Desert: The Western Tribes of Central Australia*, edited by W. Muensterberger. New York: Basic Books.

Róheim, G. 1988. *Children of the Desert II. Myths and Dreams of the Aborigines of Central Australia*, edited by J. Morton and W. Muensterberger. Sydney: Oceania Ethnographies.

Roth, W.E. 1897. *Ethnological Studies among the North-West-Central Queensland Aborigines*. Brisbane: Edmund Gregory.

Roth, W.E. 1910. Bulletin No 18: Social and individual nomenclature. *Records of the Australian Museum* 8: 79–106.

Rowse, T. 1998. *White Flour, White Power*. Cambridge: Cambridge University Press.

Rubuntja, W. with Green, J. 2002. *The Town Grew Up Dancing*. Alice Springs: Jukurrpa Books, IAD Press.

Rumsey, A. 2001. Tracks, traces and links. In A. Rumsey and J. Weiner (eds), *Emplaced Myth: Space, Narrative, and Knowledge in Aboriginal Australia and Papua New Guinea*. pp. 19–42. Honolulu: University of Hawai'i Press.

Sackett, L. 1994. *Tempi Downs and Middleton Ponds/Luritja Land Claim: Anthropologist's Report*. Alice Springs: Central Land Council.

Sackett, L. 2007. A potential pathway. *Anthropological Forum* 17(2): 173–175.

Sahlins, M. 1976. *Culture and Practical Reason*. Chicago and London: The University of Chicago Press.

Sansom, B. 2006. The brief reach of history and the limitations of recall in traditional Aboriginal societies and cultures. *Oceania* 76(2): 150–172.

Sansom, B. 2007. Yulara and future expert reports in native title cases. *Anthropological Forum* 17(1): 71–92.

Sapir, E. 1907. Herder's Ursprung der Sprache. *Modern Philology* 5: 109–142.

Sapir, E. 1917. Do we need a superorganic? *American Anthropologist* 19: 441–447.

Sapir, E. [1921] 1970. *Language: An Introduction to the Study of speech*. New York: Harcourt, Brace and Co.

Sapir, E. 1929. The status of linguistics as a science. *Language* 5: 207–214.

Sapir, E. 1933. Language. In *Encyclopaedia of the Social Sciences*, Vol. 9. pp. 155–169. The Macmillan Company.

Sapir, E. [1956] 1970. *Culture, Language and Personality: Selected Essays*, edited by D.G. Mandelbaum. Berkeley: University of California Press.

Sarg, F.C. 1911. *Die Australischen Bumerangs im Städtischen Völkermuseum*. Frankfurt am Main: Joseph Baer.

Scheffler, H.W. 1978. *Australian Kin Classification*. Cambridge: Cambridge University Press.

Scheffler, H.W. 2001. *Filiation and Affiliation*. Colorado: Westview Press.

Scherer, P.A. 1963. *Venture of Faith: An Epic in Australian Missionary History*, Tanunda: Auricht's Printing Office.

Scherer, P.A. 1994. *Select Letters from the Outback*. Tanunda: P.A. Scherer.

Scherer, P.A. 1995. *The Hermannsburg Chronicle, 1877–1933*. Tanunda: P.A. Scherer.

Schild, M. 2004a. Heading for Hermannsburg: notes on Carl Strehlow's early career path. In W. Veit (ed.), *Strehlow Research Centre Occasional Paper* 3: 51–58.

Schild, M. 2004b. Neuendettelsau pastors and Australian Lutheranism. *Journal of Friends of Lutheran Archives* 14: 19–32.

Schlichting, W. 1998. *Die Erneuerung Lutherischen Lebens duch Wilhelm Löhe: "… unter dem Winterschnee hervorgeholt"; 150 Jahre "Gesellschaft für Innere (und Äussere) Mission im Sinne der Lutherischen Kirche"*. Neuendettelsau: Freimund-Verlag.

Schmidt, P.W. 1899. Die sprachlichen Verhältnisse Ozeaniens in ihrer Bedeutung für die Ethnology. *Mitteilungen der anthropologischen Gesellschaft in Wien* 29: 245–258.

Schmidt, P.W. 1908a. Die Aranda und Loritja Stämme in Zentral-Australien. *Anthropos* 3: 622–625.

Schmidt, P.W. 1908b. Die Stellung der Aranda unter den australischen Stämmen. *Zeitschrift für Ethnologie* 40: 866–901.

Schmidt, P.W. 1911a. Is ethnological information coming from missionaries sufficiently reliable? *Anthropos* 3: 430–431.

Schmidt, P.W. 1911b. Die kulturhistorische Methode in der Ethnologie. *Anthropos* 6: 1010–1036.

Schmidt, P.W. 1912–1918. Die Gliederung der Australischen Sprachen und ihre Beziehungen zu der Gliederung des soziologschen Verhältnisse der australischen Stämme. *Anthropos* 7 (1912): 230–251, 463–497, 1014–1048; 8 (1913): 526–554; 9 1914): 980–1018; 12/13 (1917/1918): 437–493, 747–817.

Schmied-Kowarlik, W. and Stagl, J. 1993. *Grundfragen der Ethnologie*. Berlin: Dietrich Reimer Verlag.

Schneider, D. 1968. *American Kinship: A Cultural Account*. Englewood Cliffs, N.J.: Prentice Hall.

Schneider, D. 1984. *A Critique of the Study of Kinship*. Ann Arbor: University of Michigan Press.

Schoknecht, A.C. and C.P. 1997. Missionary Carl Schoknecht, Killalpaninna Mission 1871–1873. South Oakleigh, Vic: A. & C. Schoknecht.

Schulze, L. 1891. The Aborigines of the Upper and Middle Finke River: their habits and customs. *Transactions and Proceedings of the Royal Society of South Australia* 14(2): 210–246.

Schweikle, G. and I. 1990 *Metzler Literatur Lexicon. Begriffe und Definitionen*. Stuttgart: J.B. Metzlersche Verlagsbuchhandlung.

Siebert, O. 1910. Sagen und Sitten der Dieri und Nachbarstämme in Zentral Australien. *Globus* 97 (3): 44–50; (4) 53–59.

Silverman, S. 2005. The United States. In F. Barth, R. Gingrich, A. Parkin, S. Silverman, *One Discipline, Four Ways: British, German, French and American Anthropology*. pp. 258–347. Chicago: Chicago University Press.

Smith, M.A. 2005. *Peopling the Cleland Hills. Aboriginal History in Western Central Australia 1850–1980*, Aboriginal History Monograph 12. Canberra: Aboriginal History.

Smith, W.D. 1978. The social and political origins of German diffusionist ethnology. *Journal of the History of the Behavioural Sciences* 14: 103–112.

Smith, W.D. 1980. Friedrich Ratzel and the Origins of Lebensraum. *German Studies Review* 3(1): 51–68.

Smith, W.D. 1991. *Politics and the Sciences of Culture in Germany, 1840–1920*. Oxford: Oxford University Press.

Smyth, R.B. 1878. *The Aborigines of Victoria with Notes Relating to the Habits of the Natives of other Parts of Australia and Tasmania* (2 Vols). Melbourne: Government Printer.

Spencer, W.B. (ed.) 1896. *Report on the Work of the Horn Scientific Expedition to Central Australia* (4 Vols). London and Melbourne: Melville, Mullen & Slade.

Spencer, W.B. and Gillen, F.J. 1899. *The Native Tribes of Central Australia*. London: Macmillan and Co.

Spencer, W.B. and Gillen, F.J. 1904. *The Northern Tribes of Central Australia*. London: Macmillan and Co.

Spencer, W.B. and Gillen, F.J. 1927. *The Arunta* (2 Vols). London: Macmillan and Co.

Stanner, W.E.H. 1965. Aboriginal territorial organization: estate, range, domain and regime. *Oceania* 36: 1–26.

Stanner, W.E.H. 2011. *The Dreaming and Other Essays*. Collingwood: Black Inc.

Steinen, K.v.d. 1905. Gedächnisrede auf Adolf Bastian. *Zeitschrift für Ethnologie* 37(2): 236–254.

Stepan, N. 1982. *The Idea of Race in Science: Great Britain 1800–1960*. London: Macmillian Press Ltd.

Stevens, C. 1994. *White Man's Dreaming. Killalpaninna Mission 1866–1915*. Melbourne: Oxford University Press.

Stirling, E.C. 1896. *Anthropology. Report on the Work of the Horn Scientific Expedition to Central Australia*, Vol. 4. London and Melbourne: Melville, Mullen & Slade.

Stocking, G.W. 1968. *Race, Culture and Evolution: Essays in the History of Anthropology*. New York: Free Press.

Stocking, G.W. 1983. The ethnographer's magic: fieldwork in British anthropology from Tylor to Malinowski. In G.W. Stocking (ed.), *Observers Observed: Essays on Ethnographic Fieldwork*. History of Anthropology, Vol. 1. pp. 70–120. Madison: The University of Wisconsin Press.

Stocking, G.W. 1984. *Functionalism Historicized: Essays on British Social Anthropology*. History of Anthropology, Vol. 2. Madison: The University of Wisconsin Press.

Stocking, G.W. (ed.) 1985. *Objects and Others: Essays on Museums and Material Culture*. History of Anthropology, Vol. 3. Madison: The University of Wisconsin Press.

Stocking, G.W. 1987. *Victorian Anthropology*. New York: Free Press.

Stocking, G.W. (ed.) [1982] 1989. *A Franz Boas Reader: The Shaping of American Anthropology 1883–1911*. New York: Basic Books.

Stocking, G.W. 1992. *The Ethnographer's Magic and other Essays in the History of Anthropology*. Madison: University of Wisconsin Press.

Stocking, G.W. 1995. *After Tylor. British Social Anthropology 1888–1951*. Madison: The University of Wisconsin Press.

Stocking, G.W. (ed.) 1996. *Volksgeist as Method and Ethic: Essays on Boasian Ethnography and the Germans Anthropological Tradition*. History of Anthropology, Vol. 8. Madison: The University of Wisconsin Press.

Stocking, G.W. 2001. *Delimiting Anthropology: Occasional Inquiries and Reflections*. Madison: The University of Wisconsin Press.

Streck, B. 2001. Theodor Waitz. In C.F. Feest und K.H. Kohl (eds.), *Hauptwerke der Ethnologie*. pp. 503–508. Stuttgart: Alfred Kröner Verlag.

Streck, B. 2006. Zur wissenschaftlichen Zielsetzung der ehemaligen Direktoren des Frobenius-Instituts. In K.H.. Kohl und E. Platte (Hrsg.), *Gestalter und Gestalten*, pp. 215–240. Frankfurt am Main [u.a.]: Stroemfeld.

Strehlow, C. 1907-1920. *Die Aranda- und Loritja-Stämme in Zentral-Australien* (1907–1920). Translation by H. Oberscheidt. Typescript.

Strehlow, J. 2004a. Shifting focus. In M. Cawthorn (ed.), *Proceedings of the Strehlow Conference 2002*. pp. 109–119. Alice Springs: Northern Territory Government.

Strehlow, J. 2004b. Reappraising Carl Strehlow: through the Spencer-Strehlow Debate. In W. Veit (ed.), *Strehlow Research Centre Occasional Paper* 3: 59–91.

Strehlow, J. 2011. *The Tale of Frieda Keysser*. Volume I: 1875–1910. London: Wild Cat Press.

Strehlow, T.G.H. 1944. *Aranda Phonetics and Grammar*. Oceania Monograph 7. Sydney: University of Sydney.

Strehlow, T.G.H. 1947. *Aranda Traditions*. Melbourne: Melbourne University Press.

Strehlow, T.G.H. [1964] 1978. *Central Australian Religion: Monototemism in a Polytotemic Community*. Adelaide: Australian Association for the Study of Religions.

Strehlow, T.G.H. 1965. Culture, social structure and environment in Aboriginal Central Australia. In R.M. Berndt and C.H. Berndt (eds), *Aboriginal Man in Australia*. pp. 121–145. Sydney: Angus and Robertson.

Strehlow, T.G.H. 1967. *Comments on the Journals of John McDouall Stuart*. Adelaide: Libraries Board of South Australia.

Strehlow, T.G.H. [1967] 2005. Man and Language. Address to the Adelaide University Linguistic Society on 19 September 1967. In A. Kenny and S. Mitchell (eds), *Collaboration and Language,Strehlow Research Centre Occasional Paper* 4: 76–88.

Strehlow, T.G.H. 1969. *Journey to Horseshoe Bend*. Sydney: Angus and Robertson.

Strehlow, T.G.H. 1969-1970. *Handbook of Central Australian Genealogies*. Adelaide: University of Adelaide. Typescript.

Strehlow, T.G.H. 1970. Geography and the totemic landscape in Central Australia: a functional study. In R.M. Berndt (ed.), *Australian Aboriginal Anthropology*. pp. 93–140. Perth: University of Western Australia Press.

Strehlow, T.G.H. 1971. *Songs of Central Australia*. Sydney: Angus and Robertson.

Strehlow, T.G.H. 1977. *Christian Missions: Places of Refuge Concentration Centres?* Held at the Strehlow Research Centre.

Strehlow, T.G.H. [1950] 1997. Agencies of Social Control in Central Australian Aboriginal Societies. *Strehlow Research Centre Occasional Paper* 1: 1–51.

Strehlow, T.G.H. 1999. Aranda Regular and Irregular Marriages. *Strehlow Research Centre Occasional Paper* 2: 1–44.

Stuart, J.M. 1865. *Explorations in Australia: The Journals of John McDouall Stuart*. London: Saunders Otley.

Summer Institute of Linguistics 1979. *Pintupi/Luritja Kinship*. Alice Springs: Institute for Aboriginal Development.

Sutton, P. 1995. *Country: Aboriginal Boundaries and Land Ownership in Australia*. Aboriginal History Monograph 3. Canberra: Aboriginal History Inc.

Sutton, P. 1996. The robustness of Aboriginal boundaries and land tenure systems: underlying and proximate community titles. *Oceania* 67: 7–29.

Sutton, P. 2001. Kinds of Rights in Country: Recognising Customary Rights as Incidents of Native Title. Perth: NNTT (02/2001).

Sutton, P. 2003. *Native Title in Australia: An Anthropological Perspective*. Cambridge: Cambridge University Press.

Sutton, P. 2007. Norms, statistics and the Jango Case at Yulara. *Anthropological Forum* 17(2): 175–187.

Swain, T. 1985. *Interpreting Aboriginal Religion: An Historical Account*. Adelaide: Australian Association for the Study of Religion.

Swain, T. 1991. *Aboriginal Religions in Australia: A Bibliographical Survey*. New York: Greenwood Press.

Swain, T. 1993. *A Place for Strangers: Towards a History of Australian Aboriginal Being*. Melbourne: Cambridge University Press.

Swain, T. and Rose, D.B. (eds) 1988. *Aboriginal Australians and Christian Missions: Ethnographic and Historical Studies*. Adelaide: The Australian Association for the Study of Religions.

Swan, C. and Cousen, M. 1993. *A Learner's Wordlist of Pertame*. Alice Springs: IAD Press.

Synnott, A. and Howes, D. 1992. From measurement to meaning, anthropologies of the body. *Anthropos* 87: 147–166.

Szalay, M. 1983. *Ethnologie und Geschichte. Zur Gundlegung einer ethnologischen Geschichtsschreibung*. Berlin: Dietrich Reimer Verlag.

Szalay, M. 1985. Historismus und Kulturrelativismus. *Anthropos* 80: 587–604.

Taplin, G. (ed.) 1879. *The Folklore, Manners, Customs and Languages of the South AustralianAborigines*. Adelaide: Government Printer.

Thomas, M. 2004. RH Mathews and anthropological warfare: on writing the biography of a 'self-contained man'. *Aboriginal History* 28: 1–32.

Thomas, M. (ed.) 2007. *Culture in Translation: The Anthropological Legacy of R.H. Mathews*. Aboriginal History Monograph 15. Canberra: Aboriginal History Inc. and ANU E Press.

Thomas, M. 2011. *The Many Worlds of R.H. Mathews: In Search of an Australian Anthropologist*. Crows Nest: Allen & Unwin.

Thomas, N.W. 1905a. The religious ideas of the Arunta. *Folklore* 16(4): 428–433.

Thomas, N.W. 1905b. Über Kulturkreise in Australien. *Zeitschrift für Ethnologie* 37: 759–767.

Thomas, N.W. 1906a. *Kinship Organisation and Group Marriage in Australia*. Cambridge: Cambridge University Press.

Thomas, N.W. 1906b. Dr. Howitt's defence of group-marriage. *Folklore* 17(3): 294–307.

Thomas, N.W. 1909. Veröffentlichungen aus dem städtischen Voelker-Museum Frankfurt am Main: I. C. Strehlow, Die Aranda- und Loritja-Staemme in Zentral-Australien, II Teil. Frankfurt: Baer & Co., 1908. *Folklore* 20(1): 125–127.

Thorley, P.B. 1999. Regional archaeological research in the Palmer River catchment. *Australian Aboriginal Studies* 2: 62–68.

Thorley, P.B. 2001. Uncertain supplies: water permanency and regional archaeological structure in the Palmer river catchment, central Australia. *Archaeology in Oceania* 36: 1–14.

Tindale, N. 1940. Distribution of Australian Aboriginal tribes: a field survey. *Transactions of the Royal Society of South Australia* 64: 140–231 and map.

Tindale, N. 1972. The Pitjandjara. In M.G. Biccheiri (ed.), *Hunters and Gatherers Today*. New York: Holt, Rinehart and Winston.

Tindale, N. 1974. *Aboriginal Tribes of Australia: Their Terrain, Environmental Controls, Distribution, Limits and Proper Names*. Berkeley: University of California Press.

Tjalkabota, M. 2002. Appendix 2: Moses Tjalkabota. In P.G.E. Albrecht (ed.), *From Mission to Church, 1877–2002*. pp. 237-300. Adelaide: Finke River Mission.

Toohey, J. 1978. *Land Claim by Alyawarra and Kaititja*. Canberra: Australian Government Publishing Service.

Toohey, J. 1980. *Anmatjira and Alyawarra to Utopia Pastoral Lease*. Canberra: Australian Government Publishing Service.

Trabant, J. 1990. *Humboldts Traditionen*. Frankfurt am Main: Suhrkamp Verlag.

Trabant, J. 1994. Nachwort. In W.v. Humboldt, *Über die Sprache*. pp. 201–217. Tübingen und Basel: A. Francke Verlag.

Trigg, R. 1999. *Ideas of Human Nature: An Historical Introduction*. Oxford: Blackwell Publishers.

Turner, Victor. 1967. Colour classification in Ndembu Ritual: a problem in primitive classification. In *The Forest of Symbols*. pp. 59–94. Ithaca and London: Cornell University Press.

Turner, Victor. 1968. *The Drums of Affliction*. London: Oxford University Press.

Tylor, E.B. 1871. *Primitive Culture: Researches into the Development of Mythology, Philosophy, Religion, Art and Custom* (2 Vols). London: John Murray.

Vaarzon-Morel, P. and Sackett, L. 1997. *Central Mount Wedge Land Claim. Anthropologists' Report*. Alice Springs: Central Land Council.

Vallee, P. 2006. *God, Guns, Government on the Central Australian Frontier*. Canberra: Restoration Books.

Vatter, E. 1920. Preface. In C. Strehlow. 1920. *Die Aranda- und Loritja-Stämme in Zentral-Australien V. Die Materielle Kultur der Aranda- und Loritja*. Frankfurt am Main: Joseph Baer & Co.

Vatter, E. 1925. *Der australische Totemismus*. Hamburg: Museum für Völkerkunde.

Veit, W.F. 1991. In search of Carl Strehlow: Lutheran missionary and Australian anthropologist. In J. Tampke and D. Walker (eds), *From Berlin to Burdekin: The German Contribution to the Development of Australian Science, Exploration and the Arts*. Sydney: University of New South Wales Press.

Veit, W.F. 1994. Carl Strehlow, ethnologist: the Arunta and Aranda tribes in Australian ethnology. In T.R. Finlayson and G.L. McMullen (eds), *The Australian Experience of Germany*. pp. 77–100. Adelaide: Australian Association of von Humboldt Fellows, Flinders University.

Veit, W.F. 2004a. Labourers in the vineyard or the uneducated missionary. In M. Cawthorn (ed.), *Proceedings of the Strehlow Conference 2002*. pp. 136–150. Alice Springs: Northern Territory Government.

Veit, W.F. 2004b. Social anthropology versus cultural anthropology: Baldwin Walter Spencer and Carl Friedrich Theodor Strehlow in Central Australia. In W. Veit (ed.), *Strehlow Research Centre Occasional Paper* 3: 92–110.

Völker, H. 2001. Missionare als Ethnologen. Moritz Freiherr von Leonhardi, australische Mission und europäische Wissenschaft. In R. Wendt (Hrsg.), *Sammeln, Vernetzen, Auswerten. Missionare und ihr Beitrag zum Wandel europäischer Weltsicht*. pp. 173–218. Tübingen: Gunter Narr Verlag.

Von Hendy, A. 2002. *The Modern Construction of Myth*. Bloomington: Indiana University Press.

Wafer, J. 1982. *A Simple Introduction to Central Australian Kinship System*. Alice Springs: IAD Press.

Walker, G. and R. Vanderwal (eds). 1982. *The Aboriginal Photographs of Baldwin Spencer*, introduced by John Mulvaney; selected and annotated by Geoffrey Walker. Melbourne: Currey O'Neil.

Warneck, G. 1897. *Evangelische Missionslehre* (3 Vols). Gotha: Friedrich Andreas Berthes.

Weber, C. 1996. *Missionstheologie bei Wilhelm Löhe: Aufbruch zur Kirche der Zukunft*. Gütersloh: Gütersloher Verlagshaus.

Wendland-Curtis, L. 2009. Out of the Shadow: Reconstructing Frieda Strehlow as Missionary Wife in central Australia, 1895–1922. Phd Thesis. Monash University.

Wendt, R. 2001. Einleitung: Missionare als Reporter und Wissenschaftler in Übersee. In R. Wendt (Hrsg.), *Sammeln, Vernetzen, Auswerten. Missionare und ihr Beitrag zum Wandel europäischer Weltsicht*. pp. 7–22. Tübingen: Gunter Narr Verlag.

Wefelmeyer, F. 1988. Herders Kulturanthropology und die Frage nach der Geschichtlichkeit des Seelischen. In *Wegbereiter der Historischen Psychologie*. pp. 28–40. Munich: Psychologie Verlags-Union Belt.

Wenzel, M. 1990. Die Anthropologie Johann Gottfried Herders und das klassische Humanitätsideal. In G. Mann and F. Dumont (eds), *Die Natur des Menschen: Probleme der Physischen Anthropologie und Rassenkunde (1750–1850)*. pp. 137–167. Stuttgart: G. Fischer.

Whitman, J. 1984. From philology to anthropology in mid-nineteenth-century Germany. In G.W. Stocking (ed.), *Functionalism Historicized: Essays on British Social Anthropology*. pp. 214–230. Madison: The University of Wisconsin Press.

Whitton, B. 1988. Herder's critique of the Enlightenment: cultural community versus cosmopolitan rationalism. *History and Theory* 27: 146–168.

Wilbur, G.B. and W. Muensterberger (eds). 1951. *Psychoanalysis of Culture: Essays in Honor of Géza Róheim*. New York: International University Press.

Wilkins, D. 2001. Glossary. In J. Mulvaney, H. Morphy. and A. Petch (eds), *'My Dear Spencer', the Letters of F.J. Gillen to Baldwin Spencer*. pp. 487–533. Melbourne: Hyland House.

Willshire, W.H. 1888. *The Aborigines of Central Australia*. Adelaide: Government Printer.

Wilmot, H. and Koser, R. 2007. Applied Anthropology and Contemporary Arrernte Perceptions of Connection to Country. Paper read in Canberra at the AAS Conference (November). Alice Springs: Central Land Council.

Winnecke, C. 1897. *Journal of the Horn Scientific Exploring Expedition*. Adelaide: Government Printer.

Wolfe, P. 1999. *Settler Colonialism and the Transformation of Anthropology*. London: Cassell.

Woods, J.D. 1879. *The Native Tribes of South Australia*. Adelaide: E.S. Wigg and Son.

Worsnop, T. 1897. *The Prehistoric Arts, Manufactures, Works, Weapons, etc. of the Aborigines of Australia*. Adelaide: Government Printer.

Zammito, J.H. 2002. *Kant, Herder and the Birth of Anthropology*. Chicago: University of Chicago Press.

Zimmerman, A. 2001. *Anthropology and Antihumanism in Imperial Germany*. Chicago: Chicago University Press.

Index

Name Index